THE CARE AND TRAINING OF THE
MENTALLY HANDICAPPED

The care and training of the mentally handicapped

A MANUAL FOR THE CARING PROFESSIONS

Charles H. Hallas, SRN, RMN, RNMS, RNT

Formerly Chief Nursing Officer, Glasgow Western Infirmary and Gartnavel Hospital Group

William I. Fraser, MD (Glas.), FRCPsych., DPM

Senior Lecturer in Department of Psychology, University of St Andrews; Senior Lecturer in Rehabilitation Studies, University of Edinburgh

Ronald C. MacGillivray, MB (Edin.), FRCP (Glas.), DPM (Lond.), FRCPsych.

Physician Superintendent, Lennox Castle

SEVENTH EDITION

WRIGHT·PSG
Bristol London Boston
1982

ⓒ
C. H. Hallas
9 York Grove, Garstang, nr Preston PR3 1HU.
W. I. Fraser
Gogarburn Hospital, Edinburgh EH12 9BJ.
R. C. MacGillivray
Lennox Castle Hospital, Lennoxtown, Glasgow. 1982.

Published by:
John Wright & Sons Ltd, 42–44 Triangle West,
Bristol BS8 1EX, England.

John Wright PSG Inc, 545 Great Road, Littleton,
Massachusetts 01460, USA.

First edition: 1958
Second edition: 1962
Third edition: 1967
Fourth edition: 1970
Spanish translation: 1974
Japanese translation: 1975
Fifth edition: 1974
Spanish translation: 1976
Japanese translation: 1976
Sixth edition: 1978
Seventh edition: 1982

British Library Cataloguing in Publication Data
Hallas, Charles H.
    The care and training of the mentally
    handicapped.—7th ed.
    1. Mentally handicapped—Care and treatment
    I. Title   II. Fraser, William I.
    III. MacGillivray, Roland C.
    362.3   HV3004

ISBN 0 0736 0624 2

Library of Congress Catalog Card Number: 82–70097

Printed in Great Britain by
John Wright & Sons (Printing) Ltd,
at The Stonebridge Press, Bristol BS4 5NU.

*To the memory of Lionel S. Penrose
whose genius deserved respect,
but did not command it.*

Preface

IT IS ALMOST 25 years since the first edition of this book was published. As the author, my intention was to provide a comprehensive textbook which would be both helpful and challenging to those nurses involved in caring for the mentally handicapped.

Though dreams were dreamed that the care of the mentally handicapped would miraculously change, in 1958 it was difficult to see how all the prejudices could be overcome. However, changes were taking place unobtrusively.

A science which had almost totally been the prerogative of the medical and nursing professions began to interest other professional bodies and the whole field of mental handicap slowly came to life and opened up. The psychologist became more than an assessor of intelligence: his advice was sought on therapy, training, work and education. The educationalist's role broadened and he took under his wing also the severely handicapped person. The social worker became more than a reporter of home conditions. Occupational therapists, physiotherapists, speech therapists and practitioners of many other professions began also to take on a greater and more positive role.

The 1959 Mental Health Act stimulated this change, and large groups of hospitalized patients were suddenly discharged, often without adequate provision having been made for their welfare. Such is still the case, though there is now a greater awareness and appreciation of the problems which ensue, and efforts are being made to overcome them.

Like the first edition, this seventh edition contains precise information for several types of professional, spanning both education and basic nursing skills and techniques. These may currently be less fashionable to discuss than are attitudes, but they are of vital importance to the staff who care for the severely and profoundly handicapped, and for those who come into contact with mildly handicapped people who are maladjusted.

The first edition was written with little thought of its future development. It was not until after the book was published that the real need became apparent, and its popularity has continued to grow as knowledge progresses and attitudes change dramatically.

Two people have remained constant throughout these 25 years; they are my wife and my friend and colleague, Dr Ronald

MacGillivray. Throughout this time their support and encouragement have been unfailing. To them, I say, 'Thank you'.

I am grateful that Dr W. I. Fraser has been able and willing to make available his wide knowledge and expertise by joining Ronald and myself in compiling the last three editions. I would also like to say 'Thank you' to all other contributors who have helped in the success of this book.

C. H. H.

Acknowledgements

The authors are indebted to:

Dr J. A. Baird, Consultant Psychiatrist, State Hospital, Carstairs.

Gilean Blyth, Remedial Gymnast, Gogarburn Hospital.

Philip Derbyshire, Nursing Tutor, Gogarburn, and Dettol Nurse of the Year.

Paul Dickens, Principal Psychologist, Royal Scottish National Hospital.

Dr Eric Fischbacher, Associate Specialist, Gogarburn Hospital.

Fiona Grimson, Senior Occupational Therapist, Ladysbridge Hospital.

Paul Kelly, Officer-in-Charge, Ravelrig, Barnardo's.

Jenny McCardel, Adult Tutor, Gogarburn Hospital.

Dr Ann Macdonald, Lecturer, Department of Psychiatry, Edinburgh University.

Gilbert Mackay, Senior Research Fellow, Glasgow University, Department of Education.

Bobbie Paton, Principal Psychologist, Borders Health Board. (The Borders Assessment Schedule.)

Dr Morag Rennie, Consultant Psychiatrist, Lanark Health Board.

Angus Scott, Principal Psychologist, Leverndale Hospital.

Jois Stansfeld, Principal Speech Therapist, Gogarburn Hospital.

Ann Thow, Principal Social Worker, Stracathro Hospital.

June Tree, Senior Chiropodist, Lennox Castle.

Patricia Veall, Eleanor Wilkinston, Physiotherapists, Gogarburn Hospital.

Norman Watters, Dental Surgeon, Lynebank Hospital.

Contents

CHAPTER 1

Introductory

'Those who forget the past are condemned to repeat it.'

George Santayana

THERE IS REFERENCE in the *Ayurveda*, some 1400 years before the birth of Christ, to possession by demons as being the cause of insanity. Seven demons were listed: one of these rejoiced in the name Pisaka and the characteristics of this gentleman were that he was gluttonous, dirty, without memory, restless, uneasy, walked naked and tore his flesh. When there is neglect, this can be the picture today.

In ancient Greece and Rome the retarded person was viewed with horror and exposed so that he or she might perish. The word 'idiot' comes from the Greek, 'a person who cannot take part in public life and cannot carry on a conversation'. The term 'imbecile' probably had its origin in 'Bacillum', a short stick, for an imbecile was a person who could not stand unsupported. In Sparta, mentally retarded children, having first been viewed by the civic fathers, were destroyed. Similarly, parents in India were compelled to bring new-born children for examination by persons appointed for the duty, who ordered all those born with any signal defect to be put to death. The poet Marcus Valerius Martialis, who lived in the first century AD, has a number of quotations concerning mentally retarded children: *Acute capite et auribus longibus, Quae si moventur ut asellorum*—With narrow head and long ears which they moved in the manner of asses. During the Roman Empire deformed 'idiots' were kept in many households for amusement and there is also a comment in Martialis' epigrams, where the poet complains bitterly to his friend Gargilianus that, having bought an 'idiot' in the market for 20 000 sesterces he wants his money back, because the purchase proved not to be a genuine morio—that is, a retarded person. Seneca in one of his letters mentions the death of a female 'imbecile' (fatua) belonging to his wife, but, while she provided a text for philosophical reflection, the Stoic derived little amusement from the follies of the 'imbecile'.

There are frequent references in the *Bible* to insanity, but it is very difficult to single out mental deficiency, since the entire philosophy was that mental disease was due to diabolical possession. However, the Jewish *Talmud* stresses that mental disease is not due to such possession and that the physician and not the priest should be

1

consulted; it further classifies epileptics and retarded persons under one heading. Moreover, it is of note that persons suffering from mental illness were not held responsible for their actions and therefore should not be punished. The following passage from the *Koran* may refer either to the insane, to retarded persons, or to both; 'Give not unto those who are weak of understanding the substance which Allah hath appointed you to preserve for them; but maintain them thereout and clothe them and speak kindly unto them.'

Avicenna (AD 980–1037), that prince of physicians, the Persian Galen, has some comments on mental disorder. The mind, he believed, comprised firstly, common sense; secondly, imagination; thirdly, instinct; fourthly, memory; and fifthly, understanding. He classified mental disease as *'phrenitis'*; *'lethargus'*; *'delirium'*; 'disorders of memory and imagination'; 'mania'; 'melancholia'; *'lycanthropy'*; the insane form of love, *'incubus'*; the *'pathic'* disorder; and lastly *'amentia* or fatuity'. He thought that *amentia* was caused by a cold humour occupying the body of the middle ventricle. Defects of memory and imagination were similar to fatuity, although he places the former in the posterior part of the brain and the latter in the fore part. Avicenna was an interesting individual: he worked hard, liked wine and the society of females; indeed doctors have changed little since Avicenna's time.

Following Avicenna's death in 1037, little fresh appears in the medical textbooks concerning the treatment of either insanity or mental retardation. This is not surprising when one reads the article by Professor Merke of Basle published in 1960. This is entitled, *The History of Endemic Goitre and Cretinism in the 13th to the 15th centuries*. Merke reproduces what he considers to be the oldest picture of a cretin taken from the *Musterbuch* of Reun, dated 1215. It shows an obvious 'defective', cretinous with three goitres, receding forehead and small head, with the fool's staff grasped in the left hand and right hand supporting a toad.

Fools—they would now undoubtedly be classified as retarded persons—are well illustrated in illuminated psalters of the time. They are always depicted associated with the letter D. The reason they are so associated is that the 53rd Psalm begins; *Dixit insipiens in corde suo non est Deus* which means 'The foolish body has said in his heart, there is no God.'

Felix Plater (1535–1614), a Swiss physician who had travelled extensively before settling in Basle, where he held the Chairs both of Anatomy and Medicine, published between 1602 and 1608 his *Praxis Medica*. London publication was in 1644. This represents the first attempt, by modern standards, at the classification of mental disease. He distinguished four types of mental disorder: *mentis imbecilitas* (mental weakness); *mentis consternatio* (including epilepsy); *mentis alienato* (phrenitis); and *mentis defatigio* (hyperkinetic states). Here then is an early occasion where mental retardation is separated from lunacy. Furthermore, he thought heredity important. He believed that, just as clever and active people produce their like, so do the stupid produce the stupid. His treatment, however, leaves something to be desired, for although he recommended exercises of body and mind and massage to the head, he had a fondness for amulets, particularly those containing precious stones such as amethyst and beryl, which were supposed to sharpen the intellect.

Plater was a keen clinical observer. Concerning 'idiots', he considered these could be recognized from an early stage by their actions, absence of discipline, intractability and inability to learn. In addition, he described changes in physical condition: the head was abnormal, the tongue was thick, the neck enlarged. He may possibly be describing cretinism or mongolism.

With the rise of Protestantism things did not improve for the retarded person, as Calvin believed that they were filled with Satan, while Luther maintained that 'idiots' were illegitimate children of the devil, and actually recommended on one occasion that an 'imbecile' boy of 12 be drowned. Luther wrote, 'The greatest punishment that God can inflict on the wicked is to deliver them over to Satan. There are many devils in woods, waters and wildernesses ready to hurt and prejudice people. In cases of melancholia, I conclude it is merely the work of the devil.' Yet St Vincent de Paul, born only 30 years after Luther, maintained that mental disease was no different from bodily disease and that Christianity demanded that the humane and powerful should protect and relieve one as well as the other. During the fifteenth, sixteenth and seventeenth centuries the physically deformed, the fools, epileptics, psychotics and deaf mutes were all grouped along with what we would now term 'the retarded person'.

Eastern cultures at this period were more endowed with Christian humanity than their Western brothers and thus we have Constantine, Bishop of Myra, stating that the weak-minded should be clothed and looked after. In France at that time, the word 'cretin' came into use, probably as a corruption of the word 'Chrétien' or 'Christian'. In many instances retarded persons were known as God's children—les enfants du bon Dieu.

At this stage, we might glance briefly at the legal history of the 'idiot' and the 'imbecile'. The word 'lunatic' first appears in the Statute book of 1541, but for long enough the terms 'lunatic' and 'idiot' were used indiscriminately. There are also laws passed in the time of Edward I and II protecting the lands, etc., of the retarded person. There was a legal phrase Prerogativa Regis, which meant 'The King has control over the property of natural fools'. Sir Matthew Hale defined three types of mental disorder; idiocy, madness and lunacy. Madness was considered to be permanent, but lunacy was characterized by incapacity of mind associated with lucid intervals. Locke in 1689 clearly distinguished the 'lunatic' from the 'defective'. He writes, 'Madmen put wrong ideas together and so make propositions, but argue and reason right from them, but idiots make very few or no propositions and reason scarce at all.'

From Plater until 1800 there was little fresh in the way of research and understanding of the retarded person, till we come to a Parisian ear, nose and throat specialist, Jean Marie Gaspart Itard (1774–1838). In 1801 Itard published a book entitled, *De L'Education d'un Homme Sauvage*. The circumstances which gave rise to this pioneer work are worth recording. In the late 1790s, three men hunting at Aveyron came across a young boy running wild in the woods. He was handed over to Professor Bonaterre who described him as follows. 'The boy was unused to our food, selecting his food by smell, drinking by lying flat on the ground and placing his mouth in the water, tearing his garments, walking on all fours, biting, giving few indications of any intelligence and having no appearance of being able to speak. He was, however, responsive to gentle caresses.' The professor thought that the lad would furnish to philosophy and natural history important concepts on the original constitution of man and on the development of the primitive faculties, provided that the state of 'imbecility' did not offer an obstacle to instruction. He was accordingly passed to a school for deaf mutes, the work to be undertaken by an individual, Sicard. But alas, Sicard quickly gave up the struggle of attempting to educate this wild boy, who constantly threw away his clothes and tried to escape, until finally he was allowed to wander quite neglected throughout the school. Yet the boy had aroused a great deal of interest. There were two schools of thought: one, led by Pinel, distinguished Physician-in-Chief to the Insane at Bicêtre, declared emphatically that the child was an 'idiot'; the second, dominated by Itard, Physician to the Deaf Mute Institution in Paris, held that the boy was simply wild and untaught. To quote Itard's words when it was pointed out to him that the boy was idiotic, 'I did not partake of this unfavourable opinion and, despite the truthfulness of the tableau and the closeness of resemblance, I dared to conceive some hopes.' It should be realized that Itard undertook this task, not to improve or cure an 'idiot', but 'to solve the metaphysical problem of determining what might be the degree of intelligence and the nature of the ideas in a boy who, deprived from birth of all education, should have lived entirely separated from individuals of his kind'. Itard drew up a programme, firstly to endear him to social life, secondly to awaken his nervous sensibility, thirdly to extend his sphere of ideas and fourthly to teach him to speak. For over a year Itard followed this psychological programme, but without any conspicuous degree of success.

Although Itard gave up this work he was fortunate—or rather the retarded person was fortunate—in that one of his pupils, Edouard Séguin (1812–1880), picked up the torch and blazoned a path which exists to this day in the treatment and care of the retarded person. Séguin, born at Clamecy (Nièvre) in France, studied under Esquirol and Itard and in 1837 founded a small school for 'idiots', based on the work of Itard. Following this he was asked to adopt the same techniques at the Bicêtre and in 1846 published his magnum opus entitled *Traitement moral, Hygiène et Éducation des Idiots et des autres Enfants Arriérés*—a book that should be regarded as the Magna Carta for the emancipation of the 'idiot' and imbecile'. Following its publication, Esquirol remarked that Séguin had 'removed the mark of the beast from the forehead of the imbecile'.

Séguin was astute enough to separate the retarded person from the lunatic. 'Therefore we must not confound imbeciles, insane persons and epileptics. The harmless idiot sitting awkwardly, bashful or reserved at our approach: he will answer us if he can, rarely mistaking, never deceiving, but oft-times failing to understand. His mind is extremely limited, but not deranged and with no special tendency to final insanity. He has a look, not of envy at things and persons, but of abstraction, gazing far out of this world into something which neither we nor he can discern.' Of paralysis with extensive contractures, he believed that these should not necessarily be beyond our skill, and gave ample indication that he was fully aware of the importance of physiotherapy.

Séguin also gives very precise information concerning the types of building to be used to house retarded persons. 'Idiots vitiate the air very rapidly; hence the necessity of supplying them with more than an ordinary share of it, by making their rooms very high and large, very airy and easily ventilated, accessible equally to natural and artificial heat. The windows should be so placed that children can, from the tables, enjoy the view of the gardens which have purposely been laid out.' In lighter vein he mentions, 'There are no means of communication from the side, stairs or building occupied by the girls, to that of the boys.' Séguin was something of an idealist, failing to realize that even with retarded persons, love will find a way. He stressed the importance of such things as singing and drawing and the importance of having a large common assembly hall. He felt strongly that nursing reports should be accurate and that the night staff should give a full report to the day staff. In fact there is no aspect of institutional care and supervision that Séguin did not cover. He emphasized the grave responsibilities resting upon those authorities who conduct schools and institutions for the training of retarded persons. 'It is thus apparent that great responsibilities rest upon the superintendents and upon the trustees who employ them in carrying out the immediate and remote objects of the foundation of schools for idiots. Narrow eagerness in pursuit of some points in practice; remissness in analytical enquiry, neglect of the synthetical problem of physiology; dropping of the scientific and social corollaries already issuing from the doctrine of physiological treatment and education; such are some of the evils which may bring down a school for idiots to the level of a richly endowed poorhouse.'

Following the accession of Napoleon III, Séguin in 1848 emigrated to the United States. There, in 1866, he published his book *Idiocy and its Treatment by the Physiological Method*. He pays great attention to detail and wrote 'Before entering further into the generalities of training, the individuality of the child is to be secured; for respect of individuality is the first test of the fitness of a teacher. At first sight all children look much alike; at the second their countless differences appear like insurmountable obstacles, but better viewed, these differences resolve themselves into groups easily understood and not unmanageable.' He discusses the causes of 'idiocy' and appreciates the gravity of extensive paralyses and contractures which deprive a child of important means of communication and knowledge. He realized that special senses are often abnormal and devised simple methods for their training and correction. Of training and education he wrote, 'It was a work, not for one individual, but for the teacher, the nurse, the physician, the philosopher, physiologist, psychologist and moralist all to work as a team and that men who treat idiocy with talent, erudition, even genius and have no true love or dedication for this work become in the words of St Paul as sounding brass or a tinkling cymbal.'

The first 'mental defective' colony in America was at Barre, Mass., opened privately in July, 1846, while the first public institution for retarded persons commenced in October of the same year at South Boston under the guidance of Dr Howe. The leading city of New York out-voted a proposal by Dr F. Backus to have an institution in 1845 and it was not until 1857 that New York opened its first 'defective' colony at Albany.

Contemporary with Séguin was the Swiss doctor J. Guggenbuhl, who published a book on the treatment of cretins in 1835. He believed that he was investigating a malignant disease which infested some of the most beautiful valleys of the higher Alps. During his travels he 'saw an old cretin who was stammering a half-forgotten prayer before an image of the Virgin, at Seedor in the canton of Uri. This sight excited my feelings in favour of those unhappy creatures and fixed my vocation. A being still capable of conceiving the thought of God is worthy of every care and every sacrifice. These individuals of our species, these debased brothers, are they not more worthy of our interest than those races of animals which we labour to make perfect? It is all important then, that a practical experiment should be tried. Much has already been written upon this subject, but little has been done.'

Guggenbuhl chose a spot above Interlaken between lakes Thun and Brientz. Opposite was the mighty Jungfrau and there he built his hospital. He was fortunate in that Interlaken was a popular tourist resort and many distinguished visitors climbed the mountain paths to see his pioneer work. He clearly differentiated the cretin from the simple *ament*. One of his basic principles was that it is vitally important to strengthen the body before attempting to develop the mind. This concept was in reality not new; it had been stated in 1540 by John Cuidad (1495–1550) *Por los cuerpos a las almas*—through the body to the soul—a motto Cuidad, that former mercenary soldier, placed above the doorway of his asylum in Granada. In a short time Guggenbuhl had aroused considerable interest in every European capital. Although history proves he was over-optimistic in the prognosis of 'idiocy', he pioneered the approach of treating physical disease before attempting to ameliorate the mental retardation.

The third great figure of the nineteenth century is a Dr Saegert, who was in charge of the Deaf and Dumb Institute in Berlin. He acknowledged the work of Séguin and Guggenbuhl, but published his own book, entitled, *The Treatment of the Blunt Mind in a Scientific Way*. Initially he was concerned with the training of the deaf and dumb, but used his techniques to educate the 'idiot' and 'imbecile'. He wrote, 'If some unhappy body should have a mentally backward child, congenital or due to disease, he should in the first instance have physical treatment by an able doctor and mental development will follow.' He also advocated nursing by humane nurses; 'that the company of other children was desirable; that there should be careful exercises and special nurseries would be useful'. He concludes, 'Not yet do such institutions exist, neither teachers nor other means. I hope the germ of the present work may sprout, and may Heaven bless it to succeed.'

Following the work of these early pioneers, research was carried on by Froebel and Montessori. It had become obvious that many retarded persons did not require full institutional care, so that by the latter part of the nineteenth century the beginning of special classes and special schools can be traced.

The first private 'mental deficiency' colony in Britain was established by the Misses White at Bath in 1846. This was a small establishment maintained by themselves for the reception of 'idiot' children. In 1848 at Highgate was opened what is officially known as the 'first mental deficiency colony'. This was the parent institution of both the Royal Earlswood and the Royal Eastern Counties at Colchester. In Scotland it was not until 1852 that something tangible was done for retarded persons. This charitable object came to the notice of Sir John and Lady Ogilvie who very generously at their own expense erected an institution for the education of the 'imbecile' on their estate of Baldovan some 4 miles from Dundee.

The problem of mental retardation had now become so vast that in 1904 a Royal Commission was set up. This Commission interviewed between 200 and 300 witnesses, sent representatives abroad and even had the courage to come to Scotland. As a result of their deliberations, they published in 1908 a report in eight Blue Books. On the basis of this report, the Government passed the Mental Deficiency and Lunacy (Scotland) Act, 1913. A similar Act applied to England (1 April, 1914) but did not come into force until 15 May, 1914.

The 1913 Act clearly separated the retarded person from the lunatic and further subdivided the retarded person into four well-defined groups, the 'idiot', the 'imbecile' the 'feebleminded' and the 'moral imbecile'. This Act was modified, for England only, in 1927, in that the 'defect' must have existed before the age of 18; but in Scotland it merely said from birth or an early age.

By the middle of the century, uniformity of legislation was in vogue in Great Britain, although other European countries were introducing specific legislation for the mentally handicapped. Confused thinking resulted in the Mental Health Acts of 1959 and 1960, where policies more suited to psychiatry were forcibly imposed on the mental deficiency hospitals and the community—so that now in 1982 we have voluntary bodies pressing for separate legislation for the mentally retarded! It may be that certain of the civil servants and their advisers prefer to say of the great men of yesterday what Ingres said to his pupils in the Rubens Gallery of the Louvre, 'Salute them, but pay no attention to them.' It is to be hoped that this book will remove some of the confused or dogmatic thinking which has always beset the planning of provision for the mentally handicapped. Recent history has been one of continuous reform. We are now in a new epoch of community care, with the ethic of equality of opportunity and citizens' rights. Yet the social order may have a very different effect and disappointment, injury and neglect may instead be the inheritance of retarded people. Philosophies of normalization and unassailable legal and humanitarian principles should be pursued with clear-headedness about available resources, with both diplomacy and a professional awareness of the mentally handicapped person's deficits and excesses.

CHAPTER 2

Changing Attitudes

WHO ARE THE MENTALLY handicapped? How many are there? Where do they live? Where ought they to live? Why are they living where they are? Why cannot the situation be regarded as satisfactory? By whom should the retarded be cared for? What next should happen in our plans?

DEFINITIONS

There are several ways in which to define the mentally handicapped. Some, such as Bijou (1966), say that mental deficiency, as it cannot be observed but is only inferred, ought not to be defined, rather each person's predicament described. Mental subnormality in the English Mental Handicap Act recognizes two degrees of mental subnormality; severe subnormality and subnormality, which are defined as follows; severe subnormality is 'a state of arrested or incomplete development of mind which includes subnormality of intelligence and is of such a nature or degree that the patient is incapable of living an independent life or of guarding himself against serious exploitation or will be so incapable when of an age to do so'. Subnormality is 'a state of arrested or incomplete development of the mind (not amounting to severe subnormality) which includes subnormality of intelligence and is of a nature or degree which requires or is susceptible to medical treatment or other special care of training and occupation'. The Mental Health (Scotland) Act considers mental deficiency as 'a condition of arrested or incomplete development of mind occurring at birth or at an early age, however caused or manifested'. These legalistic limited definitions are incompatible with current ideas about mental handicap, and the most acceptable definition currently available is that in the terminology manual of the American Association on Mental Deficiency, which states that (Grossman, 1973), mental retardation is 'significantly subaverage general intellectual functioning existing concurrently with deficits in adaptive behaviour, and manifesting during the development period'. Each key term is defined in the manual, e.g. 'significantly subaverage' is less than IQ 70 and the 'development period' stops at 18 years. Crucial emphasis is put on 'adaptive behaviour', which is how well a person copes with individual independence and responsibility, consistent with his age and culture.

So society is moving towards a model of mental handicap based on the following further points:

1. The importance of social criteria of functioning and performance, coping and adaptive behaviour in evaluation and classification.

2. The irrelevance of medical labels from a rehabilitation standpoint and the necessity for a classification based upon current observable behaviour.

3. The acceptance that low intelligence is a necessary but insufficient criterion of mental retardation.

4. Recognition of the humanitarian and legal principle of 'normalization'. (This point will be amplified later.)

5. Recognition of the effects of the expectations of others in influencing the behaviour of mentally retarded people. The retarded behave in the way they do partly as the result of living in large groups, partly as the result of being second class citizens, and partly as the result of inappropriate linguistic experience and opportunity.

NUMBERS AND LOCATION

How many mentally handicapped are there? And how many need special residential provision? That is to say, what are the true prevalence and the administrative prevalence, respectively? The usual rule of thumb is that 3 per cent of the population have IQs below 70; but the number of retarded people is much fewer and is different at different ages, as can be seen in *Table 1* (which is the mean prevalence from various surveys in the United Kingdom).

Table 1. Prevalence of Mental Handicap

Age	Severe[a] (IQ 0–50)	Overall (IQ 0–70)
United Kingdom 7-year-olds	2·4 per 1000	7–19 per 1000
United Kingdom 11–18-year-olds	3·8 per 1000	21·2 per 1000

[a] One third are mongols. 10% of mongols IQ 50+.

More retarded people in Britain live in hospitals than do in most other similarly wealthy countries. More in Britain live at home than in other similarly wealthy countries. This is partly the result of medical labelling and the historical predominance of the medical position in the field. There has been a change in society's view of the mentally handicapped and a change in the label, from 'subnormal' to a 'person with learning difficulties'. There is a change in threshold for acceptance; as Duke describes 'in a whole variety of ways communities are overcoming the temptation to segregate people', taking the risk of integration and discovering their own resources. Mental handicap is a multiprofessional business. The view of Stephens is now widely held: 'In most countries it is generally accepted that the care of the mentally handicapped can no longer be regarded as the sole responsibility of one discipline.' The multidisciplinary approach (of which more will be said later) has obvious advantages, as has the use, as often as possible, of ordinary professionals in ordinary settings. The use of ordinary environments and services wherever possible is encompassed in the Normalization Philosophy, which is not incompatible with hospital care, as the mentally handicapped commonly have severe additional physical illness or handicap. There was a fashion in the early 1970s to vilify all institutions, whatever their concern for personalized care, and unfeeling pressure was put on parents, whatever their resources, to undertake home training or to participate intensively in the construction of a community support service. As Gibson says, 'professionals were advised to tell parents that institutions of any kind were unhealthy, and home care uniformly preferable. Attention shifted from the parents to, ostensibly, the physical and psychological wellbeing of the retarded.'

THE NORMALIZATION PHILOSOPHY

The Normalization Philosophy entails normalizing the mentally handicapped person's relationships as much as possible, regarding him as a developing person, minimizing the effects of handicap and maximizing his similarities to other people. This principle entails tailoring down many of the special facilities which in the past were thought necessary for handicapped people and emphasizing care in the small group. It means non-standardized care, living in a world of both sexes, having a normal rhythm of day, week, year and life cycle. The principle of normalization encompasses the concept of 'the dignity of risk'. This concept may seem couched rather pompously for British readers, but it involves the process of learning through risk taking and the avoidance of over-protection.

Changeover

Until 30 years ago there was a world-wide trend towards institutionalizing the handicapped for good and humanitarian reasons; but in the late twentieth century a different approach developed, a trend towards community care, due to increasing child-centred attitudes and the unfeasibility of keeping the larger institutions staffed whilst maintaining standards comparable with those they had enjoyed at their inception. Community care means providing a service as close to the home of the handicapped person as is reasonable. It means providing a comprehensive service, a life-long service, a co-ordinated service; and it faces several initial hurdles, not least the economic costs of changeover ('start-up' double costs are considerable) from the institutional services. We have at present hospital and hostel provisions—often in the wrong places for the residential care and training of the mentally handicapped—but the momentum of discharge from hospital has become increasingly fast. In the United States this has been further accelerated by legal decisions. The National (American) Association of Retarded Citizens (NARC), for example, have formulated the useful guideline for gauging the suitability of placement of the mentally handicapped, '*the least restrictive setting*'; and several large institutions, e.g. Willowbrook, in New York State, have faced legal judgements compelling them to decrease radically their population. These legal requirements have been under-written by funds to enable their implementation. The Eastern Nebraska Community Office of Retardation (ENCOR) has pioneered a complete community alternative to institutional care, where now only a handful of profoundly handicapped children live in hospital-based (but not hospital-like) premises. In Canada, the Canadian Association of Mental Retardation (CAMR) has managed a partnership between professionals and citizens; CAMR sponsors the efforts, and expertise is offered by the National Institute of Mental Retardation (NIMR) in the form of technical advice and research. CAMR has produced *comserv*, comprehensive community service systems (North America has a surfeit of acronyms) which are now operating in parts of Ontario, in Quebec, Alberta and British Columbia and are intended to co-ordinate services. In the USA, as a result of President Kennedy's initiative, there is a standing Presidential Committee on Mental Retardation, which tries to co-ordinate interests and point the way forward; but, like many watch-dog committees in the United Kingdom, it lacks legal teeth, although it is a federal body.

Continued Use of Hospitals

The expectation that hospitals for the retarded will become irrelevant has not, in the early 1980s, shown much sign of being justified. There seems little doubt that, as regards children, the need for hospital care is evaporating, except for specific treatment (short term) or for the care of the profoundly handicapped decorticate or deteriorating child. Fostering (short- or long-term) is a better alternative and is increasing rapidly. For adults, however—assuming that hospitals will be part of the mentally handicapped scene for some time, in a climate of economic recession and governmental vacillation—all one can look forward to is the development of common elements in the training of nurses and social workers and the concentration of physical resources on priorities (such as secure units) and the maximization of those advantages that institutions do possess. In particular, the number of inhabitants warrant technical facilities such as a gymnasium, a swimming pool, sheltered workshops, physiotherapy, speech therapy, specialized dental care, and the provision of remedial gymnasts and beauticians. A mark of the mentally handicapped woman is, commonly, frumpish hair and dress and schoolgirl socks, and this is intolerable either inside an institution or in the community.

Places will also be needed in the foreseeable future for the permanent care of the multiply-handicapped in hospital. Such wards may well be part of children's hospitals, under paediatric supervision. The principle here is that a mentally handicapped child should only be hospitalized if he would also be in hospital had he been of normal intelligence.

One third of the intellectually retarded have a physical handicap, most often a neurological condition which was probably the primary cause of their retardation, while more than a fifth have a psychiatric disability. As only one in ten of the intellectually retarded are without other handicap, it should be abundantly clear that most intellectually handicapped children present multiple problems, and these are not merely ones directly related to their learning difficulties.

The severely handicapped adults will in many countries remain the hospital's responsibility—those too physically handicapped, too behaviourally disturbed, those requiring treatment of a temporary physical or mental nature, or those perhaps too institutionalized for it to be humane to eject them from what they regard as their 'home'. This is yet a questionable ethical point. Many of us have times of insecurity and almost everyone nowadays leaves home or moves home on at least one occasion during his life. This can be a growing experience, although painful at the time, whether we are handicapped or not; and perhaps mentally handicapped children and adults should have a right to at least one change of home and doctor during their lives. It is in the nursing of the severely handicapped that normalization is most effective, paradoxically. Even the most handicapped can have home-like conditions—non-standardization of care, access to choices and risks. Flowers and soft furnishings can make the ward home-like—not just one or two vases of plastic flowers (since one would possibly be destroyed it is better to exhibit several vases at once); also knives and forks and having the other sex to sit beside at lunch-time, with recurring outings and walks, so that, eventually, the ideal of pattern foresight and planning may arise. For the less profoundly handicapped, living in such a ward of partial segregation helps them at least to enjoy the benefit of a tablecloth and a tidy lunch. Nevertheless the constant aim should be present to bring up the messy eaters to a tablecloth situation. Normalization does not mean that we should assume that the tastes of the mentally handicapped will be identical to ours. For instance, most of us would prefer tranquil music in ward settings, but evidence is that the mentally handicapped, like the young child, prefer a thumped-out rhythm and repetitive noisy music, but only for a little while!

DAY CARE

Day hospital care is a valuable adjunct to inpatient treatment. Often regarded by the hospital as inconvenient and troublesome, it in fact should be part of the hospital services to the community. The hospital can also provide evening recreation for the mentally handicapped, if no community centre is available, and further education classes, if these are not available under the Education Authority's auspices. It should be remembered that the usual age of school leaving (16 years) in the United Kingdom is also the age when the mentally handicapped person is becoming optimally motivated and ready for formal education. It is often part of nursing duties (usually for a specified nursing officer) to liaise with community organizations, such as the Hospital Friends, the National Societies for the Mentally Handicapped and MENCAP, to increase and ease visiting, outings, holidays and benefits for the residents. Hospital nurses are also participating increasingly in outpatient clinics and following up their patients in their homes. As specialized community nurses they do not conflict with a Health Visitor's duties.

OBJECTIVES

Hospitals which care for the mentally handicapped are, for the foreseeable future, likely to continue to have the mixed purposes of being places of treatment, education and residence (SHHD/SED 1972—Jay, 1979). Such objectives as treatment and creating home-like conditions are equally important. We see the hospital for the mentally handicapped as both a resource and a residential treatment centre, offering short and medium stay for several categories of mentally handicapped people; the particularly profoundly handi-capped child in need of continuous nursing care; the severely handicapped child with additional handicaps, whether physical or behavioural, such as restlessness and sleep disturbance; the adoles-cent with conduct problems; and the multiply-handicapped adult who requires intermittent or continuous hospital facilities. Many of these categories may only require day-care or periodic admission;

medical effort is towards continuous assessment and rehabilitation, but the targets may necessarily be very limited, e.g. self-help and toilet training in an institutional setting. Mentally handicapped people ought not to be admitted on purely social grounds (Cmnd. 104, 1965), but it is often impossible to make fine distinctions, and relief on mainly social grounds is often cost-effective to other medical agencies, such as doctors and health visitors, in view of the high incidence of associated breakdowns of parents of handicapped children. Therefore, hospital care of the mentally handicapped is a continuum from short-term admission to paediatric units for diagnosis, to residential treatment centres in mental handicap hospitals, where a team of doctors from a range of backgrounds in child-care or mental health collaborate with teachers and social workers to provide an optimum living environment for severely handicapped and psychologically sick mentally handicapped. The existence of, and the resources offered by, the mental handicap hospital depend on local needs and on facilities already provided. The hospital may, for instance, provide day-care, five-day wards and holiday relief, but what is crucially important is that the resident should have access both to the full range of medical services and to educational and social services which match those medical services in their comprehensiveness.

RANGE OF SERVICES

The range of services provided by the various departments of a mental handicap hospital include Special Teaching Units for all children; speech and language programmes; physiotherapy clinics, as the commonest and least treated disability in the mentally handi-capped population is communication disorder—the mentally handi-capped person grossly underfunctions in language; remedial gymnas-tic clinics; dental clinics; chiropody clinics; toy banks and toy libraries; and a joint-user service with the Local Authority for Adult Training Centres, dovetailing with leisure centres for adolescents and adults, advice centres, home-sitting services, foster-care and re-sidential care in the community. A Mental Handicap 'hospital' complex must provide a psychology service; analysis of absent or lost skills in brain-damaged individuals and the supply of recording techniques; teaching machines for the over sixteens; 'time-out', token economy systems; conditioning; even aversion therapy—used for self-mutilation, unpleasant but successful. Nurses should be involved in the new technologies of ethology, altering territoriality, exploiting grooming and manual signing and time-sampling with event recorders.

Despite many hindrances to the development of such services, and the burden of those not requiring hospital care, mental handicap hospitals over the past decade have increasingly been developing *family-supportive* as well as *family-replacement* services. The locations of the family supportive services and clinics vary. The mental handicap clinic may not be physically situated in a mental handicap hospital, but it must be closely connected with the mental handicap hospital by shared staff. The hospital and community services should have access to the same array of personnel, comprising paediatrician, psychiatrist (one or both of whom should have special knowledge of learning disorders), psychologist, visiting school-health doctors and therapists, with a reserve of specialist social workers. The mental handicap clinic ought to be multidisciplinary, in the sense that open consultation should be a feature ; yet modes of practice have to be left to individuals.

There is real danger that community care is becoming a slogan concealing policies of neglect rather than positive, intensive care. At least minimum standards are likely to exist in hospitals. The difference between the relative uniformity of standards of care in institutions and the variability in the community is an inevitable result of the nature of the organizations responsible. Patients in hospital are both visible and accessible, and responsibility for care standards is therefore assignable. The difference in administrative style that results is clear. A hospital desperately short of nursing staff will go to a Nursing Agency. Similarly, the Hospital Advisory Service and the Mental Welfare Commission for Scotland can provide trenchant criticism of hospital services, unless there has been careful and comprehensive planned integration. Community units can become claustrophobic institutions, undersupervised, over-crowded, with both low resident and high staff turnover.

Priorities and Parents

A comprehensive Mental Handicap Service must have a list of priorities. The first is *prevention*, which is dealt with in other chapters; but the mention of one aspect cannot at this juncture be deferred—the increasing realization of the importance of psycho-social disadvantage in causing mental handicap. In some regions of the UK one child in six is gravely deprived of the chance to learn. This simple amentia or 'subcultural mental deficiency' can be prevented by early intervention, if powerful enough. In the Mil-waukee experiment by teaching and encouraging subcultural mothers to become good 'first teachers', the communicative competence and IQ of their offspring was significantly raised. The connection between poverty and cultural–familial retardation has been established, notably in the vast urban ghettos of Scotland. Such children have no specific stigmata or unifying characteristics except the tendency to equate repeated failure with being a 'write-off'.

The second priority is *early identification,* which involves a multi-disciplinary team locating and helping the parents through the process of the initial shock, disbelief, anger and the period of reactive depression, to the period of gradual adaptation and to the realities of making plans and orientating themselves to the future. Priority three—*intervention*— means offering parents respite: short-term care in, ideally, community hostels such as the alternative living units (ALUS) provided by Barnardo's and other charitable bodies such as SSMH and MENCAP; emergency care perhaps in hospitals; and the promise of continuity of care during the child's progression to adult life and, eventually, some form of employment. Also of assistance are the use of specialist community nurses who work flexible hours; and the responsibility and accountability which a 'named person' (*see* Appendix 1) provides, as foreseen in the Warnock Report (1978).

The Down's Baby Project based on the Hester Adrian Unit has shown the advantage of training parents as educators, and demonstrated that the decline in IQ which the Down's anomaly shows can be minimized.

Differences do *Exist*

Normalization is a humanitarian and legal principle. It is not a factor in psychological and medical assessment. It does not deny the existence of differences between retarded and average people, nor the possibility of deterioration. A bland optimism or dodging of the differences in learning processes between retarded and normal children is also now realized as being as professionally unacceptable as the previous inflexible and inappropriate labelling on IQ basis was. A Down's child of 'IQ 70' is not the same as a normal child of 'IQ 70'. Retarded children have cognitive deficits which differentiate them, qualitatively, not simply quantitatively on an IQ curve (with the possible exception of the uncomplicated socially disadvantaged child). Normal children are constantly engaged with vim, in manufacturing new games to perfect their competence in mastery of their environment; the retarded child not so. Normal children are noted for their rapt attention; retarded children have impaired attention-denoting and are distractable—they moreover often have trouble shifting from one stimulus to another—this is not rapt attention but perseveration. Retarded children often lack the ability to make connections, either linguistic or perceptual. Normal children are driven by curiosity to explore, investigate, try out, and change their circumstances. The retarded person often shows passivity in problem solving. He has little imagination, he lives in the here-and-now. He has memory problems, not in remembering isolated facts but in flexible memorizing, so that spontaneous transfer and strategies are not acquired. There is usually also un-selective perception so that the ability to focus on one aspect while keeping others in perspective, to organize and analyse situations, is impaired. When one asks the retarded person to describe a picture often one simply gets a list of items as a response. Recognition of barriers to learning is the first step to overcoming them.

ACCOMMODATION

Domiciliary support for adult mentally handicapped persons also involves the provision of advice, relief in emergencies for adults and continuous support, with the development of specialized units for the blind deaf and for the aged mentally handicapped, whose numbers are increasing. And, in hospitals, *improving quality of the residents' lives* is the next priority, firstly, by recognizing that friendship ties are vital, that people should not be unceremoniously moved from one ward to another, that occupation is a right for all, and that endowment funds and patients' funds may, with the patients' democratic agreement, be used to increase their pleasures rather than their bank balances. It should be recognized that staff need for their own morale, as well as their enlightenment, to see some turnover in their charges and to go on courses. We should look forward eventually to a national training college for treatment and education of the mentally handicapped. Each inpatient needs an *individual plan* and at least yearly reappraisal; this should not simply be done by one discipline. *Co-ordination* is also a priority. The overall accommodation, occupational and educational services available in an area should be co-ordinated and the criteria for entry to each agreed upon by a Joint Care Planning Team as suggested by the National Development Group (NDG). The National Development Group for the Mentally Handicapped, an independent advisory body, was set up by the Secretary of State for social services in England and Wales in 1975 to advise on the development and implementation of services. It ceased functioning in 1980. In its 5 years existence it produced a wealth of ideas, suggestions and educative notions to help care-givers who had some power to consider and implement sensible change. The National Development Group's last act was to draw up a checklist which reviewed meticulously every aspect of health and social service care. Implementation of these standards in the checklist of good practice has not yet occurred. The checklist has (to date) not yet received the imprimatur of government and the approach is open to local interpretation. The National Development Group recommended three principal issues to which Joint Care Planning Teams should address themselves:

1. The assessment of availability of residential places in all sectors and the calculation of the appropriate overall level of short-term residential care provision.

2. The identification and designation of the facilities to be used for short-term care. Ideally these will be distributed throughout each area so that links with the family and the community are easily established and maintained.

3. The formulation of criteria for admission to and discharge from such provisions. These must be acceptable to all staff concerned and agreed with senior management of both the NHS and the Local Authority.

In other countries such teams can use the Programme Analysis of Service Systems (PASS)—another acronym! The procedure is for the objective measurement of the quality of a wide range of human management services and moves on from the stage of identification of needs to evaluating services, analysing the quality and adequacy of services, continuously assessing services and accrediting services. In certain American states, service providers do not qualify for state funds unless they pass the PASS! The broad bases of the ratings are on proximity to population centres, access, physical context, the size of the facilities, the programme's appropriateness, contact with the community and other socially integrative opportunities. Of these factors, the greatest failure in the care of the mentally handicapped has been the sizes of the groups cared for. Large groups are accompanied by behaviour problems and lower social competence, the mentally handicapped becoming more handicapped by the perplexing chaotic environment shared with many other people. Thus, Grunewald writes, 'It's not so much that we have retarded people as that we have retarded environments.' For those who are not sick there must be various forms and choices of 'small group living'. The most innovative practice recently has been that of retarded people and students sharing accommodation supported by the Manpower Services Commission and Cardiff University Student Settlement (CUSS).

Both the Education Authorities and charitable bodies, e.g. Barnardo's, provide residential schools for handicapped children. The Social Work Department, Foster Homes and a 'Share-the-Care' for retarded children and adults, e.g. in Camden, London, also have a part to play. Social Work Departments provide for adult 'hostels'—a hostel has a turnover connotation. Such a hostel will probably house 25–30 people, promote independence training and often will be attached to an Adult Training Centre in rural areas. For the more competent, sheltered housing, e.g. the Ark Housing Association, and, for the most able group, homes where supervision consists of a visiting social worker or community nurse may be available. In North America the term 'Group Home' may apply to 'boarding houses', 'hostels', 'halfway houses' and modified motels and hotels; such board or care facilities may cater for 30–50 residents. 'Community Homes' are smaller, 4–10 residents, and approximate to the British meaning of Group Home or sheltered accommodation. Village communities, e.g. Steiner and L'Arche, also play an important part in the range of services in the UK.

EMPLOYMENT

The path to competitive employment is nowadays almost un-navigable for the retarded youth, but the range of alternative temporizing facilities has expanded. On leaving school, like many of their contemporaries, mentally retarded persons can start by spending some time on the Youth Opportunities Programme (YOP) which offers work experience on employers' premises, project-based work, community service programmes, training workshops, work intro-duction courses and courses in basic employment skills. Some Employment Rehabilitation Centres offer Young Persons' Work Preparation Courses (YPWPC), and some Colleges of Further Education now offer Link Courses to Special School pupils (which involve, during the last year of school, a day per week at college) and 1- or 2-year full-time courses for mentally handicapped school leavers (extension courses). These extension courses followed by YPWPC and then by YOP give the retarded youth time to mature and to realize that previous failure does not mean he is a 'write-off'. Some retarded young people who are registered disabled can join sheltered workshops or Sheltered Industrial Groups (SIG). A SIG involves the 'firm', which pays for the work done, and the Manpower Services Commission, which contributes a grant.

For the severely mentally handicapped there are hospital in-dustrial therapy units and, again, an increasing variety of training centres. The emphasis in Training Centres will be less on meeting contracts and more on improving independence and on craft and art work, where the mentally handicapped worker can have the reward of seeing the product of his labours. Staff are expensive; repetitive occupational skills are cheap. Therefore it saves money: it is not simply humane to make the mentally handicapped as independent as possible. Training Centres often include bathing facilities and sometimes a model home for domestic training so that a mentally handicapped person who has been grossly overprotected by his parents can start at the lowest rung in the Centre, by learning for example to make a cup of tea without burning himself, on the road to living in a local authority hostel.

Integrating the handicapped does not mean fitting the mentally handicapped into our economic system 'at all cost'. The 'productivity' basis of industry and the pace required may be too much. We should not promote the mentally handicapped to incompetence by placing him in a job where he is only just coping, having to work at peak performance all the time, and is too fatigued for leisure. Social workers and health care staff can spend time more profitably than in striving officiously to place an occasional retarded man in open employment which he is unfit to hold. As professionals we have to bear in mind that whatever the ethics of equality and citizenship say, society may have a different view. We should avoid allowing the retarded person to face unnecessary disappointment or rejection. In the current watchwords of the American Association on Mental Deficiency this is *A Decade of Change: From Rights to Realities.*

CHAPTER 3

Methods of Assessment. 'A Multidisciplinary Business'

1. HISTORY

There may be an absence of reliable subjective information from the mentally handicapped person himself, depending upon the degree of handicap. The examiner therefore has to depend upon other means to provide him with important facts. Taking a history is an art and requires great skill and patience: the whole process is fraught with difficulties. The relatives may not have appreciated sufficiently the significance of developmental landmarks to have noted them, or they may have forgotten them. In families where there are three or four children important facts may be incorrectly ascribed to one or other of the siblings. Some parents, in their anxiety and desire to make their offspring appear brighter than he actually is, will unknowingly distort the facts, while others may exaggerate their difficulties and distort them in other ways.

a. *Personal History*

This should be a very comprehensive report and no detail about the mentally handicapped person should be dismissed without consideration as being unimportant. It should contain information about:

i. BIRTH

Place of birth in the family; age of parents, mother's state during pregnancy, whether the delivery was normal or whether it was accompanied by some abnormality; the appearance of the child at birth; whether he breathed normally or whether there was some delay.

ii. PROGRESS THROUGH CHILDHOOD

A record outlining the milestones of his progress should be made, for instance; feeding, the age at which he smiled, raised his head, sat up, crawled and walked alone; the age at which he was weaned, when he talked and when he became toilet trained; behaviour and personality as a toddler and pre-school behaviour. (*See* Development Assessment.)

iii. SCHOOL AND NURSERY REPORTS

These reports are considered and should include the age of entry and the age of leaving, the child's degree of competence in handling subjects taught and any truancy, maladjustment or unsociability recorded during his school-going career.

iv. SELF-CARE

It is important to report on the child's habits as fully as possible. The nature of these will give an indication of his self-care ability.

v. SEPARATION

There may have been factors necessitating the separation of the child from his mother, or periods when the mother displayed inability to tolerate physical contact. In such cases the reason and the duration should be investigated.

vi. EMPLOYABILITY

The nature of his employment and the reasons for any changes that may have occured.

vii. PREVIOUS HEALTH

What physical illnesses and accidents has he had and at what age did they occur? It is important that the following be reported upon in detail: meningitis, concussion, fainting attacks, chorea, venereal disease, epilepsy and any of the virus infections.

viii CIRCUMSTANCES LEADING TO ADMISSION

Whether due to change in family circumstances or the mentally handicapped person's behaviour and, if so, the nature of this.

b. *Family History*

Relationship and any great disparity in ages of parents should be noted. Inquiry into the temperament of the parents and for signs of mental instability in either one should be made. Are there any cases in the family of insanity, mentally handicap, or fits?

2. INFORMATION

Information is largely acquired through the combined efforts of the doctor, the nurse and social worker.

A careful routine physical examination is of great importance, and investigation of all systems should be directed towards ascertaining the existence of malnutrition, disease, deformity or special-sense defect which might be responsible for mental handicap, and towards the detection of the presence of developmental anomalies and stigmata.

a. *The Skin*

The state of the skin will suggest the mentally handicapped person's ability to provide his own self-care or that of others to provide it for him; information relating to the standard of his general nutrition, whether his diet is adequate, or if too much of one class of food is being given and too little of others.

b. *Hearing*

If the patient is being examined for deafness, it is important that he is also examined for high-frequency deafness. This could quite easily be the cause of his lack of mental development.

c. *Sight*

Though the patient can see, it may be that he can only see things in detail when they are at a certain distance away from him, and he may as a result miss quite a lot of information due to tunnel vision.

d. *Central Nervous System*

A full and thorough examination of this system is important, as it may show an underlying degenerative disease which may not have affected the more recent generations of the family, but is nevertheless present in the family tree.

Other facts concerning the mentally handicapped person's reactions, degree of mental handicap and feelings are equally important and need observing so that an accurate assessment can be made.

The points to be noted on interview with the patient are:

1. How well developed is his speech? Can he use words in their right context, and is his vocabulary extensive or limited?

2. Is the mentally handicapped person relaxed and at ease during the interview, or does he appear to be insecure and strained? The message that people verbally transmit is usually amplified or at least modified by their non-verbal behaviour. It serves as a complementary function to verbal behaviour; both are part of communication. Eye contact is one of the most important aspects of non-verbal

communication. Interviewers who engage in a large amount of eye contact to gain positive feedback are judged as most likeable by interviewees.

Mentally handicapped people often avoid eye contact, either not knowing how to obtain social feedback or else to hide their feelings and to avoid being recognized as a person. Eye blink rate increases as the amount of threat to handicapped persons increases. The 'grammar of posture' is a phrase now applied to the defining of a person's emotional state by his body movements and positions.

Positive head nods and smiles are associated with approval seeking, and negative head nods with avoidance of approval. Mentally handicapped persons under stress will show more trunk and leg movements but less hand and arm movements, their hands and arms moving into a closed position. On the part of the interviewer a forward lean of the torso towards the mentally handicapped person tends to show a more positive, warmer attitude, and an orientation directly towards the person also shows more warmth. It is important that the interviewer shows self-awareness of the mentally handicapped person's position both in terms of social status and in terms of the actual situation and presentation at interview.

3. What account can he give of himself? For instance, can he say when he had his last meal and what he had for it? Which school did he go to, what subjects did he do and with what success? What information can he give of his friends and his work? All these questions will have to be prepared and presented according to the person's age and obvious ability.

4. Is the mentally handicapped person orientated as to time and place? Does he understand what day, and the time of the day it is, and does he appreciate where he is?

5. Routine questions such as the mentally handicapped person's name, age, address, etc., are asked.

6. General information questions are asked to see if the mentally handicapped person is as well informed as a normal child of his age should be, or to gauge the degree of subnormality present. Questions will include those of everyday usage, such as money sense—if he goes into a shop to buy an article costing 5 new pence with a 10p piece, how much change will he have? In what day and in which year is he living? His sense of number will also be tested by asking him to multiply 2×2 and subtract 2 from 4.

7. The mentally handicapped person's 'feeling tone' will be investigated by observing his mood. Is it in keeping with his circumstances? Is he anxious, depressed or elated? Is he suffering from a psychosis masquerading as mental handicap? Has the mentally handicapped person the ability to form a relationship with the examiner, or does he remain flat and uninterested?

8. The examiner will encourage the mentally handicapped person to explain any statements made about him by others, especially with regard to impulsive actions and eccentricities of conduct. An attempt will be made to trace out each symptom to its origin.

3. OBJECTIVE INFORMATION

This information is given by any or all of the following people who have direct and close contact with the mentally handicapped person: the parents of the mentally handicapped person, the officer in charge of the mentally handicapped person's unit and the occupational therapist. The information so submitted deals with the same aspects of the mentally handicapped person's abilities, progress or regression.

The points dealt with below are continually being observed, assessed and reported upon.

a. *Capacity for Self-care*

i. FEEDING

Can the mentally handicapped person feed himself? If so, what degree of efficiency can he attain? Lack of manipulative power, such as being unable to raise the spoon to his mouth, may indicate spasticity and athetosis.

ii DRESSING

The degree of skill he achieves in dressing and undressing himself with or without assistance, and the manipulative power of his hands in fastening his buttons, shoe laces, etc.

iii. TOILETING

Is he continent and able to attend to his own toileting?

b. *Physical Ability*

Reports on the power of the mentally handicapped person's muscular co-ordinations are necessary. If the mentally handicapped person can walk, does he do so with a normal gait? Can he run and climb?

c. *Intellectual Ability*

Speech is important and it can vary in degree of efficiency amongst the mentally handicapped. All aspects of the mentally handicapped person's ability to use this special sense should be reported upon. Does he speak distinctly, and is his speech normal? How great is his vocabulary? Are short phrases used in an attempt to overcome the difficulties of speech? The ability to read and write, though not essential for self-care, is nevertheless important, and the degree of competency in reading, writing and spelling should be investigated.

d. *Working Ability*

What degree of working efficiency has the mentally handicapped person achieved? What kind of work does he like doing best? What skill has been acquired in handling tools associated with his work?

e. *Relationships*

Notes on the mentally handicapped person's relationships with other mentally handicapped people. What is his attitude towards his social life? Is he solitary or sociable? Interested or uninterested in other people? Has he an equable temperament or does he suffer from temper tantrums? Is he simple, docile and tractable?

f. *Social Activities*

Does the mentally handicapped person enjoy taking part in social activities? If so, what type? Active or passive? Or does he prefer to watch other people taking part in them?

g. *General Work Record*

This report will only be necessary for those mentally handicapped people working away from the hospital and should include the mentally handicapped person's capacity for accepting reasonable authority, and whether he is amenable to, or hostile towards, authority.

4. SPECIAL INVESTIGATIONS

These are carried out for diagnostic purposes and include: (1) Intelligence and personality tests; (2) School reports; (3) Electro-encephalography; (4) Blood analysis; (5) Urine analysis, including chromatography; (6) Buccal smears; (7) Chromosomal investigation; (8) Hormonal investigation.

Annually the whole team—nurse, psychologist, doctor, teacher and therapists—meet to review progress. It is important that there is a baseline for this purpose. The most common baseline is the Adaptive Behaviour Scale (Nihira, 1969), which provides better information about the coping behaviour of mentally handicapped people than previous assessment schedule rating scales. It identifies those who could achieve self-sufficiency and points out the excesses and deficits of persons. A new check list, Paton's Borders Assessment Schedule, is particularly flexible and versatile (Appendix 4).

EARLY SIGNS OF MENTAL HANDICAP

All the procedures described in this chapter have the common aim of securing information so that the diagnosis can be soundly based. Though it is important to make a formulation of mental handicap as early in life as possible, it is only possible to do this in the early months of life in the cases where there are gross deformities and in certain metabolic disorders. It is estimated that, of the cases recognizable at birth, between 70 and 80 percent are either born dead or die within the first few days, and those that survive are usually severely handicapped. However, it is highly important that an early diagnosis is made in such cases as the metabolic disorders, phenylketonuria, galactosaemia etc., and in the case of cretinism. It is possible to make an early diagnosis in these cases, and prompt treatment has the possibility of success. Mild cases of mental handicap tend to go unnoticed until the children begin to show failure in school, and some even escape notice until they have left school, when their social incapacity becomes apparent due to their rapid changeover of jobs and frequent involvement with authority.

MULTIDISCIPLINARY ASSESSMENT AND CASE RECORDS

The assessment of the mentally handicapped child is a particularly multidisciplinary effort, as the child is almost certain to be the responsibility of (and problem for) several agencies, for example, the Hospital Authorities, the Education Authorities and the Social Services. The same multidisciplinary approach should of course also be applied to the adult mentally handicapped.

DEVELOPMENTAL ASSESSMENT

The ability to take a developmental history ought to be part of staff training. It is only then that the mentally handicapped person's existence, his encounters, and his individuality can be documented so that we can obtain clues as to how he is trying to find meaning in the world.

Staff from different professions will place different emphasis on areas of developmental assessment. Medical emphasis will be placed on the family history; the possibility of sex-linked illnesses; the pregnancy, in particular the first trimester and perinatal period; the immediate neonatal period (as at that point the child is more likely to display signs than in the few months when brain damage in particular may vanish in the 'latent period'). Did the child have convulsions in the first 5 days or after the 8th (likely primary brain damage?), or between the 5th and 8th day (likely metabolic?)— the outcome being worse in the former. How was mother's health in the perinatal period? What about social and psychomotor sequences or the vital period about 28 weeks when love becomes reserved for mother? What are the language milestones—babble amount; character; time of first words and two-word utterances and sentences? How and when did toilet training occur? What about play interests, toys and relations with transitional objects?

However, the interdisciplinary historian-practitioner will ask it all again in a different way and form a different perspective. He will ask of the mother chronologically: what do you remember during the pregnancy; at the breast; or of the child in the incubator; when he was one year old; when he was 2; when he was 3? The child's medical history: complications, convulsions, hospitalizations, the number of times the doctor came to the house; his predominant mood? Was he a 'twittery' baby; was his activity purposeful or purposeless; was there sleep disturbance; his relationship with siblings; his fears, specific and non-specific; phobias, tics, fads and nightmares; his relationship with peers and his achievements; what was he good at? All this against the background of a family, its moods, ambitions, rearing practices and idols.

In a developmental assessment of a young person, there is a major dichotomy to be borne in mind. Medicine is divided into *disease states* and *developmental disorders*. The child's failure to walk may be simple developmental retardation of the mechanisms of walking, or it may be muscular dystrophy, cerebral palsy or a brain tumour. The medical team has sapiential authority here.

Growth and Development

A child's journey into adulthood involves two processes: *growth* and *development*. To see a child in the playroom without considering growth would be utterly wrong. It is a measure that you can quantify. There are tables available; the standard deviations of weight, height, head circumference, bone age, onset of secondary sex characteristics. The principle of normal distribution of such parameters is equally applicable to development. One need not investigate a child's slow speech if it is within normal limits for his age. Malnutrition is not a problem in twentieth century Britain (obesity in Social Class 5 certainly is, and the clock is set by the age of 7). At birth there is little or no nerve insulation (myelin), which with environmental stimulation increases rapidly. If during a certain period the nervous system does not receive timely stimulation, it is likely that insulating will not arise. This is the principle of the 'Sensitive' period (Brown, 1971).

We know that the child between 6 months and 5 years requires a close maternal relationship and that character disorder may result from lack of such maternal interaction. If a child does not hear the normal range of speech sounds in the first year, he will build in his own modules to speak adequately. We know that if a child suffers brain damage in the dominant hemisphere before the age of 8 he will recover speech. If damaged after the age of 8 he will not recover fully.

The acquisition of *dominance* means the complete over-ruling of one side of the brain, necessary for independent movement of one side—dominance is not usually fully achieved until about the age of 8; though the child often seems to be right or left handed at one year, this can shift. There is a relationship between cross-laterality, left handedness, late dominance and poor reading/writing. In the small child one limb cannot move independently of another. Associated (overflow) movements are common. These are the basis of many of the flappings, grimacing and blinks in the mentally handicapped. Enuresis can often be regarded as a developmental disorder. One must always remember the statistics behind the individual: one child in nine is a persistant bedwetter at age eleven. Two percent are ascertained as educationaly subnormal. If a child has fits after the age of five, he stands a ninety-three percent chance of being maladjusted. The people most in need are least likely to get the required services or obtain them so late that the clumsiness, behaviour and speech problems have crystallized. If only the emphasis on the diagnosis of currently rare and largely untreatable metabolic disease could be put on reliable developmental screening for those vast numbers of multiply handicapped children!

One should remember that if you find one handicap the odds are you will find another. Most children who have got a developmental disorder (for example a squint) will have more than one disorder and these should be looked for. Does the child suffer from chronic catarrh?; perhaps a 'glue' ear and high frequency deafness? We should not so much just 'test' as *ask* as well.

Little attention is paid to *perceptual motor development*, however sophisticated our facilities. An exception is clark's study of body image and motor skills in the handicapped. This study shows that normal people show a range of accuracy in their self-perception of their body image, physiotherapists and remedial gymnasts tending to be the most accurate on tests employing distorted mirrors. Mentally handicapped people use proprioceptive (motor/touch) cues rather than visual ones, while normal adults do the opposite. Children use proprioceptive cues. This is independent of intelligence, but is dependent on development. Thus, the mentally handicapped person is less accurate at assessing his body image with his eyes than the normal person at estimating his body image! Developmental maturity is the crucial factor, not intelligence.

Day care centres for children and the handicapped must pay particular attention to *motor development*: to the child sitting and standing and walking and lying, prone and supine; to his head control, and whether he shows posturing or tonus in gross movements; to the child's overall motoric output and tempo and purpose, whether the movements of his body are global or partial; the finer motor movements, the stereotypic movements, the associated movements; to the child's overall motor output and tempo and purpose, cybernetic systems; the postural controls—the Extra Pyramidal System—and the 'willed-movement'—the Pyramidal System. As regards postural control, the questions are whether there are signs of abnormal persistence of primitive postural reflexes (the Moro; the tonic neck reflexes; the stepping reflexes; ventral suspension reflexes) or whether there is a lack of appearance of mature postural reflexes (such as the parachute, the landau, the propping reactions). Is there correct super-imposition of the child's willed motor skills? Can he bring his hands to the middle; can he grasp; how is his fine finger manipulation; can he 'cruise'; and how does he get from hitching or scooting to cruising, walking or hopping? In the absence of a specific motor disability, almost all severely handicapped children learn to walk; and 'shoogliness' and mannerisms, those immediate antecedents of prejudice and discrimination, are understandable and therefore not frightening when the care-worker has developmental expertise.

Deficiencies in *perceptual motor skills* are often now remediable. Physiotherapists can exploit persistent postures. Systematic assessment procedures, such as the Frostig programme, have led to forms of controversial perceptual training. It is, however, not yet possible to differentiate with certainty between developmental delay and brain injury using these instruments and treatment. Often such differentiation is not necessary.

Different categories of staff will place different emphasis on *social development*. Particularly for child-orientated services, special attention must be paid to relationships with peers; whether he ignores or imitates them; whether he plays in parallel or co-operates; whether he understands rules; his relationship with adults; whether he shows over-dependence; whether he shows eye avoidance. One wishes to know how he relates to toys; whether he notices them; whether he has specific toys; the quality of his play; his fantasy play; his social abilities; smiling, feeding, toileting; his emotional development, the overall integration of his personality, his ego, his mechanisms of defence. In the case of the severely handicapped adult, the Borders Assessment Schedule (Appendix 4) should be scored and at least one agency in the area should be operating a Token Economy Social Competency Programme.

Language development should be considered along with speech development and hearing assessment. It is important to know if there is an amplitude defect or a frequency defect; if the person can hear conversationally; if he can locate the sound source. Sheridan screening with Stycar vocabulary and high frequency cards will indicate possible defects, and perhaps could be used in day centres.

Hospital and day care staff ought to have some understanding of the development of communication, and its common medical and social deviations. They should be taught to be aware of whether their charge, child, trainee or client is producing only infantile phonemes and babble, one-word sentences, or two-word utterances; telegramatic speech; whether the mentally handicapped person can decide what the staff members say, whether the mentally handicapped person's comprehension is greater than his speech production, whether the mentally handicapped person has articulation problems or whether the problems are of grammar. The staff member should know if the mentally handicapped person is accurately signalling messages and emotions with his face and with his intonations, and of great importance is the staff's ability to personally provide good speaker/listener discourse. Some staff with expertise in manual sign language are invaluable.

Examination and Testing

The extent and rigour of the neurological examination depend on the results of developmental testing, which is increasingly becoming a part of every health centre and Local Authority's functions, as part of an Integrated Child Health Service. The framework used is generally the 'Key Date Method' of Egan, Illingworth, and McKeith, which consists of testing a child for threshold items which a child should pass at key dates of 16 weeks, 6, 9, 12 and 18 months, 2, 3, 4, and 5 years. For example, a child should follow a dangling ball 23–25 cm from the eye through a quarter of a circle at 6 weeks, and turn to a high pitch rattle and smile at mother at 6 weeks. At 6 months he should reach for toys, taking everything to his mouth, but should forget it all when it falls. At 9 months he should look for a falling toy. At 12 months he should know his own name and babble tunefully. At 18 months he should point to his hair or feet and lift a cup between two hands. At 2 years he should put on hat and shoes, and at 3 years give full name and sex. At 4 he should be able to copy a cross and to hop on one foot. At 5 he should be able to skip on alternate feet.

As part of this screening, Stycar testing of the child's vision and hearing is carried out. The vision test consists of rolling graded balls in front of the child, if he is between the age of 6 months and 2 years; showing him matched toys at 3 m between the ages of 2 and 4; and over the age of 3, showing him letter tests at 3 m which he can match with letters in front of him. At 5 years, nine-lettered charts at 6 m are used. The Stycar hearing tests consist of: (*a*) baby tests—rattles, hand-bells, etc.; (*b*) 2-year tests—toys and cubes; and (*c*) 3–7-year-old tests—picture cards and cubes. The cube tests consist of putting cubes into and out of cups.

POMR

The increasing bulk of case records, the formation of multi-disciplinary teams, as described, the increased integration of health functions and the problem of communicating information has inspired a new look at recording systems and POMR (Problem Orientated Medical Records—the Weed System) has developed. This involves restructuring of the case sheets and making them of a more standard design and quality, making them subject to 'auditing' and able to be fitted into computer technology.

The first section consists of the *data base* which corresponds to the traditional history and physical examination, but as far as content, is not fixed and depends upon the doctor. It can include such things as behavioural and social details.

The next section is the *problem list*—a table of contents by which all the mentally handicapped person's problems, social, medical or psychological, are listed.

A problem is defined as anything which is relevant to the care of the mentally handicapped person—a cause for concern for the health services. Problems are noted as 'active' (which require action) and 'inactive' (which require watching).

The third section of the POMR is a set of *initial plans* which are required for every active problem formulated from the data base.

The next section is *progress notes*, which again are structured into subjective—what the mentally handicapped person says he feels, objective—what the nurse notes, the physical signs and laboratory results.

Lastly comes *interpretation* of subjective or objective reports, *therapy* and *plans*.

Out of the data base gathered by the doctor from the social worker's report, the developmental examination, the psychologist's assessment and the nurse's observations, the problem list and records might be compiled as follows:

PATIENT X
> *Data base contents*
> Age 5
> *Problem list*:

1. Aggression towards other children	Active
2. Tonsillectomy, 1971	Inactive
3. Seizures (× 2 per day)	Active
4. Nursery school refusal	Inactive
5. Developmental delay (speech)	Active
(motor dexterity)	Active
(social competence)	Active
6. Intellectual retardation (IQ 52)	Active
7. Overprotective mother	Active

As regards *each* Active problem there should clearly follow:
> *Initial Plan* (e.g. (3) Seizures—EEG investigation).

Follow-up notes written under the headings: (1) Subjective (2) Objective. Any member of the team contributes.

> *Follow-up Notes*:   Subjective: Patient complains of 'funny taste in mouth' × 2 per day.
>   Objective: EEG—focus in temporal lobe.
> *Interpretation*:   Temporal lobe epilepsy.
> *Therapy and Plans*:   Tegretol 125 mg. t.d.s.

PROGNOSIS

The influence of the environment in augmenting or minimizing the child's mental handicap and the capacity of the human beings associated with him to make the most of his potential will greatly influence the prognosis.

A mentally handicapped child brought up in a family in which the parents play with him and stimulate his motor development will be much less retarded than the child who is left without maternal attention.

Parental attention and training will make an enormous difference to the rate at which handicapped children will develop. They will thrive on patient, repetitive training, and, if steadily pressed by their parents, will learn to do things, which, if left to themselves, would be outside their compass.

One of the difficulties in estimating the potential prognosis is in estimating to what extent environmental factors at the time of diagnosis have stimulated the child to act at his optimal capacity.

Bowlby suggests that human maternal behaviour is brought out by five distinctive responses which the baby makes to his mother; crying, smiling, following, clinging and sucking. It may be that these responses have to occur within certain critical periods for the mother's instinctual reactions to be aroused. Some mothers miss out on developing such instinctual reactions during the critical period and may as a result be over-solicitous. Staff become more understanding of parent's hostility when they are taught how instinctively such reactions arise.

Very often the parents' anxiety and self-criticism will result in their rejection of the child and adversely affect the prognosis. It is often common for the rejection to take the form of general neglect and apathy, a feeling that nothing can be done and that the handicapped child must take his chance along with everybody else. This is particularly true of the attitudes among the so-called 'social problem families' who are incapable of effective action.

On the other hand, rejection may be replaced by overcompensation. This can take the form of denying that the child is mentally handicapped or of the parents accepting the diagnosis and, by their will-power and domination, trying to prove the doctors wrong, only to cause the child's prognosis to be worse instead of better.

Prior to recent years mental handicap was considered hopeless and beyond man's efforts to help; therefore, as far as treatment and training were concerned, the mentally handicapped person was neglected. Nowadays, the training of the mentally handicapped person is occupying more and more of the civilized nations' efforts. It has now become apparent that very few mentally handicapped people are beyond help. There has been a break-through in communication disorders and in psychology so it is now technically feasible to improve almost any child's communication, no matter how mentally handicapped he or she might be.

MULTIPROFESSIONAL ASSESSMENT—SOME THOUGHTS ON THE TEAM APPROACH

Multiprofessional team is a 'porridge phrase'—a very useful, meaningless statement requiring further detail and refinement. The term multiprofessional team is applied usually in a vague way, when what is meant is simply a network of professionals whose working paths occasionally converge. Full team-work is rarely required. The idea that all members of the team are always equal is confused. The term has become, occasionally, an unreflected orthodoxy, sometimes used fraudulently.

At the outset let us make two definitions:

1. A *team* is a small, clearly-banded group, trained in identity over a long period of time. In face-to-face work they are often together, share values and outlook and have a specific institutional base. There is always an issue of leadership.

2. A *network* is the interaction between a range of professional who may not know each other personally and do not have to consider each other's acceptability. No permanent or definite face-to-face group exists—individuals may come and go (according to duty systems, shifts, etc).

These terms come from the Brunel Institute of Organization and Social Studies. It should be noted that the team is close-knit and expensive, and it is usually in the network that professionals meet. Let us consider some examples of where teams are necessary—where we have significantly improved care, where the outcome is more than the sum total of members. The best examples are research teams, for example, psychiatric research teams, where advances in the past decade have been wholly due to team-work—psychologists, statisticians, chemists and clinical psychiatrists. Significant advances in the study of psychoses will more likely occur in the area of neuro-humoral transmitters than the cell membrane: the psychiatrist, therefore, is quite likely to be the junior member of such a team.

Changes in society have meant that previous medical practice in the field of handicap has also had to change and the mentally handicapped management model is now a team-work one. Previously, institutions were enormously wasteful of health service resources. Teachers, doctors and nurses should in the main do what only teachers, doctors and nurses can do, but in the field of mental handicap there has to be a sharing of many other skills. This is sometimes called a 'trans-disciplinary approach', and it requires considerable self-respect and self-confidence as regards the individual's own professional identity.

So, the management model of the hospital is changed by transforming, for example, the community specialist nurse, who may be sent on a course of training in behaviour therapy and receive also training in delivering home-based parent participation programmes. She then can receive referrals from health visitors and educationalists which she can bring back to the Mental Handicap Team initially based on the traditional institution. She sees the family in flexible hours, advising, arranging relief and training. A Portage Development Kit may be used where structured advice is needed. High-level expertise is available to her from the team. The cost is the ratification of one nurse as a car user and the 'opportunity-cost' of a team meeting once a week for an hour, set against the referrals of each of these cases independently to these 'members'.

What the consumer often refers to as Dr X's so-called 'team', often appears to consist of an unaccountable medley of staff, seemingly endlessly on holiday or on middle management courses.

Psychologists inevitably plan autonomous departments. Letters to other teams are unaccountably delayed to the chagrin of the team-leader and the indifference of other members. This way of working is not a team, it is a loose network which the leader consults when he gets the chance. The first retort to this sort of description, of course, is that the leader must be a 'poor manager', or not a good 'team member', or 'undemocratic'. The traditional medical model is one where the consultant always leads the team, is always the final arbiter on matters pertaining to his specialty; he is trained in such a way that he has profound knowledge and technical experience in his chosen specialty, and is equipped with a knowledge of allied disciplines so that he can assess the quality of other people's work. In the case of primarily health care work this is indisputably true, legally and practically. However, in the case of mental handicap, this is only true in respect of medical aspects of care, where he is the final arbiter on clinical judgements. There is a sociological categorization, available from the Brunel Institute of Organisation and Social Studies, which describes three relationships for the leader of the team. (1) *The managerial relationship*, involving assigning work, allocating and appraising perfomance and developing and applying authority to select staff, describe and ascribe work and initiate promotion. (2) *The co-ordinating relationship*, involving preparing and issuing detailed plans and programmes, attempting to overcome obstacles and setbacks and applying authority to gain information about progress, but which does not employ authority to over-ride sustained disagreements, or appraise personnel perfomance or ability to set new directions. (3) A *prescribing relationship*, employing the right to set a specific task to be carried out and the right to check this up but no other right to manage, supervise or direct. The multiprofessional team in the field of mental handicap has big problems of accountability which can only be worked adequately amongst members of the same profession. To complicate matters, in the UK medical doctors are legally responsible for all three relationships. This does not mean that he can arbitrarily admit a dangerous criminal to your establishment, but rather that in the case of a sick retarded person he seeks an admission by a process of consultation. There are in the British Health Service 3 levels of multiprofessional working:

Level 1—*corporate management.*

Where each member manager is responsible for his colleagues' managerial decisions, but not professional decisions—as for example at Area, District or Board level.

Level 2—*mutliprofessional watchdog and planning committees.*

Level 3—*the treatment of sick patient level.*

It is assumed in corporate management that the contribution of each member always carries equal weight, wisdom, expertise and authority. Each member has equal power, but not equal account-ability. Such formulae become nonsense when individuals with vastly different qualifications have equal authority. (Let us not get the idea that this is a sociological plot. The Brunel Institute are very clear about the distinctions between trainees, practitioners, consult-ants and principals.) As regards Level 2, there seem to be no ground rules as regards representation, balance or accountability except the general obligation of each member not to impede business. Yet one prima donna from another profession can stop everything.

There are three social systems working constantly against multi-professional teams—authority systems, career systems and political or power-game systems. Now, one profession simply does not understand the authority structure of another profession; for example, the nurse does not know the authority structure of the education departments, nor the social work departments: the nurse does not know how senior an officer in charge of a hostel is, or a district co-ordinating social worker (teaching adviser). We do not know other profession's legal bases. Ambition, moreover, cuts across any multiprofessional team. Here is an everyday example. A family is involved with a multiprofessional group in assessing its child. The headmaster gives a seminar in a parents' workshop for handicapped children; the other professionals are all clinical. The parents rate the headmaster's contribution tops, the speech therapist walks out furious, the headmaster has upstaged her by promising miracle educational cures. Well, the headmaster was the most senior in the team, interested primarily in demonstrating his ability as a polished performer and the power of his educational technology in competition with health service skills and technology. His 'miracle cure' statements were encouraged by the presence of a Local Authority Councillor. This is the power game of ignorance and ambition. Yet another smaller problem-solving group of a transport manager, a junior doctor, a Mr Fix-It and a teacher, without any planning may solve many problems, i.e. a network working well.

This is also the age of the fraudulent use of language. The term 'multiprofessional' can be used to camouflage authority. The vaca-tion student worker is not in an *inter-pares* position with the charge nurse; his assessment is not of equal value. When there is failure of central or local government to provide funds, a multiprofessional team is inserted as a remedy, when the real need is cash. This is particularly noticeable at national level. There have recently been 27 multiprofessional working parties in the field of mental handicap. They are all said to be representative, but all have been to some extent 'fixed' at the start as regards the relative power of the disciplines represented, and the representatives of the disciplines.

Multiprofessional practice is not a great humanitarian reform. As regards Level 3, the doctor must treat the individual *sick* patient, and the nurse *must* be quite clear that every statute and law is unequivoval—other professions are consulted or invited to participate. (The healthy retarded person is an entirely different matter.) Clinical leadership can be delegated but authority cannot.

This may be a cynical way to end, but it is not meant to be so. With proper knowledge of the organizational and legal basis of the multiprofessional team, and given experience of working in such teams, this is one of the most potent ways of helping handicapped people.

CHAPTER 4

The Admission of a Mentally Handicapped Person to Care

ATTITUDE ON ADMISSION

Psychological Needs

DURING HIS DEVELOPMENT a child has certain needs, such as adequate nourishment, clothing and shelter. Equally vital is his need for affection and a feeling of security within the family group. The love of his mother is the child's most important requirement, and, in the absence of a mother, a mother-substitute is necessary to take her place.

When a mentally handicapped person is sent to hospital or admitted to care, he is usually being separated from his mother for the first time in his life. He will receive all the specialized care available, but although the nurse tries in every way to prove a substitute for the mother the child may fret and show emotional upsets, as would a normal child. He may fret openly and be inconsolable in his tears, or inwardly and become quiet, withdrawn and morose. Consider how a handicapped child must feel when he loses contact with maternal warmth and security. His security has been undermined, he is struggling to overcome a wave of depressing grief, and he is confused and bewildered in his loyalty to his mother, who, it would seem, has committed him to a strange environment amidst a host of strangers.

No normal child likes to feel that he is loved only on a selective basis. Almost unconsciously he is driven to test by provocative behaviour the affection offered to him. He is finding out for himself if he will be loved while he remains co-operative and well behaved, and rejected when naughty and disobedient. By deliberately provoking adults he is judging the reactions of those who promise affection and security. If he is still accepted when he is badly behaved, he feels he can safely put his trust in those who are caring for him.

If they satisfy the mentally handicapped person's psychological needs, he will develop a state of mind which will enable him to accept the problems and disappointments he receives in his daily life. It is important that he is accepted by his group, as this will be an important stabilizing influence.

When a nurse admits a mentally handicapped person to the ward, formalities should be kept to a minimum. The importance of first impressions must not be overlooked. The unconscientious nurse

40

will merely fill in the form of particulars, transport the mentally handicapped person to his ward and bed, and casually dismiss the parents. The nurse should, however, be sympathetic and recognize the parents' problems, which will in all probability be of an emotional nature. It must be remembered that the mother is bringing her own flesh and blood into a hospital which cares for the mentally handicapped child. She realizes that there may be no cure available and that as a result her child may have to spend the rest of his life in such a place.

Most of the parents, because they have not been forewarned, have been unable to act decisively; because of their lack of knowledge of mental handicap they do not appreciate the true nature of their problem.

Following the birth of a mentally handicapped child the parents may spend many anxious years searching for help and true guidance. Even after having her child admitted to hospital, the mother still requires reassurance. The nurse can do much to give the parent peace of mind and, in return for this, may ask for her full co-operation. Nurses have a wonderful opportunity to be of service to these people in their hour of need. Parent and child should be received with expectancy and a friendly welcome. One method of approach to the child and relatives is first of all for the nurse to take time to make a proper introduction, never appearing to hurry, and to address them by name if their names are known. The first meeting can have a lasting effect and it does help the child to feel that he is not a stranger. Opportunity for parents and child to look round the child's new home together should be arranged and the mother should be given an insight into the care and training her child will receive. Not until a firm, friendly foundation has been prepared between the nurse and parent should any conditions or instructions be given. Once a mother's confidence is gained it will be easy for her to accede to the hospital's wishes. Visiting days and hours of visiting, times of buses and the number of the bus, the telephone number of the hospital, suggestions about food parcels and clothing, and any other information parents may need should be given clearly.

It is the rule in some hospitals for parents to visit the hospital before the child is admitted. There is much to be commended in this system, as it tends to break down the parents' fears of the unknown.

Physical Needs

Early in the period of welcoming the new patient, the nurse must ascertain whether he has had a recent meal. If not, arrangements must be made to provide him with an appetizing meal as soon as possible. Quite often all that is required is a friendly welcome, attention to small needs and possibly a picture-book to interest him for the moment.

Once the patient has settled down and gained confidence in his surroundings he can be bathed in the manner Sister considers most suitable. It is usually necessary to help him in this, and vital relationships can be strengthened if the nurse shows tact and thoughtfulness during the carrying out of the procedure. Any obvious physical abnormality can easily be noted while the patient is being bathed, and should be reported to the Ward Sister as soon as the procedure is completed.

Discretion should be used as to whether the child's hair is fine toothcombed or not. If such a duty has to be carried out, a little tactful explanation will be necessary in the case of children who are likely to feel embarrassment over it; it will in most cases prevent surprised indignation.

The child's bed should be clean, warmed and invitingly turned down. These simple but important touches will help him to gain confidence in his surroundings and in the nursing staff responsible for his care. When the child expresses a desire to visit the toilet, it is usual to collect a specimen of urine for a routine test.

OBSERVATION OF CHARACTERISTICS

During the days immediately after admission it will be important to note the following characteristics and report on them as necessary:

1. *Health Habits*

BREATHING

The correct way to breathe is through the nose, not the mouth. Mentally handicapped children suffering from a deflected septum, enlarged adenoids or catarrh will breathe through the mouth because of the difficulty experienced with nose breathing.

SLEEP

A record of the child's sleep should include observations on its duration and character. Is it restful or fitful? Is there difficulty in getting off to sleep? Do dreams and nightmares disturb the sleep? Does the child appear to be rested on waking in the morning?

TOILET HABITS

Regularity of bowel action, frequency of micturition and whether these functions are carried out with ease or if they cause distress should be noted. Are the toilet habits clean or do they require correction?

EATING HABITS

Some mentally handicapped children bolt their food without properly chewing it, others may be more particular and be slow and methodical in their eating. The nurse must make sure that every child has adequate time allowed for eating his food. It may be necessary to seat all those who are slow eaters together to make it easier for the nurse to pay attention to them. A report should be submitted on the quantity of food a new child eats, and whether he shows a lack of interest in it. He will show his mechanical and dextrous ability in his handling of cutlery at meal times.

PERSONAL CLEANLINESS

Most mentally handicapped people take a pride in their appearance if given encouragement. Where this encouragement has been missing in their previous environment, it may be found that they respond with a slovenly, untidy appearance.

From these early observations the nurse is made aware of the extent of the task of the child's health education.

2. *Physical Symptoms*

BRUISES

These must be noticed early and reported immediately.

COMPLEXION

Notice whether the face is flushed, pale or cyanosed.

COUGH

Any cough is significant and must be reported.

DISCHARGES

Report any discharge from any orifice.

EXCITEMENT AND OVERACTIVENESS

A report on these may direct attention towards a possible superimposed mental disorder.

EXCRETA

Observations on the excretion of faeces and urine and on expectoration should include the amount, colour and smell; any incontinence should also be reported.

INFLAMMATION

The presence of redness and swelling of a part should be reported upon immediately so that treatment can be instituted without delay.

MENSTRUATION

Irregularity or absence of the menstrual periods amongst female mentally handicapped patients is common. The duration, amount, character, odour and any accompanying discomfort or pain should be reported.

TEMPERATURE

Slight variations occur according to the time of day or the amount of exercise taken, the normal range being between 36 °C (97 °F) and 37 °C (99 °F). The temperature of a mentally handicapped person should be taken in the axilla, care being taken that the axilla is dry and that the bulb of the thermometer is between folds of skin and not clothing.

PULSE

Wherever an artery is near the surface of the body and crosses over a bone, the wave of blood can be felt and is called a pulse. The nurse should note its frequency, regularity and fullness, and the condition of the artery.

WEIGHT

A very important record, which through any abnormal variation in weight will indicate the state of the mentally handicapped person's health.

3. *Speech and Language Deficits*

Abnormalities of speech are common among mentally handicapped people, and may be due to defective hearing or functional ability.

DEFECTIVE HEARING

A mentally handicapped person who from birth has been unable to hear will also be unable to speak owing to lack of experience of the spoken word. Deafness occurring before the age of 2 years will have the same results. The vocabulary acquired at that age is so small as to be useless and is easily forgotten unless special teaching is instituted early.

DEFECTIVE FUNCTIONAL ABILITY

Anatomical defects, such as cleft palate, hare lip and muscular and nervous conditions, will cause any of the following disabilities:

a. Dysarthria: Flaccid dysarthria, due to bulbar palsy, causes hypernasality and imprecise consonant pronunciation; spastic dysarthria causes insufficiency of pitch and loudness; and 'ataxic dysarthria' due to cerebellum damage, causes inaccuracy and randomness in speech; and the prosody particularly to be affected.

b. Dysphonia or Aphonia: The patient is unable to speak louder than a whisper, in spite of his efforts to strengthen his voice due to weakness of the vocal cords.

c. Stammering: Muscular spasm interrupts speech. Nervousness increases the struggle involved and there are three stages: (1) repetition or stuttering, (2) clonic spasm and (3) avoidance of speech situations.

d. Cluttering: Very rapid speech, with omission or slurring, stumbling over or separation of syllables, or leaving sentences unfinished. Usually improved by drawing the person's attention to his dilapidated speech.

e. Dyspraxia: Loss of purposeful movements without obvious detectable defect. No elementary motor disturbance.

LANGUAGE DEFECT

The most common problem retarded people display is *non-specific retarded language development* (*see* Chapter 8). The patient's language stage will be an earlier one than that anticipated on the basis of his Mental Age (MA). He shows 'slow motion' development in reaching linguistic milestones. Severe social deprivation can also cause this.

Specific developmental language disorders are due to defective development of the speech centres. The Developmental Language disorder syndromes (the dysphasias) and Early Childhood autism which affect grammar and cause bizarre intonation are described in Chapter 8. *Elective mutism*, deliberate and manipulative silence, is rarely sustained by the mentally handicapped person for more than a few hours. *Psychotic speech* breaks the rules of cohesion—the patient jumps from one topic to another without adequate textual links. In both autistic and psychotic speech neologisms (idiosyncratic private words), paragrammatism (distorted syntax structure) and echolalia (repeating back the end of a sentence without comprehension) occur.

4. *Gait, Posture and Movement*

DEFINITIONS

In studying gait, posture and movement, the following are important definitions:

Hemiplegia—paralysis of one half of the body.

Diplegia—paralysis of the lower limbs.

Cerebral palsy—a persistent but not unchanging disorder of posture and movement due to dysfunction of the brain, excluding that due to progressive disease present before its growth and development are completed. Many other clinical features may also be present.

Posture—the relative disposition of parts of the body.

Tone—the sustained contraction of living muscle serving posture and movement.

Spasticity—a persistent increase of the stretch reflexes resulting in a disorder of tone, usually with increased muscular resistance and stretch.

Dystonia—abnormal postures and movements with disordered distribution of tone involving the trunk and often characterized by extreme degrees of flexion and extension in the extremities.

Dyskinesia—a disorder of movement.

Athetosis—irrepressible slow writhing movements, the result of imperfectly co-ordinated activity of the muscles, exacerbated by voluntary movements.

Choreic movements—irrepressible non-repetitive abrupt movements of roughly normal pattern resembling incompleted gestures.

Tremor—uncontrolled, alternating, fine rhythmic movements.

Rigidity—sustained increase in muscular resistance for the duration of passive movements in all directions.

Ataxia—a particular kind of unsteadiness of movement in which patterns are normal *per se*, but not adjusted to the outside world. There may be associated imperfect balance, inco-ordination and intention tremor.

5. *Muscular Co-ordination*

By muscular co-ordination is meant the harmonious working of separate muscles or groups of muscles in order to carry out a definite function. If this co-operation is absent or imperfect the carrying out of the function becomes difficult and without rhythm or it becomes impossible.

CURVATURES OF THE SPINE

The curvature may be in an anterior, posterior or lateral direction. An abnormal forward curve in the lumbar spine is called 'lordosis'. A posterior curvature of the spine is known as 'kyphosis' or 'hunchback'. An abnormal lateral deviation of the spine is called 'scoliosis'. Proper positioning in infancy prevents this.

6. *Interests*

Once a knowledge of a mentally handicapped person's interests is gained, the gateway to rehabilitation is open. Conversation will be the main channel through which potential interests will be discovered. In thinking of the mentally handicapped person as a person, his home, his life, his experiences, and the things he likes or enjoys are important, and they will help in understanding him.

When planning conversation it is important to appreciate when it is out of place and what subjects are dangerous. Intelligent silence and attentive listening will often produce equally satisfying results.

7. *Activity*

Does the mentally handicapped person move quickly and rhythmically or are his movements slow and lethargic? Is he alert or does he sit in a corner with apparent lack of interest? Often it seems impossible to arouse interest in a mentally handicapped person who is antagonistic towards all the nurse's efforts. The preliminary step is to make activity necessary. Regardless of the mentally handicapped person's behaviour, the nurse should keep working towards objectives that are within the mentally handicapped person's capabilities.

8. *Sociability*

The nurse's report on the mentally handicapped person should contain a record of his attitude towards other mentally handicapped people and staff. For instance, does he take an interest in his surroundings? Does he associate with other mentally handicapped people and join in their games, or does he remain apart? Does he accept authority? Is he aggressive towards anyone representing it?

CHAPTER 5

Classification of the Clinical Varieties of Mental Handicap

CATEGORIZATION

THE CLINICAL VARIETIES of mental handicap may be considered as follows:

1. *Mental Handicap Following Infections*
   a. Gastro-enteritis in the newborn.
   b. Meningitis.
   c. Congenital syphilis.
   d. Encephalitis.
   e. Congenital rubella syndrome.
   f. Cytomegalic inclusion disease.
   g. Toxoplasmosis.

2. *Mental Handicap Following Injury or Physical Agents*
   a. Pre-eclampsia and eclampsia.
   b. Excessive intra-uterine irradiation.
   c. Birth injury.
   d. Rhesus incompatibility.
   e. Drugs and the newborn.
   f. Lead poisoning.

3. *Mental Handicap Associated with Disorders of Metabolism*
   a. Disorders of lipid metabolism:
      i. Amaurotic family idiocy (cerebromacular degeneration).
      ii. Niemann–Pick disease.
      iii. Gaucher's disease.
      iv. Metachromatic leucodystrophy (sulphatide lipidosis).
   b. Disorders of amino-acid metabolism:
      i. Phenylketonuria.
      ii. Tyrosinaemia.
      iii. Homocystinuria.
      iv. Histidinaemia.
      v. Maple syrup urine disease.
      vi. Hartnup disease.
      vii. Hyperuricaemia.

   c. Disorders of carbohydrate metabolism:
      i. Gargoylism.
      ii. Galactosaemia.
      iii. Hypoglycaemia.
   d. Disorders of endocrine metabolism:
     Cretinism.
   e. Disorders of mineral and electrolyte metabolism:
      i. Wilson's disease (hepatolenticular degeneration).
      ii. Diabetes insipidus (nephrogenic).
      iii. Hypomagnesaemia.
   f. Disorders of nutrition in the infant:
     Malnutrition.

4. *Mental Handicap Associated with Brain Disease*

   a. Neurofibromatosis.
   b. Sturge–Weber's syndrome.
   c. Tuberous sclerosis.
   d. Schilder's disease.

5. *Mental Handicap Associated with Disease and Conditions due to Prenatal Factors*

   a. Acrocephalosyndactyly.
   b. Craniostenosis.
   c. Hydrocephalus.
   d. Hypertelorism.
   e. Microcephaly.
   f. Laurence–Moon–Biedl syndrome.
   g. Ichthyosis.
   h. Prader–Willi syndrome.
   i De Lange syndrome.
   j. Rubenstein–Taybi syndrome.
   k. Smith–Lemli–Opitz syndrome.

6. *Mental Handicap with Chromosomal Abnormalities*

   a. Down's syndrome.
      i. Regular (trisomy).
      ii. Translocation.
      iii. Mosaic.
   b. Cat-cry syndrome.
   c. Trisomy 13–15 (Patau syndrome).
   d. Trisomy 16–18 (Edwards syndrome).

    e. Sex chromosome abnormalities:
        i. Klinefelter's syndrome.
        ii. Turner's syndrome.
        iii. Triple-X syndrome.
        iv. XYY syndrome.
        v. Fragile X.

7. *Mental Handicap Associated with Prematurity*
    a. Prematurity.
    b. Kernicterus.
    c. Cerebral palsy.

8. *Unclassified Mental Handicap*

1. MENTAL HANDICAP FOLLOWING INFECTIONS

a. *Gastro-enteritis in the Newborn*

In the newborn fluid-loss and dehydration in gastro-enteritis may be so severe that brain damage with permanent mental handicap results. Intracranial venous thromboses are usually found in such cases.

b. *Meningitis*

Meningitis is an infection of the coverings of the brain. The common types are pyogenic and tuberculous meningitis.

    The onset in pyogenic meningitis is acute, with headache, increasing irritability and pyrexia. Projectile vomiting occurs. Muscle rigidity is found with stiffness of the neck. Mental handicap may develop as a direct result of meningitis causing severe brain damage or following the development of hydrocephalus, when inflammatory lesions block the flow of cerebrospinal fluid.

TUBERCULOUS MENINGITIS

This usually develops insidiously. Irritability alternates with drowsiness. There is loss of appetite with vomiting and constipation. During the terminal stage hyperpyrexia occurs with coma and paralysis. With antituberculous drugs the majority of infants recover from the infection, but damage to the central nervous system and mental handicap are still too often found in many children.

c. *Congenital Syphilis*

Congenital syphilis is now rare in the United Kingdom. Infection occurs before birth and is due to the passage of the organism, *Treponema pallidum*, across the placenta from the mother to the infant. Shortly after birth the infected infant becomes pale and wasted and fails to thrive. A rash is visible on the skin and the nail-beds are infected. There are usually moist lesions on the skin around the mouth, anus and genitals. A characteristic feature is 'snuffles' due to infection of the bones of the nose, with nasal obstruction and purulent and blood-stained discharge; collapse of the nasal bridge occurs with the formation of the saddle-nose deformity. When the nervous system is involved, signs of meningeal irritation develop and convulsions and hydrocephalus may occur. Late manifestations of syphilis may appear from 1 to 10 years after birth, with maldevelopment of the teeth, damage to the eyes, spastic paralysis, convulsions and mental handicap. Thorough antisyphilitic treatment is essential when the diagnosis has been made.

d. *Encephalitis*

Encephalitis is an infection of the brain substance. It may occur following infections with measles, rubella, chicken-pox, mumps, encephalitis lethargica, cytomegalic inclusion disease and toxoplasmosis. The onset of encephalitis is usually sudden with severe headache and drowsiness, progressing to deep coma. However, the onset can be insidious with a gradually increasing headache, convulsions or behaviour disorders. In young infants mental handicap, nerve palsies and behaviour disorders are likely to be severe and permanent.

e. *Congenital Rubella Syndrome*

Rubella (German measles), if contracted within the first 3 months of pregnancy, may cause in the infant mental handicap, deafness, cataract and congenital heart disease. Vaccination which is now available should reduce the incidence. It is estimated that about 200 rubella-infected babies are born in the United Kingdom in non-epidemic years.

f. *Cytomegalic Inclusion Disease*

This virus disease in the mother is usually mild. Infection of the fetus, however, gives rise to mental handicap, often with microcephaly and enlargement of the liver and spleen with jaundice. Inclusion bodies can be recognized in tissue cells and in urine and cerebrospinal fluid. Some 800 damaged infants are born in the United Kingdom annually, this infection being the commonest cause of microbial central nervous system defects.

g. *Toxoplasmosis*

Infection with a boat-shaped protozoon is transmitted to the offspring either late in pregnancy or at birth. It causes mild hydrocephalus or microcephaly, spastic deformities, convulsions and enlargement of liver and spleen. Diagnosis is made by blood and skin tests. The condition is rare in the United Kingdom—about 70 cases per year, but in France the incidence is ten times greater, perhaps reflecting the popularity of undercooked meat which favours viability of tissue cysts.

2. MENTAL HANDICAP FOLLOWING INJURY OR PHYSICAL AGENTS

a. *Pre-eclampsia and Eclampsia*

Pre-eclampsia and eclampsia are conditions which may affect a mother in the last 3 months of pregnancy. There is a rise in maternal blood-pressure accompanied by severe headache and oedema of the limbs with kidney and liver disorders. Continuous epileptic seizures occur in eclampsia. Stillbirths are common in this condition and live births may show severe brain damage with mental handicap and epileptic attacks later in life.

b. *Excessive Intra-uterine Irradiation*

During the first 3 months of pregnancy irradiation of the uterus may result in microcephaly and mental handicap of ranging degrees of severity. This is becoming much less common now that pregnancy tests are carried out as a routine before irradiating a woman of child-bearing age.

c. *Birth Injury*

Prematurity, anoxia (an inadequate supply of oxygen to the tissues) and difficult labour are important factors in birth injury. Prematurity itself may be a cause of intracranial haemorrhage and anoxia is common in premature infants. Anoxia due to delay in breathing after birth can cause direct damage to the brain cells and gives rise to spastic paralysis and mental handicap. Anoxia can result from the administration of large doses of anaesthetic to the mother, from the inhalation of mucus or from the constriction of the windpipe (trachea) by the cord being twined tightly around the neck of the infant. Other obstetric difficulties, such as instrumental delivery, precipitate labour or breech delivery, may produce damage to the brain of the baby.

d. Rhesus Incompatibility

About 85 per cent of people carry the Rhesus factor in their red cells ('Rh positive'). The other 15 per cent do not have this factor and are called 'Rh negative'. The condition of rhesus incompatibility occurs when the mother (usually Rh negative) and the fetus (usually Rh positive) are of different groups. Fetal blood enters the mother's circulation and stimulates the production of substances called 'antibodies'. Later in pregnancy these antibodies return across the placenta to destroy the fetal red blood-cells; a condition known as 'haemolytic disease in the newborn'. Recently it has been discovered that injection of mothers with antibodies obtained from previously immunized mothers prevents the formation of antibodies in a subsequent pregnancy. With improved antenatal care and advances in treatment by exchange transfusion we see far fewer 'rhesus imbeciles' nowadays.

e. Drugs and the Newborn

Some drugs taken by the mother during pregnancy and by the infant after birth can affect the development of the infant and give rise to mental handicap.

Excessive intake of vitamin D can cause infantile hypercalcaemia. Children so affected become ill shortly after birth with vomiting and constipation. Muscle weakness occurs with thirst and increased output of urine. The blood calcium is raised. Many of these children have elfin faces with low-set ears and prominent epicanthic folds. Heart murmurs are found and the child is usually mentally handicapped.

Enzyme systems in the liver of the infant can be affected by excess of vitamin K and by some antibodies giving rise to jaundice and kernicterus with possible brain damage.

Drugs given to the mother to control endocrine, physical or emotional disorders may cause fetal damage. Hypoglycaemia (low blood-sugar) usually occurs in these infants and brain damage may follow.

Cretinism may develop in the child of a mother who has had treatment for hyperthyroidism (oversecretion of the thyroid hormone) during her pregnancy.

f. Foetal Alcoholism

There are around 75 000 women alcoholics of child-bearing age in Britain today, whose pregnancies are likely to result in babies with some mental retardation and physical abnormalities. The first twelve weeks of pregnancy, as usual, is the most critical period. At birth a degree of microcephaly is common, physical and mental growth is slow and they never catch up with their contemporaries. They sleep badly, shake and cry a lot, a situation that can go on for years and one that many alcoholic mothers find difficult to cope with, resulting in baby battering, child neglect and accidents in the home.

Drugs in pregnancy should be avoided except where absolutely necessary. A recent Edinburgh survey showed 80 per cent of women were taking drugs of various kinds other than iron in pregnancy. Smoking in pregnancy should be avoided because of its effect in causing growth retardation in the fetus and increasing the risk of a still birth, but it is not so far known to be associated with other abnormalities.

g. *Lead poisoning*

Ingestion of lead by children may lead to mental handicap. Lead may be absorbed from paint, toys, ointments and cosmetics. The symptoms include loss of appetite, constipation, headache, irritability, delirium and convulsions. Diagnosis is by estimation of lead in blood and urine and treatment by chelating drugs after withdrawal from exposure. It has recently been suggested that the association between lead and mental retardation extends over a wider range than hitherto considered and that small amounts of lead can be an aetiological factor in mild and borderline cases of mental handicap. It is therefore suggested that raised lead levels should be considered in the examination of all children suspected of mental retardation.

3. MENTAL HANDICAP ASSOCIATED WITH DISORDERS OF METABOLISM

An ever-increasing number of discrete metabolic diseases are now known where abnormalities of lipid, protein or carbohydrate metabolism are associated with mental defect. Some can be detected by simple urine tests, others require elaborate biochemical procedures.

a. *Disorders of Lipid Metabolism*

These conditions form a group of diffuse and progressive disorders of childhood which have a common feature of progressive mental deterioration. They are storage diseases in which various lipids are deposited in the cells of the central nervous system and the tissues of the body.

i. AMAUROTIC FAMILY IDIOCY

One example is Tay–Sachs disease. This is a rare condition due to a single recessive gene. Both sexes are affected equally. There is a deposition of a lipid material within the nerve-cells leading to their degeneration. Tay–Sachs disease is the commonest form and is a disease which mostly affects the Jewish race. The child is normal at birth and develops normally until about the end of the third month when spasticity, generalized weakness, and muscle wasting occur. A characteristic feature is that the infant is easily startled by loud noises. There is progressive loss of vision leading to complete blindness. A 'cherry-red' spot is found in the macula of the retina. Death usually takes place within 4 years of the onset of the disease. Other types of amaurotic family idiocy have similar presentations but develop later in life. There is no treatment.

ii. NIEMANN–PICK DISEASE

The onset of this disease caused by a recessive gene is during infancy and death often occurs before the second year. The disease is characterized by mental deterioration and handicap with the physical features of wasting, profuse sweating and yellowish pigmentation of the skin. The liver, spleen and lymph-glands are enlarged. There is loss of vision and hearing. A cherry-red spot at the macula as seen in amaurotic family idiocy is present in less than half the patients.

iii. GAUCHER'S DISEASE

This is an uncommon disorder of lipid metabolism. The cells of the reticulo-endothelial system contain deposits of lipid material which lead to an enlargement of the liver, spleen and lymph-nodes. In cases with an acute onset the brain may be involved, resulting in mental handicap. The disease is due to an autosomal recessive gene or to a simple dominant character and about one-third of the reported cases are familial.

iv. METACHROMATIC LEUCODYSTROPHY (SULPHATIDE LIPIDOSIS)

Metachromatic leucodystrophy is a familial disease found in late infancy which causes severe brain damage. The child appears normal for the first year or two but then progressive muscular weakness and inco-ordination develop. Death usually occurs between the third and sixth years in this disease. Sulphatides accumulate in the brain and kidney and the accumulation of these substances interferes with normal brain function. A screening test using fresh urine is available. A diet with low vitamin A content has been suggested.

b. *Disorders of Amino-acid Metabolism*

i. PHENYLKETONURIA

Phenylketonuria is an inborn error of metabolism due to an autosomal recessive gene and commonly accompanied by severe mental handicap. The basic fault is deficiency of the enzyme normally responsible for converting the amino-acid phenylalanine to the amino-acid tyrosine so that phenylalanine, phenylpyruvic acid and their toxic products accumulate in the blood and are subsequently excreted in the urine.

The patient affected with phenylketonuria is nearly always fair-haired with light blue eyes, from pigment deficiency. The skin is fair, soft, smooth and fine in texture. There is frequent occurrence of eczema and there is often cyanosis of the hands and feet due to poor circulation. The patient is dwarfed and a slightly reduced head circumference is not uncommon. The gait is stiff, short-stepped and on a broad base. The incisor teeth are widely spaced. Some phenylketonurics show stiffness in their limbs. Epilepsy occurs in the majority of patients. Repetitive finger movements are seen in the lower-grade patient. Dermatitis is not unusual.

Mass screening for amino-acid and other abnormalities in the newborn is at present proceeding in many centres. The Guthrie test which is a bacteriological method detects raised levels of phenylalanine. When the *blood* phenylalanine concentration rises above 4 mg/100 ml (240 µmol/litre) a diagnosis of phenylketonuria is considered.

Phenylketonuria, when detected at birth, is treated with a low phenylalanine diet which prevents mental, physical and neurological complications so that affected individuals may live a normal life span.

ii. TYROSINAEMIA

There are two types of disorder of tyrosine metabolism in the newborn. Transient tyrosinaemia is the condition in which there are elevated plasma tyrosine levels which decrease as the child gets older. Usually the only reason why these infants come to notice is that a positive test for tyrosinaemia is found when testing for phenylketonuria in the newborn. Infants with transient tyrosinaemia are physically normal in all respects. The more permanent disorder of tyrosine metabolism is tyrosinosis. Within a few days of birth children affected with this disorder develop severe vomiting and diarrhoea. They fail to thrive and progressive liver failure and severe kidney damage occur. Children who survive may suffer from mental handicap. Treatment is by diet low in phenylalanine and tyrosine with additional vitamin D.

iii. HOMOCYSTINURIA

Homocystinuria is an inborn error of sulphur amino-acid metabolism. The amino-acid methionine is increased in the blood and the amino-acid homocystine appears in the urine. In homocystinuria the patient has certain signs and symptoms, some mild, some severe. These symptoms are dislocated lenses, fine, sparse hair, convulsions, malar flush, knock-knees and mental handicap.

Affected patients can be detected by a simple urine test and dietary treatment is now employed.

iv. HISTIDINAEMIA

Histidinaemia is caused by an enzyme defect in the metabolism of the amino-acid histidine. Urine from these patients shows a positive test with Phenistix, but phenylpyruvic acid is not present in the urine. Affected patients have a speech defect and some are mentally handicapped.

v. MAPLE SYRUP URINE DISEASE

This condition is so called because the sweet-smell of the urine is said to resemble the smell of maple syrup. The blood and urine contain abnormal amounts of the amino-acids valine, leucine and isoleucine.

Affected patients show clinical symptoms shortly after birth. There is difficulty in feeding and respiration is irregular. Stiffness of the limbs is found. Rapid physical deterioration occurs and the infants die within a few weeks or months.

The condition can be treated with a diet which is deficient in the amino-acids valine, leucine and isoleucine.

vi. HARTNUP DISEASE

This condition resembles pellagra and is an abnormality in the metabolism of the amino-acid tryptophane leading to a pellagra-like skin rash, temporary cerebellar ataxia, constant amino-aciduria and the excretion of large amounts of indole substances. Some patients affected have been mentally handicapped while others are emotionally unstable or even psychotic. Treatment is by nicotinamide and riboflavine supplements.

vii. HYPERURICAEMIA (LESCH–NYHAN DISEASE)

Only male infants have been described with this condition. The child is normal at birth, but after a few weeks develops hypertonic attacks. Increasing spasticity develops and with eruption of teeth these children mutilate their fingers and bite their lips away. As in gout, the serum acid levels are high and the urine shows a heavy deposit of orange urates. Urinary calculi are frequent.

Treatment is by restraint to prevent self-destruction, by keeping the urine alkaline, and by drugs to reduce the blood uric acid level.

c. *Disorders of Carbohydrate Metabolism*

i. GARGOYLISM

Gargoylism is a rare type of mental handicap caused by a single recessive gene and characterized by the deposition of mucopolysaccharide in the tissue cells of the brain, liver, heart, lungs and spleen. There are two main types of gargoylism. In the first type, autosomal recessive, both males and females are equally affected and cousin marriages are frequent precipitating factors. Clouding of the cornea and dwarfism occur. The second type is a sex-linked recessive. Only males are affected. Corneal clouding does not occur and only one-third of patients are small of stature. Half of the patients affected are deaf.

The name 'gargoylism' is evocative and describes the grotesque appearance of the affected patients. The head is enlarged and the forehead protrudes. The eyebrows are bushy and the nose is saddle-shaped. The abdomen is protuberant and there is usually an umbilical hernia. Considerable enlargement of the liver and spleen is found. The degree of mental handicap varies. Urine tests are useful in diagnosis. There is no real treatment for gargoylism.

ii. GALACTOSAEMIA

This is a rare congenital and familial disorder in which the sugar galactose is not converted into glucose in the normal manner due to enzyme defect. It is caused by a single autosomal recessive gene. The infant with this condition appears normal at birth but after a few days' milk feeding loses his appetite and has persistent vomiting. In severe cases death occurs from malnutrition. Those who survive are, at 3 months of age, undernourished and small in stature. Mental handicap and cataracts occur. Examination of the urine shows a constant presence of the sugar galactose and an increased excretion of amino-acids and protein. If diagnosed shortly after birth a galactose-free diet should be instituted and maintained until puberty.

iii. HYPOGLYCAEMIA IN THE NEWBORN

Hypoglycaemia or low blood-sugar in the newborn has many causes. It is found in premature infants and in twins and is more common in male than in female births. It can be familial and mothers with diabetes mellitus and toxaemia of pregnancy may give birth to infants with hypoglycaemia.

Infants with hypoglycaemia are pale and reluctant to feed. They are irritable and the infant is said to be 'jittery'. Convulsions may occur. Treatment is by correction of the cause, by diet, ACTH and sometimes partial pancreatectomy.

d. *Disorders of Endocrine Metabolism*

CRETINISM

The condition of cretinism is due to a defect of the thyroid gland resulting from various enzyme disturbances. The early signs of the disease are feeding difficulties, noisy respiration, constipation and jaundice. The child's growth is retarded. He is apathetic and he does not readily smile or laugh and is slow to suck. The tongue becomes large and protrudes as the condition progresses. The skin becomes yellowish, loose and wrinkled, with marked puffiness of the eyes and thickening of the eyelids, nostrils, lips, hands, feet and back of neck. Prominence of the abdomen with an umbilical hernia is common. The hair on the scalp and eyebrows is often very scant. The child has a peculiar hoarse cry. With the lapse of time the child makes little attempt to sit up, stand or walk. Speech may not appear until 7 or 8 years of age. The characteristic features of untreated cases are severe mental handicap, dwarfed stature, bowed small legs and stumpy hands and feet. The eyes are set widely apart and the lips are pouting. The nose is broad and flattened. Puberty is usually late and the external genitals remain infantile.

About 150 babies will be born with hypothyroidism in the UK this year. Only a few will be diagnosed by the age of four weeks, and perhaps fifteen others will be diagnosed so late that severe mental handicap will result in a life spent in an institution. In the past there have been differences of medical opinion on the general application of screening every new-born baby for neonatal cretinism, but its value is now generally agreed.

It has always been difficult to recognize the features of cretinism because many, in particular mental handicap, become apparent only in the months after birth as the baby grows. Consequently, detection has commonly been late and treatment then delayed until after brain damage has occurred. Now a new development, a screening test, promises to ensure that all cretins are detected and treated by the age of four weeks.

The screening test was developed in Quebec in 1973 and is based on the radioimmunoassay of thyroxin (T_4). The beauty of the new assay is that it can be done on a tiny sample of dried blood, i.e. on one of the samples of heel-prick capillary blood that is at present collected from infants on a piece of filter paper for the screening of phenylketonuria. The new test has been evaluated in several countries and has been found to be a reliable indicator of those babies who have a T_4 level below the third centile, who then need further detailed investigations to confirm the diagnosis of hypothyroidism. [A more difficult and expensive radioimmunoassay for thyroid-stimulating hormone (TSH) can be done on selected dried blood samples.]

With good organization the diagnosis can be confirmed before the baby is four weeks old, and thyroxin replacement therapy instituted. The early follow-up results confirm the expectation that such babies will grow up normally and will not incur brain damage. Longer follow-up will be required before it is certain that there are no minor neuro-developmental problems as a result of thyroxin deficiency before the start of treatment.

The test is now routine in twelve states of the USA and in several areas of Europe. Large scale regional laboratories seem to provide the most efficient and economical service, the cost being about 50p per baby screened (including the cost of consultation and investigation for the children with suspect levels). As the incidence of cretinism is about one in 5000 births, the cost of detecting a cretin comes to about £2500, which is cost effective.

Criticism is already being voiced about the delay in implementing the screening test for every baby born in the UK. A number of British centres have completed pilot surveys and there is considerable experience of assays. Although there is debate about the most suitable initial screening test and, in particular, the role of TSH assay, we know that it would be feasible to start a screening service now, and that it is needed. Unless the Departments of Health take the initiative there is a danger of less efficient, less comprehensive and more costly local screening services becoming established in different parts of the country.

Replacement therapy with thyroid hormone is indicated. Thyroxine given orally has the advantage over desiccated thyroid of being a stable preparation with long shelf life and constant biological activity. Prompt treatment of the young infant is essential to avoid residual or further brain damage. Levels of TSH should be monitored during treatment and maintained within the normal range.

In the majority of cases thyroid treatment is effective if diagnosis is made at an early stage. Patients in whom cretinism appears after 1 year of age have the best prognosis. Replacement therapy is not indicated in the adolescent since such medication merely agitates the patient.

e. *Disorders of Mineral and Electrolyte Metabolism*

i. WILSON'S DISEASE (HEPATOLENTICULAR DEGENERATION)

This condition is accompanied by a decrease of blood copper and the virtual disappearance of the copper-containing protein, caerulo-plasmin, in the serum. Urine copper excretion is increased. The age of onset can be from 5 to 40 years, with ascites, jaundice and enlarged liver. Involuntary choreiform movements and tremor develop with progressive difficulty in articulation and swallowing. Rigidity of the muscles of limbs, trunk and face occur resulting in contractures and muscle wasting. A smoky brownish ring (Kayser–Fleischer ring) forms at the outer margin of the cornea. There is progressive mental and physical deterioration. Prognosis is poor in spite of the use of chelating agents, penicillamine or dimercaprol to remove copper.

ii. NEPHROGENIC DIABETES INSIPIDUS

This condition is due to a sex-linked recessive gene. It affects males who are unable to control the passage of water from the blood to the kidneys. In early infancy the child develops an excessive thirst and passes large amounts of urine. He becomes dehydrated and may run erratic fevers. This condition is prevented by continuous large intakes of water and administration of ethacrynic acid.

iii. HYPOMAGNESAEMIA

Infants born to mothers who are suffering from magnesium defici-ency may develop convulsions in the neonatal period. Hypomag-nesaemia also develops when severe malnutrition is complicated by chronic diarrhoea. These convulsions, especially if complicated by dehydration and malnutrition, are liable to cause permanent brain damage. Adequate replacement of the deficient magnesium rapidly relieves the condition.

f. *Disorders of Nutrition in the Infant*

i. MALNUTRITION

There is considerable experimental evidence that vitamin deficiencies in pregnant rats and rabbits may result in brain damage in the offspring, similar to that seen in human infants. The possibility that protein malnutrition may be a factor in limiting mental development has also been put forward and this might act antenatally or postnatally. The occurrence of severe impairment of brain growth has been documented in infants subjected to severe protein mal-nutrition for socio-economic reasons and this limitation of mental capacity means in the end an impossibility of improving socio-economic development.

4. MENTAL HANDICAP ASSOCIATED WITH BRAIN DISEASE

a. *Neurofibromatosis (von Recklinghausen's Disease)*

This is a rare hereditary disease characterized by pigmentation of the skin and tumours of the nerve-trunks and skin. Malignancy may develop in both skin and nerve tumours. About 20 per cent of cases are mentally handicapped.

b. *Sturge–Weber's Syndrome (Naevoid Amentia)*

The causative factor is unknown. The condition is characterized by naevus of the face on one side only, meningeal angioma, possible calcification in this and the cerebral cortex, epilepsy, contralateral hemiplegia and often severe mental handicap. Treat the epilepsy; neurosurgery for removal of the naevus.

c. *Tuberous Sclerosis (Epiloia)*

This condition is due to a single dominant gene or to mutation. The three classic signs of this condition are mental handicap, epilepsy and adenoma sebaceum, although on occasion all may be absent.

Most patients are severely mentally handicapped and, as they grow, they undergo progressive mental deterioration and many die before reaching maturity. Epileptic fits, which may be major, minor or Jacksonian, occur from the first year of life and continue with increased severity. Nodular growths occur in the brain and may undergo malignant change. Status epilepticus is a common cause of death. Adenoma sebaceum (butterfly rash) is a rash arranged symmetrically on both cheeks and involving the nose. It is due to an overgrowth of sebaceous glands of the skin. Post-mortem examination often reveals multiple tumours of various internal organs and of the brain. Treat the epilepsy; sometimes neurosurgery is indicated for removal of the nodules. Radiotherapy is sometimes employed to stop the growth of sclerotic nodules which may otherwise become malignant in the brain.

d. *Schilder's Disease*

The condition is due to a recessive gene. Defective synthesis of myelin is associated with axon degeneration and neuronal overgrowth.

This disease usually makes its appearance in childhood or adolescence. Clinical features, which vary considerably, consist of progressive failure of vision and hearing, spastic paralysis, convulsive attacks, muscular inco-ordination of limbs, and tonic and clonic spasms. Difficulty in swallowing and speaking may be experienced by some patients. Mental impairment is progressive and the condition always ends fatally.

5. MENTAL HANDICAP ASSOCIATED WITH DISEASES AND CONDITIONS DUE TO PRENATAL FACTORS

a. *Acrocephalosyndactyly*

A rare condition due sometimes to a dominant gene and showing marked association with paternal age. The two commonest features are an abnormally high or pointed head and varying degree of fusion of fingers and toes. Not all cases are mentally handicapped. Reconstructive hand and foot surgery is frequently indicated.

b. *Craniostenosis*

This is an uncommon condition occurring predominantly in males. There is premature closure of the cranial sutures resulting in malformations of the skull with secondary effects on brain and eyes. Mental handicap and cranial nerve defects follow. Cleft palate, syndactyly and congenital heart disease are sometimes associated. Treatment, by surgical creation of artificial sutures in the early months, is not generally accepted.

c. *Hydrocephalus*

Hydrocephalus ('water on the brain') refers to an increased volume of cerebrospinal fluid within the skull. The excess cerebrospinal fluid may be within the ventricles or in the subarachnoid space. In the infant the head expands to accommodate the excess fluid; as a result the circumference of the head may increase to as much as 90 cm, the normal average adult circumference being 55 cm. A genetic factor is sometimes involved, while intracranial haemorrhage at or around birth may lead to hydrocephalus. Rare causes are tumours or cysts in childhood.

The hydrocephalus may be primary or secondary. Primary hydrocephalus results from developmental abnormalities causing excessive secretion of the cerebrospinal fluid and a low or absent absorption of the secreted fluids. Secondary hydrocephalus is caused by lesions within the system of ducts which drain away the cerebrospinal fluid. Blockage of these ducts causes an obstruction to the flow of fluids. Those commonly affected are the aqueduct of Sylvius and the foramina of Luschka and Magendie. Hydrocephalus at birth is usually associated with meningomyelocele. The hydrocephalus may be active, producing progressive deterioration. The patient will suffer from blindness, deafness and convulsions, be severely wasted, bedridden and paralysed. Death usually takes place very early in life. In patients who survive, the condition is only slowly progressive and is often arrested, leaving the patient with varying degrees of mental and physical disability. In surgical treatment an artificial shunt is inserted between the lateral ventricles of the brain and the right atrium of the heart via the jugular vein. Through this the exessive cerebrospinal fluid is drained off, passing through a valve (Spitz–Holter). This operation is effective if done early, and careful follow-up is required.

d. Hypertelorism (Greig's Syndrome)

Hypertelorism is a rare form of mental handicap. There is abnormal development of part of the sphenoid bone of the skull and this thrusts the brow forward, separating the nasal bones more widely than normal. The distance between the eyes is increased and in extreme cases the eyes tend to appear on the side of the face. Hare-lip, congenital heart disease, and cleft palate may occur.

Ocular hypertelorism occurs more frequently as part of other syndromes involving the upper mid-face than as an isolated defect. These include Down's syndrome, gargoylism and acrocephalo-syndactyly.

e. Microcephaly

Microcephaly is the name applied to mentally handicapped persons whose cranium on completion of development is less than 42·5 cm in circumference. This condition may be due to a single recessive gene which determines the inability of the brain to develop to its normal size or be secondary to exposure to radioactive substances.

The head is reduced in size so that a relatively normal nose and chin and large ears contrast with the receding forehead and flattened back of head. There is overlapping of the sutures of the skull and thick ridges of bone can be felt. The scalp is sometimes loose and wrinkled longitudinally as though too big for the skull. Spastic diplegia is common. About 50 per cent of such persons are epileptic. Mentally they vary from severely to moderately handicapped and may be restless and vivacious with considerable powers of mimicry.

Microcephaly is not always a specific disease. It is often a feature of other clinical types of mental handicap such as Down's syndrome or phenylketonuria. It has been reported following maternal rubella.

f. Laurence–Moon–Biedl Syndrome

This is a very rare condition thought to be due to a recessive gene and characterized by obesity, hypogenitalism, extra fingers and toes, eye defects—which include pigmentary degeneration of the retina, nystagmus, optic atrophy, poor night vision and progressive visual defect—and severe mental handicap. Close relatives of the patients may show some of the signs.

g. *Ichthyosis*

Ichthyosis is a congenital skin disease characterized by scaling and hyperkeratosis and is a common complaint in the general population. Several genes may cause it. The most frequent is an autosomal dominant. There are two syndromes associated with mental handicap of which ichthyosis is an essential part. The Sjögren–Larsson syndrome is characterized by spastic diplegia, ichthyosis and mental handicap. Rud's syndrome is characterized by ichthyosis, sexual infantilism, epilepsy and varying degrees of mental handicap.

h. *Prader–Willi Syndrome*

Associated mental handicap ranges from mild to severe, the main clinical features in the child being obesity, hypogonadism, short-stature and high incidence of diabetes mellitus. Hypotonia is a prominent early sign, and this disorder and Down's syndrome provide good examples of the association of cerebral intellectual defect and profound infantile hypotonia. The genetics are not clear.

i. *De Lange Syndrome*

This syndrome consists of severe mental handicap, short stature, bushy confluent eyebrows and general hirsutism, wide prominent upper lip and abnormalities of digits. No consistent cytogenetic abnormality or known pattern of inheritance has been found.

j. *Rubinstein–Taybi Syndrome*

This is a complex of congenital defects which is indicated by the findings of pathologically broad out-turned thumbs and toes, narrow beaked nose, epicanthal folds and downward-slanting eyes, in association with moderate to severe mental handicap. There is no known chromosome abnormality, although affected siblings are reported.

k. *Smith–Lemli–Opitz Syndrome*

This syndrome shows itself in infancy with vomiting and failure to thrive. Ears are low set; there are epicanthal folds associated with a wide nasolabial distance and abnormalities of the digits. The most distinctive feature is hypospadias and cryptorchidism, but the genitalia are normal in females. There is some evidence of autosomal recessive inheritance.

6. MENTAL HANDICAP WITH CHROMOSOMAL ABNORMALITIES

A human being originates in the union of two sex cells (gametes), the ovum and the spermatozoon, and is built up of single units called 'cells'. Each cell is composed of a cell membrane surrounding the complex cell structures which include the cytoplasm (a substance surrounding the nucleus) and the nucleus itself—a compact object containing the hereditary material, chromosomes, in the form of strands of desoxyribonucleic acid, a substance commonly known as DNA.

DNA is the main compound of the chromosomes, but they also contain ribonucleic acid (RNA) and protein. Other indefinite structures are present also and are called 'genes'. Genes are 'blueprints' for the development of the individual. The position of the gene on the chromosome is called its 'locus'. Genes occasionally change their character giving rise to new genes. This process is called 'mutation'.

The hereditary material in the cells of man is divided into 46 sections of varying lengths making 23 pairs of different chromosomes. When the genes of a pair of like chromosomes ('homologous') contain comparable sets of loci then they are said to be 'homozygous'. If they do not agree they are 'heterozygous'.

These arrangements apply to 22 pairs of chromosomes (the 'autosomes'); the sex chromosomes in the male differ, one being an X and the other Y, whilst in the female they are a homologous pair XX.

Transmission of the hereditary material from one generation to another takes place through the germ cells, the spermatozoa in the male and the ova in the female. These cells, unlike the other cells of the body, have each only one-half the normal complement of chromosomes, 23 in number. When fertilization takes place the sperm and the ovum unite together to form a new individual and this is called the 'zygote'. Thus each individual has received one-half of his chromosomes from each of his parents.

Some genes are capable of producing dominant and recessive traits. A dominant trait is the result of a defective gene in one or both parents and has the following characteristics:

1. Every affected person has an affected parent.
2. The affected person is easily distinguishable.

3. In every affected family one-half of the children will be affected.

The importance of new mutation must be remembered, which is said by some to be the rule rather than the exception in tuberous sclerosis.

Recessive traits are caused by the occurrence of two similarly defective genes, one from each parent, and have the following characteristics:

1. The parents are carriers of the defective gene.

2. The parents are normal with respect to the defective trait.

3. In every affected family one-quarter of the children will be affected; one-half will be carriers of the defective trait.

Genes may be linked to sex and whether an individual develops normally or abnormally may depend upon the sex of the individual.

Altogether about 3·5 per cent of all human conceptions show chromosome faults gross enough for microscopic detection and it has been said that nature is 90 per cent efficient in getting rid of the abnormal fetus, but some abnormalities are better tolerated than others! In early spontaneous abortion the rate of chromosomal faults is as high as 60 per cent and the fetal abnormalities represented are severe, but both rate and severity decline as pregnancy advances.

By amniotic puncture (amniocentesis) it is possible to obtain a specimen of the fluid surrounding the fetus and to examine the cells and biochemistry. This makes it possible to tell in early pregnancy whether a baby is suffering from certain conditions, such as translocation mongolism, where the risk of a second affected child is high. A decision about termination may then depend on the mother's feelings, and the law. At present antenatal diagnosis by amniocentesis is available at a number of centres, but it is highly desirable that a nation-wide service be developed and such screenings may soon become as common as antenatal tests for diabetes and venereal disease. The procedure is usually not carried out before the 15th week; results are not usually available for 3 to 4 weeks; and culture of cells may fail, so that the procedure may have to be repeated. The overall risk of causing an abortion is 1–2 per cent. Parents must know the risks of amniocentesis, small as they are. Advanced maternal age is the chief indication; when a woman is over 40 the risk of an abnormal fetus may be as high as 1 in 8.

Examination of the unborn baby is also sometimes carried out by ultrasonic waves or visual inspection by a fetusscope.

a. Down's Syndrome (Mongolism)

Although Langdon Down first described mongolism more than a hundred years ago it is only recently that it has been recognized that the condition is the result of chromosome abnormality. It is now known that Down's syndrome is caused by the presence of an extra chromosome in pair 21. Three types of Down's syndrome occur:

1. REGULAR (TRISOMY)

The chromosome count is 47 instead of the normal 46, the extra chromosome being one of the smaller chromosomes.

2. TRANSLOCATION

The chromosome count remains at 46; the extra small chromosome has become attached to another chromosome making the chromosomal count appear normal.

3. MOSAIC

The chromosome count is 46 in some cells and 47 in other cells.

Down's syndrome accounts for 10 per cent of all patients admitted to hospitals for the mentally handicapped. The incidence in the general population is 1 per 660 births. Cases tend to be born at the end of large families and the frequency is related closely to the age of the mother, the risk of giving birth to a child with Down's syndrome rising with the age of the mother. From work carried out in Australia it seems that infective hepatitis may cause the fault in the ovum which leads to the syndrome. More than one case can occur in a family. Other chromosomal abnormalities such as Klinefelter's syndrome, Triple-X syndrome and Turner's syndrome have been found in association with Down's syndrome. Leukaemia and cancer are more prevalent in Down's syndrome than in the general population.

PRINCIPAL FEATURES OF DOWN'S SYNDROME

These are stunted growth, a small round head with flat face and occiput, florid complexion and obliquely set eyelids, with upper lids having an extra fold at the inner margin (epicanthic fold). There may be eye defects such as squint, nystagmus, cataract and speckled iris ('Brushfield's spots'). The ears are small and do not possess the natural folds. The nose is stubby and depressed at the bridge; the tongue in most cases is large and flabby with well-defined fissures. The hair is dry and scanty. The hands are broad and clumsy-looking and have a curious 'boggy' feeling. The little finger is curved and ends midway between the last and middle interphalangeal joints of the third finger. The palm creases are abnormal; a single transverse crease often runs across the palm of the hand. The feet are marked by a large cleft between the first and second toes and often a crease runs from this cleft down the sole of the foot. Supernumerary toes and webbing of the toes are seen occasionally. The abdomen is protuberant and umbilical hernia is common. The joints have abnormal range of movement due to laxity of the ligaments and hypotonus of the muscles. The more 'floppy', the worse the prognosis. The circulation is usually poor, the extremities being blue and cold and susceptible to chilblains. Congenital heart disease is common. Mongols are usually mouth breathers and are prone to respiratory infections.

The traditional stereotype of Down's syndrome, of equable temperament and loving disposition, is only statistically true for females aged 3–12 years.

b. *Cat-cry Syndrome (Cri-du-chat)*

In this condition affected infants are severely mentally handicapped and have a characteristic mewing cry from which the syndrome gets its name. In appearance they are obviously abnormal, with small heads, wide-spaced eyes, epicanthic folds, abnormalities of the ears and mouth, and eyes slanting downwards. The condition is due to partial deletion of the short arm of chromosome No. 5.

c. *Trisomy 13–15 (Patau Syndrome)*

This chromosome defect is not only always associated with profound mental handicap, but also with early death. The characteristic features are seen in the face and consist of broad nose, cleft-palate and micrognathia. Microcephaly is the rule. The infants are small for age and associated abnormalities of the ear, heart, kidneys are common, as are polydactyly and microphthalmia. Some have patches of atrophic hairless skin on the scalp. It occurs in about 1 per 5000 births. Diagnosis is by cytogenetic examination. The trait is not inherited.

d. *Trisomy 16–18 (Edwards Syndrome)*

Diagnosis is contingent upon cytogenetic study. Again there is profound mental handicap and early mortality. Mid-line facial defects are common, as well as micrognathia. The head is microcephalic sometimes with a prominent occiput. The nose takes off from the forehead and is straight or upturned. The index finger overlays the third finger in a characteristic fashion. Associated anomalies of heart and kidneys are known. Occurrence rate is about 1 in 4500 births and the trait is not inherited.

e. *Sex Chromosome Abnormalities*

The true genetic sex of an individual can be determined by obtaining preparations from the cells lining the inside of the mouth (buccal smear) and examining them for the presence of the sex chromatin body. This body is found in the nuclei of females (chromatin positive) and is absent in males (chromatin negative).

The sex chromosome abnormalities are:

i. KLINEFELTER'S SYNDROME

The patient is a male whose sex chromatin is positive. The sex chromosome constitution is XXY and the total chromosome count is 47. After puberty, patients with this constitution present with sterility and have small testicles. The breasts may be feminine in appearance and eunuchoidism may occur. Ten per cent are diabetic and asthma is common. The degree of mental handicap varies but is usually mild; often intelligence is within the normal range.

ii. TURNER'S SYNDROME

The patient is female with absent sex chromatin. The cells have only a single X chromosome and the total chromosome count is 45. The patients are dwarfed and congenital abnormalities are found, particularly webbing of the neck. At puberty secondary sexual development is absent due to lack of ovarian tissue and hormones. The degree of mental handicap is usually mild. Often intelligence is within the normal range. Personality traits include passivity, vagueness and tomboyishness. Treatment is by oestrogen-replacement therapy.

iii. TRIPLE-X SYNDROME

The patient is female and there are no abnormal physical characteristics. The sex chromosome constitution is XXX and the total chromosome count is 47. The tissue cells are chromatin positive and some cells contain two sex chromatin bodies.

The mental state varies from severe mental handicap to normal intelligence. Various psychotic disorders may be found. Cardiac, skeletal and neurological abnormalities are more common in cases suffering from severe mental handicap.

iv. XYY SYNDROME

These patients are of interest, as the majority have been diagnosed in the maximum security hospitals. They are unusually tall, over 6 feet in height, with a tendency towards aggression and violence. As in

Klinefelter's syndrome there is often deviant behaviour and sometimes a reduction in intelligence.

v. FRAGILE X CHROMOSOME

The reason for the excess of males over females affected by mental handicap may be an X-linked genetic defect called the fragile X chromosome, characterized in most cases by a tiny almost detached piece towards the end of the long arm of the X-chromosome. It had been suggested for many years, that X-linked genes should be considered in the causation of non-specific mental handicap, but only recently have laboratory methods become fastidious enough to demonstrate the fragile site on the X-chromosome.

There appear to be at least three distinct forms of X-linked mental handicap which breed true in families. Firstly, boys with the marker X chromosome tend to have large heads, large ears and lower jaws. The most specific finding is macro-orchidism generally present at puberty, but sometimes at birth. Specific speech delay is common and the boys often have a characteristic speech rhythm called litany speech. Epilepsy is only found in the most severely retarded. Secondly, there are members of families who do not show the marker chromosome, but have the above clinical features without the macro-orchidism. Thirdly, Renpenning seems to have described a separate syndrome with microcephaly, small testes, severe mental handicap and no marker chromosome.

As with any X-linked condition the implications are important for female relatives and the fragile site can be detected in a proportion of female carriers. Recent studies in British Columbia gave an incidence of at least 1·83 per 1000 males for X-linked non-specific mental retardation so that the condition is an important one and may be second only to Down's syndrome in prevalence.

The fragile X chromosome has been demonstrated in cultured amniotic cells, thus opening the way to antenatal diagnosis. It has also been recently suggested that fragile X may show a significant frequency of association with autism.

7. MENTAL HANDICAP ASSOCIATED WITH PREMATURITY

a. *Prematurity*

By definition any infant weighing 2500 g or less at birth is premature; 5–10 per cent of all births are in this category. Premature infants are particularly liable to develop severe respiratory distress at birth and this is associated with a higher mortality-rate. Infants with a birth-weight less than 1500 g show an association between respiratory distress and the development of mental handicap and neurological abnormalities. Prematurity may be found in association with maternal toxaemia, congenital anomalies and multiple pregnancy. Premature children also have a liability to kernicterus and also hypoglycaemia which may lead to mental handicap. It has been said that intensive care of premature babies could mean that only 14 per cent of those who survive will suffer brain damage instead of the 33–70 per cent who develop with handicap at present.

Hypoxic premature babies suffer much greater structural brain damage than hypoxic full term deliveries. The latter often only have damage to the 'watershed' areas of blood supply which include the language areas and memory areas such as the hippocampus and mamillary bodies, while hypoxic prematures often suffer destruction of major structures such as the cortex, or parts of the thalamus. They may therefore fail to thrive or be wholly decorticate.

b. *Kernicterus*

Kernicterus, or jaundice of the newborn with brain damage, occurs in prematurity, infantile malnutrition and when some drugs are given to the infant or to the mother. Sepsis and congenital cirrhosis of the liver may also be factors. Kernicterus may also occur in haemolytic disease of the newborn especially when there is Rhesus antibody incompatibility. The affected infant may be obviously jaundiced at birth or becomes jaundiced a few days later. The infant is severely ill and fails to thrive properly. There is respiratory distress and death may occur at this stage in respiratory failure. The liver and spleen are enlarged. Cyanotic attacks occur and in some cases severe anaemia results from haemolysis. With recovery, athetoid movements may be noted as early as 6 months of age. Motor development is poor, high-tone deafness is frequent, disorders of balance and epilepsy may occur during early childhood.

c. *Cerebral Palsy*

Cerebral palsy is a permanent disorder of movement and posture, due to a non-progressive defect of the brain occurring in early life. The incidence of cerebral palsy is about 1 per 500 live births. Mental handicap and cerebral palsy are commonly found together, the same cerebral insult accounting for both effects. Neurologically, pyramidal signs are most commonly observed and may show as hemiplegia, diplegia, quadriplegia and as a variety of clinical pictures. In some cases extrapyramidal signs are seen including ataxia and athetoid movements. Many patients are epileptic.

Cerebral palsy may be found in association with prematurity, difficult birth, multiple birth and kernicterus. It is sometimes transmitted as a recessive gene defect or it may appear as part of the clinical picture in conditions associated with mental handicap such as microcephaly.

8. UNCLASSIFIED MENTAL HANDICAP

Unclassified mental handicap applies to those cases in which there is no gross evidence of structural or biochemical abnormality. Approximately 65 per cent of all cases of mental handicap still have to be placed in this 'unknown' group. However, recent more sophisticated microscopic examination of the neocortex showed that there are in many cases insufficient branching and spines on the nerve axons and what is described as 'ectopic' dendrogenesis (connections in the wrong places).

Unclassified mental handicap can be divided into two groups. In the genetic group heredity plays an important part. Children can show different levels of intellectual development from their parents, and parents who are themselves below average in intelligence may produce children who are above or below their own measured intelligence. Many of the higher grades of unclassified mental handicap belong to the genetic group. The subcultural group is more complex and comprises a mixture of genetic and environmental factors. Below-average parents and adverse home circumstances and upbringing give rise to this subcultural group of mentally handicapped with intelligence quotients in the range of 50–70. Social changes should eventually bring about a reduction in this type of mental handicap.

Usually of normal appearance, they have no grasp of the principles which govern human behaviour. This partly results from their mentally unstable background; they are easily led, being exploited either sexually or by unscrupulous employers. They rebel against their special school and there are frequently social complications on leaving there.

CHAPTER 6

Care of the Mentally Handicapped

DENTAL CARE

THE IMPORTANCE OF dental health is self-evident. Not only the teeth themselves are to be rendered healthy but also the supporting structures, *dental* health and *perio-* or *parodontal* health, respectively.

Sepsis, finding its origin either in the teeth or in the surrounding tissues, has too frequently been the cause of serious breakdown elsewhere in the body, e.g. subacute bacterial endocarditis results from 'silent' dental abscesses, which are detectable first only on X-ray and harbour *Streptococcus viridans*. Many serious, even fatal diseases have had their origin in the oral structures.

Consequently, those caring for the mentally handicapped will appreciate the importance of oral hygiene, so that further distress will not, at least through neglect, be added to the mental affliction.

Dental hygiene for the mentally handicapped person is the same as for normals in so far as the powers of communication, capability and perseverance permit.

The brushing of the teeth is best achieved by holding the brush firmly in the clenched fist and applying a wrist movement to it. Each jaw is brushed separately and in the one direction only, as follows— downwards in the upper jaw and upwards in the lower jaw, never up and down. Brushing is commenced at the base of the gum and directed to the teeth. This massages and stimulates the gum and cleanses the teeth of sticky particles. Likewise, brushing is carried out on the palate and tongue side of the teeth. Across or lengthwise brushing is permissible only on the biting surface of the teeth, otherwise injury to the gum margins may well result. Remember to renew toothbrushes every 4–6 weeks.

Electric toothbrushes are efficient cleansers of the teeth but they may cause more gum margin injury than manual toothbrushing.

Whatever toothbrush is used, a follow-up with an oral irrigating machine is always advisable, as it will flush clean all those crevices not accessible to a toothbrush. Indeed, with low-grade mentally handicapped patients this may well prove to be the only cleansing process possible apart from cleaning the mouth under a general anaesthetic.

Mentally handicapped people vary in their susceptibility to dental disease, either decay or oral stagnation. The profoundly handicapped on a liquid-feed diet are remarkably free of dental disease compared to those conventionally nourished.

74

The dentist should be informed by the accompanying nurse at each visit of the dental symptoms of the mentally handicapped person. In many low-grade cases these may amount only to a suspicion as to the cause of some unusual behaviour pattern in the patient.

The dentist likewise must be informed as to any clinical conditions such as coughs, colds, heart murmurs (common in mongols), blood disorders, diabetes, etc. Where such conditions exist and patient co-operation allows, treatment under local anaesthesia is preferred.

However, in many cases, particularly low-grade mentally handicapped people, general anaesthesia is necessary to give the dentist access to examine and treat the mouth. Again, advance information as to the person's clinical condition, in respect of heart, respiratory system, blood, epilepsy, diabetes, etc., is necessary, so that pre- and post-operative medication, as required, may be given. So the nurse must consult the dentist *and* the anaesthetist several days beforehand.

In Down's, the tendency to mouth breathing gives rise to oral stagnation, so that periodontal disease is common. However, in mongoloid children there is a greater resistance to actual decay of the teeth than one may expect. This may be due to compensatory self-cleansing of a limited extent from the tendency to spaces between individual teeth arising from a deficiency in the normal supply of teeth. The upper lateral teeth, for example, are frequently absent altogether. The mouth breathing is due to lack of muscle tone in the lips, so that 'cracks' and 'fissures' of a persistent nature occur in the lower lip, and 'fissures' in the resultant protruded tongue with tissue enlargement of that organ anteriorly (although the tongue itself is basically normal in size) which are not easily susceptible to cure.

Due to the frequent heart defects and above-average infective foci in the local oral condition, treatment necessitates pre-operative antibiotic cover. Most dental treatment for mongols is of a basic preventative nature and ambitious treatment in respect of crowns, orthodontics, etc., is contra-indicated.

Epileptic people's only specific abnormality, dentally, is due to the drug, Epanutin, which gives rise to gross enlargement of the gum margins, known as 'hyperplasia'. Change of drug is usually the only necessary measure, but surgery may be required to restore the gum contour if sufficient patient co-operation is obtainable to suggest success, as the dentist and his staff cannot cure this condition, which is dependent upon the post-operative oral hygiene procedures being carried out by the mentally handicapped person.

In the condition of osteogenesis imperfecta it is important to note that bone fragility is high, so that conservative dental treatment to prevent extractions is highly desirable and will make for peace of mind for all concerned.

The condition of cystic fibrosis has certain interesting oral manifestations. Due to the barrage of tetracycline therapy in infancy and early childhood when the teeth are also undergoing calcification, marked yellow discoloration of the teeth occurs. The author has no knowledge that this affects the resistance of the teeth to decay one way or the other. A further consequence of the disease is an increased mucus secretion from the submaxillary and sublingual salivary glands giving rise to an inferior quality saliva. It is axiomatic with this disease that pulmonary secretion is high, so that general anaesthesia is not the method of choice and dental care is strongly preventative and conservative under local anaesthesia.

Sometimes dental pain in the upper premolar and molar area may be due to sinusitis, as the sinuses are likewise over-productive of secretions, although it will be for the dentist to determine that. There is also a possibility that the mentally handicapped person is deficient in vitamins, and if extraction of a tooth is contemplated a prior course of vitamin K is helpful, as haemorrhage is copious where insufficient vitamin K is in the system. The bleeding time should be checked in advance.

Spastic people are susceptible to inflammation of the gums, often increased by the dilantin group of drugs. Oral hygiene is poor and the measures necessary to maintain a clean mouth are so difficult by normal means that it is in these cases most of all that use of an oral irrigating machine is strongly recommended.

In those mentally handicapped people with athetosis, involuntary grinding of the teeth leads to their being worn down to a dramatic extent—that is, virtually down to the roots. This condition is known dentally as 'bruxism'.

In general, people with a degree of cerebral palsy are not good subjects for dentures, and for this reason one must try to meet the challenge of preserving the dentition as best as one can, although success cannot be measured in anywhere near normal terms with the severely afflicted.

In diabetes the timing of meals and insulin injections before a visit are important and dental appointments should be postponed if the blood-sugar has recently been unstable.

Finally, there are many other mental disorders with no dental connexion specifically, but emotionally disturbed people are prone to self-neglect and frequently apprehensive of dentistry. Bruxism occurs in neurotic and in normal people, although the tooth-grinding is usual only during the unconscious hours of sleep. If the nervous tension is prolonged, the bruxism leads to traumatic bone-support loss for the teeth. Its social side-effects are identical to snoring. However, for the one who is obviously neurotic during waking hours, they have the added burden of vivid imagination given to exaggerating pain not yet afflicted. To many such people dentistry is akin to 'execution'! In fact, not even the dentist likes having dental treatment, but he knows that pain nowadays need not go beyond a very tolerable degree. It is paramount, therefore, for those connected with caring for the mentally disturbed or handicapped to refrain from recounting their own 'fear' of dentistry or painful experiences thereby, even in jest, in the presence of one whose tensions are currently high and who is incapable of calling upon a reserve of courage. Quiet encouragement, little fuss and an air of calm towards a visit to the dentist virtually ensures continued attendance and eventual success of treatment. The end justifies the means of regular visits to the dentist, since the general health of the mentally handicapped person can only be maintained by a healthy mouth.

NEEDS OF MENTALLY HANDICAPPED PEOPLE IN HOSPITAL

It is sad that in the 1980s living standards for the handicapped still require the following self-evident principles to be emphasized.

We frequently hear that it is important to meet the needs of our mentally handicapped people. The hospital can satisfy some needs such as food, clothing and shelter. Other needs can only be satisfied by the active striving of the mentally handicapped people themselves. The hospital can help and encourage by providing a good environment, but this is treating needs not meeting them.

Food and fluid are essential physiological needs to relieve the tension of hunger and thirst. It is important to provide a diet that ensures a proper number of calories for the normally active, the sedentary, the over-active and those engaged in heavy manual labour. The well-fed are less irritable, and a snack at bedtime helps some to sleep better.

Fluids in adequate amounts are also essential. Efforts should be made to serve food that would be acceptable in the community. Variety in the diet should be provided and menu planning should aim at avoiding dishes appearing on predictable days. Food must be well cooked and attractively presented and look enticing on the plate. The dining room should be clean, quiet and attractive, and correct tableware should be available. Every effort should be made to obtain a high standard of hygiene to ensure that food is safe and uncontaminated.

Mentally handicapped people living in hospital have a heightened interest in food. When hunger is pleasantly satisfied it makes life more bearable. Deprived people may gain more satisfaction from oral gratification than just that of sustenance.

Shelter may protect one from the elements, and thus meet a primitive need. Fortunately the tendency is to build more spacious wards with fewer people occupying them, with clean attractive adequate furnishing and lighting to present-day requirements.

A proper bed with firm springs and clean bedding assures comfort and is a necessity.

Mentally handicapped people should be dressed in the manner they would be in the community. Clean clothing in sufficient quantities to maintain self-esteem is a minimal requirement.

Micturition and defaecation result in part from a reflex action arising from the accumulation of waste material. Traumatic emotional experiences and great tensions may alter the excretory pattern. Some mentally handicapped people use excretory products aggressively, some may retain excreta. It is important that adequate sanitary accommodation which is clean, warm and well lighted and ventilated be available. It should be possible to go to the toilet when necessary and without an audience. It should also be possible to take a bath in reasonable privacy and daily if necessary. In our culture, where social custom decrees and acceptance demands that the individual 'smells sweet and looks good', no self-respecting poor person would be without these necessities of life.

The importance of resources to maintain acceptable standards of personal hygiene and to ensure good grooming cannot be over-emphasized. Baths, shaving, hair care, access to cosmetics and appropriate clothing are essential to the maintenance of dignity and self-esteem. Mentally handicapped people should be encouraged and instructed how to use 'make-up' and how to dress their hair. Clothes should be of the current fashion.

Most men need to shave daily to look neat. An ordinary safety razor, some shaving soap, water and a mirror are the resources needed. Those who are too infirm or disturbed to shave themselves will need to be shaved by the nurse.

Hair cuts are required every three or four weeks to keep men looking neat. The hairdresser is helped to prepare a regular schedule for service to each ward to ensure that he meets the demands of the mentally handicapped men.

Women and girls enjoy regular visits to the hairdressing salon. Beauty parlours can be most attractive and friendly places that are greatly appreciated for relaxation and socialization. A shampoo, a trim and an attractive set or blow-dry helps restore self-esteem.

Brushing of teeth after meals or twice daily is a wholesome practice. Not all mentally handicapped people have formed regular mouth hygiene and many cannot manage without help from the nurse. For those whose gums are easily damaged a 'Water Pick' is available on the market. This instrument produces a fine water jet which can be directed onto the teeth and gums washing away all particles of food. The nurse should inspect the skin and hair weekly and should see that equipment is available for finger- and toe-nail care.

CHIROPODY

The proportion of mentally handicapped people requiring chiropody treatment may be as high as 60%. The conditions seen are varied and numerous ranging from simple problems such as callous, corns, mycological infection and verrucae to complex lesions and ulceration developing with such anatomical abnormalities as talipes equino-varus.

People suffering from well-defined syndromes such as Down's invariably follow a definite pattern. The foot is commonly triangular in shape with a narrow heel and broad splayed forefoot. Metatarsus primus varus, accompanied in adult life by hallux valgus, can cause problems in these people. A deep transverse cleft between the first and second metatarsal joints may be seen. The feet are abnormally broad for their length and great care is required when fitting shoes. Anhidrotic skin and poor circulation are often evident.

Spasticity, hemiplegia, syndactylism, fusion or omission of joints, supernumery toes and bones, accompanied by poor posture and gait, offer the chiropodist a challenge in both skill and ingenuity.

Liaison is essential between all disciplines if chiropody treatment is to be successful. Nursing staff or relatives need to keep a close vigilance over foot hygiene, with careful washing and drying of the feet, particularly between the toes. Tinea pedis is common and, if allowed to progress unchecked, may become widespread, with secondary bacterial infection. Bare feet are not advisable, except under supervision, as the risk of foreign bodies becoming implanted in the sole of the foot, particularly where a degree of anaesthesia is present, may lead to unnecessary pain and infection.

Toe nails should always be cut straight across and not too short: careless cutting can cause an extremely painful onychocryptosis, which may necessitate nail avulsion. Some patients are compulsive nail pickers and if this cannot be cured it is often more successful to avulse the nail and destroy the matrix.

With the co-operation of the physiotherapist many problems with gait can be helped with a programme of exercises to strengthen the muscles of the thigh, leg and foot. Discussion is also important when choosing surgical shoes, splints and prostheses.

Chiropody treatment must always be progressive, aiming for corrective measures in the young and paliative in the elderly or those too infirm to co-operate. With regular visits to the chiropodist and carefully measured, well-fitting hosiery and shoes, the mentally handicapped person can be kept relatively free of problems. Treatment should never be rushed and the operator must remain patient and good humoured. Several visits may be necessary before the client will actually receive a treatment, but this is always worthwhile, as even the most stubborn person will eventually succumb and in fact enjoy the excursion to the chiropodist.

PHYSIOTHERAPY IN THE MENTAL HANDICAP HOSPITAL

The hospital population is subject to many conditions which require treatment by physiotherapy, including recent injuries, arthritis, chest infections, mobility problems from the geriatric wards, and neurological disorders. However, the major handicap requiring referral is cerebral palsy, in all degrees and in all age ranges.

Cerebral Palsy in Children

Although most mentally handicapped people are admitted at an age when they have fixed motor patterns with various secondary conditions, the physiotherapist is still concerned with training more normal postures and movements, particularly in the early years, when maximum improvement is likely. The aim is to integrate this training into the child's daily life in the ward and at school, so that nurses, teachers and other paramedical staff become valuable allies in helping the child to gain increasing control of movement.

MODERATELY HANDICAPPED CHILDREN WITH CEREBRAL PALSY

The physiotherapist can avail herself of a range of treatment methods, as widely diverse as the traditional orthopaedic approach, various neuro-developmental techniques, and others which advocate using the therapist in a combination of roles.

Often a carefully planned starting position used during treatment can also be created by supplying the right aid and will enable a range of useful functions to be performed which would otherwise be impossible. For example, a child who has precarious trunk control and the typical posture of a spastic diplegia, cannot use her hands when seated on an unstable surface (see Fig. 1). Alternatively, as shown in Fig. 2, sitting on the right size of a special chair, with feet and thighs well supported and her weight on the buttocks rather than the lower back, allows useful control of head and arms.

Group work can supplement formal physiotherapy and is also aimed at introducing the sequences of motor control experienced by all normal children. Helpers can include untrained as well as professional people, though whenever possible each child should have the same familiar adult handling him in the class. Thus child and helper together learn how to inhibit disabling primitive reflex patterns and to elicit the more mature reactions and skills as they

Fig. 1. Child on a beanbag, unable to use her hands.

make their appearance. Carefully chosen music is an essential part of such a class, which should be devised and conducted by a physiotherapist.

CHILDREN WITH SEVERE MULTIPLE HANDICAPS

In children with the most severe brain damage, resulting in grossly abnormal postural reflexes with limited or absent motor control, positional deformities are an ever-present problem. Passive movements are often used, in total patterns rather than singly, to

Fig. 2. Correct sitting, allowing useful control of head and arms.

maintain joint and muscle range, but these are a poor substitute for active movements.

The physiotherapist can advise on a suitable regime of good positions for each child, to cover the whole daily programme of sleeping, feeding and playing, and also on handling techniques for dressing, carrying etc. If these programmes can be consistently carried through, deformities should be kept within manageable limits in all but a few extreme cases.

Should orthopaedic intervention prove necessary, the physiotherapist will play an active part in post-operative management, and help with supervision of appliances. Often the orthopaedic surgeon will provide a modified Milwaukee jacket made in Plastozote.

Positioning at night-time is of great importance, because the child will otherwise revert to an asymmetrical position dictated by his abnormal postural reflexes, and may stay in this position of deformity for as long as 14 hours out of the 24.

It has been found that lying on the back usually produces the worst deformities. The corrective sleeping positions are individually planned, and maintained with sandbags and shaped high density foam supports. Diagrams over the bed show all staff what to do. The example in Fig. 3 shows how a scoliosis and chest asymmetry and a 'windswept' hip deformity can develop from an uncorrected resting position.

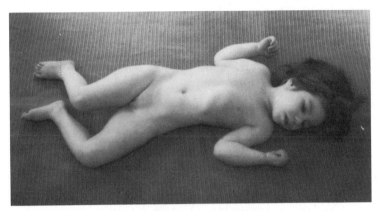

Fig. 3. Scoliosis and chest asymmetry and a 'windswept' posture resulting from an uncorrected resting position.

Lying Supine

Figures 4 and 6 show examples of poor positions, which are then corrected and the improved positions, shown in Figs. 5 and 7,

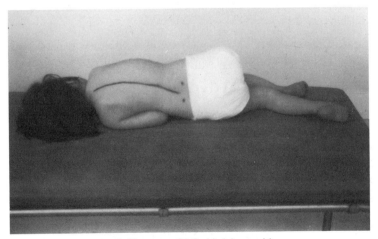

Fig. 4. Uncorrected left-side lying position.

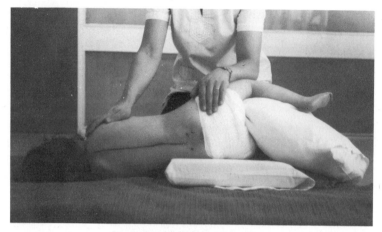

Fig. 5. Good left-side lying position.

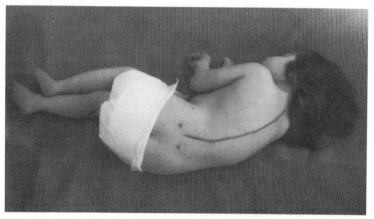

Fig. 6. Uncorrected right-side lying position.

maintained with sandbags and foam trunk and leg supports (not shown).

Late Adolescent and Adult Cerebral Palsy of all Degrees and Allied Conditions

It has been noted that mature mentally handicapped people may resent or become bored with too much formal physiotherapy, knowing perfectly well that further physical improvement is rare. However, physiotherapy should not be discontinued but should change to meet their needs which are to maintain former motor

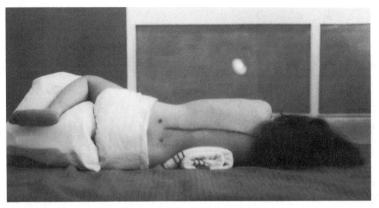

Fig. 7. Good right-side lying position.

gains and general physical fitness; to develop social skills through various activities, to provide motivation for continued physical effort; and carefully to follow-up all cases receiving orthopaedic surgery. Individual programmes may include group work, hydrotherapy or swimming, gymnastics and trampoline, pony riding, wheelchair dancing and athletics. Some people prefer to perfect skills, while others are motivated by use of the numerous award schemes in sports for the disabled; a surprising number enjoy competitive events, which in turn provides excellent experience in the community.

Finally, much time is spent by the physiotherapist in ordering, maintaining and adapting wheelchairs, assisting in the fitting of spinal jackets, splints for various purposes, helmets for the epileptics and surgical footwear.

THE REMEDIAL GYMNAST

The Role of Remedial Gymnasts in a Hospital for the Mentally Handicapped

There is little or no dividing line between the work of a remedial gymnast and a physiotherapist in this type of hospital. The professions work in close collaboration both in the wards and the department, often working together or 'sharing' patients, using identical or similar forms of treatment. Here the aim of the remedial gymnast is to gain as much active movement as possible from the mentally handicapped person and to instil the will and initiative to carry out the exercises without help, and ultimately to make the mentally handicapped person more comfortable within his own condition.

Because a high proportion of mentally handicapped people have a poor concentration span, the work schedule must be interesting and stimulating; though the presentation of movements must frequently change, the muscle groups being exercised may remain the same, and this ultimately leads to some improvement in the physical status. One of the best ways of holding the attention of those people is to utilize game situations, either by down-grading major games, e.g. football, or by incorporating minor games related to the desired movements, all corresponding to the patient's capabilities. This method can be used for the whole range of mentally and physically handicapped people, even those who are capable of performing only limited movements. With middle grades of intelligence it is often possible to progress on to formal work as their powers of concentration improve during exercise, in turn enabling the therapist to work specifically on one part of the body at a time.

A problem encountered in work with mentally handicapped people is the fact that they are loath to use inner and outer range movements in everyday activities, movements frequently being confined to middle range, e.g. it is common to find a mentally handicapped person, who should be physically normal, unable to lift his arm in full elevation above his head.

Another common problem is poor posture from 'bad habit,' often resulting in arthritic changes in early middle age, or else leading to the development of cervical spondylosis due to habitually walking with neck flexion and a secondary kyphosis and never being required to use the joints and muscles through their full range. This is one of the unfortunate results of institutionalism where much of the day may be spent sitting or aimlessly wandering, and it is particularly noticeable in the older patients.

With the higher grade hyperactive adolescents or children, it is important to keep them fit for the same reasons as there are for giving physical education in school—to get rid of excess energy and teach them to channel the body's capabilities in useful activities.

The more severely physically handicapped the mentally handicapped person, the more individual the work must become; however, the person if at all able must be encouraged to use any available movement. Only as a final resort do we turn to passive movements, and whenever possible they are used in conjunction with voluntary movements.

The remedial gymnast and physiotherapist also work together in various sports, such as swimming, training for the cerebral palsy games, pony riding, table tennis, etc., plus a variety of group activities which involve other professional bodies with similar aims. Coaching is also given in individual badge work and in competitive events, and this approach has proved to have considerable psychological benefits, as well as producing physical improvements.

OCCUPATIONAL THERAPY

Occupational therapy has much to offer the mentally handicapped of all ages and abilities, not only in the delivery of the therapist's many practical skills, but also in the opportunities within occupational therapy for providing new learning situations for the mentally handicapped person to respond to, both within and without the Occupational Therapy Department. A skilful occupational therapist will be able to assist in the habilitation of the mentally handicapped in many varied ways.

Initially, with the use of carefully chosen activities, the therapist will be able to determine her patient's level of functioning in most areas of his daily living, and thereby assist in the mentally handicapped person's overall assessment. Thereafter her training in occupational therapy treatment skills and planning will allow the therapist to prescribe and implement a programme of activities designed to effect some improvement or change in that person's performance, A well-run Occupational Therapy Department in which the therapist's skills, both practical and personal, are utilized to their maximum, will offer much to the mentally handicapped.

The Occupational Therapy Department

It is essential that the Occupational Therapy Department should offer the right kind of environment to those attending for treatment. Physically the building must be sufficiently spacious to allow not only for work areas, but also to provide space for non-work activities. Adequate storage is essential and the building must be suitable for the needs of the multiply handicapped.

Good working conditions are necessary for serious concentration; this includes good lighting, ventilation and comfortable furniture. The atmosphere of the Occupational Therapy Department, though light and airy, must be kept informal and cosy. A cold and cheerless, clinical-looking department will never achieve its purpose. People must feel both welcome and comfortably at home in order to relax and give of their best.

The Occupational Therapy Department offers the mentally handicapped person an opportunity of finding his place in an environment other than his usual living setting. The department, therefore, should offer surroundings very different from those with which he is already familiar, remembering, however, how much reassurance some people will require in this new situation. Although routine is not only necessary but also beneficial, the occupational therapy routine should be kept as informal and relaxed as possible, in an environment which is both stimulating and cheerful.

The Occupational Therapist

The occupational therapist working with the mentally handicapped must be patient, flexible and imaginative. She must not expect quick results from her labours or she will be disappointed. Duration of treatment is long, relative to other fields of occupational therapy; new activity ideas must, therefore, continually be thought out and put into practice to avoid repetition and boredom.

The therapist must feel at ease in an informal department with no props to her status. Ideally no uniforms or other badges of authority should be worn. Thus the mentally handicapped person is offered the opportunity to form a different kind of relationship from that which he has already experienced with uniformed authority, thereby promoting his skills in making satisfactory inter-personal relationships. An astute therapist will be able to build up trusting and friendly relationships with the mentally handicapped people attending her department and, while these are valuable in themselves, they will also help motivate them to co-operate in their treatment programmes.

Many professions are involved in the overall habilitation of the mentally handicapped person. The occupational therapist, as part of this team of workers, must conscientiously consult and co-operate with nurses, medical staff, speech therapists, physiotherapists, psychologists, educational and administrative staff, heads of service departments and any other members of staff involved with those she treats, in order to offer them the most effective therapy. The occupational therapist must willingly share her assessments of mentally handicapped people's functioning with other professions and must be able to re-use and adapt her activity programmes in accordance with their changing needs.

The Occupational Therapist's Aims

The occupational therapist, through the medium of a variety of activities, assists mentally handicapped people to function as well as their limitations will allow in many aspects of their daily lives, thereby contributing to their overall habilitation. Interesting work and recreational activities serve to stimulate and motivate the mentally handicapped. Success in these activities serves to increase self-confidence sufficiently to encourage the tackling of harder tasks. Occupational therapy provides opportunities for lower dependency people to train for hostel living or just for greater independence within the hospital. Good work habits are encouraged. The mentally handicapped person finally has the freedom within the Occupational Therapy Department to discover his own gifts and talents.

Higher dependency patients will find the reality of a day-to-day routine stimulating and very important to their psychological well-being. Initiative and a sense of responsibility are encouraged under friendly supervision.

The occupational therapist is the ideal person to introduce the mentally handicapped to the community outside the hospital. For example, a shopping trip may be an ordeal for the mentally handicapped: however, planned excursions into the community with the support of the occupational therapy staff will familiarize them with what is expected of them in many previously strange situations, thereby increasing their independence and self-confidence.

The occupational therapist is also a very suitable person to introduce the mentally handicapped to themselves. Using many activities designed to encourage self-awareness and awareness of the people round about him—for example, varied art techniques, puppet role-playing, discussion groups and movement to music— the occupational therapist will encourage the mentally handicapped person to see himself as an individual with many positive attributes as well as negative ones. Gradually, he will be able to foster a more truthful and positive self-image.

Lastly, the many aspects of occupational therapy, both within and without the department, offer varied opportunities for socialization in the differing work, recreational and training activities, thereby encouraging appropriate behaviour and good social habits in many changing situations.

Areas of Activity

I WITHIN THE OCCUPATIONAL THERAPY DEPARTMENT

a. Handcraft Workrooms—well-equipped handcraft workrooms are essential to any occupational therapy department for the mentally handicapped. Ideally these should be divided into two categories—light and heavy workrooms.

The former should be given over to fairly clean, light activities, some of which may be the following: sewing tasks, varying from teaching people how to mend their own clothes—for example, sewing on buttons—to teaching more able patients the elements of dress-making or how to handle an electric sewing machine; also included would be fancy stitch work, which is easily graded according to ability—for example, simple canvas embroidery, assembling soft toys, tapestry work, and more complicated needle-work projects like appliqué and florentine embroidery; knitting; crochet; leatherwork; macramé; and rug-making. Not only individual projects may be undertaken: learning to work with others is important and group projects such as making Christmas crackers or masks for Hallowe'en are valuable learning experiences.

However, more traditionally male-orientated activities should be arranged together in a separate work area, preferably soundproofed. The following are suitable activities for this heavy workshop: woodwork, with tasks ranging from the simple assembly of stools and toys to more complicated carpentry projects, which can be undertaken by mentally handicapped people under the supervision of the occupational therapist with the assistance of technical instructors, such as picture framing—this is an activity favoured by many Occupational Therapy Departments as providing the mentally handicapped people with training in a variety of basic woodwork skills as well as providing contact with the general public as they bring in their pictures to be framed and collect the finished product; metalwork, including wrought iron work; stone polishing; enamel jewellery making; and concrete-slab production.

b. Social and Personal Area—Teaching the basic principles of self-care is an important aspect of occupational therapy and with co-operation from the ward staff programmes can be devised for mentally handicapped people on, for example, foot-care, hygiene, looking after teeth and other aspects of health and personal care. Also in this area of activity, the mentally handicapped person can, through various projects, become better acquainted with himself, his peers, the area in which he lives and the skills he requires to feel at home in his environment. Here are some examples:-

i. Learning about time, shapes, colours, numbers and money.

ii. Documentation of personal statistics followed by comparison of them with those of others—height, weight, colour of hair and eyes, size of shoes etc— ending the project perhaps with a self-portrait, which again can be compared with those done by others.

iii. Learning about his local community, his country and getting out and about to see for himself.

iv. Learning how to communicate with others, far and near; use of the telephone, writing letters, pen-friends, conversation, eye contact, non-verbal communication—very important as a high percentage of the mentally handicapped have difficulty with verbal communication.

v. Learning how to behave in an emergency—fire, accidents etc.

Due to the slow rate of development of the mentally handicapped person there is real value for some in pursuing academic subjects beyond school years. The occupational therapist is well poised to help. Reading and writing is of no value to the mentally handicapped if learned 'parrot-fashion' with no understanding; but a basic recognition and comprehension of certain, socially-useful, words may give independence to the mentally handicapped in some areas of his life.

c. Domestic Area—Competence in domestic tasks is advantageous to both sexes. In this area the aim would be to give mentally handicapped people a training experience in all types of domestic duties, some of which may be the following:

i. Cooking and baking safely and competently;

ii. Bedspreading, shopping and simple nutrition;

iii. Care of personal clothing and domestic linen—how and when to wash them;

iv. Housewifery.

d. Art Area—Art activities are invaluable to occupational therapists, not only in providing a creative medium and a useful means of expression, but also as an aid to sensory experience. Many varied techniques can be used—for example, painting with brushes or fingers, claywork, wax scratching, group frieze painting, plaster of Paris modelling and papier maché. Art activities are easily adapted for people of mixed abilities and are ideal for either group or individual work.

e. Recreational Area—Recreation is an important aspect of occupational therapy for the mentally handicapped. For this, a large area is essential, equipped with an imaginative supply of records, percussion instruments, table games, balls, large and small, hoops and bean bags. Using these, the skilful occupational therapist will channel physical energies into constructive recreational activities, amongst which may be included team games, marching, dancing, competitive tournaments, five-a-side football, keep fit exercises, community singing and action songs. Careful planning and organization is essential, but free movement and self-expression must not be stifled.

Ball games, rounders, races and other sports can be taken outside in fine weather and these, along with venture trails, berry-foraging trips and so on will provide healthy activity in the fresh air—a helpful aid to physical fitness.

II OUTSIDE THE OCCUPATIONAL THERAPY DEPARTMENT

Many mentally handicapped people have undergone useful training within the various service departments of the hospital or training centre. In most cases the following hospital departments are suitable, and may be very willing, to accept patient trainees and to provide them with adequate support and supervision, reporting back regularly to the Occupational Therapist on any improvement or change in the patient's performance:

i. Laundry;

ii. Maintenance departments;

iii. Gardens;

iv. Hospital farm;

v. Kitchens.

While placed in these departments the mentally handicapped trainee will not only pick up skills which may be useful to him in future employment, but will also learn what would be expected of him in terms of his attitude towards authority, acceptable social behaviour, punctuality and appropriate dress.

Occupational Therapy Programme Planning

When planning a programme of activities for the mentally handicapped, the occupational therapist must bear in mind the nature of their problems. Their concentration lapses quickly and they are easily bored and distracted. The mentally handicapped respond well to a series of changes within a secure framework of activity. A suitable and effective occupational therapy programme will therefore consist of a number of well-organized and varied activities, involving a mixture of physical exercises, self-expression, and differing social situations and learning experiences, both passive and active.

Teaching new skills to the mentally handicapped is most effective in small groups, but the person must also learn how to react appropriately in large groups where he is only one of a crowd. The size of the group should therefore vary. However, regardless of how many are in her group, the occupational therapist must never lose sight of each person's individuality.

Occupational therapists are assisted in the implementation of treatment programmes by staff not necessarily registered as occupational therapists. These include occupational therapy helpers, technical instructors and teachers of handcrafts. They are responsible to the Head Occupational Therapist and make a valuable contribution to the work of the Occupational Therapy Department.

The Domiciliary Occupational Therapists

A domiciliary occupational therapist, as part of a social work team, will be involved in the care of the mentally handicapped person when he is discharged from hospital. Her task is to visit the mentally handicapped person in his new surroundings and assess any associated problems. Where there is physical disability overlying the person's mental handicap, the occupational therapist may be able to prescribe adaptations to his home or hostel (e.g. widening doorways to take wheelchairs) or aids to daily living (e.g. support rails beside the toilet) thereby allowing him greater independence within his home. The hospital-based occupational therapist must therefore, work in co-operation with the domiciliary occupational therapist so that any adaptations to houses or prescriptions for aids are taken care of *before* the patient is discharged from hospital.

EDUCATIONAL PROVISION IN A HOSPITAL SETTING

Most educational provision within hospitals for the mentally handicapped falls within the area now called *Adult Basic Education*, which is itself part of *Continuing Education*. Continuing Education sees learning as a life-long process, rather than as something only undertaken before the age of 16—which unfortunately is still the case for most mentally handicapped students. This traditional or school view of education is particularly unhelpful for the mentally handicapped, since many of them are commencing their best years of learning ability at the point when statutory education ceases.

Adult Basic Education tries to be responsive to the student's needs as an individual and to determine the essential skills needed by a particular person. This involves a process of assessment, programme negotiation with both the student and supporting staff and a focus on what will enhance personal self-reliance. Another aspect of Adult Basic Education is that teaching is seen as an activity that all concerned staff can practise, leaving the role of the adult education tutor as programme co-ordinator, assessor and animator.

However, in practice there is likely to be a 'lingering-on' of traditional ideas, both from the students, who will often see the adult education tutor as 'the reading teacher' and from some hospital staff, who expect the tutor to concentrate on reading, writing and arithmetic. The traditional literacy skills do have an important part to play—particularly in raising a student's confidence—but reading, writing and numeracy now tend to be integrated into purposeful activities like cooking, shopping and budgeting.

With improvements in materials and techniques, and a lowering of the threshold of functional literacy to include basic social sight words like *TOILET, PAY HERE, EXIT,* and *DANGER*, it has become possible to teach socially useful signs to students who would a few years ago have been considered ineducable.

The student who has learnt to recognize words on sight may be ready to move into 'phonics', to learn the relationship between sounds and letters. This will give the student a strategy for dealing with words they do not recognize. They can then concentrate on reading for meaning and on reading useful social documents like labels, TV guides, menus, forms and recipes, rather than 'readers' of the traditional kind. For those students who have developed reading skills to the point where they can follow narrative, they are able to maintain their skills by attending regular Readers' Circle sessions.

The writing skills have undergone a similar review and are now seen more pragmatically, focusing on signatures and form filling, letter and post-card writing. Pen-pals are encouraged and a hospital magazine can offer students the opportunity to put their views and comments across to those servicing their needs, in addition to giving them the satisfaction of seeing their writing in print.

Many students lack confidence in handling money either because they have little experience in shopping or because they have never been taught to transfer to the decimal system. Before they can handle money many students have to be taught number recognition and counting.

Simple social skills are a fundamental part of the educational programme. The acquisition of skills like time-telling, how to use a pay phone or go on a bus alone can lead to a greater independence for the student. BBC series *Let's Go* can provide the basis for a useful social-skills training programme. The series is aimed at the moderately handicapped in adult training centres, hospitals and hostels.

The skills already mentioned depend for their acquisition on good communication abilities. In many large institutions with inadequate staffing, students are rarely involved in conversation, but hear only instructions and comments, which can mean that they have a very limited idea of interactive language use. As a result they may have to be taught the skills of initiating a conversation, taking turns, changing topic, expressing an opinion and feelings in socially accepted ways. However, these skills cannot be taught in isolation from normal activities and events—that is, from those things that supply the content of normal conversation. Large institutions by their very nature may deprive students of essential stimulation and experience, which may mean that a tutor will have to generate events and make extended use of calendar events such as Easter and Christmas so that activities and conversational content will have a base in everyday life. These events can be used as the basis for a programme. For example, Christmas could be anticipated by the making of a Christmas pudding. This could involve the reading of recipes, the writing of shopping lists, a shopping expedition, the writing of invitations followed by the celebration of its eating.

Any teaching programme should include regular visits to shopping centres and other community venues to practise real-life situations. Learning a skill in the educational department is a rehearsal for genuine application elsewhere.

CHAPTER 7

Helping the Mentally Handicapped to Learn

INTRODUCTION

DIFFICULTY WITH LEARNING is the most universal characteristic of mental handicap. On the surface, this statement seems too obvious to be worth making. Yet it is important, for all developed societies have official educational systems for helping children and young adults to learn. Therefore, people who have difficulty with learning offer a challenge to the system, and few offer more of a challenge than do the mentally handicapped. As a result, the educational systems of the developed countries have been expanded in an attempt to make provision for the learning difficulties of the mentally handicapped. This chapter takes examples from the educational system of Great Britain to describe the provision which is made for the mentally handicapped, and to explain some of the changes which have taken place (and are continuing to take place) with the passage of the years.

DEVELOPMENT OF EDUCATIONAL PROVISION FOR THE MENTALLY HANDICAPPED

Background

Schools have existed in Great Britain for over a thousand years. However, it is convenient to date the birth of the present educational system in the 1870s with the passing of two major Acts of Parliament. Even before that time, the Lunacy (Scotland) Act of 1862 made it clear that the provision of facilities for training the mentally handicapped was a matter of serious concern. Thus it is not surprising to discover that a debate about the nature of educational provision for the mentally handicapped should have begun in the closing years of the nineteenth century. Several important themes emerged in the course of that debate, and it is interesting to note their recurrence in debates about special education ever since.

One of these themes was that education for mentally handicapped children might require changes in the 'normal' system of education. Initially, this concern was expressed for the least handicapped group of children (then termed the 'feeble-minded'). In time, the debate expanded to include all groups, no matter how severe their handicap.

Another theme is that of discriminating between children who are educable and those who are ineducable. As a result, educators are continually trying to develop fairer and more adequate methods of assessing children's ability. They also concern themselves with trying to define education itself. For, if they do not know what education is, how will they know who is ineducable?

A third theme which emerges just before the start of the twentieth century is that the mental handicap of some children is so severe that their education cannot be carried on inside the ordinary schools. This concern led to the creation of segregated special schools and, inevitably, to the debate about whether this segregation was morally or educationally sound.

Like most people, special educators are fond of remarking on the way history tends to repeat itself. For example, the themes mentioned above are virtually identical to debates which still preoccupy us in the last quarter of the twentieth century. We are still concerned that our modern tests may not discriminate between children who need special help and those who do not. We still debate whether to build better schools or to integrate as many handicapped children as possible into the ordinary school system.

Significant Influences on the Development of Educational Provision

Yet history never can repeat itself exactly. Even if the themes are old the circumstances in which they occur are different and call for a different sort of response. For example, in 1910 la Page made many useful suggestions for the education and training of 'feeble-minded' children and some of these suggestions still seem remarkably up-to-date. But la Page was writing at a time when there was no parental or professional lobby compaigning for (or even attempting to describe) the rights of handicapped people. Moreover, in 1910 it would have been very difficult for an educator to plan a scheme of activities for stimulating the mental skills of a nonverbal, severely handicapped child. After all, Jean Piaget, the Swiss psychologist who has had such a great influence on the psychology of education, did not publish his *Language and Thought of the Child* until 1923.

In short, though the mentally handicapped child's basic difficulty with learning has not changed, and though cycles and fashions in educational thought are very likely to recur, the twentieth century has seen some very significant changes in attitudes towards the mentally handicapped. In particular, three of these should be identified.

THE INFLUENCE OF PRESSURE GROUPS

The first major force for change was the development of voluntary organizations, such as parents' associations, who have acted as pressure groups aiming to secure better public understanding of the problems and needs associated with mental handicap. The National Association for Mentally Handicapped Children and the Scottish Society for the Mentally Handicapped are two of the best known. Such groups can and do draw on academic research to support their pleas for better services, but their claim to be listened to is stronger than that. It is that they represent the rights of the parents of children who are to be specially educated, and thus they are in a unique position to make claims on behalf of the children's emotional well-being and for their opportunity to lead as full a life as possible. The understandable reluctance of parents to part with their children, leaving them in the care of the mental deficiency hospitals, has made the public more acutely aware of the learning difficulties in mental handicap and, consequently, of the need for the educational system to make an adequate response to it.

DEVELOPMENTS IN EDUCATIONAL THINKING

A second major influence on the development of educational provision for the mentally handicapped has been the growth of thinking about the curriculum. What does happen in schools and what should happen in schools are among the oldest questions in education and probably will continue to be so. Not surprisingly, the vast majority of books which have been written about the theory of education have been concerned with the education of children in the ordinary school system. However, it is often illuminating to examine the aims and practice of education meant for mentally handicapped people in the same terms, for there is a high degree of similarity between the two systems. For example, many 'ordinary' educators are concerned about the conflict which can often exist between the notions of preparing a child for life in the outside world and of drawing out the child's potential to the highest level of which he is capable. This is a real problem for special educators too. At a practical level, for instance, they may have to work out how much time should be spent on reading, writing or music at the expense of time which could be used learning how to tie shoelaces, use the bus service or bandage a cut.

At a more theoretical level, one recent document (Scottish Education Department, 1977) written for the ordinary school system recommends that the school curriculum should help a child to (a) acquire knowledge and understanding, (b) develop skills which will be useful outside the school, (c) develop emotionally and artistically and (d) be equipped for the demands society will make on him once he has left school. It is not difficult to see that the same priniciples can apply to the education of the mentally handicapped. Indeed, it is conceivable that these principles can be realized more easily with the mentally handicapped as their education is not subject to the pressures of an examination system. Because of this, idealism probably has a better chance to flourish in special education than it has in general education. In time we may even see general education looking to special education for illumination of the issues which concern it.

DEVELOPMENTS IN PSYCHOLOGY

The third major influence on the education of the mentally handicapped that has taken place during the twentieth century has been the growth of understanding about child development, learning and relationships between people.

Very many severely mentally handicapped children do not advance beyond a stage at which they are able to solve the kinds of puzzles which can be tackled by most other children before they go to school. Thanks to the work of *developmental psychologists* our understanding of how young children make sense of the world and communicate with other people in it has greatly increased. As a result, it has become possible to think quite constructively about activities which can sensibly be tailored to the intellectual level of children whose ability to solve problems is much lower than their age would suggest. Of course, these activities must also be sufficiently interesting for the children; mental handicap does not always prevent a child from realizing that he is being 'talked-down to'.

The *psychology of learning* has also played an important part in developing the quality of education which is provided for the mentally handicapped. This branch of psychology is sometimes criticized for basing its insights on studies which have been carried out on rats, pigeons and other animals. However, it has to be recognized that these insights have been very valuable for increasing our understanding of how people learn. As a result, educators have begun to pay attention to how interesting may be the tasks that they ask people to do, for without a basic interest in what is happening the child or adult will not be encouraged to learn. Psychologists interested in learning have also shown how important it is to use the skills which a person already has as a basis for building more advanced skills. In addition there is abundant evidence to show how important 'reinforcement' is in teaching and learning. Quite simply, reinforcement consists of giving the child encouragement to produce new behaviour more frequently and more accurately.

The best-known and most controversial product of the psychology of learning is behaviour modification. Behaviour modification is a highly structured form of teaching which requires the teacher to (a) create circumstances in which learning can take place, (b) present carefully graded tasks which have to be learned, and (c) reinforce (or punish, as appropriate) the learner for his responses. Behaviour modification has been used successfully to teach a variety of skills from toilet-training to language, and from behaving courteously to behaving assertively. It is controversial because some people feel that it reduces both teacher and learner to the status of machines which have to follow mindlessly 'programmes' thought up by someone else. It is also criticized because it is used too frequently to subdue undesirable behaviour rather than to increase new, desirable skills. Criticisms such as these can often be justified. However, behaviour modification cannot be dismissed out of hand as it demonstrates very effectively the importance of planning and careful attention to all aspects of teaching a skill or of imparting knowledge. Not everyone can be a 'modifier'; everyone can be a thoughtful, systematic teacher.

Psychology and sociology concerned with the *development of personality and the formation of relationships* have also made an important contribution to the development of educational provision for the mentally handicapped. For example, with very young children it is important to pay adequate attention to helping the child form an attachment to an adult. Of course this adult will usually be the child's mother, but if the child has been moved into institutional care then the highly important role of 'mother' passes to the nurse or care officer who is in charge of the child. The importance of this is difficult to understate, especially when hospital or domestic routines are at cross-purposes with the emotional needs of individual children. At the other end of the age-scale, people have also begun paying attention to the emotional needs of mentally-handicapped teenagers and young adults. It is very easy to carry on treating a mentally-handicapped adolescent or adult as if he were still a child of primary school age. Yet this is not the kind of treatment which we would expect to be dealt out to leavers from the ordinary school system. As a result, special educators must work to reconcile the principle of protecting the weaker members of society with the principle of encouraging people to develop to the fullness of their power and to be as independent as possible. This is one aspect of education which is a very long way from having been explored fully and which will offer educators many challenges for years to come.

Warnock and After
In November 1973 Mrs Margaret Thatcher, then Secretary of State for Education and Science, announced her intention to appoint a committee which would review the provision of special education in England, Scotland and Wales and which would make recommendations about its future course. The committee, headed by Mrs Mary Warnock, eventually made its report in the summer of 1978.

Although the Warnock Report is concerned with the entire range of disabling conditions which cause children to have special educational needs, it is clear that the needs of children who are mentally handicapped figured prominently in the committee's deliberations. They certainly figured prominently in the three areas of education which the committee considered should be tackled as a matter of 'first priority'.

These three areas were the provision of educational treatment for children of under five years of age; the planning and provision of genuinely *education* programmes of work for the post-sixteen mentally handicapped; and a comprehensive assault on teacher-training to provide changes ranging from major improvements in existing training courses to the inclusion of a special education component in the basic training of *all* teachers.

It is not difficult to see connections between Warnock's areas of influences on the development of special education which were outlined above. For example, the proposal of educational provision for the under-fives is a response to parental pressure, and to the clearest of research findings indicating that treatment to prevent a 'disability from becoming a handicap' should be begun at as early a stage as possible. It is also a reponse to developments in psychology and the curriculum which make it possible for us to state what should be the components of educational programmes for the under-fives.

The plea for education for the over-sixteens has a similar base to that for the under-fives. Parents who were active in drawing attention to the need for help for their mentally-handicapped children are now claiming the same rights for their mentally-handicapped young adults. These pleas are supported by research workers who draw attention to the case for continuing educational treatment to which children had become receptive in middle and late adolescence. This proposal is also in line with the thinking of educators who see education as a process which continues throughout life and in which the mentally-handicapped have a right to share.

Finally, the recommendations in respect of teacher-training can be seen as a response to the ethical issues of excluding some children from the education system; to the need for teacher-training to take cognisance of research findings and advances in the philosophy of special education; and to the fact that many children considered 'normal' by virtue of their attendance at an 'ordinary' school where they are taught by 'ordinary' teachers are likely to have special educational needs.

The Warnock Report is rightly regarded as a major blueprint for the future of special education through to the end of the twentieth century. However, the official response to it at the time of writing this chapter has been quite disappointing. Certainly, two White Papers have been produced (Department of Education and Science, 1980; Scottish Education Department, 1980) but at best they serve only to legitimize trends which were already well under way before their publication.

The recommendations of the White Papers cover three areas. The first of these is that the statutory list of handicapping conditions (nine in Scotland, ten in England and Wales) should cease to be the main determinant of the educational placement of a child who has some form of disability. Instead, placement would depend on the child's 'special educational needs'—which was of course the title of the Warnock Report. Thus, educators are to be concerned less with classifying a child and more with describing what he can do and what are his needs.

The second major area covered by the White Papers concerns the concept of 'learning disability'. Traditionally, one percent of the school population of Britain has received education in a special school or unit. However, Warnock drew attention to the fact that as many as 20% of the school population were likely to require special educational provision of some sort at some point in their career. The White Papers suggest that the Government intends to recognize this fact more specifically by requiring education authorities to make provision for the special educational needs of all children in the community, including those who attend (and always will attend) the ordinary school.

The third area covered by the White Papers concerns the role of parents as partners in the education of their children. Approval is given to those local authorities who encourage parents to participate in the overall assessment procedure of their children who may require special educational treatment.* This is done formally in some authorities by providing parents with a form on which to make their own statement. However, the White Papers stop short of requiring (or even recommending) that local authorities should adopt this procedure as standard policy.

A much more clear recognition of the rights of parents is given in respect of their children's placement in special schools. Parents of children attending special schools are now being given the same opportunity as other parents to state which schools they would like their children to attend. It is likely that they will also have the right (not open to parents of other children) to ask that their children be placed in a grant-aided or independent school at local authority

---

* Children are usually admitted to special education after they have gone through a procedure known as 'ascertainment'. Local authorities decide if a child's need for special education has been 'ascertained' on the basis of examinations carried out by an educational psychologist and a school doctor, and, whenever possible, on the basis of a report from the child's headteacher.

expense if they believe that there is no appropriate special educational treatment available for their children locally.

Parents will also have the right of appeal against decisions about special educational treatment proposed by the local authorities. The form of this appeal proposed for Scotland is a significant change from the existing practice in which such appeals are currently directed to the Secretary of State. It is now proposed that Scottish parents who do not accept the findings of their local authority or of the local appeals committee will have the right to take their case to the Sheriff Court. Ultimately therefore the Sheriff will be the final arbiter of children's special educational placements. Superficially, this appears to be a significant improvement in parents' rights. However, the plan may backfire if parents are reluctant to go through the procedures of initiating a court case—a procedure which may be very much more complicated than the former practice of appealing to the Secretary of State. One of the Scottish teachers' unions is also expressing concern on this issue (Educational Institute of Scotland, 1981) in that the proposed legislation would empower a legal officer to make educational decisions.

EDUCATIONAL PROVISION FOR THE MENTALLY HANDICAPPED

Local government education committees in Great Britain are required to provide education for mentally handicapped children. This provision takes the form of special schools and of teachers (and others) to staff them.

Provision of Schools

The more common method of providing schools for the mentally handicapped has been to relate types of provision to degree of handicap. Thus, a pattern has emerged of providing three types of school for children who live at home.

SPECIAL SCHOOLS

The first type of school is often called, simply, a 'special school'. The pupils who attend special schools were formally described as 'mildly mentally handicapped' (Scotland) or 'ESN'/'educationally subnormal' (England and Wales), though as a result of the Warnock Committee's recommendations it is likely that these children will now be known as 'children with moderate learning disabilities'. Children who attend special schools have usually encountered severe difficulty in keeping up with the work of their age group in ordinary schools, though it is only rarely that their difficulties with learning are the result of any obvious clinical condition. Indeed, many people have expressed anxiety that a considerable proportion of the children in this group have been placed in special schools as a result of difficult behaviour in their ordinary schools.

When the topic of 'integrating' children receiving special education into the ordinary school system is discussed, the most obvious group for integration are those who attend special schools for the mildly handicapped or ESN. The curriculum followed by these children in their special schools is very similar to that followed by slower learners in the ordinary schools, and some people would claim that the wider range of educational opportunities together with the higher level of expectation of output from children in the ordinary schools would make greater integration of these handicapped pupils an attractive proposition. However, it can also be argued that there will continue to be a role for the special school. It is, after all, an establishment which claims to make special provision for the educational needs of slower learners, and this is an ideal which many special schools attain quite readily. Furthermore, the absence of an examination system in the special schools inevitably means that teachers have more scope to develop a flexible curriculum, and anxious pupils have less chance of being worried by prospects of failure.

JUNIOR OCCUPATION(AL) CENTRES—SCHOOLS FOR THE SEVERELY MENTALLY HANDICAPPED

Occupation(al) centres were established as a result of the 1945 (Scotland) Education Act and the 1967 (England and Wales) Education Act. Their purpose was to make provision for children who were described formally as 'trainable but ineducable'. In Scotland these children were later described as 'severely mentally handicapped' and in England and Wales as 'SSN'/'severely subnormal' or 'ESN'(S)'/'educationally subnormal (severe)'. Children attending occupational centres invariably showed severe difficulties in learning compared with what would be expected from other children of the same age. Almost invariably also, their handicap would be the result of some clinical disorder. Children with Down's Syndrome (Mongolism) are perhaps the group which most people would think of when the severely mentally handicapped are being discussed.

Since 1945 in Scotland and 1970 in England and Wales, education authorities have been responsible for the provision and oversight of occupational centres.

Throughout Great Britain occupational centres are now termed 'schools'. This is a progressive step as it recognizes that children with severe learning difficulties are educable. However, this step also requires parents and the staff of schools to look carefully at what is meant by 'education'. The change of labels from 'centre' to 'school' and from 'ineducable' to 'with severe learning difficulties' does not mean that the new schools will offer a curriculum which apes the curriculum of the ordinary schools. The task of working out what is meant by education for the severely handicapped offers one of the most exciting challenges to the community in the coming years.

DAY CARE CENTRES OR SPECIAL CARE CENTRES

These centres care for children who were formerly described as 'ineducable and untrainable'. It is now more common to refer to the children as 'most severely mentally handicapped' or 'profoundly mentally handicapped', though if the Warnock terminology takes hold, they will probably become known as 'children with the most severe learning difficulties'.

Although these centres are intended to make provision for the most severely handicapped children in the community, the interpretation of what constitutes 'most severely handicapped' is subject to great variation among authorities and even among schools within an authority. Some educators will accept that a child is profoundly mentally handicapped only when he is unresponsive, bed-bound and appears to spend most of his life in a coma. However, other educators are prepared to regard children as profoundly handicapped even when these children are able to walk and talk. Arbitrary borderlines such as 'mental level of lower than one year' have also been proposed, but even this is not so clear cut as it may seem at first. For example, the one year borderline would be unfairly biased against young children who could be expected to pass through it later in their school career. The one year border also indicates perhaps too confident a reliance on measures of mental age as the main determinant of a child's educational treatment.

Responsibility for day care centres passed from health to education authorities in 1970 in England and Wales, and from social work to education departments in Scotland from 1974. A considerable number of day care centres were run by voluntary agencies, but, while these agencies retain ownership of buildings, the funding of staff salaries and equipment and other running costs have been taken over by the local authorities.

ALTERNATIVE EDUCATIONAL PROVISION

The paragraphs above have dealt with the most easily described provisions of schools for the mentally handicapped. They have detailed the usual forms of day provision which can be found in most urban areas throughout Britain and in many rural areas also. However, this standard pattern is subject to regional variations depending on various causes such as local educational policies and the numbers of children who are to be served by the special educational provision.

For example, some local authorities will arrange the special education of two or even three of the above groups of mentally handicapped children in the one building. This can make sound economic sense in rural communities where relatively few children may require special educational treatment. However, other local authorities have found that this all-in provision makes good educational sense also and are attempting to establish schools which can be regarded as centres of excellence for the provision of special educational treatment. Still other local authorities have adopted the policy of establishing special schools or classes on the sites of existing larger primary or secondary schools. Once again, this can make good economic sense as well as providing opportunities for breaking down the barriers of segregation between the ordinary and special school systems.

The statutory requirements for local authorities to provide day-school provision for the mentally handicapped has made it accepted that the majority of mentally handicapped children will spend at least their years of childhood in the parental home. However, residential accommodation is still required for a considerable number of the mentally handicapped. The majority of children who require institutional care as a result of mental handicap, primarily, are the severely and profoundly mentally handicapped. Certainly some children with milder learning difficulties also find themselves in institutional care but in their case the main cause of their placement is likely to be some sensory, physical, behavioural or psychiatric problem. However, the degree of handicap and the cause of placement in the institution are irrelevant to the fact that education has to be provided for these children too. Teachers appointed from the local education department serve the hospitals in their area. Residential schools and children's homes with teaching units attached also have teachers appointed to them, but the responsibility for making this provision will depend on whether the school is under the auspices of the local authority or is grant-aided or independent.

A small proportion of mentally-handicapped children of school age still spend all their time at home. A typical example would be a profoundly handicapped child for whom there was no adequate day-care provision in his home area and whose parents did not want him to be taken into institutional care. The other group of mentally handicapped children who remain at home, of course, are the under-fives. Many local authorities have established an itinerant teaching service for children like this, so that the children can receive appropriate systematic education. In such circumstances parents have an especially important role to play as educators of their own children. Therefore, one of the skills that the itinerant teachers must develop is how to transmit their ideas about teaching to the parents so that schemes of activities can be carried on between the teachers' visits.

Provision of Educational Staff

Even in an area as compact geographically as the mainland of Great Britain, there is considerable variation among the qualifications and training of staff in schools for the mentally handicapped. Broadly speaking, these members of staff can be divided into two groups, depending on whether or not they have a professional teacher's qualification. However, even within the teacher and non-teacher divisions there is little standardization in qualifications, as the following two sections will show.

TEACHERS

The traditional route to becoming a teacher of the mentally handicapped has been to qualify as a primary or secondary teacher within the normal school sector first of all and then to transfer to special education. Colleges of education provide three-or-four year diploma courses which enable people to obtain a basic qualification in teaching. University graduates, however, can obtain certificates of education entitling them to teach after one year of study. Teachers who have decided to move from primary or secondary education to special education may return to college of education at a later date to study for a post-experience diploma in special education though, normally, this qualification is not insisted upon by local authorities. Recent years have seen a growing interest in providing a genuinely educational curriculum for the severely mentally handicapped and as a result more and more colleges of education are providing entire courses, or special modules within the post-experience diploma, which will encourage teachers to develop special expertise in working with the most severely handicapped groups of children.

In England and Wales it is possible to undertake initial teacher-training in the field of special education alone. This means that after three years teachers are entitled and qualified to work immediately with the mentally handicapped. At present, this qualification is not recognized in Scotland unless the teacher has also undertaken approved training in primary or secondary education. In Scotland all teachers working in state schools must register with the General Teaching Council for Scotland, and this Council recognizes qualifications in primary or secondary education only. The Council takes the view that teachers should have a grounding in the ordinary educational system before transferring to special education.

STAFF WITHOUT QUALIFICATIONS IN TEACHING

Throughout Great Britain, staff other than teachers are appointed by education authorities to work with mentally-handicapped children. Some of these staff carry out ancillary duties such as escort duty on school transport, and assistance with feeding and toileting the children.

Other 'non-teaching' staff, such as nursery nurses, work alongside the teachers, participating in all aspects of the children's education. However, whereas the overall direction of the school is the responsibility of a teacher in England and Wales, in Scotland it may be the responsibility of an instructor who is not a qualified teacher. The appointment of instructors to senior positions has been carried over from the days when the occupational centres provided 'care and training' rather than 'education'—and care and training can be given without a teaching qualification! In 1973 the Melville Committee proposed that a two-year full-time training course should be established for instructors and that teachers should direct the running of schools for the mentally handicapped. To date, a one-year full-time course has been established, and teachers are gradually being appointed as heads of schools. The future structure of staffing in Scotland raises problems which are unique among the educational systems of Britain and which must be handled delicately if they are to have an amicable solution.

THE CONTENT OF EDUCATION FOR THE MENTALLY HANDICAPPED

Introduction

It is easy to say that mentally-handicapped children should be educated. It is not so easy to state why we want them to learn and what we want them to learn. However, the Warnock Report (1978) does provide some useful guidance when it states that the aims of education are ... '... to increase the child's knowledge of the world and ... to let him develop as much independence and self-sufficiency as he is capable of'.

At first these aims of education should seem to be commonsense and non-controversial, but in fact they offer a considerable challenge. For example, how do you increase the 'knowledge of the world' of a profoundly mentally-handicapped child who seems to be in permanent coma? Moreover, do you really want a long-stay hospital patient to become self-sufficient when self-sufficiency is at cross-purposes with hospital procedures and the whole notion of a community apart?

The rest of this chapter will be spent looking at what activities can be used to help mentally-handicapped children learn. It is based on the belief that education mainly consists of helping children to learn about the world, and of helping them to learn how to do things. 'Learning about the world' is concerned with acquiring knowledge and understanding. 'Learning how to do things' is concerned with acquiring skills.

Knowledge and Understanding

The mentally handicapped person's need to acquire knowledge depends on his degree of handicap and the circumstances in which he is living. A fourteen year old Down's child who can walk and talk, for example, will need to know different things from a fourteen year old profoundly handicapped child who is unable to lift his head. Furthermore, a fourteen year old Down's child living in a hospital will need to know quite a different set of things from a fourteen year old Down's child who is living at home. Therefore, the aim of this section is to suggest some of the kinds of knowledge which people acquire as they grow up.

One of the earliest things a child has to learn is simply that he exists. If a child is very young, for example, or if he is very profoundly handicapped, it is important that he should become as aware as possible of the fact that there are objects and people all around him, and that these objects and people are not part of him.

The child becomes aware of these facts by stimulation of his senses. Thus, even before we can be sure that the child is responding to his surroundings, we do everything possible to make him aware of them. This can be done by systematically examining the ways in which he can be stimulated and by finding activities which will provide that stimulation. Here are some examples:—

STIMULATION OF THE SENSE OF VISION

Moving brightly coloured toys within the child's visual field (if he can see) will let him pick out the details of the object, and will let him experience colour and movement. It is important to work person-to-person with the child as this will help him to build up relationships (*see below*), but of course there is not always time for this. Therefore, when there is not time for individual work visual stimulation can still be provided by letting toys on strings dangle in front of the child, for example, or by letting him lie or sit near an open window overlooking a playground or by laying or seating him near a tank of tropical fish.

STIMULATION OF THE SENSE OF HEARING

Let the child hear a wide variety of sounds such as those which can be produced by cymbals, tambourines, drums, bells and squeezy toys. There are plenty of these materials available in the shops but it is possible to make just as effective ones using materials which can be found around the home. Once again, person-to-person work is very valuable, but the child's sense of hearing can also be stimulated at times when there is no individual contact if a radio, gramophone or musical box can be left playing near him. However, do not let this background music take the place of individual contact altogether, and do not let background music play all the time as it will soon hardly be noticed.

STIMULATION OF THE SENSE OF TOUCH

Let the child experience a wide range of textures. For example, he can lie on a plastic mattress, a gymnastics mat, a woollen blanket, and it may even be possible to take him into a swimming pool. Of course, around a house, school or ward there will also be many materials with interesting textures and these can be rubbed against the child's skin or (if he is able) be placed in his hand for him to manipulate. Such textured substances include towels, dusters, crinkly paper from biscuit tins, brushes and a variety of clothing.

The child's sense of touch can also be used to help him understand where his body ends. For example, brown paper or newspaper can be laid underneath his legs and his feet can be dropped onto it. This activity may help him to realize that he has legs and that they are a (comparatively) long way away from his face which in turn can be stimulated by gentle brushing by a towel or duster. Nursery rhymes with actions are another good way of stimulating the sense of touch (for example, *This Little Piggy. . .*), and at the same time give the child experience of an adult's company and the world of language.

STIMULATION OF THE SENSE OF MOVEMENT

If possible, get a physiotherapist's advice on suitable activities for the child. At a very basic level the child's sense of movement may be stimulated by changing his position of lying from one side of the body to the other, or from lying on his back to lying on his tummy. More advanced are activities in which his limbs are moved to new positions and in which he is swung. However, before attempting any of these it is important to know that they will not cause him injury. Nancy Finnie's book (referred to in the Bibliography) is a good source of ideas for movement activities.

STIMULATION OF THE SENSES OF TASTE AND SMELL

The taste-buds on our tongues respond to saltiness, sweetness, sourness and bitterness. These flavours are mixed together in a great variety of foods which can be found around any house. Assuming that it is safe for the child to swallow any of them (check this with his records first of all) they can be presented to him in various ways. If he can chew, of course, the variety is limitless, but many things can be mixed into pastes which can be placed on his tongue using teaspoon handles or spatulas. Surgical bulb-end droppers can be used to let drops of a variety of flavoured liquids fall on his tongue. The best way of stimulating the child's sense of smell is probably to give him experience of being taken round different rooms in a house or school unit, as the different purposes for which each room is used will often give it a distinctive set of smells. Trips to the open air are also valuable: hospitals are often thought to be restrictive environments, yet many hospitals have farms and several kinds of work units in their grounds, and all of these would let a child experience a different set of smells from those in the wards.

Many other examples of activities for stimulating a child's senses can be found in the books which are referred to at the end of this book.

THE CHILD WHO HAS BEGUN TO MAKE CONTACT WITH THE WORLD

It is often difficult to guess where stimulation exercises are leading. This is especially the case with the most profoundly handicapped children, but it is possible to look further ahead when the child shows some signs of being responsive.

The child may show his responsiveness by becoming excited when an adult comes to work with him, by holding out his hand to be lifted, or by appearing to try to do something with the toys and equipment that are being used. When things like this appear, it is possible to begin much more constructive work aimed at developing the child's knowledge and understanding. Even before a child begins to talk he is showing various kinds of intellectual activity which can be developed further by thoughtful teaching. *Table 2* lists some of these intellectual skills and gives examples of activities which can exercise them. Only a small number of these activities can be noted in the space available.

THE INFLUENCE OF LANGUAGE

The ability to understand speech and the ability to use it are extremely important developments in the child's progress towards a greater understanding of his world. The child's experience, his ideas and his language combine to form a very powerful tool that lets him reason without having to take part in an activity. He will still

Table 2. Activities for developing children's understanding of the world even before they have begun to speak

Targets for work The child should learn to:	What to do Use activities such as:
Watch and find things	Following moving objects with his gaze Looking for favourite toys which have been hidden
Act for himself	Reaching for food Pulling along a toy which is tied to a string
Understand cause and effect	Discovering how to work a Jack-in-the-Box Learning how to wind up a mechanical toy
Understand the positioning of objects	Building steady towers of bricks Pushing objects into a toy posting-box
Handle objects	Squeezing crinkly paper Banging a drum
Imitate	Pretending to feed a doll Joining in music and movement
Respond to sound	Looking for a hidden alarm-clock which is ringing Dancing to music

continue to learn by doing things, of course, but he now has power to make greater sense of his activity. By his own actions the child will already have begun to classify objects and experiences. For example, he will probably be able to divide the world into objects which are small enough to put in his mouth and objects which are too big to put in his mouth; there will be people whom he recognizes and people whom he does not recognize. However, by learning to understand the language of the culture in which he lives, his own thought patterns will be influenced by the ideas of other people and he will become able to understand the world even more effectively.

EDUCATION OUTSIDE THE CLASSROOM

There is a danger that the provision of education in classrooms and school units may lead to a belief that this provides the child with sufficient experience of the world. The world of the classroom can only be an inadequate representation of the wider world outside. Thus, it is important that the child should become aware of as wide a range of surroundings as possible. Even for a child who is in permanent institutional care this is not difficult to achieve. For example, it is worth taking an honest look at the childrens' opportunities for discovering how much of the world exists outside their hospital or even outside their ward and classrooms. Do the children know that food has a history—that is, it has to be prepared, and that it looks quite different before it has been cooked? Do they know that food dishes are to be cleaned after they have been used? And there is the world beyond the boundaries of the institution. Trips to shops, to the countryside, to the seashore, to the cinema, to sports events, and so on may seem like an easy day out for teaching and care-staff yet the educational advantages of these to the children should not be under-estimated.

While experience is probably the most useful vehicle for extending a child's knowledge, there is also valuable 'second-hand' experience to be acquired through effective use of television, film, pictures, telling stories and so on. However, for experience to be stored as knowledge, skills have to be exercised, and the final section of the chapter deals with the range of skills which the educators have to consider if the child is going to be provided with an all-round education.

RELIGIOUS KNOWLEDGE

Religious education takes place in many schools and units for the mentally handicapped. It may take the form of simple observances such as hymn-singing or of ceremonies associated with festivals such as Easter or Christmas.

Staff who are religiously committed have important questions to answer if they believe that the mentally handicapped should have a religious element in their education. For example, is there a difference between religious education and the teaching of moral values? How can deep and complex ideas be conveyed to children whose understanding of words is very limited?

One answer to problems like this is that religious understanding should grow out of an understanding of relationships between people. For example, the Judaeo–Christian idea of 'God the Father' can grow from the children's own experience of relationships with a father. Of course this is easier said than done. Children living in institutions may have no experience of family life on which to base such an understanding. Their understanding of love, responsibility, right and wrong can grow only from the attitudes and behaviour of the staff who care for them.

Skills

COMMUNICATION

The skills of communication are perhaps the most universally useful of all skills which a person acquires. Long before a child has begun to speak his ability to communicate with others has begun to develop. The first, and possibly the most important relationship, is between mother and infant, and much subsequent skill at communication develops out of this relationship. Simply to be with a young child, to play with him and to encourage him to exercise the types of thinking (described in *Table 2*) which appear before the child has begun to speak is as effective a way of developing his communication as any other. However, we usually think of communication as a contact between people which involves some kind of language system, and so it is not surprising that many books and schemes of activity have been written to provide ideas for helping people find activities which will encourage children to talk. Most schemes of activity focus on the two most striking features of the use of language, namely, the ability to understand it and the ability to use it. It is common to try to teach children to understand words before they learn to produce them, though it has to be said that the first words which children produce are not necessarily the words which adults had been teaching them to understand! All the same, it is quite clear that understanding speech is every bit as important as producing it, if true communication is to take place.

Now, it may seem that teaching a person to understand words must be very difficult; but there are a few simple rules which make this quite a practical proposition. For example, it is helpful to concentrate on just one or two words to be learned at a time and to mention these words frequently and naturally (through play) when talking to the child. In addition, it is important to remember not to use too long sentences or to try to say the same things in too many different ways using different words, as this can cause confusion. Good advice on the use of this technique is given in *The First Words Language Programme* by Bill Gillham (1979).

Helping children to produce words may also seem to be a very difficult task, but even this can be simplified. If a child is really interested in an activity it is possible to leave out words at the end of short sentences and hope that the child will provide the missing word. Similarly, children who enjoy the rhythm and sound of nursery rhymes and songs will often supply words which adults have missed out at strategic points. A good general rule which applies to all activities is to take the child's lead as a basis for activities. If the child is already keen to take part in an activity there is a good chance he will want to continue it particularly if it seems to have caught the interest of an adult or of other children as well.

When the child has begun to speak he can begin to extend the range of words whose meaning he knows, and to use the words he knows in real-life settings. There are many teaching activities in which these skills can be developed. For example, simple bakery lessons, 'buying' and 'selling' at a shop which can be set up in the class, and playing together in a Wendy House, are all suitable. The advantages of these activities are that they seem more like play than teaching, and thus may encourage the more inhibited children to come out of their shells and talk to the others.

However, all this work on communication is not going to be put to good use if the children do not have an opportunity to use it in real life. Thus, it is important for teachers, instructors and others to decide what are the likely real-life experiences in which children are going to have to communicate. It is not possible to give specific advice on this for, clearly, children or young adults whose life is going to be spent in an institution will experience a quite different range of situations in which they have to communicate than will children and adults living in the larger community. Similarly, mentally-handicapped people living in rural areas will use their communication in circumstances which are quite different from those who live in the town. However, some rough guidance can be given.

For example, communication is often used to obtain things. Common examples would be bus tickets, food and clothing from shops, hair-cutting, and food and drink in cafes. Communication is used to give and obtain information. Common examples might be asking the way to another building, asking what programmes come next on television, and asking what the time is. Finally communication is used for social purposes, to make relationships between people more friendly and relaxed. This kind of communicative skill is clearly important on social occasions such as dances and club meetings but of course it is also important in everyday affairs whenever two or more people are living and working together.

These advanced communicative skills can be learned in two important ways. The first way is to teach them directly. For example, it is not difficult to set up a shop in a school or teaching unit so that the mentally handicapped can have practice in buying things. They have to learn how to make choices, and, having made them, how to let their preferences and needs be made known to the shop assistants. In addition they have to learn some of the rules of polite conversation which, though quite artificial in themselves, make conversation and communication more natural. For example, it is usually better to use 'please' and 'thank-you' than to miss them out, and 'could I have' is often more acceptable than 'give me'. Many mentally handicapped people also may have to learn to look at (but not stare at) the people they are speaking to. And they must learn not to feel discouraged if they are asked to repeat what they have just said, or if the other person in the conversation is trying to be awkward.

A very important method by which mentally handicapped people learn to communicate is by copying the example of the adults who are responsible for them. A mentally handicapped person who is able to talk will certainly be able to imitate, and as a result he will be able to imitate the rules of communication if he can see them being practised by the people who care for him. In turn, teachers and instructors may begin to see that some of the 'rules' which they want the mentally handicapped to learn are really quite artificial and would be better to be dropped. A good example of this is insisting that children should 'answer in sentences'. Thus, children are taught to reply 'My name is . . .' in response to the question 'What is your name?', whereas the standard non-handicapped person's reply is simply to state his or her name.

Mention should be made here of the use of alternative systems of communication for helping mentally handicapped people to communicate. In many parts of the country modified forms of hand-sign languages used by deaf people have been taught very successfully to mentally handicapped people who are not themselves deaf. Perhaps the best known of these is the Makaton vocabulary, which is a systematic approach to learning some of the most useful signs of British Sign Language. There is plenty of evidence to show that some mentally handicapped people who have been unable to acquire conventional language are able to pick up signs systems such as Makaton. The decision to use a sign language should not be seen as a last resort when everything else has failed. Perhaps the worry that is sometimes expressed about using sign languages is that parents, teachers and instructors fear that this is one step further away from the child being able to pick up conventional language. However, the opposite seems to be the case; teaching a child to read and to produce sign language may well encourage him to begin using conventional speech also.

SCHOLASTIC SKILLS

Many people still see the principal aim of education as being to teach people to read, write and count. So, it is not surprising to discover that reading, writing and arithmetic appear frequently on school syllabi for the mentally handicapped. Attempts to teach conventional scholastic skills like these may help some school staff to feel that what they are providing for children is 'real education'. Many parents also are pleased to see their children with a reading book as this encourages them to think that the children are perhaps not so handicapped after all. However, the case for teaching these scholastic skills is not as strong as it may appear.

Let us take the example of reading. Mentally handicapped children can certainly be taught to identify words appearing in print, but is this reading? One way to discover the answer is to ask the child to tell you about what he has been reading. For instance, can he tell you the main events of a short story? If he cannot, then it is likely that the passage he has been reading is too difficult for him to understand. But if he cannot understand, then why is he reading at all? Non-handicapped people usually read mainly, for two reasons, to obtain information and for recreation. But when we look at the world of the mentally handicapped the opportunity and the necessity to read for information or recreation are often lacking. And so, if teachers believe that reading should be taught to the mentally handicapped they must first show that there is a good reason for this, and they must then create the materials and experiences through which the skill will be taught and used. This is a very difficult problem for teachers to solve, but unless they do, they will continue to be frustrated by the experience of being unable to help mentally handicapped children and adults to cross the barrier which exists between 'barking at print' and genuine reading.

Handling money is the mathematical skill which is most frequently taught to the mentally handicapped. The fact that money enables us to obtain things gives the learning of this skill a built-in interest, and the fact that numbers are less complex than words visually may make it easier to acquire than reading. Once again, however, it is important that teachers should base their lessons on the situations in which the child will use money in real life. A make-believe shop in the classroom provides a good training-ground for what will actually happen in the high street.

Other mathematical skills which lend themselves to practical usefulness are measurement and simple geometry. Their development can be encouraged in a variety of activities including baking, cooking, handicrafts and gardening.

Thus the principle behind the teaching of scholastic skills to the mentally handicapped is quite clear. If a skill has some genuine practical application, then teach it. If it is of theoretical interest only, do not—unless of course the child or adult is attracted towards it of his own accord.

VISUAL SKILLS

Visual skills develop from the various types of thought process (described in *Table 2*) which appear in early childhood. These skills enable the child to make sense of the world with his eyes. In the early months of life children can be seen focusing their gaze on objects and watching them move. Later they are able to distinguish familiar objects from unfamiliar ones as a result of their growing powers of memory and discrimination. A vast amount of educational equipment has been produced for training children in these skills, and it is easy to lose track of the purpose which that equipment is intended to serve. The following paragraphs have been written to indicate some of the varieties of visual skill which educational treatment aims to develop.

Hand–eye Co-ordination The child learns to make increasingly fine movements of his fingers and hands so that he can carry out precise tasks. Dropping bricks into a box would be an early example of this activity. Colouring in pictures or writing would be much more advanced examples.

Form Perception Most babies are able to recognize familiar objects well before the first year of life. As this skill increases they become able to make more and more fine distinctions, for example between a circle and an oval or between a five and six-point star. Form-boards, with wooden or plastic cut-out shapes, are a good example of an activity which combines hand–eye co-ordination with form-perception. They also provide some of the best examples of thoughtless teaching. Too often, children are expected to work at form-boards which are too difficult for them. Too often, children are expected to continue to take an interest in form-boards which they have mastered weeks, months and even years previously.

Relating Parts to Wholes Jig-saw puzzles are a good example of this type of visual skill. The child learns to see how various parts can be fitted together to form a whole picture. While many mentally-handicapped people can eventually tackle difficult jig-saws success-fully it is necessary to provide much more simple examples in the early stages. These simple jig-saws might consist of a line drawing (or a very clear photograph) of a face or of an animal cut in half. All the child has to do is push the halves together. At a rather more difficult level the child could be asked to fit cut-out arms, legs and head to the correct places on the trunk; a large wooden jig-saw like this is made commercially.

A variant of this skill is the ability to copy abstract shapes using, for example, mosaic pieces. This again calls for the ability to see that parts fit together to form a whole pattern. It also calls for the ability to recognize that shapes may have to be turned upside-down or roundabout if they are to match a pattern exactly. At a more complex level, people who can read have to use this skill when they recognize that the letter 'b' is not 'd' or 'p'.

Sorting This skill is used when children group objects into categories. One of the first aspects of this skill to develop is the recognition of form which has been mentioned already; for example, the child learns that all circles can be placed in one box, all triangles in another and all squares in a third. Recognition of colour is another skill which appears quite early, and long before the names of the colours are understood or spoken. As the child develops he is able to pay attention to more than one quality at a time. For example, he will be able to sort out red circles from blue circles and from red squares. Later still he will be able to sort into more complicated categories such as animal/non-animal, living/not living and so on.

Other Visual Skills   As children develop it becomes increasingly difficult to distinguish visual skills from the skills of mathematics. For example, being able to arrange a row of dolls from tallest to shortest is a visual skill, but it also calls for awareness of the fact that objects can vary in size. Being able to sort animals standing on two legs from animals standing on four requires the use of vision, but also an awareness of quantity. Activities such as those seem quite simple to an adult as they are normally associated with pre-school work. However, it is important to recognize how many different skills they are actually tapping, as they may seem quite complicated to a mentally handicapped child. One of the skills of sensitive, professional teaching is to be alert to difficulties like this and to be able to reduce the degree of complication in complex tasks.

SELF-HELP SKILLS

The self-help skills which are most useful to the mentally handicapped person depend on age and degree of handicap.

The earliest self-help skill, and the one which is probably the most vital for life, is of course *feeding*. Like most of the skills in this group, feeding can be taught very successfully using the procedures of systematic teaching. Almost any indication the child gives that he is reaching for food or trying to bring it towards his mouth can be used as a basis for 'shaping' it towards a more mature and self-sufficient standard of feeding, such as holding a cup or eating from a spoon. More advanced skills still will lead on from this.

Toilet-training   can also be acquired by using any of several techniques of systematic teaching—assuming, of course, that the child is physically capable of bowel and bladder control. Toilet-training is often achieved by establishing regular times of elimination, by praising the child for toileting at those times and for keeping clean in-between times, but by avoiding causing anxiety when the child soils or is wet.

The first sign that a child is taking an interest in *dressing* is when he moves in sympathy with an adult's efforts to dress or undress him, or when he begins to remove the 'easiest' clothes such as shoes, socks or hat. The technique of 'chaining' is frequently used in helping children teach themselves to dress. This involves breaking the act of, say, pulling on a jumper, into the various smaller acts of which it is made up (e.g. putting one's head through the hole, reaching for the arms, pulling the jumper down over one's body, etc.). Each of these component acts is taught individually, often beginning with the last act first—in the case of putting the jumper on, pulling it down over the body. Then the child is taught to string the acts together into a complete movement.

Quite complicated acts such as shoelace-tying, fastening buttons and zipping up an anorak can all be taught by the same technique.

Skills which are probably a little more difficult to acquire include washing and drying, brushing teeth, grooming hair, brushing shoes and hanging up clothes. These will all be carried out more quickly if the adult who is looking after the child does it for him. However, this cannot be done if he is to become as self-sufficient as possible.

More creative self-help skills can be added as the child becomes older. These include baking and other forms of food preparation, gardening, simple joinery, cleaning and tidying the house, and using domestic appliances.

In adolescence girls will have to learn to cope with menstruation and boys with shaving. In both cases their self-sufficiency can also be assisted by encouraging them to participate in choosing and buying new clothes, in recognizing when they need to visit the hairdresser, and in learning how to take pride in their appearance.

Much more advanced self-help skills should be acquired by young adults, especially if they are living in semi-independence, for example in 'half-way houses', in the community. People in this type of situation require the ability to obtain a sufficiently nutritious diet, to use first aid and medicines, to use money responsibly, and (if they are in employment) to be punctual.

If men and women are living in the same establishment, the expression of sexuality is an unavoidable topic. Of course, adult sexuality is also concerned with matters of knowledge and ethics; but social skills are required too, especially the skills of communication and of caring for other people. This is a controversial and delicate matter, but it must be confronted if there is a sincere commitment to letting the mentally handicapped live as normal a life as possible.

PHYSICAL SKILLS

The earliest physical skills which can be taught are mainly concerned with the control of large body movements and with awareness and control of balance. In institutions this training is usually the responsibility of physiotherapists, but they are often willing to advise other staff on schemes of appropriate activities, especially when it is not possible for children to have regular individual sessions of physiotherapy.

There are many standard classroom activities for increasing the physical skills of children who are mobile. Music and movement is very popular as it encourages the exercises of various skills including physical agility, listening and the ability to imitate. There is also an excellent selection of commercially-produced apparatus for developing children's strength and agility.

The finer physical skills of manual dexterity can be encouraged in many ways, beginning at the simple level of picking up, then dropping small objects. Later, this skill can become more complicated through activities such as pouring, brick-building, and work with peg-boards. Children who can be encouraged to draw, paint, colour-in, or perhaps write, will require even greater skills.

Many mentally handicapped people have difficulty in understanding the idea of competitiveness and working together as a team against other people. Perhaps this is no bad thing! Terry Orlick's *Cooperative Sports and Games Book* (1978) contains ideas for activities in which the competitive element is low and the idea of everyone helping everyone else is encouraged.

One activity which can be competitive but also purely recreational is of course swimming. This provides excellent opportunities for developing physical skills as well as for developing strength and stamina. Many institutions have their own pools, but, if not, time can be booked at school swimming pools or the public baths.

CONCLUSION

This chapter has traced the development of present thinking about the education of the mentally handicapped and has described the educational provision which is a response to that thinking. It has also shown that there is a wide range of knowledge and skills which can be taught even to people with very severe degrees of handicap.

The task of working out educational policies for all mentally handicapped people in the community is still very far from complete.

However, there is evidence of an increasing awareness and clarification of central issues both by professional workers and by the elected representatives of the public. The time has passed when 'care and protection' were all that could rightly be expected from schools and centres for the mentally handicapped. We can look forward confidently to the steady growth of provision which has a right to be called 'education', with all the forward-looking connotations which that word implies.

CHAPTER 8

Communicating with the Mentally Handicapped

PERHAPS THE MOST CRIPPLING problem for the mentally handicapped is communication. Communication can be either vocal or non-vocal (gestural) and vocal communication can be either verbal (words) or non-verbal (emphasis, stress, intonation, shouts).

Verbal communication is commonly sub-divided into *speech* and *language*. The mentally handicapped suffer from a large variety of speech disorders. They show a high incidence of stuttering (dysrhythmia), and do not develop, or are late in developing, normal articulation (dysarthria). Down's anomalies tend to have low pitched and hoarse voices (dysphonia). The organs of speech are uniquely highly developed in man. Air flow through these organs produces the two major types of sounds, vowels and consonants. Vowels are produced by air flowing through the vocal cords plus the movement of the tongue. Consonants by air being stopped by the tongue, palate, teeth or lips. The configuration of the infant's vocal tract is quite different from that of adults. This is also true of his inner ear position with respect to his outer ear. There is probably also a considerable difference in the infant's neurophysiological control of the relevant parts of the nervous system from that of adults, and certainly this is so in the mentally handicapped. Down's anomalies are particularly handicapped in infancy by tongue thrust. Infants' earliest sounds—crying, fussing, burping, swallowing—are 'vegetative' and not under their control. More controlled noises—cooing and chuckling—can express contentedness and pleasure, and come later.

THE MARCH OF LANGUAGE

The First Year

To understand the language of the mentally handicapped, the stages of normal speech development must first be understood. The acquisition of language follows distinct milestones (Table 3). The mentally handicapped child goes through these stages at a slower rate, like a slow motion film. These first vocalizations are involuntary and start with the process of birth; they are vowels. The only cry which can be distinguished in the first few weeks is the colic cry; but, even at this stage, there is effective dialogue between child and mother. She recognizes many of the child's needs, by the context of his crying rather than by the actual sound (*see later*); her voice stops

Table 3. Milestones of speech and language acquisition

Average Age		Approximate mental age correlated at age 14
Birth	Vocalizations	Profoundly subnormal
6 months	Babble	
10 months	Reduplications appear: 'Ma-ma'—'Ba-ba'	IQ 18
1 year	One-word sentences	IQ 20
18 months	Two-word utterances	Severely subnormal
20 months	Telegrammatic speech	IQ 30
2 years	Pre-sleep monologues	
2½ years	50-word lexicon. 5-word sentences. I, personal pronoun	
3 years	Plurals established. 250 words	IQ 40
3½ years	'p', 'b', 'm', 'w', 'h' pronounced. How? Why? questions	
4 years	Tells story; still many morphological errors	
4½ years	't', 'k', 'd', 'ng', 'y' pronounced. Asks what words mean	IQ 45
5½ years	'f', 'z', 's', 'v' pronounced	Language established
6½ years	'sh', 'zh', 'l', 'th' pronounced. Adult morphology complete. Listens to another's standpoint in conversation	IQ 72+
8 years	'ch', 'r', 'wh' pronounced	Normal intelligence

the crying much more effectively than a mechanical buzzer does even in the earliest days of infancy. The child is sensitive to intonational patterns, such as in the word 'No', very early in his life.

In the first year the child develops almost all the sounds of the human voice. Partly by reinforcement certain sounds become dominant and at about five months babble starts. Syllable-like sounds are made. Lots of sounds are never heard again in the English language—German umlauts and African clicks—they vanish because they are never reinforced by the parents. Cooing and chuckling is added to by reduplicative babble, i.e. the repetition of uniform sequences of simple syllables—a da, a da, a da. Next comes non-duplicative babble—ba, da, ga, dug—and later on expressive jargon in which a variety of meaningful patterns are superimposed on babble sequences.

It is to be noted that the child cannot yet produce on demand a given word but by now is very sensitive to parents' voice quality and intonation, and adults, particularly mother, are producing complex baby talk, or 'motherese', which are exaggerated sounds slowed in certain respects, and which represent an important dialogue between the mother and the child.

There is often a gap at this point between babbling and true speech, between playing with sounds and planned sounds communicating (for babble is essentially a practice activity, not a communication activity). Babble is produced by the child, for the child, largely because it is enjoyable. During the hesitation between playing with sounds and planned sounds, between babbling and true speech, the child will be automating such processes as walking so that he can get on with the next hurdle—the acquisition of words and grammar. Deaf children may cease to babble prematurely, as do severely mentally handicapped children who lapse into stereotyped vocalizations and echolalia.

Echolalia is simply the echoing back of sounds that the child hears but does not understand; usually it is the last portion of a sentence which he picks up. Echolalia is very similar to the speaking of a parrot and this occurs briefly in normal toddlers, but may be maintained in the mentally handicapped as a means of superficial contact in the vocal realm into adult life. During the period of practice babble communicative interaction continues using predominantly non-vocal channels. We do not know whether the motivation that starts the child's babble is his desire to sound like adults long before he knows what sounds can do for him or whether it is simply interest in the products of his own solitary activity or whether it is a specific linguistic innate drive. The next stage is for the child to use word-like sounds. The child takes his meanings and sounds from his caretaker's speech and from his earlier vocal behaviour which was reinforced by his parents. Most parents don't understand their child's proto-language, although there is meaning in it. Investigators with time to pour over each episode have shown that there is system and method in the proto-language.

The Second Year

At the end of the first year the space between two sounds is split and in most languages, much the same way throughout the world, 'mama' and 'dada' appear. These single though duplicated words are really *one word sentences* (*see Table 4*). The word performs the function of a sentence: 'mama' means 'come here', 'mama don't go', 'mama where are you?'. Words are strongly linked to action and are rather ambiguous in their meaning. 'Dada' is not a claim to paternity but applies to every male. Mentally handicapped people with mental ages between one year and eighteen months are likely to

Table 4. Examples of early speech from mentally handicapped adult subjects

One-word sentences	Hullo!
	Bye
	Nurse
	Smoke?
Two-word utterances (pivot and open)	No high
	Shut door
	Wan'(t) swee'(t)
	No dirty
Telegrammatic utterances	See Panda car!
	Wan' grub hot
	Anne give kiss

develop only this primitive type of language. It is commonly seen in settings where the profoundly handicapped live.

It should be emphasized that it is neither nature nor nurture alone which determines the infant's linguistic progress. Certainly there are innate or natural aspects, for instance, the child's extraordinary interest in human faces and the human (and other primates') extraordinary interest in talking to infants. The acquisition of language depends crucially on the fact that the child and his caretakers have a strong propensity to take an interest in each other's subjective states from birth. And present linguistic theory suggests that *language development builds on earlier 'intersubjective development'*. The mother acts as a sort of scaffolding for the child's development; and infant dialogue, the emphasis on 'turn-taking' on the 'I–Thou' relationship, is the foundation of later communication. The evidence is against the idea that the 'mother understands everything the child says'. The child does not communicate his intentions accurately. Mother does not always know best. (This is evident from twins' and siblings' ability to interpret baby's speech better than mum does sometimes.)

The normal child at around eighteen months crosses a language watershed. He starts to link words together. This is also the time when he is beginning to link objects and ideas together and when he has developed the idea of the permanency of objects so he can put on labels. The two-word utterances usually consist of a *pivot word* (commonly an action word) and an *open word* which is often a new noun that he has learned. When the mentally handicapped child shows the development of two-word utterances, this is a good prognostic feature and the child has shown his ability to acquire *grammatical devices*. Children throughout the world, speaking a range of different languages, develop a two-word stage where they employ only a small number of semantic operations—between eight and fifteen relationships. The kind of meanings that are usually grammatically encoded are, in order of frequency; nomination; recurrence; non-existence; agent and action; agent and object; agent and action and object; action and locative; entity and locative; possessor and possession; entity and demonstrative. This order is based on 'frequency'; and, as Hoogenrad has pointed out, this means the frequency as recorded during repetitive activities such as play and reading, and might be a different order of frequency during other activities such as bathing and feeding.

No matter how this system, or group, of words was gathered it has the advantage of giving us a 'first lexicon'—an early dictionary—to teach mentally handicapped children. This has been documented by Gilham who has shown in more detail that such early dictionaries do not much differ in the mentally handicapped from those of normal toddlers. Most of the words we put in early lists are relational ones, such as rejection—no; non-existence—all gone away; cessation of action—stop; prohibition of action—stop; recurrence of objects—again, more, another; noting existence and identifying objects—this, there, that; actions on objects—do, hit; requests—wanna, more; attributes of objects—big, hot, dirty, heavy; and persons associated with objects—person's names.

After the age of eighteen months (or mental age $1\frac{1}{2}$ years), patterns of speech and vocabulary develop; also at this time the child practices his new words, speech devices and patterns in pre-sleep monologues or soliloquies which are charmingly unique and often poetic. The child has now developed a general principle that things have names and that he has got the mechanism (grammar) to use these names. He is developing a word dictionary instead of, as in the one-word stage, a one-word sentence dictionary.

The Third Year and On

About two years personal pronouns start to appear, usually in the order of 'my', 'me', 'you' and 'I'. 'We' starts at about three years. The two year old *learns* words, and then the three year old starts to *use* them. He fits words to actions and actions to words, before he has the grammatical organization of how and why questions. When these start the interest is on how the answers fit his thoughts.

By the time he is five his language is almost free of childhood mistakes, but he still makes morphological errors, inflectional errors, such as 'I buyed', 'the goodest'. Although development of language follows a pre-determined order, there is great variation even amongst normal children in the time at which they produce their first words, in which words they produce, and in their abilities to pronounce words. Many children go through a phase of simplifying the phonological structure of words; they simplify clusters by reducing them to a single consonant, e.g. 'phant' for elephant, 'bid' for biscuit, 'bo' for ball; they drop the distinctions between voiced and unvoiced consonants, e.g. tb for p, and make consonants harmonize, e.g. gog for dog. Not all children go through such stages or do so as vividly: some are taciturn and hardly speak, but, when they finally do, they then speak with little variation and often great competence.

When the child starts to develop multiple-word sentences he is using telegrammatic speech. High information words, content words, and nouns are retained and 'functor' words—like possessors and plurals, adverbs and prepositions—are disregarded, as if there were a premium on the important words, as in a telegram. The immediate question arises; should the parent, nurse or houseparent correct this little telegram, which the normal child or mentally handicapped person uses? 'Ada puddy' commonly results in the nurse or parent saying, 'Yes, that is the pussy'. This is expanding the sentence, but parents might be wrong! The child might mean 'That's my pussy' or 'My pudding'. There is some evidence to suggest that modelling—that is, saying something else to allow modelling around the likely theme, the pussy—is preferable to constant grammatical correcting. That is, the nurse or mother should say, 'Yes that is the pussy; it's got a big tail, is that what you mean?'

Now the normal child is a pattern learner. He tends at first to over-regularize rules, e.g. one sheep, two sheeps; but his mistakes tend to vanish by the age of seven years. The mentally handicapped person may continue to make mistakes; he may obstinately make mistakes about plurals and pronouns and past tenses. When you press him you realize that he often knows the rules—yet he does show impulsiveness in language, he seeks the easy way out. Occasionally, normal adult competence (in some aspects of language) will never be reached. The author remembers the wretchedness of not being able to pronounce the letter r, particularly important in Scotland. Instead he lisped and produced the seemingly affected English 'w' until he was ten years old! The normal child extends control over the prosodic system, the grammatical system and the phonological system in a piecemeal fashion, bringing one aspect under control at a time. Prosody is under control early, by $1\frac{1}{2}$ years normally, but it may be eight or nine years before the child can cope with the more complex consonant clusters.

THE EFFECTS OF LOW INTELLIGENCE.

A mentally handicapped child is rather like one of us in a foreign country. They often cannot understand much of what is said and seek, silently, solutions by judging things by the way they look and in the way they are accustomed. They often show erroneous pragmatic presupposition. Just like the ordinary child the mentally handicapped person is driven more by visual and contextual cues than by language. It is only gradually that words come to serve as symbols and as useful representations to map his world. The mentally handicapped person's visual attention is often better than his auditory attention. There is some evidence (but only for the severely subnormal) that it is better to direct their visual attention to an object prior to naming it, and certainly it seems that their ability to use language depends on the complexity of what they are looking at, i.e. they are slow in acquiring prepositions both because prepositions involve more complex situations and because it is more difficult to demonstrate prepositions. You can hardly show an 'under' or 'beside' in the same way as a horse or lorry!

Language in the Mildly Handicapped

The mildly mentally handicapped person's main communication problems are likely to be 'socio-linguistic'. Just as two different geographical areas have different dialects, so have different social classes different language codes, and the 'subcultural' defective commonly uses a restricted language code of Social Class V, which means that the mildly handicapped person has learned little well-formed language in childhood and is not able to form long phrases or complete sentences. He does not know some essential words. He will speak with more emphasis on rapport than on logic and keeps to familiar topics. Language is for him more for the purpose of communicating emotion than achieving solidarity and information! He will break his speech with lots of repetitions, hesitation phrases, such as 'Do you know?.' The teacher and nurse must identify this restricted language and avoid using middle-class constructions with which the handicapped person may be unfamiliar. Both hospitals and schools tend, therefore, to use a rather different language code from that which the subcultural handicapped person has acquired prior to admission and will require after rehabilitation in his work environment.

Language in the Severely Handicapped

The severely mentally handicapped person's communication problems are widespread. It is not simply a problem of not knowing enough words. They have poor articulation, less opportunity to pick up words and certain clinical categories are also backward in their grammar. The mentally handicapped are often poor at signalling non-verbally, either in their intonation, their prosody or with their faces, or by manual gestures. They are also often poor at decoding other people's non-verbal gestures. They are particularly poor at managing interactions, so that you seldom hear a mentally handicapped person who has acquired the skills of what are called 'locutionary acts', i.e. he has never had the opportunity to make requests, ask for qualification, ask for a repetition of what was said, or break into dialogue at the proper time; and the topics in which he is competent are limited, so that often he gives a misleading impression of competence, when he is talking about, for example, his training centre football team or his own work. He also has certain problems with 'interactional synchrony', i.e. the way that people of average intelligence (from the same culture) adjust their postures to fit in with their conversant's position, social status, viewpoint or predicament. *Table 5* shows some points where communication between the mentally handicapped and the average person breaks down. Below IQ 50 the grammar of the mentally handicapped does differ in some respects from that of normals. It is more likely to be more primitive and to be at one of the stages, e.g. telegrammatic, two-word utterances, one-word utterances, that we have mentioned above (*see Table 4*). Moreover, speech feedback is increasingly likely to be poor, mother should be speaking to a child of one year at mother-distance, but if the child's mental age is one year and he is overactive, and his chronological age is four years, speech to him is likely to be at a great distance, shouted and perhaps irritable and not adapted to his mental age.

The mentally handicapped are more backward in language than can be accounted for in terms of intelligence alone. They perform even more poorly in speaking than their intelligence should allow: they underfunction in language. Yet language still begins in much the same way and develops in much the same way in the handicapped as in normals, but it may be arrested permanently at any of the stages shown in *Table 3*. This is because there seems to be a 'sensitive period' for the acquisition of language. After the age of twelve you cannot 'pick up' a language effortlessly, just as if you miss your mother's affection in infancy, you cannot pick it up later: there is a critical period for emotional bonding between six months and five years, after which you have 'missed the boat'. Similarly, just as there is a diary for events in language there are 'deadlines'— after the age of one year is too late to acquire prosody and after the twelfth year to acquire language easily, although the backward person can still develop his vocabulary well into adult life.

Mentally handicapped people in institutions give an even poorer account of themselves in communication than they should for their intelligence, partly because the institutions in which they are reared may be quite inimical to language acquisition. The noise-to-signal ratio in a hospital, for instance, is much too large for the focus commonly to be on the language signal. Children benefit linguistically from a child-centred social organization.

As mentioned above, the mentally handicapped are limited across the range of language skills. There is some evidence that mongols are particularly slow in understanding negation. So if a 3-year-old mongol is shown a picture of a boy on a bicycle and a picture of a boy beside a bicycle, and asked, 'Show me the boy *not* on the bicycle', he will usually point to the boy on the bike, even when the negative is strongly emphasized! Those mentally handicapped people who have spent their lifetime in an institution often have a limited vocabulary. They tend to use a small number of 'heavy-duty words'. The researchers Mein and O'Connor have produced a vocabulary of institution words, which is a very useful little dictionary. O'Connor has further shown that the mentally handicapped's language defect is one of acquisition rather than poor perception, retention or transfer ability, and this is, at least partly, because of an inability to focus attention on the correct stimulus. *'The severly mentally handicapped cannot begin to learn until he has found out what it is that he should learn.'*

On present findings it is impossible to tell whether subnormals are particularly handicapped with respect to language or not; that they underfunction, however, is indisputable; that they have lots of other handicaps which make the language poorer, such as impaired hearing, and the inadequate way that adults talk to them, emphasizing names for objects, etc., is also certain.

Deafness

Deaf children are not mentally handicapped by reason of their deafness, although typically deaf children are retarded by about 1 year in their education, due to their experience of the world being unavoidably limited by their absence of hearing. Deaf children do as well, comparably, as hearing children on intelligence tests which do not involve language in any way: there are, however very few tests which do not involve language in some way. Deaf children without language can acquire concepts, compare sizes, remember sequences and associations, and solve simple problems involving forms and colours. There is a form of 'thought' without language and treatment should be by specialists in the first instance—otalaryngologists and audiometricians. Some mentally handicapped children who are profoundly deaf will not wear hearing aids unless they are incorporated in crash helmets; others can be taught to tolerate them by the psychologist rewarding them for wearing the hearing aid under a crash helmet, with sweets or other desirable objects. There may be, however, instead of a conforming response by the child, an explosive reaction. With restriction of comforting, communication, fantasy and memory an attempt is made to get rid of the source of frustration. Normal failures of adaptation are greeted with rage and tantrums: the birth of a sibling; changes of routine; admission to hospital; or separation with the absence of mother; these may be overwhelming and incomprehensible and lead to violent outbursts. In his egocentric view of himself there may be long-standing resentment at the relationships the parents have either together or with the sibling. He may find sharing difficult and try to control the family. Socialization and toilet training may become a battle ground. Attacks may be directed against the self, biting and scratching.

It is important that deaf children should have bilateral hearing aids, so that they can locate sounds in space and also hear the entire range of sounds before their first birthday. Inability to hear the higher frequencies means that the child does not hear consonants, particularly l, r and fricatives (f, v). Deaf mentally handicapped children may be able to cope with lip reading, but they usually require a mixture of reading and fairly simple signing, e.g. the Makaton system. The more complicated Paget Gorman sign language, which involves syntax, is often beyond their capabilities. It is best that they should not have to rely solely on one channel of communication. Deaf children of average IQ are in a position not unlike hearing people from an extremely impoverished social environment. Given the words they will perform as well intellectually.

Table 5. Suggested model of communication

BREAKDOWN POINTS		
Linguistic Components	*Paralinguistic Components*	*Interaction Management*
Grammar	Non-vocal (e.g gesture,	With peers
	eye contact,	With adults
Vocabulary:	facial expression)	
Output,		In large groups
Input		In small groups
Phonology	Vocal (e.g.	
	voice quality,	
	rate)	

The model in *Table 5* takes a practical view of communication skills rather than more traditional emphasis on grammatical skills and points particularly to the importance of managing interactions. The mentally handicapped are often claimed to be unresponsive, when what is happening rather is that there are several kinds of communication which are socially functional: speaking (overt) and strategic (covert), e.g. aggression and withdrawal, which is regarded as 'unresponsiveness'. The manner in which retarded persons choose to affect their audiences largely depends upon their social relationship to the listener, in particular upon the distribution of power in the relationship, its 'negotiability'. Departures from overt communication are commonly adaptations to distorted communicative situations. The sullen fire-raiser, the unpredictable retardate on an unrelenting belligerent path, the person in a state of unfathomable wretchedness, or the person who has become electively mute for the past fifteen years following the death of a friend or the birth of a dethroning younger sibling.

Does his Cry mean he is in Pain?

Mothers of normal children are fairly aware of their offspring's subjective states from the child's crying. There are three main aspects which influence the cry signal. They are:
1. The internal state of the infant;
2. The age of the infant; and
3. The situation in which the infant is involved.

A fourth factor—the clinical disorder from which mentally handicapped children may be suffering—also has to be taken into account when the child is mentally handicapped. Mothers of Down's Syndromes are often concerned that they are not sure how to respond to the child as the cry is sometimes so different from that of a normal child that they have some difficulty in using a cry as an indicator of distress. So differences between normal and abnormal cries can be usefully documented. We know, from the work of Reece, that mothers of normal children when asked to distinguish their own infant's cry cannot distinguish their own infants from other infants but can distinguish the message. Mothers of autistic children can distinguish their own children's abnormal cry but not often the message. We know from the work of Sirvio, Michelson, Wasz–Hockert and colleagues in Helsinki that the cries of premature children, brain-damaged children, and children with hyperbilirubinaemia are higher pitched, but Down's anomalies cries are low pitched. From our own work we know that de Lange dwarves' cries tend to sound low and have an unusual glottal throb. The best future method for systematically studying cries is likely to be a combination of the spectrograph and the Cry Index, which is calculated by multiplying two components, amplitude and density, together. Amplitude is a measure of the loudness and density is a measure of the amount of time spent crying. The informal method that parents use is to utilize the child's cry as an alerting device, by detecting a change in its causal characteristics. The child is then observed and the setting in which the crying is occurring and examined to decide whether he is in pain and why. In rough order of likelihood causes of pain are: locomotor discomfort; eyelash in eye; sore throat; sore ear; colic; oesophagitis; sphincter spasm; voluntary muscle spasm; joint pain; and so on.

Early Childhood Autism

Almost all autistic children show retarded language development (very occasionally a child may have overcorrect grammar and prosody and yet have all the other features of autism). Yet musical abilities are normally preserved and other islets of competence such as visual short-term memory and memory for faces and topography, whilst impaired functions include auditory attention, auditory verbal memory and verbal reasoning and fluency. The work of O'Connor, Hermelin and Frith has suggested a satisfactory intact superficial or immediate memory store. This is believed to house a phonological component which gives physical shape to utterances, i.e. stress and emphasis in intonations. The deep memory store is believed to house a syntactic component which is used for analysing word strings and making new utterances. Early childhood autistics show a marked tendency to echolalia; it is as if they have an echo-box memory. It is only with difficulty that they decode sentences to get the meaning. A series of particularly illuminating studies have been carried out by Balthaxe, who investigated the linguistic competence of autistic children by means of their bedtime soliloquies. These are free from situational and linguistic distractions and intrusions. Balthaxe found no evidence of a dialogue with an interlocuter such as one usually finds in pre-sleep soliloquies. No altercation took place. Autistic subjects seem to break phonological syntactic and semantic constraints—there was little attention to deep or internal structure. Their language appeared to show only surface structure and operations. In another study Balthaxe has shown that in the more able autistic, the situational rules were broken; most commonly seen as a switching from an inappropriate 'formal' code to an inappropriate 'informal' code. For example, from an intelligent autistic, a letter to his guardian: 'Please read my dietary restraints—I must have only beans in all my life—Please give me protein only in all my life. In all my life I shall keep to my diet, where in Hell is my goddam beans?' When autistic children of normal or near normal intelligence acquire adult speech, deficits are still noticeable. In addition to continuously breaking situational constraints, such as is shown above, their prosody (by which is meant stress, rhythm and intonation) still remains quaint. Balthaxe has recently commented that their speech is improperly modulated, produced with overprecision: they string words together as if they were in isolation. Their speech is flat, colourless.

THE ASSESSMENT AND TREATMENT OF COMMUNICATION DISORDERS

Firstly, deafness must be excluded. An audiogram should be performed to assess amplitude and frequency deficits. In the case of the profoundly handicapped or the very young, this may have to be an evoked potential EEG/audiogram under sedation. The speech therapist will analyse the phonological deficits, working particularly with the mother or mother-substitute. Do the child's language abilities match mother's complexity of speech? Is the discrepancy between his understanding and mother's speech so great that he does not bother to attend? Is the signal-to-noise ratio so large in that house, with banging doors and raucous television sets, that the child shows habitual inattention? Is the mother mentally or emotionally such a limited speaker that the child is suffering from sensory deprivation—from actual lack of data? The speech therapist may use the Edinburgh Articulation Test, which covers the age range 3–6, and involves presenting, as a naming game, relative stages in articulatory development.

Tangible reward operant conditioning (TROCA) which includes 'impedance-audiometry' and 'operant-audiometry' involving speech discrimination using a range of stimulation from pure tones and clicks to normal conversation with a background of 9 decibels noise, is becoming an increasingly-applied technique in the United States and the United Kingdom.

Language may be measured by the Reynell Test (*see* Appendix) and the mean length of utterance (MLU) and mean length of response (MLR) are common predictors of degree of language development.

How can the adult best further the child's language environment? Firstly, in one way language is like a golf swing (although the latter certainly is not effortless!) Do not 'cramp your style' by reading too many 'Dos and Don'ts', because you may lose your natural *intonation* which carries so much meaning for the young child. There are reasons to believe that small families provide a better adult/child language environment; the child gets more personal attention; the adult (usually the mother) will select more meaningful sounds from the child's repertoire and refine them and expand them and provide models for his next utterances. The adult should make direct verbal demands on the child or mentally handicapped person, and offer explanations for questions—'Don't slam the door, Johnny— because you'll break the glass in it', not just, 'Because I say so'. Sanctions should not just consist of *imperatives* (i.e. slaps and simple refusals and don't-do-its), but should also make a *personal* appeal. A slap might work in behaviourist terms if a child were slapped immediately after he was found drawing on a newly papered wall. However, he is much more likely to get slapped when mother finds this out a few hours later, by which time he will associate the slap with some quite harmless activity that he was indulging in. A more effective approach is, 'Look what you've done, you've drawn on the wall again. This has made me very angry. It's wrong to do this because everybody gets upset by the mess and the cost.' This is a personal appeal. It shows that what he is doing is harming others and if he draws on the wall again, i.e. is defiant, he is not now challenging mother's authority directly, but rather the principle behind her authority. It is similarly wrong for any nurse, or mother, or care-worker to threaten to bring in a larger authority if this cannot be implemented. Contempt of the police in many of our delinquents may have arisen out of threats like 'If you don't stop that I'll bring in the policeman'.

The adult should teach the child by language to require others to act—'Go and bring Robert to the duty room.' The child should be read to at night and given fun rhymes that express feeling. The Ladybird picture book series help with naming. Mentally handicapped children will usually like looking at and naming from mail order catalogues from which the parent or nurse can build a scrap book of words. At table the nurse or parent should encourage every day the saying of the names of the people at the table, widening this to naming things on the table. The nurse and the mother should be encouraging the child to find out about the world by questions which involve relationships such as 'or', 'on' and 'under', and not simply by asking for labels. The child may not understand the passive or convoluted sentence. Wherever possible for the younger child, teaching should occur in the one-to-one situation, at 'mother-distance'. For the child who is aphasic or so autistic or profoundly handicapped that speech is out of the question, American Sign Language (ASL) may be taught. The speech therapist's opinion will, of course, be sought before this is implemented. The child will then, in effect, have abandoned a vocal communication channel and be using a type of semaphore (non-vocal communication channel). Speech therapy is a specialist area but the nurse can help at least the stammerer by removing his attention from his speech. 'Shadowing' is a refinement of this.

It is no use trying to make a child progress to a language stage that he is not yet mature enough to accomplish. If he has not acquired the nervous mechanisms to walk and he is not spastic, it is unlikely that he will be mature enough to speak. If his mental age is 1 year only, it is highly unlikely that he will develop two-word utterances, which would occur at 18 months. The staff of any group home or hospital should examine their language-stimulus environment. Noise should be reduced to a minimum and signals maximized. Maintenance is a lesser priority than absence of reflected noise. Tiles and high ceilings and blaring television sets should be replaced by acoustic plaster, soft furnishings and adjusted, discriminate television sets. If there is a public address system, the residents should be using it as much as the staff for disc programmes, hospital news, etc. For residents at infantile level, records of mother/child interactions might help. Television is a largely unexplored medium. Its severest limitation is that it is not sensitive to a child's behaviour. Videotapes are, in some centres, being used with some promise.

PARENT PARTICIPATION

Parent workshops are a useful method for developing self-help skills in mentally handicapped, autistic, emotionally disturbed children and children with other learning disorders, but courses and propaganda on workshops often underplay problems of administration, selection and the emotional overtones and intricacies.

Nevertheless, the greatest single need of parents of mentally handicapped children is constructive, professional counselling at various stages in the child's life. Neil Yule makes the point that if you teach parents treatment techniques, it is only a small step in their minds to infer that there has been something deficient in their care and thus promote further guilt. Tottering workshops are seldom reported.

In 1971, the Hester Adrian Research Centre conducted a systematic series of workshops for parents of mentally handicapped children. The aim of the workshops was to arrive at an approach to, and to demonstrate the feasibility of, workshops for parents of mentally handicapped children. Courses were primarily aimed at helping parents to help the child.

The greatest need of parents is to feel that they are doing something to help their own child. Yet, seeking this, courses, articles and lectures on parent participation can reinforce frustration to despondence—more so when these courses offer practical help which does not help. The content of Hester Adrian courses involves training the parent to observe the child. Observation leads to task-analysis, then to treatment-strategies. Workshops are particularly geared to parents attempting educational tasks rather than modifying behaviour disorders. Parents facing the behaviour disorders, more common in a hospital population, need a course content which includes a personal element. The Hester Adrian workshop's primary objective is that parents will internalize a teaching model. By internalizing is meant that parents achieve a skill in applying both principles and concepts, so that they need not overtly articulate each step on each occasion, but can intuitively react to the child.

Parents' educational level does not affect parents' performance in training their child; Jeffree's opinion is that parents of lower intellectual groups appear most able to accept the fact of having a handicapped child, whereas those of high intelligence are apt to place greater emphasis on intelligence in their value systems and therefore find acceptance more difficult. One lesson is that a child should not be placed in a workshop unless there is certainty of at least some improvement. Therefore, children should be involved as early as possible, and those outside the language-sensitive age, 12, should not be included in a language workshop with under-twelves. Parents require a familiar setting, as well as one-way screens and tutorial rooms for coffee and informal discussion.

Parents generally need to utilize the time they are already spending with their child more effectively, rather than simply spending more time with their child. A social worker is essential in the team. Too often the handicapped child is a recipient rather than a participant in family activity. Unsolved problems include the level of expertise to which parents should be trained—whether they should be instructed up to professional level or should just be given brief introduction to techniques—and of attracting the less motivated, the less intelligent, and those parents with limited resources. Further problems are ones of support, how and when to end the course, and what to do afterwards, and particularly problems of parents' emotions. Parents need continued support from outside agencies. There are many cases when the parents and family circumstances cannot be expected to enter into a complex, time-consuming training programme for the child.

Parents are taught as regards communication:

1. Make it enjoyable for the child—practice where the child produces best, e.g. the bath.

2. Do it regularly.

3. Do not cramp your style by too much formality.

4. Be an opportunist—sing; act; whistle; change your voice gear and speech.

5. Use consistent labels.

6. Take small steps, and do not reach for a level beyond the child's development.

7. Remember to signal vigorously with your face and do not forget the child does not signal well back!

8. If he is not looking, he is not likely to be listening.

9. Give him time to answer.

10. Cue him by his name.

11. The onus is on you to ensure you are understood.

TOY LIBRARIES

Out of a real personal need the idea of borrowing toys for physically and mentally handicapped children developed and, in 1967, 'The Enfield Society for the Mentally Handicapped' followed up the idea and started lending out toys to all handicapped children who would benefit by them.

Much hard work was done, the co-operation of toy manufacturers was sought, and, by 1973, the Toy Library was registered as a charity and, having received a grant from the 'Kings Fund', was able to extend its work.

The aims of the Toy Library Association are:

1. To assist the development of all handicapped children, from their earliest age and whatever the handicap.

2. To provide the best possible toys.

3. To foster the understanding of the play needs of handicapped children.

4. To give guidance on the selection of toys and play materials.

5. To work with manufacturers, designers and other interested bodies to maintain communication with professional workers and organizations.

In 1975 there were approximately 300 toy libraries in the United Kingdom and 200 more developing. Overseas toy libraries are being established in Canada, Australia, South Africa and Norway.

The address of the Toy Libraries Association in the United Kingdom is—

Toy Libraries Association
Sumley House
10 Gunthorpe Street
London E1 7RW

WRITING

The written word (orthography) is outside the sphere of the nurse, being primarily the teacher's responsibility. Speech has primacy over the written word but mental handicap does not preclude a child from learning to read, though a severely handicapped child never will. Social and emotional deprivation, poor eyesight and diffuse brain damage can all retard reading. Dyslexia is no longer regarded as a discrete entity but as a group of conditions which result in difficulty in reading and writing, in which a reversal of letters, which normal children do in any case when they start to write, occurs, but more severely. There is an association with confusion over right and left handedness.

Children with mixed laterality are not the only children with writing problems. Some children, regardless of their laterality, suffer from motor praxic or emotional difficulties which can lead to genuine trouble in the developing of writing. Such problems are those of balance or of spatial orientation, or in learning language and reading, or behaviour disorders, or anxiety or nervousness. Writing only becomes possible around the age of 7, when a certain level of motor control and co-ordination in space (praxis) has been attained, and also a certain level of language ability is reached. In the purer forms of dyslexia, a child will show difficulty in telling the time until a relatively late age (the normal being seven), ambiguity about right and lefthandedness and a tendency to confuse lateral dimensions in space until adult life. There is a familial background to this disease. Children with non-specific learning disability often suffer from minimal cerebral damage. To exclude this it is necessary to be very sure about early history (Critchley, 1974).

The best way in which to teach children to read is controversial. The recognition of words as a whole from their shape is the basis of the *Look and See Method*. This enables the child to build a provisional vocabulary of key words. The *Sentence Method* starts with groups of words. The simple sentence is the basis. Children have to learn letters eventually but not to name letters in order to learn to read. The old *Sound Methods*—A is for Apple, B is for Boy—are not favoured nowadays. As regards spelling, various methods have been tried to modify the ambiguities, such as the simplified spelling of the Initial Teaching Alphabet, which adds a further 18 symbols on to the 26 of the ordinary alphabet. Coloured keys are also used. For the pre-school child and for most of our mentally handicapped population, however, the best introduction is the bedtime story, letting the child follow the text with his eyes as well as listening.

The more that we can get the mentally handicapped to use language, the more they will communicate their feelings with others by words rather than by actions, the more explicable their behaviour will be to others and the more they will be able to use language to control their own actions and make *themselves* less impulsive, by internalized unspoken speech.

CHAPTER 9

Non-Speech Systems of Communication Used with Mentally Handicapped People

NON-SPEECH SYSTEMS of communication have only become widely accepted as methods of improving communication skills in recent years, and there is still some controversy over their use with many client groups. Systems can be used as a complete alternative to verbal communication, or as a supplement to verbal language, to comprehension and/or expressive skills.

MODES

There are two modes into which non-speech systems fall:

A. *Manual Systems*
   1. Finger spelling (British or American).
   2. Signed English
     a. Paget Gorman Sign System (PGSS) (British).
     b. Linguistics Of Visual English (LOVE) ⎫
       Manual English.   ⎬ (American)
       Seeing Essential English (SEE_1).
       Signing Exact English (SEE_2).
       Signed English (SINGLISH). ⎭
   3. Native sign languages
     a. American Sign Language (ASL)
     b. British Sign Language (BSL)*
   4. Key word signing—The Makaton Vocabulary. (British)
   5. Signal system—Amer-Ind. (American)

B. *Symbol Systems*
   1. Written word—produced manually or by machine.
   2. Ideographs and pictographs
     a. Premack system.   ⎫
     b. Non-speech language initiation programme ⎬ (American)
       (Non SLIP).
     c. Blissymbolics. (Canadian)   ⎭

*Note: There are also Australian, Danish, French, Irish, Israeli and Swedish sign languages, amongst others.

    d. Rebuses.
3. Pictures—photo or picture boards.

A. MANUAL SYSTEMS

1. *Finger Spelling*
In Britain a two handed system is most commonly used, while in the USA there is a one handed system. One sign is used for each letter of the alphabet Fig. 8.

Fig. 8. British and American finger spelling. Courtesy Martin A. Connell, Mary Brennan, Martin D. Colville, Lillian K. Lawson: after illustrations in *Words in Hand: A Structural Analysis of the Signs of British Sign Language.*

    Disadvantages
    i. It is a slow form of communication.
    ii. A knowledge of the written language is required, by reducing its value to mentally handicapped people greatly.

    Advantages
    i. It is useful for names and initials.
    ii. It can make meaning absolutely clear.

    Some form of finger spelling is used to supplement most forms of signing at times (Grove, 1980a).

2. *Signed English*
There are one major British system and several American systems which share very similar characteristics.

a. PAGET GORMAN SIGN SYSTEM (PGSS) (BRITISH)
This is an artificially designed language (Paget et al. 1968) which aims to be an almost exact translation of English. There is one sign for each morpheme (unit of meaning) and irregularities of English are removed, e.g.

shop + s ⎫
        ⎬ both use two signs to indicate plurality.
sheep + s ⎭

Disadvantages
- *i.* Extremely fine finger control is required for many of the signs.
- *ii.* There are over 3000 signs: it is therefore inconceivable that a mentally handicapped person could learn the full form.
- *iii.* The system must be learned by everyone in the environment if it is to be an efficient form of communication.
- *iv.* It is in very limited use in Britain.

Advantages
- *i.* It is logical: signs have a root and other signs develop from the root Fig. 9.
- *ii.* In its complete form it should indicate all the subleties of spoken English.

Animal   Giraffe   Meat

Fig. 9. Examples from the Paget–Gorman Sign System. Courtesy The Association for Experiment in Deaf Education Limited (Paget–Gorman Sign System).

b. AMERICAN SYSTEMS

Linguistics of Visual English (Love)

Manual English
Seeing Essential English (SEE$_1$)
Signing Exact English (SEE$_2$)
Signed English (SINGLISH)

Each of these is a system of signed English, with the same advantages and disadvantages as PGSS.

3. *Native Sign Languages*

a. AMERICAN SIGN LANGUAGE (ASL)

b. BRITISH SIGN LANGUAGE (BSL)

These were evolved and are used by the native deaf populations of the USA and Britain, and the deaf populations of many other countries also have their own sign languages (Grove, 1980b).

ASL and BSL have very similar motor and cognitive characteristics, because they are natural and not artificial languages (Kiernan, 1977). ASL tends to have many signs using both hands performing mirrored gestures, while BSL has more one-handed signs. Each language varies through a continuum, from using signs, a few finger spellings, limited lip movements, vocalizations, and a great deal of facial expression, to 'total communication', where all modalities are used as fully as possible. There is also a 'pidgin' form of signing, using just key concept signs and facial expression.

Signing was suppressed, particularly in schools for the hearing handicapped, until recently because it was regarded as a poor and ungrammatical attempt to translate verbal language. In fact, sign languages have their own intrinsic grammars, using changes of speed, size of gesture, and direction to express grammatical distinctions (Stokoe, 1978; Kilma and Bellugi, 1979), but these do not easily translate into English. They should generally be regarded as different, and not inferior in terms of the semantic and syntactic information they carry.

Disadvantages
  i. The grammatical structure cannot easily be translated into verbal language.
  ii. The system must be learned by everyone in the environment if it is to be an efficient form of communication.

Advantages
  i. Signs often represent broader concepts than a single word.
  ii. Once learned, signing is a quick form of communication.

4. Key Word Signing
THE MAKATON VOCABULARY

Makaton is a complete language programme, derived from the signs in BSL (above), but following the word ordering of English (Walker and Armfield, 1981). Key words are signed, always accompanied by grammatical spoken English. Facial expression and body language is used to increase intelligibility (Walker, 1973). Originally designed specifically for deaf mentally handicapped people, it is the most common signing system used with mentally handicapped people (with or without hearing handicap) in Britain. It is becoming accepted in other parts of the world, using the signs from the native sign languages.

Disadvantages
  i. There is not a direct correspondence with spoken English.
  ii. There is not a direct correspondence with BSL.
  iii. Everyone in the environment needs to learn the system, if the mentally handicapped person is to use Makaton to communicate efficiently.

Advantages
  i. It can reduce the level of frustration at not being able to communicate.
 ii. The vocabulary is progressively more advanced, following developmental guidelines.
iii. In the early stages, signs are mimes and are easy to understand.
 iv. It is relatively easy to learn, and language programmes are available to facilitate teaching (Walker, 1976).
  v. Signs often express a more general meaning than the corresponding word, e.g. Fig. 10.

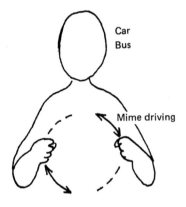

Fig. 10. 'Drive the car' in the Makaton vocabulary. Courtesy Mrs Margaret Walker and the Makaton Vocabulary Development Project.

It would appear from the literature that the attempts to introduce ASL to mentally handicapped people usually fall into the same category as Makaton (Grove, 1980a), with key words being introduced, using English word ordering and accompanied by grammatical English, thus not introducing ASL as a language in its own right.

5. *Signal System*

AMER-IND

Developed from American Indian Hand Talk (Skelly, 1979), Amer-Ind is a gesture system of signals. Each gesture represents a single concept, which can be translated into its verbal equivalent. Strings of gestures can be used to form sentences, and agglutination of two or more gestures can produce new ideas.

Disadvantages:
   i. It only uses concrete concepts and operates at a very limited symbolic level.
   ii. There are no true grammatical or structural rules.

Advantages:
   i. There are only a limited number of signs.
   ii. It is easily interpreted by the untrained observer.

The major problem with the sign systems is that they are mutually incompatible.

B. SYMBOL SYSTEMS

1. *Written Word*

This is of extremely limited value as a first line of communication for mentally handicapped people. Those who can read and write can, almost without exception, also communicate verbally and therefore do not require an alternative system of communication. The rare exception is generally a person originally of normal intelligence who is suffering progressive physical and mental deterioration for some reason. In such a case, the written word may be used in some form temporarily, if, for instance, the speech musculature fails before intellectual deterioration becomes too severe. There are a variety of machines on the market which aid written communication.

Possum produce modified electric typewriters, electric word boards, letter boards, and other 'environment control' systems to enable a severely physically handicapped patient to communicate. Some of the aids are available on the National Health Service, or through the Social Services Department. The machines require some controlled body movement to operate, but this may be as minimal as the ability to control breath flow.

Electric Typewriter—requires the ability to move the fingers and to scan to find the correct keys, but not such heavy pressure is required as for a manual typewriter.

Cannon Communicator—a typewriter-like machine which straps to the wrist and produces a ticker-tape message when the letter keys are touched.

Lite-Writer—typewriter-like keys allow the user to produce a written message of up to a limited number of items which move across a screen in a light display. Occasionally available on the NHS.

Splink—uses microchip technology to associate a word board, the alphabet, and some commonly used phrases (pre-programmed into the board), with one or two TV screens. The user touches the word, phrase, or letter key, and the screen displays the required message.

2. *Ideographs and Pictographs*
These use either mobile or static 3D or 2D displays of symbols to represent different concepts or ideas.

a. PREMACK SYSTEM (USA)
This was originally designed to teach language skills to chimpanzees. It uses behaviour modification techniques to teach symbolic representation, using the 3D colour coded symbols, which can then be combined to produce limited grammatical structures (Premack and Premack, 1974).

b. NON-SPEECH LANGUAGE INITIATION PROGRAMME (non-SLIP) (USA)
This was developed from the Premack system, using 3D colour coded plastic chips to teach tactics for functional communication (Carrier, 1977).

Disadvantages (for *a* and *b* above):
  i. Visual perception skills are required to recognize the difference in colour, size, shape and thickness of the chips.
  ii. Fine finger movements are required to manipulate them.
  iii. Everyone in the environment would need to recognize the meanings of the symbols.
  iv. The abstraction of chips is an unnecessarily complex method of introducing concepts.
  v. There is no evidence that a neurologically intact chimpanzee is comparable with a neurologically deficient (mentally handicapped) human. (Carrier, 1977).

Advantages
None apparent over other symbol systems for mentally handicapped people.

c. BLISSYMBOLICS (CANADA)
A system originally designed (Bliss, 1966) as a form of written Esperanto, this has since been developed for use mainly with physically handicapped people. Some of the symbols are pictographic but the majority ideographic (abstract). It is the most widely

used symbol system in Britain, and is also used in many other countries. Grammatical word ordering is attempted, and the basic vocabulary taught follows a normal developmental pattern. Symbols have logical roots, and several symbols can be combined to produce new words. For details of this system *see* Blissymbolics Communication, 1975; 1976.

Disadvantages
   i. A minimum mental age of $3-3\frac{1}{2}$ is required for Blissymbolics to be introduced successfully, so the systems is of limited use with mentally handicapped people.
   ii. Any visual or visual perception problems can interfere with communication.
   iii. Some body movement control is required to indicate signs.
   iv. The communication boards can be bulky.

Advantages
   i. Introducing the system can prove that a severely physically handicapped person is capable of communication.
   ii. It is relatively easy to learn.
   iii. There is a logical base to the symbols.
   iv. Composite meanings are possible.
   v. Symbols are pre-drawn and static.
   iv. Each symbol has the corresponding word written below it, and therefore the recipient does not need to know the symbols.

d. REBUSES
Any pictographic system uses Rebuses, e.g. Fig. 11.

House (Concrete)   Down (relational)

Fig. 11. Rebuses.

They are often used to interest children in learning to read, as code-breaking exercises, e.g. Fig. 12, but the form/meaning conflicts

I   ran   home   for   tea

Fig. 12. Use of rebuses as a code-breaking exercise.

can cause confusion for mentally handicapped people, e.g. Fig. 13.

= eye or I   4 = four or for

Fig. 13. Conflicts caused in use of rebuses.

Therefore Rebuses are not widely accepted as useful as communication systems for mentally handicapped people (Grove, 1980a).

3. *Picture Systems*

Picture and photo-boards are produced by the Chest and Heart Foundation, the College of Speech Therapists, and Photographic Teaching Materials Ltd., amongst others, although it is often more suitable to design one individually for a particular patient (Fig. 14). They are useful for those people not able enough to communicate by the higher symbolic functions of writing or symbol systems.

Disadvantages
  i. Communication is necessarily at a fairly concrete level.
  ii. Grammar is abandoned to all intents and purposes.
  iii. The patient requires to attract attention before he can use the board to indicate his needs.

Advantages
  i. Communication is at a lower symbolic level than writing or Blissymbolics.
  ii. It can be easily understood by others.
  iii. It is easy to learn.
  iv. It can motivate further communication.

CONCLUSION

There are some disadvantages which are common to most alternative systems of communication:

  i. Spoken language is more adaptable and socially acceptable.
  ii. Alternative systems are conspicuous.
  iii. Sign and symbol languages tend to cut off the user from the general population.
  iv. Alternative systems may be seen by some people as proof that the patient will not talk.
  v. Comprehension of signs and symbols precedes expressive use, and this can cause patients, parents, care-staff etc., to become discouraged because they expect too much of the system.

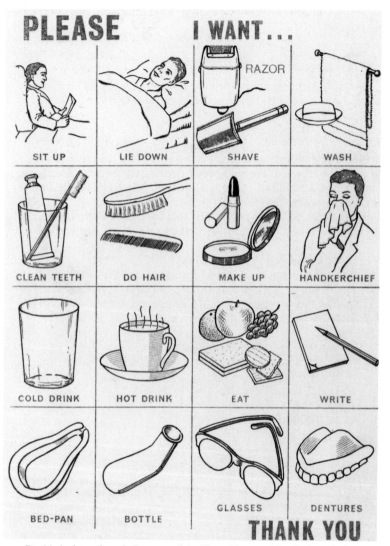

Fig. 14. A picture board. Courtesy of the Chest, Heart and Stroke Association.

vi. Signing should be the main medium of communication for everyone in a signer's environment, and this rarely occurs. Difficulty in motivating (e.g.) staff to learn signing has long been known.

The following criteria are basic prerequisites for any of the above systems to be successful:

i. The mentally handicapped person should be able to establish and maintain eye contact.

ii. He/she should have reached at least the cognitive development necessary to appreciate object permanance.

iii. He/she must be able to attend for at least a short period.

iv. There must be some motivation to communicate.

The above list of alternative systems of communication is not exhaustive, but includes most of the ones in wide use with the mentally handicapped today. For further information *see* Grove, 1980a and b.

CHAPTER 10

An Alternative Living Unit

IN 1973 DR BARNARDO'S Scottish Office decided to re-adapt an old manor house near Edinburgh to offer four independent living areas for small family groups of handicapped children. In June 1977 Ravelrig was opened.

One group of the children is classed as being profoundly mentally handicapped, mostly with assessable IQ levels. The top group of children have mental age levels of around 3–6 years, with chronological ages of 10–18 years. The middle two groups, each of four children, are in between these two extremes: mainly they are younger children who could eventually acquire the skills, through treatment and training, to reach the top group level in the unit.

The policy of the unit is to help children achieve their full potential and to encourage all children in the unit to become independent in some measure. For example, it is hoped that the top group of children will be able to achieve independence within the community, some with minimum supervision. In the profoundly handicapped group, children with severe disabilities will never achieve real independence, and will need some form of residential care for the rest of their lives. The unit hopes to achieve a basic style of independence within this group through treatment programmes and assessment and to achieve social skills and to control behaviour through behaviour modification techniques. This is an account of one alternative way of living for mentally handicapped children.

ADMISSION AND ASSESSMENT

Children are referred between the ages of 5 and 14 years. Referrals are usually made by Local Authority Social Work and Education Departments. When a child is referred, a case conference discussion is set up to assess the possibilities of admission. Although the unit caters for a wide range of mental handicap, the main criteria for admission is to decide whether or not the child has potential to develop and whether there is a vacancy in a particular group suitable to cater for the child's emotional and physical needs and abilities. After the initial referral conference, the child's parents are invited to the unit to meet the staff, and to then become part of the decision making process concerned with the admission of the child. At this point as much information as possible is gleaned directly from the family in order to assess how best both the family, social worker and residential staff can become supportive. The initial case conference is also the first step in deciding which group within the home would best cater for the child's needs. A visit from an experienced member of staff is arranged so that a first hand assessment can be made to calculate the child's suitability for inclusion in one of the unit's groups. The visit usually takes place within the child's current school situation so that the information obtained from teachers, parents, local authority social workers, psychologists and psychiatrists may be pooled, and that all these people may become involved.

The unit has an open door to parents, who are encouraged as much as possible to take part in the care of their child at whatever level they feel they are able to participate. The residential staff and family social worker help parents to cope with problems that they face in the home with their mentally handicapped child, through the use of Portage as a technique, which so far has had some successes in helping parents to deal with practical day to day problems. The system consists of a very thorough but simple way of helping parents to assess their own children and, after assessment, pinpoints exact areas of concern and action, so that a simple treatment plan can be systematized to allow the family to cope with the special problems they face with their particular child.

The unit's full time family social worker is very much part of the staff team. She visits parents on a regular basis, and brings information and problems gleaned from the family to the staff team, where they will be evaluated at their regular weekly meeting. She also takes information from the residential staff areas into the family, and utilizes the resources available in order to encourage parents to cope more ably with visits home from the children. Parents have regular contact with the unit and their child.

After a child has been admitted assessment continues to play a major role in treatment and care. During the first month or so after admission, the child undergoes a simple assessment programme in which he is observed in a host of different situations and information about every aspect of the child's life in the unit is gathered. A written assessment is then compiled which is designed to give a detailed picture of the child and his abilities or disabilities. The process is therefore designed to highlight specific areas for concern and action to enable a treatment programme to be formulated, which is immediately put into action.

Firstly, the areas of a child's behaviour repertoire which are causing immediate concern are identified and a sequence of priorities formed. It is important to be selective at this stage: the child would only become confused and perhaps fail to learn if an attempt were made to change his whole behaviour pattern in one move. Next, each section of the assessment is assimilated and an approach to each problem worked out. Assessment is continuous; each child goes through at first monthly and then 3-monthly assessments throughout his stay at the unit. After each assessment the treatment programme is re-designed to suit the child's changing needs.

The potential success of the programme lies in the fact that the treatment plan provides guidelines for all the staff to follow, so that the child is treated in a consistent manner and learning is, in that way, systematized. Research into learning theory and behaviour modification technique has taught us that it is this systematization that brings about optimal learning.

LIFE IN GROUP I

Space permits description only of one group, Group I, the adolescent area of the unit with present chronological age range of 12–18 years. The children are classified as being severely to moderately mentally handicapped, with mental ages of 3–6 years, IQs being between 40 and 65. The adolescent area is housed in a large self-contained flat within the main building. It has its own lounge, kitchen and dining facilities, where children are encouraged to prepare some of their own food. Bedroom accommodation consists of single and twin-bedded rooms, with a small games room for snooker and pop music recreations. The object of Group I is, basically, to help children achieve a high level of domestic and social independence so that residents will be able to be discharged into the community. For example, it is hoped that at least two of the children will be able to survive within some form of simple open employment and live in semi-detached housing with minimal supervision. The more limited end of the scale in Group I will perhaps require hostel accommodation with observation and supervision. Occupation for these particular children is at present envisaged as being in an adult training setting or some form of sheltered employment.

Domestic Activities

Where domestic activity is concerned the adolescent children are encouraged to become involved in as many normal experiences as possible: for example purchasing their own food, setting up menus for simple survival-cookery, and learning how to handle cash, how to wash and prepare food, and to cater for guests—for whom the children occasionally cook within their living area. Domestic skills also include caring for their own accommodation—learning how to use cleaning materials and vacuum cleaners, make beds and so on.

The dangers that come with allowing children to have more independence and to become proficient at these skills must be borne in mind: for example, some of the dangers involved in using electricity, cooking and preparing meals—knives are sharp—and dealing with chemical cleaners. It is important that the children concerned be given an insight into these daily dangers and taught care in the use of equipment and materials.

Social Life

Children in Group I area are encouraged to participate in social activities such as horse riding, ice skating, swimming, attending the various clubs and discotheques, most of which have been set up specifically for young, handicapped people. Children are encouraged not just to spend time with other handicapped youngsters but to participate in events where normal young people are involved, such as local school youth clubs and play schemes, and to hold social events in the unit where they can invite both other handicapped people and normal youngsters to enjoy the facilities available. The children have attracted a number of friends from the local community who are continually on Group I's invitation lists.

As with other group areas in the unit, a number of children in this area suffer from communication difficulties, mainly because of their limited conversational vocabulary. To overcome this the staff of Group I set up regular meetings where children are able to discuss their interests, daily experiences etc. over a cup of coffee or else during the daily evening meal. Games situations have also been used to encourage spontaneous discussion; also outings where things of interest are pointed out and discussed either during the event, or on the group's return home to the unit, are of help.

Case History

The following case history will illustrate the lifestyle of the unit and the work being undertaken with children in Group I.

Jane has now been resident in Group I for two and a half years. As with all children in the unit, Jane undergoes regular three-monthly assessments. Before admission Jane was known to be a very aggressive, disturbed young lady within the environments of ward, school and speech therapy unit. She was admitted to Group I in April, 1978 after spending the years from the age of 6 in a local hospital for the mentally subnormal, where she had been in a large children's ward.

Before coming to the unit Jane had rarely been visited by any of her family: she had not even been home for a number of years, because of her very disturbed, unmanageable behaviour.

CASE NOTES

Date of Admission   10/4/1978

Age at Admission   10 years 6 months

Self-help Skills

Dressing   Can put clothes on in correct order without prompting and assistance, but often pretends she cannot do so. Able to fasten buttons, zips, poppers and catches. Shoe buckles present difficulties. Sometimes put shoes on wrong feet, but she can undress herself without assistance.

Meals   Has ability to use knife and fork to good purpose when she concentrates, but sometimes holds knife the wrong way up. She can cut food into reasonable size for eating but often does not bother to do so in order to draw attention to herself. She can pour a drink from a jug without spilling or overfilling the cup. She is able to pour a cup of tea and add milk, and sugar. She is able to position table napkin and keep it in place until she has finished. She can spread butter and jam onto bread but tends to make a mess. She often puts bread directly onto the table instead of using side-plate. She likes to help at mealtimes—laying the table, serving food, and clearing up.

Toileting   She is able to indicate her toileting needs to the staff, and can go alone. She can perform the whole sequence adequately, however if she thinks she is unobserved she fails to wash her hands and flush the toilet. She asks for assistance in undoing clothes but can actually manage this herself, and she can also refasten her clothes. Jane is never incontinent.

Washing   When requested she washes her hands, using soap, and will dry her hands with a towel. Face-washing tends to be cursory and avoided if possible. She can clean her teeth without assistance, but sometimes fails to rinse her mouth out. Jane is able to bath herself without assistance, although this too tends to be cursory. She performs this task better if she is not closely supervised.

Bedtime   She undresses herself and puts on her nightdress.

Social Skills

Speech and Communication   Jane has no real speech, but has some vowel sounds. She vocalizes constantly and is able to indicate most of her needs to the staff and to some of the children, either by using existing sign language (Jane's own) or by improvising until she is understood. If one person fails to understand, she will seek out someone who does. She shows anger and frustration when nobody understands her. Sign language is now used less than on arrival.

Social Relationships   The child settled in quickly. She plays with other children but often prefers her own company or that of an individual member of staff, especially for indoor games. She is very helpful and enjoys running errands and helping out when she realizes help is required.

Mobility   This is generally good: she can run, skip, and play football.

Medical/Behavioural Disorders   Jane has been diagnosed as an epileptic, but has had no fits since admission to the unit. She gets 'high' quite easily, when good humour quickly turns to manifestations of aggression demonstrated by punching, kicking and loud screeching. However, attention can be turned quite easily to some more constructive activity, provided this is available.

Summary

Jane possesses most of the basic self-help skills, although she will often pretend that she does not and will ask for assistance. If this is refused, she will usually undertake the task herself although not always with good grace. Table etiquette could be improved.

There have been no signs yet of her family wishing to contact or visit. Social workers are planning to visit the parents in the near future.

PROGRESS

On admission Jane settled almost immediately, showing great delight in her bedroom and surroundings. She appeared to be a cheerful and active child, who demanded constant attention. She was unwilling to carry out many of the activities she was capable of doing without staff supervision, and seemed dependent on approval for everything she did.

She had no spoken language but was able to communicate comparatively easily with her sign language, making accompanying noises. However, she often became frustrated, being limited in the number of signs she was able to use.

Jane's intelligence was very difficult to assess because of her problems of communication, but it became increasingly obvious that her learning processes had been hampered by her lack of speech, and that she was far brighter than at first she appeared to be.

She loved to show her knowledge of words, and colours, for instance, and to compare one with another, and she could become extremely frustrated when she was not understood, moving from one member of staff to another seeking approval. Jane's comprehension of language was very good, which made her own inability to speak even more frustrating for her.

From these points it became obvious that Jane needed help in two areas; first in her communication ability and secondly in helping her to gain some independence.

It was decided to start teaching Jane the Bliss Communication System. She immediately showed an interest in this, probably realizing that it might help her relate to people, and she also desperately wanted to learn. Within six months she learned approximately 30 symbols, but was unable to use them in everyday terms, still relying on her sign language. The next move was to encourage Jane to use the system to communicate. This involved her in carrying her Bliss Board everywhere with her. It was also felt that if Jane could be taught to write, her problem of communication would be further alleviated, so this was carried out in conjunction with her learning of the Bliss system. She was already able to read to a certain extent. She could recognize names and knew every letter of the alphabet, and she was able to put the first letter to the beginning of a word.

However, she was not confident about writing, and although she enjoyed trying to write letters, she would not attempt to form words. It was felt that once she realized the value of writing as a means of communication, she would put all her efforts into this.

The second area of concern with Jane was to help her gain some sort of independence. The problem was not to teach her self-help skills, most of which she could carry out competently, but to help her to carry them out on her own. One particular aspect that was concentrated upon was trying to encourage her to bath herself. After several attempts it became obvious that leaving her to do it alone brought no success. She would merely wait for someone to appear. We therefore broke it down into several stages: first asking her to go and get her nightdress, then asking her to run the bath, and finally to undress etc.

RELATIONSHIPS

Jane enjoyed the company of others, constantly seeking their approval, even in her relationships with other children. She, however, preferred adult company if given the choice. She found it very difficult to sit doing nothing, and liked to be physically or mentally active at all times. She felt compelled to be 'in on' everything. Her understanding of sharing steadily improved; she would voluntarily give up something with which she was playing, (e.g. a bicycle) because it was someone else's turn.

She sought alliances with other children (i.e. 'You and I will do . . .') but could also be aggressive towards them if she did not get her own way. She was rarely aggressive with adults, but resorted to obscene gestures and derogatory noises. Jane often found it difficult to react appropriately in pleasant situations; for instance, if she were taken out for a treat she would scream, swear and so on, almost as if she were reacting against something pleasurable so that she was 'covered' if it were taken away. She reacted similarly if given a present, ignoring it at first, then indicating she did not want it. However, once she accepted that it would not be taken away she would become attached to it.

Jane had a good sense of humour, enjoying hiding things, or pretending that she was unable to do a puzzle.

CONCLUSION

Our work during the two years with this child fell naturally into three separate yet inter-related areas of concern.

1. Development of the basic self-help and domestic skills so that Jane could ultimately become as independent as possible.

2. Helping Jane to come to terms with her communication difficulties by encouraging alternative methods of non-verbal communication.

3. Encouraging Jane's social and emotional development in the hope that she would be able to make and sustain meaningful relationships which could be used to help her through the problems of adolescence that might well be exacerbated by her communication difficulties.

Her family, over the past 2 years, gradually restored contact, taking her home every weekend. Jane re-established a very good relationship with her two teenage sisters at home and a warm, loving relationship with her mother, and she became ready to move back with her family full time. She no longer presented a management problem and never had any aggressive outbursts during her last two years in the unit. She became well able to cope with adults in almost all situations. Jane was supervised on an individual basis by staff for two days each week and the teachers reported that her reading had improved immensely and that she was now beginning to discard the 300 Bliss symbols for use of the written word and tackling first, second and third stage reading books. She began to combine letters in writing, and there has been a great improvement in number concept. She counts competently using counters and she can now do simple addition. She was given a watch and became very interested in trying to relate to actual time rather than routine time. This indicated real scope for her personal independence as she would eventually, if she could relate to the time of day, be able to use Public Transport, and a wealth of community interaction could evolve if Jane were able to relate time in a constructive fashion.

Jane's ultimate unit review discussed her in relation to her family circumstances and the group made a decision to discharge her home to her family on Christmas Eve, 1980. The family was offered respite care as and when required and a bed was made available on weekends should any form of stress be obvious in her mother or her family to the visiting social workers.

It appeared that this arrangement ideally suited Jane as she was able to maintain contact with the residential unit both on a respite care basis and for two days of each school week, when also she has lunch at the unit with the staff and children. We also managed to maintain the speech therapy input. Jane continued to attend the speech therapy department, which works in conjunction with the local community school. Jane's family are also allowed to visit these areas so that changes in Jane's speech therapy needs can be monitored and used constructively to help Jane and her family keep pace with the developments which lie ahead in terms of her communication progress.

Jane was indeed reunited with her family on Christmas Eve, 1980.

CHAPTER 11

Families and Social Services

RESPONSIBILITIES OF THE STATUTORY AND VOLUNTARY SERVICES

Statutory Services

SERVICES TO THE MENTALLY HANDICAPPED and their families should be available, as to any other group in the community, on the basis of need, with access to resources, personnel and personal help. In accord with this principle, Regional Social Work Departments offering a generic service to the mentally handicapped and their families are now well established in Britain. This reorganization of the services followed the acceptance of the Seebohm Committee's recommendations (HMSO, 1968) in England and Wales, the Social Work (Scotland) Act 1968 and the adoption of the government White Paper *Better Services for the Mentally Handicapped* (DHSS, 1971).

Generic social work departments are geographically based in local area offices. Social workers seconded to hospitals, health centres, child guidance centres and child development centres or employed by voluntary societies continue to offer a service to those families or adults referred for specialist advice, treatment or care; but many hospitals for the handicapped are still without social work departments as an integral part of the service. Groups such as the National Development Group for the Handicapped set up in 1975, and reports such as those of the Court Committee's (1976) on the Child Health Services and the Warnock Committee's enquiry into the educational needs of handicapped children and young people, have promoted active co-operation between services in order to meet the complex needs of the handicapped. Legislation, such as the Housing and Homeless Persons Act 1977, has reinforced this and joint financing between Health and Social Services has provided opportunities.

Nevertheless, lack of co-ordination between the relevant medical, educational and social services still remains a problem for families. The parents of a mentally handicapped child may find that they themselves are the co-ordinators and have to find their way through services, often at a time when their own strength is undermined and it is difficult to ask for help. Information and advice can come from professionals of different disciplines—doctors, health visitors, psychologists and social workers. The help they offer can be biased by their own personal beliefs and sometimes limited by their lack of knowledge of existing resources. It can conflict with the families' personal and economic values or their instinctive needs, resulting in confusion and sometimes withdrawal from services. The handicapped adult of limited verbal ability and understanding of 'systems' may find it even more confusing.

The Family Fund Analysis (National Children's Bureau, 1979) still showed that 'Apart from the Attendance Allowance and medical attention a majority of families still experience a lack of meaningful contact with official services'. 'Counselling' can still be haphazard, depending on the family's initiative, local resources and statutory and voluntary expertise. The effectiveness of social work help to the handicapped depends on the variety, accessibility and range of specialized resources and functions which can be provided and which the family needs at a particular time. Social Workers have to be in a position to give accurate information on the community resources and the specialized help that is available.

Social work departments have increased their visible resources. There are more training centres for the adult handicapped with or without hostel accommodation, more short term care in voluntary homes or specially chosen foster homes and more use of resource centres for placing handicapped children. There is more active dissemination of information on opportunity groups, nursery facilities, child-minders and financial benefits. Financial benefits—the Attendance Allowance, the Mobility Allowance, the Invalid Care Allowance, the Family Fund—can help meet the extra financial burden on parents who often do not expect that any of the broadly defined categories apply to them. Fewer children attending nurseries has meant an increased intake of handicapped children. Advocacy in obtaining or establishing entitlement to benefits has become increasingly a task undertaken by social workers, community workers, or welfare rights workers. Some authorities, in co-operation with local education or health authorities, provide special nursery and day centres for the severely handicapped, which include specialist psychologist and paramedical services, such as speech therapy and physiotherapy. Recent studies indicated that 'demonstrating the techniques with the child is probably the most effective approach for all parents' (Nay, 1975). Two of the many dilemmas for parents with severely handicapped children are the accessibility of resources and whether routine family care is 'good enough'. For most parents the main component of counselling is 'What can I do for my child?'

Social workers can best help if they have accurate knowledge of the handicapping condition and how it affects normal development from childhood to adulthood. They must learn about the complexities and the effect of handicap, physical and mental, from contact with nursing, psychology and medical colleagues looking after the multiply handicapped child or adult. The nature of the handicap will affect parents' initial reactions to their own child. It will also affect decisions about placement away from home if the primary handicap leads to behavioural or medical problems affecting family stability. Medical problems, educational acceptance, fears about sexuality and the burden of long-term dependency can be uppermost at any time. At times, professional advice may influence the parents less than 'the stigma' of a particular handicap and the opinion of near relatives and friends. More flexible and regular arrangements for temporary care for the handicapped member has to be an integral part of the social work department's service rather than a response to a crisis.

Social workers must be aware of the ambitions and values of a particular family: circumstances can exist where the well-being of a family as a whole takes precedence over that of the handicapped member at any time. Concern for the handicapped and their families remains the continuing responsibility of the social services, whether the help required is educational, medical or social.

Social work departments offer a variety of personal services from ancillary workers, home helps and family helpers. Occupational therapists are employed by local authorities. Speech therapists, physiotherapists and health visitors are employed by the health authorities. Often the handicapped person's initial contact with the department will be for aids for their handicapped member and advice about housing or adaptations to the home. The Court Committee report says that 'Parents have their own special service needs, for they face problems in bringing up a handicapped child which are additional to and to some extent different from the problems facing all parents.'

For a small number of families immediate practical relief and instant placement may be necessary and right. It is the job of a social worker to identify those families; help to enable them to live through this period may be necessary, whatever the placement—hospital, home, hostel or foster home.

Parents may ask 'Why help for me, when the problem is my handicapped child?' Many parents of handicapped children develop inner resources of fortitude without professional help. Although no drug therapy, counselling or practical help can eliminate the problem, support at times of crisis can prevent undue suffering and maladjustment. Social workers should be sensitive to the distress, anger and guilt which are essentially normal and which can be the motivating force in the seeking of solutions.

Voluntary Services

Most national voluntary societies for the handicapped have branches in every part of the country. Many families will wish to belong to such a society so that they can meet others facing adversity, as well as receive special guidance about particular handicaps and the resources set up to help them. Local authorities should make sure that information is easily available at local centres, health centres, toy libraries, hospitals and schools where parents meet. Not every parent can help another, not every parent can absorb the implications through reading guidance leaflets and information. Most parents with a handicapped member feel isolated by the problems which they consider others do not have.

Information is simply a starting point from which to base later decisions realistically. Social Workers will often initiate meetings of parents. There are advantages in individual and group therapy to both the professional and the parent, but they are not always the same advantages. The sharing of experience and information in groups can be helpful, but care must be taken in small groups to avoid further stress on some parents and handicapped adults. Volunteers have a part to play in increasing familiarity with handicap in the community, which can influence parental attitudes, as well as in providing practical help.

The younger, more vociferous generation of parents, the parent associations and voluntary societies, often in co-operation with the statutory services, have done much to highlight the gaps in services. In some instances they have introduced the handicapped into the community and provided innovatory schemes (e.g. Barnardo's Chorley Project) of great benefit to families. The critical evaluation and continuity of the professional services are equally important for the handicapped.

PARENTS' DILEMMAS AND THE EFFECT OF FAMILY LIFE

Birth and the Disclosure of Facts

Although 'Patterns of family life are not so easily disrupted as one might expect by a young handicapped child' (Younghusband, 1970) parents may be overwhelmed by the birth of a handicapped child. In common with all parents there will have been some expectation of ideal parenthood which has suddenly been replaced by something unknown. The unknown is fearful and only facts can allay the fears. However, the well documented literature on how to disclose the facts to parents is often not matched in practice in busy maternity wards or GPs' consulting rooms. No formula can fit all cases, but awareness of the impact is necessary. This involves not only doctors but the whole way the treatment of mother and child is initially organized. Most mothers will be quick to sense 'differences', both in the infant and in the attitude of those around her. 'Everyone was upset. People appeared from nowhere;' said one mother, while another maintained 'I tried to be around so that I could ask but no-one wanted to say anything.' When the doctor is certain of the diagnosis and the degree of handicap he should explain the truth to both parents, comprehensively. Conflicts and misunderstandings arise if parents learn facts separately, or are given bare facts by someone ignorant of what to do or of what help is available.

One factor promoting early hospitalization of severely handi-capped children has been when a 'hopeless' (as seen by the parent) diagnosis was given, not *how* or *when* parents were told, but *what*. There is a difference between forthrightness and bluntness: those unable to undertake the task of accurately and kindly imparting full information should hand over to those who can. Unpleasant clinical or genetic facts are distorted by feelings which make such in-formation unbearable. Unfamiliar language contributes to parents' feeling of having 'been told nothing'. The first reaction may be one of 'novelty shock' as described by Wolfensberger. The cold facts have to be repeated when parents are less shocked and able to ask questions.

The doctor, or whoever tells the parents, has to be able to respond to questions of prognosis which should not go unanswered. However, unreasoned hope will continue and should not be dispel-led lightly until it can be replaced by realistic solutions. Such hope will carry parents through the ordeal of suspense, the waiting for medical opinion if the diagnosis is uncertain, and the explanations to and acceptance by families and friends. The type of syndrome will be an important determinant of the strength or direction of the parents' feelings, as also will be their past experiences. One mother telephon-ing the hospital after the emergency admission of her two year old profoundly handicapped daughter was told that she was 'alright now'. Until she reached the ward she was certain that this meant that the normal child she had expected during her nine-months preg-nancy had been restored to her. Perhaps oddly, a study by Gibson (1978) of parents of Down's syndrome children concluded that, 'previous experience of the family with the syndrome was a negative contributor to the parents' reaction.'

Later Information and Adjustment

Unfortunate timing in the giving of information can, however, be made good. The initial rejection of information is not irrevocable. Information giving can modify attitudes and help to ease disturbed feelings. Reaction to initial disclosure and reaction to later in-formation are two different things. It is always especially devastating to feel helpless towards one's own child: opportunities for helping the child should be thoroughly aired. Craft (1979) notes that two important elements of 'counselling' will be the technical qualification in all aspects of the syndrome, of those responding to parents' questions, and the opportunities for parents to help the child.

Questions can come at any time and not always to those technically qualified to answer them satisfactorily: 'What does the continual screaming mean?' 'Is he distressed?', was asked of a technician at an EEG appointment! A social worker accompanying a mother with a hyperactive child on some of her many clinic appointments can be faced with the exasperated question, 'What is hyperactivity, anyway? He won't go for a walk, sits down in the street, but runs around here and in the house all the time. Can't it be treated?' Social workers in the past have been more prone to accept the parents' feelings of self reproach than the parents' anger and need for information in order to find their own solutions. Parents should be allowed to have feelings of resentment, frustration and rejection of the unacceptable and *time* to readjust their values.

This second period of adjustment has been called by Wolfensberger (1970) a 'value crisis'. It comes after the shock of discovery and involves the search for a cause, or a 'magical' cure, and for a new identity as parents of a handicapped child: and the gradual realization that life will never be the same again. They will look to others facing adversity—particularly other parents of handicapped children. In some cases counselling has not continued beyond telling parents their child is handicapped. Social workers in hospital and in the community must be in a position to respond to parents' expectations and to their understanding of what is going on. Many parents will turn to the services for the handicapped with dread. Timing of information and introduction to resources is important.

Initially the mother may be the most vulnerable, and also the most influential in the decisions taken. One mother, a nurse herself, wanted to know what nurses in the field of mental handicap felt about the grown-up handicapped patients. Her child was only three, but she was thinking of the future. Social workers and nurses can help at this stage by sharing the burden of anxiety—particularly if admission to hospital is necessary—and by listening to the parents. Extreme martyrdom of the mother is rare nowadays, but can happen. Martyrdom will eventually exclude the father's participation. His helplessness to change the situation, his need to adjust to reduced expectations, may be harder for him to bear. He may be afraid to care for the child physically. Non-participating fathers, it has been noted in several surveys, are a factor in early hospitalization. The father's own role of setting limits to behaviour and showing firmness and discipline to the young handicapped child should not be undermined as he struggles with his own feelings of responsibility or reparation. It is easy for anger at the event to turn into anger with the actual handicapped child.

Mrs B had a high expectation of both her children, who had the slightly wary look of children who have to live in the adult world too early. They were unremarkable, unless it were noticed that they never appeared either grubby or relaxed. The family appeared isolated, but they were a service family who had moved around according to the needs of the army, rather than from choice.

Deborah, their third child, was born abroad. Pregnancy and delivery were said to be normal. The mother appeared at the surgery at intervals suggesting tentatively that the baby was slow and, in particular, difficult to feed. Deborah was taken twice to the casualty department at different hospitals. On the second occasion she had a cut lip and was admitted for observation. Some degree of hypotonia was diagnosed, but no mention was made of the cut lip. The next admission was three months later; Deborah had a fractured skull and the explanation was that a clothes pole had fallen on her. The hospital requested intervention by the local authority. The shock of being told by the Social Worker that the child would be taken into legal custody by means of a Place of Safety Order drew from the parents the admission that the mother had 'lost her temper'. Later the mother was to say that she felt the baby rejected her and, perhaps more telling, 'would not learn'.

Fortunately, the vulnerability of the mother's parenting and the reduced responsiveness of the child, as illustrated in the previous paragraph, do not always coincide so tragically. Handicap and its consequences are disruptive to a greater or lesser degree and the social worker must know not only the child, but the parents' hopes and fears for that child.

Facing Reality

A third stage which parents eventually face are the day-to-day demands on them and their families, called by Wolfensberger 'The reality crisis'. Such realities include medical complications, the endless irritating, hyperactivity of a brain damaged child, temper tantrums—particularly when speech or movement is minimal—and disturbed sleep, all of which distort relationships and undermine the family's ability to manage.

Ruth was a paediatric nurse, who gave up her profession to take on another, that of caring for handicapped children in her own home. Her practical problems changed with each child placed with her. They ranged from adapting clothing for an older child unable to walk to visiting clinics for anything from running repairs to splints to speech therapy. For her, too, there was anxiety about the future of a deaf and partially sighted child and the guilt she felt about having ultimately to send him to an institution.

Normal siblings may have their own perceptions of the problems and model themselves on the behaviour of the handicapped child to gain attention. At times they may be aware of two sets of rules in the family, their outings may have to be curtailed and they themselves may be unwilling to entertain friends. All these factors may cause resentment, and yet separation from the handicapped sibling or his illness may arouse fears.

Social workers should be alert to changes in the family's attitudes and circumstances. The strongest influence on the siblings will be the parents' attitudes to the handicapped member of the family. Social workers however can help to effect changes in the attitude of parents and in the other family members, as can volunteers; but practical relief from day-to-day caring must be available, as this allows space and time for family members to lead more extrovert lives if they wish, or to pursue their own activities without being dominated by the deadening routine which so many families experience. Single and separated parents may have particular problems. Some parents may need to be told that alternative good group care with specialist help can benefit their child. Some changes will be healthy ones and siblings can develop an understanding which may later influence their choice of vocation. Some parents will find new resources in themselves and new meaning in life, as many of the books written by them show.

IMPLICATIONS OF HANDICAP FOR PARENTS AND DECISIONS ABOUT CARE

Diagnosis of mental handicap should always lead to assessments of actual and potential developments, and that assessment should be continuous.

Intervention should be as early as possible, since there is considerable evidence that help can often prevent the occurrence of secondary handicap and that parents of mentally handicapped children are willing to spend much time and effort in helping their own child.

Parent Training and Home-Based Care

There have been various approaches to parent training (Cunningham, 1979) and studies of stimulating the infant and young child with particular handicaps. These may involve regular home visiting and demonstrating the techniques to the mother, or special nurseries involving the parents, or workshops, or even residential periods for the whole family. Early services are not yet consistently available to parents and are therefore difficult to evaluate. Stress on families and on the child may be considerable, for the optimum duration and the intensity of stimulation for useful gains is not yet known.

Parents will still need support. The longing for normality will continue and will be particularly acute when normal milestones such as school entry are reached. Inconsistencies of handling may have arisen through initial parental uncertainty; the child's early life may have been disrupted by separations in hospital. Integrated nurseries and early education may be available for the less handicapped, but a child's own unreadiness for competition or physical frailty may be a problem. If special education or hospital services are some distance away, parents may be faced with a dilemma about residential care, and compromises have to be worked out. Social workers, with others, have to help the family in making a balanced decision: the needs of the family and of the child, what the family wants and what is available, are complex.

Integrated programmes in the community during the school holidays may have benefits for the handicapped child as well as the parents. Problems may arise for the handicapped child as a healthy response to his own inability to manage his own environment at school, or may arise at home in response to parents' fear about his need for independence or growing sexuality. A breakdown in the tolerance of the family or the school, in the health of parents or in their social circumstances may lead to requests for help and placement away from home. The social workers' job may be to create conditions for consultation with other specialists—doctors, psychologists, teachers—to help to arrange for flexible short term care. Any member of this group may be concerned with the family at any time. In each case solutions are different, but it is only by a combination of skills that we can hope to offer constructive help.

Placement of the Child in Residential Care

A minority of families need early placement of the handicapped child, their needs arising perhaps from disturbed behaviour, severe physical impairment or both. There are few residential units in the community for either severely disturbed or severely physically handicapped children. With increased knowledge of the handicap parents may find it difficult to consider placement for their handicapped child and they may need to know that anxiety caused by the separation may be felt more by them than their children. Decisions about placement should involve the whole family, but each member will base his decision on different information. Consultation with hospital or residential staff prior to placement is essential. Residential community services are at present a patchwork of voluntary and statutory services. It is hoped that in future there will be better planning of community residential services, clearly related to other services for the mentally handicapped. Co-ordination would then be easier and not in the hands of any one social worker, psychologist or doctor.

A small number of children who endanger themselves or others may be the subject of a supervision requirement. The social worker involved must be aware of the resources and practical choices open to them on making recommendations to the Court or, in Scotland, to the Children's Panel. The supervision requirement may include admission to hospital.

There are times when admission to hospital is the only answer. Nursing help may be required for the severely physically handicapped. The specialized programme of the psychologists which cannot be obtained in the community may be essential for the young handicapped adult who may be in conflict with the law and need special training in social or vocational skills.

There are other problems when parents themselves grow too old to look after the handicapped member of the family. 'Chronic sorrow is not a neurotic reaction but a natural response to a tragic event' and 'lasts as long as the child lives' (Olshansky, 1965). It will be deepest when the child is so handicapped that hospitalization has to be considered. This is rarely seen as a positive choice for the benefit of the handicapped. The family must make the choice, but some of the barriers against hospitalization are overcome by frank discussions with professional staff involved. Total rejection of the child is rare, but rejection of an intolerable situation may occur, resulting in the flight of a parent or the inability to visit once care has been handed over. All parents of handicapped children may find more difficulty in expressing their negative feelings in case they are seen as rejecting. The pressure to be impossibly good becomes intolerable: their feelings of inadequacy are confirmed if they see nurses as the perfect parents they are expected to be.

Distress
Distress is not automatically relieved by hospitalization. It can itself create new and conflicting emotions. The threat may be to the integrity of the family or it may be experienced as acute loss which has its sequel in mourning and depression. Many families experience the admission of their child to hospital as a kind of death, deprived finally of their hopes for the fulfilment of their child and suffering the actual loss of being responsible for meeting his needs. One father, whose handicapped child was admitted at weekends, which was all the mother could tolerate, said, 'It's like having a funeral every Saturday.' The nurse and social worker can help promote discussion of these feelings and identify those who may be more vulnerable to this loss. Help to live through this time may be necessary once the

decision is reached. Early contact with staff may prevent misunder-standings later when difficulties arise. Each family's problem is different. For some, it may be whether to sustain a relationship with a child not able to recognize or respond to them. For others it may be how to help the child retain some trust in them and in the adult world. Whether the care is temporary or long term it has its implications for the parents. Social workers, in partnership with hospital staff, may be best placed to help the parents with their dilemmas.

Young adults are sometimes admitted to hospital when the less desirable features of a syndrome affect family stability or offend society's standards. The social worker may have to be concerned with recommending compulsory admission or involved with the family and young person in accepting this as a necessary step. The intellectually and emotionally immature young person may accept this 'punishment' as right, but may come into hospital simply bewildered by his own feelings which need to be expressed. With the family's consent the social worker should contribute special data to the hospital and not lose sight of the handicapped person and their possible return to the community. For many parents the alternatives to hospital care are not available or not yet 'good enough'. Their guilt should not be compounded by operatic soliloquies on either system.

YOUNG ADULTS

Gibson, talking about Down's Syndrome, has said that future debate will be about the care system for adolescents and young adults. This is also applicable to other syndromes. It is now recognized that the young adult, like his contemporaries, should have the chance to leave home, have friends of his own age and interests outside the home. Leaving home and the search for a marriage partner are stressful periods in any life—all the more so for the handicapped and their families. The father may regret the meagreness of the opportunities for the handicapped member to earn a living wage; the mother may express her sadness at the offspring's lack of marriage prospects. These topics will remain a preoccupation of parents and may result in parents changing their whole way of life in an attempt to provide these opportunities for their handicapped child. Certainly the fact that more handicapped children are remaining at home and that parents have more knowledge of handicap has resulted in the handicapped being less stigmatized in their own community. If the choice to live in the community is to be open to the handicapped and if custodial care is to be avoided, more professional help needs to be offered in adolescence as they move out of the home.

Hostels and Group Homes

The number of hostels and group homes, for both sexes, in the community has increased but social work departments have not yet reached government targets. Some hostels are used for periods of social adjustment, while the handicapped person attends a training centre, or simply as homes to relieve parents and handicapped alike. Shortage of such accommodation however will often still mean, for the social worker, a choice between giving a place to an older bereaved adult or training for a young adult.

Some adult residential training services and homes are provided in communities or villages for the handicapped, set up by voluntary societies, both national and international. The standard and stability of staff, the availability of programmes for the handicapped, as well as the opportunity to leave home, are legitimate concerns of the parents. Small units in the community can rarely provide specialist services, psychological, educational and recreational. Some can if linked to centres such as Hospitals for the handicapped or if they make use of community resources such as colleges of education or community centres. Social workers and community workers should work to promote these links. Opting for home care for the handicapped child can be influenced by the prospect of what will be available for the young adult. The factors influencing requests for care outside the home in the earlier years are better known than those contributing to later decisions for some kind of institutional care.

Hospital

Social workers have not yet in the main acquired expertise in planning programmes for the handicapped, although training centre staff and residential social workers are acquiring such skills. Expertise in caring for the multiply handicapped and those with severe behavioural problems remains in the hospital.

Planned discharges from hospital are more frequent, but for many handicapped the difference between hospital life and living in the community is too great. Lack of places in training centres, problems of distance and travel, often preclude a gradual introduction to community living. Different management structures and priorities make it difficult to share resources and expertise. The imaginative use of volunteers who can enhance the handicapped person's view of himself has had considerable benefits for the handicapped. The natural ability to find a friend or counsellor has often proved to be the real indicator of whether a handicapped person remains in the community, particularly when professional resources have been lacking.

Sexual Needs

The sexual needs of the handicapped are not often raised by parents, but the subject should not be left unaired. To do so will result in sexual ignorance and might make parents' unspoken fears of sexual deviance a self-fulfilling prophecy. For the more handicapped there may be more need for warmth and companionship, holding hands and cuddling, but they may need to know when and where this is acceptable for adults.

Loring has pointed out that 'the vast majority of institutions for disabled people are so constructed as to make a close personal relationship with another resident extremely difficult. Personal relationships remain undeveloped or, if developed, have a slightly coarse and comic quality about them.'

Social workers may be asked for advice by parents and may need to help parents accept the normal risks and opportunities of a group home or hostel. Both staff and parents have protective feelings towards the handicapped. As part of the parents' unwillingness to let them leave childhood they may have been denied sex education and the opportunities for learning to cope socially. Siblings at this stage may be more self-conscious about the handicapped member of the family, or parents themselves may restrict the behaviour of the handicapped unnecessarily. Inability to protect them from the consequences of their behaviour may influence parents to ask for medical intervention to protect their children, particularly if integration into the community is their main aim.

The issue of sex cannot be dealt with by a rigid approach. Sex education should be planned in a variety of ways, in schools, training centres, hospitals and hostels, in groups and in response to specific situations. Anyone—parent, teacher, nurse, social worker or volunteer—can find himself in the role of counsellor. Not everyone has learned to communicate easily with the handicapped person. Pre-marital counselling and greater availability of different contraceptive advice and methods need to be given by designated individuals.

Child Rearing by Mentally Handicapped Parents

Mentally handicapped parents from subcultural backgrounds will have trouble rearing their children unless they have considerable support. Many social work departments employ family aides and social work assistants to give practical help to all subcultural groups with child rearing problems

The Ws are a family of six whose problems are reflected in the number and kinds of contact they have with the Housing Department, Department of Health and Social Security, Health and Social Services and the police.

Their income was from State Benefits. Mrs W had been a semi-skilled worker and received Invalidity Benefit. Mr W was in and out of casual employment and receiving Unemployment Benefit or Social Security payments. Their income was uncertain and fluctuating. Readjustments to it because of periods of casual work, sickness or separations were common but incomprehensible to the parents. They lived in substandard rented property having been evicted from local authority housing.

The eldest boy, Patrick, (17 years) was referred to the services for the mentally handicapped while awaiting trial for serious assault. Robert (10 years) became known after being involved in a road traffic accident. He developed epilepsy and was hemiplegic. Attendance Allowance was granted on his discharge from hospital and assistance from the Family Fund was given for clothing and frequent hospital out-patient appointments. The younger boys came to the notice of the police by their dangerous interest in cars and escapades on their frequent absences from school.

Finally, the mother's admission to the psychiatric hospital brought Mr W to the Social Work Department with the threat of abandoning the children if Mrs W was not discharged.

The institution to which the family related best was the hospital for the mentally handicapped.

Benefits

Social Workers have a definite role in promoting the claims of the handicapped for housing, employment and financial benefits. The Housing and Homeless Persons Act (1979) has enabled closer co-operation with housing authorities in the provision of accommodation, sheltered and main-stream housing for the handicapped.

Those discharged from hospital to group homes, sheltered housing or other accommodation may need immediate help with rent rebates, changes in Invalidity and Sickness Benefits and Supplementary Benefits for special needs. Practical implementation of 'normalization' includes the utilization of all these services for the benefit of the handicapped.

Planning

The wide range of handicap means the handicapped cannot be planned for as a homogenous group of people. Common sense dictates that for some the pressure to be 'normal' can harrass more than help and some kind of institutional care of the severely handicapped, the disordered and the deviant will still be necessary.

Many older parents face particular anxiety about the future of their handicapped relative after their death. They need to know that there are likely to be changes in the community provision. Some may also need to visit the hospital in their area.

Younger parents are more hopeful of changes but continue to resent, more deeply than any gaps in services, the treatment of their child, by any professional person or service, as handicapped first rather than as a child, their young person as a trainee only, or the multiply handicapped member of their family as less than an individual.

Doctors, social workers, psychologists, nurses and teachers share the knowledge of the practical and emotional needs of the handicapped, the fears real and imagined of the families and of the handicapped themselves. Each, with the family, has special skills which can help the handicapped to self-fulfillment in the community or in institutional care.

NON-CONTRIBUTORY BENEFITS FOR THE HANDICAPPED IN GREAT BRITAIN

Attendance Allowance

This is available for those who are severely disabled, over two years of age, and who require frequent or continual supervision by day and/or night. The disability must have lasted for six months. This allowance is non-taxable and not treated as income for other benefits. No earnings rule applies. The decision can be reviewed within three months.

Invalid Care Allowance

This is available for people of working age who remain at home to care for relatives in receipt of attendance allowance for at least 35 hours a week. A married woman living with her husband or in receipt of maintenance is not eligible. This allowance is taxable and is treated as income for other benefits. There is an earnings rule.

Mobility Allowance

People unable, or virtually unable, to walk, aged five years or more but under pension age, and those whose health or life could be endangered by walking may claim Mobility Allowance, although they must be capable of going out to make use of the allowance. A payment made before pension age will continue until the age of 75 years. The allowance is not taxable but not treated as income for other benefits. Appeals can be made on medical or non-medical grounds. No earnings rule applies.

Non-contributory Invalidity Pension

A Non-contributory Invalidity Pension is available for people of working age who have been incapable of work for 28 weeks and who do not qualify for full contributory invalidity pension. This includes married women incapable of performing household duties. This allowance is not taxable but is treated as income for other benefits: therapeutic earning are discounted.

Housing Benefits

Housing benefits can be claimed by local authority and private tenants (rent rebate/allowances) including those who pay rates plus rent (rates rebate). Claims are made through the housing departments. Types of benefit are: *mobility housing*, which may include special features such as ramps/wide doors; *independent wheelchair housing*, which is special housing for those totally dependent on a wheelchair; and *Sheltered housing*, which may be suitable to your needs if you are disabled and require a warden service.

The Family Fund

The Family Fund intended to help those families with severely disabled children under 16 years. The fund is administered on behalf of the government by the Rowntree Memorial Trust and is designed to help mainly in situations not covered by other benefits. Assistance has been given with transport problems, laundry equipment, unusual aides or adaptations, holidays and the installation of telephones.

Other Financial Help

Exemption from road tax and garage rates may be made if you are severely disabled and own a car driven by someone else for your benefit. Application for this can be made through your local authority or nearest limb-fitting centre.

A car badge for the disabled entitles you to freedom from parking restrictions.

Supplementary Benefits

Supplementary benefit can be paid at an ordinary or long-term rate (this for pensioners, claimants not required to register for work or after one year). Forms are available at post offices, DHSS offices or, if unemployed, at the unemployment benefits office. The rates are increased for registered blind people aged 16 and over.

ADDITIONAL REQUIREMENTS

For a person living in someone else's household a standard rent addition is given. For boarders a board and lodging charge is payable, if reasonable. Eating-out allowances are also payable.

The commonest additional requirements may be for special diets, a heating allowance (automatic for those on mobility, attendance or constant attendance allowance), laundry (where this cannot be done at home or there is an unusually large amount), regular hospital visits, and private domestic help.

Income is calculated on gross weekly income from all sources, including child benefit, national insurance benefits (i.e. sickness, unemployment and maintenance) but *excludes*:

i. A proportion of part-time earnings or single parents' earnings.

ii. Any attendance/mobility allowance, or an education-maintenance allowance.

FAMILY INCOME SUPPLEMENT

Family Income Supplement is paid to low income families where the head of the household works full time (30 hours) or single parents (24 hours). It is also based on gross family income but *excludes*: child benefit; rent/rate rebates; attendance/mobility allowance; war disablement pension; and income of children, other than maintenance.

CAPITAL

The first £2000 of a claimant's capital is ignored and the value of the house if lived in by the claimant.

OTHER SOCIAL BENEFITS

Social benefits should be checked with the local education/social services departments such as Home Help Service, meals service, mechanical and other aides for the handicapped (including adaptations to the home, telephone installation), and particular services such as assistance with school journeys and holidays for the handicapped). Dental/optical/chiropody services are free.

HOSPITAL ADMISSIONS

Most benefits are reduced during periods spent in hospital after eight weeks. The exceptions are the Attendance Allowance and the Invalid Care Allowance, which are reduced after four weeks. Supplementary benefit is liable to reduction on admission.

Mobility Allowance is payable at the full rate during a stay in hospital, provided conditions for eligibility remain the same. It is payable to a child's parent or guardian provided it is being used for the child's benefit.

CONTRIBUTORY BENEFITS

Invalidity

Invalidity pension is paid in place of *Sickness Benefit* if a person continues to be incapable of work after 28 weeks. *Invalidity Allowance* is paid with the pension if the person has become incapable of work while there is still a large part of working life ahead.

Unemployment Benefit

To qualify for this a person must have sufficient contributions in the relevant tax year. A claimant must initially attend at the Unemployment Office. Sickness Benefit will only be paid after an absence of 4 days and on production of a medical certificate.

CHAPTER 12

Ethical Aspects of Mental Handicap

THERE ARE ETHICAL DILEMMAS throughout medicine; some, however, are peculiar to the field of mental handicap. The wide range—in social, physical and intellectual terms—of people known as being mentally handicapped lends itself to an equally wide range of problems. The child with an IQ of 20, with gross physical dependence, will present quite different ethical dilemmas from the young adult of IQ 68 with no physical handicap. One of the more general differences is that responsibility for the former will rest totally with other people, whilst the latter will be expected to be responsible, at least in some areas of their life, for themselves.

PHYSICAL CARE

We will consider first the aspects of the mentally handicappeds' physical care which give cause for consideration of ethical problems. We are therefore, concerning ourselves mostly with those who are severely handicapped, often physically as well as mentally.

The ethical problems are similar to those which arise with any group of people, but complicated by the incomprehension of the mentally handicapped and by their inability to express their needs. Other people, therefore, have to take responsibility for them, and there is endless debate as to who should most suitably do this. Parents are responsible for any child and, if mentally handicapped, often into adulthood. But how much should doctors, nurses, lawyers and even politicians be concerned, answerable or influential?

To Live or Not to Live?

Some of the problems start in the womb. With the possibility of detecting some abnormalities, should the pregnancy be terminated or not? Legally, if there are medical indications for termination, it is the parents' decision. Their religious and cultural views will affect their decision. A similar decision may be necessary when handicap can be predicted before conception. Take, for instance, a family of six children, five of them being microcephalic as a result of an autosomally recessive genetic disorder. The only normal child is a girl. The parents have great difficulty in caring for the family. They are given genetic counselling but continue to have children because they want a normal son. How far should the counselling extend?

For many the handicap is unpredictable but obvious at birth because of physical deformity. Clearly we are right into the area of euthanasia, active or passive, which is so hotly debated in other areas of medicine. The medical decision is how much help, if any, to give to the infant to support life. But should doctors make that decision? There is little hard data available with which to form the basis for such a decision. If a parent kills a deformed child, it is legally murder, though commonly called a 'mercy killing', and may well incur a nominal sentence for infanticide. Should the parents have to bear such an onerous responsibility? And how much say in the decision should the nurses—who will, after all, care for the child and be the closest to him in his living or dying—have in the matter?

Some advocate decisions be made objectively, for instance, by lawyers or politicians. In arguments against euthanasia, in any form, the decision by politicians in Second-World-War Germany is recalled. This resulted in the mass extermination of the mentally retarded. This was little attacked, but 'naturally' progressed to other groups of people. It seems unlikely that total objectivity is possible or reasonable in such a very human decision.

Duff and Campbell (1973) have written at length on these problems and give account of a decision-making process involving parents and medical and nursing staff from the earliest days on the best course of action for the individual child. Of 300 consecutive deaths in a special care nursery, 14 per cent were related to the withholding of treatment. The decision is rarely clear cut. Considerations are: the child's physical and emotional future; the parents' moral and religious beliefs; their wishes and abilities; the strength of their marriage; the effect on their other children; and (the study being in America) their financial situation. Even with the quantity of research which has been done to help such predictions, the decision remains one laden with value judgements and compromise.

Other Decisions

In any case, a decision at any one point in time is inadequate, even if not as dramatic as one concerning a life or death matter. What, for instance, about the severely handicapped adolescent with undescended testes? Should surgery, with its attendant risks, be undertaken as it might be with a normal adolescent? The decision is the more difficult because the person involved may be totally unaware of the problem—it may be incomprehensible to him—or he may be unable to communicate. The onus is often on the nurse or doctor to take note of the problem and meet it with the various people involved. There is rarely a 'right' answer, but the issues need to be kept open.

QUALITY OF LIFE

Then what about quality of life? It is long known that any person, mentally handicapped or otherwise, may or may not achieve their potential, and just putting them in an institution is not enough. Physical exercise and perhaps physiotherapy are important both to prevent contractures and for physical fitness, but how much should be encouraged? Education is given to every child in this country, but how far should a child be pushed? How much, physically or intellectually, should be expected? What about, for instance, the Doman—Delacato system of patterning which is the subject of much controversy? It is the basis of treatment in the Institutes of Human Potential in the United States and in the United Kingdom.

The system is based on the principle that the neurological development of the mentally retarded child has been arrested. Treatment aims at developing lower level functions fully before leading on to higher ones. There is little difference here to normal care and indeed many exercises are used in ordinary hospitals. However, proponents of the system raise expectations of change in parents and demand enormous time and energy, whilst 'normal' care is seen as achieving a possibly low potential and maintenance at as good a level as possible. Abuse of exercises is difficult to define. The patterning used is basically a good physiotherapy exercise—but what, for instance, about 'masking'? In this, exhaled air is re-breathed on the rationale that increased blood carbon dioxide increases cerebral blood flow and hence the flow of oxygen to the brain—a theory of debatable validity.

Sparrow and Zigler (1978) conducted a well controlled trial comparing the Doman—Delacato system with a motivational control group and a 'no treatment' group having normal institutional care. The motivational control group were given more individual attention and interest but no specialized system. All three groups showed some improvement after a year, but the Doman—Delacato group were no more greatly improved than their motivational control counterparts. It is always difficult to tell what, in treatment, is effective, but parents and children should be protected from unreasonable research, and treatment should be a balance of the most help with the least harm: a difficult line to draw.

Social and Sexual Life

In the social area, there are also ethical problems. The law is designed to protect the mentally handicapped person from exploitation and danger. The Mental Health Act allows for the mentally handicapped person to be detained compulsorily in hospital and the Sexual Offences Act protects the severely subnormal against sexual intercourse.

It is certainly reasonable to protect the mentally handicapped from physical exploitation, but it is difficult to apply such laws taking individuality into account. The same laws that protect someone can be applied in such a way as to diminish that person's rights. A severely subnormal person cannot, in theory, validly give consent to homosexual or heterosexual acts, anal or oral sex. Since convictions are rarely made in practice, it is arguable how much the law protects and how much it inhibits.

The mentally handicapped person in hospital is at a disadvantage anyway, whether severely handicapped or not. His keepers, the doctors and nurses, have the constant dilemma of whether to allow socially unacceptable behaviours, such as open masturbation, to occur in the ward setting. This behaviour will, if repeated in public, be severely restricted and may result in prosecution for indecent exposure. The problem is that the person rarely has the opportunity for privacy by the very nature of communal facilities. The same factor gives no opportunity for private sexual intercourse and, with homosexual acts illegal except in private, effectively prohibits homosexual relationships. The mentally handicapped person in hospital, therefore, has fewer rights than the average person.

People looking after the mentally handicapped need to be aware of these difficulties, so that the impossible is not asked. If they are to be encouraged to lead a 'normal' life, we should be clear what that means, what it entails and how far it can reasonably be expected in given circumstances. Should the environment be geared to the possibility of as wide a range of relationships, good or bad, as the 'average person'? Should sex education be given and what form should this take? What about contraceptive cover? Who is responsible for the decision? In practice, this involves everyone from hospital planners and administrators to medical and nursing staff. The general issue needs to be clear, as well as the individual.

CONTRACEPTION

When the decision concerns, for instance, contraception for an individual, expert consultation should be made, as well as that of the patient and relatives, and the medical, psychological, educational and social problems of the individual considered with all those involved. All methods have their drawbacks and the least dangerous and most effective method should be chosen to suit. The right to have children should be remembered even if it seems ill-advised, and especially so when irreversible measures are considered such as sterilization. Such circumstances are rare.

SEX EDUCATION

Sex education is difficult to effect, but how best should one communicate the essentials to those handicapped mentally? In any case, what are the essentials? They will learn so much more easily practically, but how legal or ethical is it, for instance, for a nurse to physically teach a boy to masturbate or for surrogates to be used for education? If we do not teach, how much do we add to their troubles in the world? How much will our own moral standards and value judgements creep in?

MARRIAGE

Marriage becomes increasingly common, but it is advised that the responsible medical officer states in writing that the person under-stands the nature of the undertaking. This is indeed a responsibility and it is open to question whether the doctor is capable of such a value judgement and indeed whether it allows the mentally handi-capped as much opportunity for personal, if idiosyncratic, choice as the rest of us. In practice, will the hospital be prepared to provide the support necessary and the facilities to allow the couple to live together and not to have to return to their respective wards, whether they approve of the liaison or not?

CONCLUSION

We have asked a lot of questions on ethical aspects of various areas of the mentally handicapped person's life. There are no absolute answers, but only answers made in the context of individuals and their situation and environment.

CHAPTER 13

Planning and Delivery of Total Nursing Care

BEFORE THE NURSE begins to consider the details of planning and giving nursing care she must first have a clear idea of what her role and functions are in relation to the mentally handicapped people under her care.

THE ROLE OF THE NURSE

What then is the role of the nurse? Virginia Henderson, (1960) Emeritus Professor of Nursing at Yale, gave us this most accurate and comprehensive description of what the nurse's unique function is: 'The unique function of the nurse is to assist the individual, sick or well, in the performance of those activities contributing to health or its recovery (or to peaceful death) that he would perform unaided if he had the necessary strength, will or knowledge and to do this in such a way as to help him gain independence as rapidly as possible.' Henderson adds, 'This aspect of her work, this part of her function, she initiates and controls; of this she is master'.

This definition of the nurse's function is so central to the provision of good nursing care that it is well worth considering in detail its relevance to mental handicap nursing. 'The unique function of the nurse is to assist the individual.'

Two concepts are embodied here which mental handicap nurses must understand. The nurse's function is to assist the individual, to help him towards reaching a goal. Her function is not to do everything to or for the resident, especially when the resident is capable of performing the task or learning to perform it for himself. It is far more time consuming for the nurse to encourage a mentally handicapped person to feed or dress himself than for the nurse to do it for him, but fostering this dependence on nurses and preventing him from learning more independence is the antithesis of assisting the individual.

The concept of the individuality of the mentally handicapped person is vital for the nurse to grasp. In any hospital where mentally handicapped people are being cared for it is all too easy to see instances of their individuality being ignored, usually to make the running of the hospital 'easier'; obvious examples include communal clothing, lack of any personal belongings and task-centred nursing where, for instance, a nurse will be allocated to 'bathing duties' or to 'feeding duties', instead of being given responsibility for the care of a group of people.

The nurse must constantly ask herself when performing a task, 'Is this fostering the mentally handicapped person's individuality, or is it simply being done in such a way as to get the work finished quickly?'

Another habit which nurses must avoid is that of 'labelling' people in their care: this reduces them to the level of a collection of signs and symptoms and denies their individuality. Few things sound worse than hearing a nurse describe her ward as containing so many mongols, Amsterdam dwarfs, happy puppets etc. One immediately asks oneself if there are any *people* living there?

Sick or well   This is another concept which it is important for mental handicap nurses to understand. Nursing is not confined to the curing of people who are physically ill. Mental handicap nurses are no less nurses than general or paediatric nurses; the principles and practice of good nursing care do not change according to the type of patient being nursed.

The misconception that 'real' nurses work with sick people and, by implication, that any nurses who do not are somehow lesser nurses has been responsible for much low morale among mental handicap nurses.

Those Activities Leading to Health or its Recovery   Nurses tend to view health as merely absence of illness. This again is to take a very narrow view.

The WHO define health as: 'A state of complete physical mental and social well-being and not merely the absence of disease or infirmity.' For many people, including most of the mentally handicapped, this condition will not be realistically achievable, but this concept of health is a worthwhile goal to aspire to.

Or to Peaceful Death   Here Henderson points out that the nurse's function is not always to preserve life at all costs. There are occasions when nursing will involve the care of a dying patient and trying to ensure that death, when it comes, is as dignified, peaceful and painless for that person as the nurse can make it.

The Strength, Will or Knowledge   People will require nursing care for a wide variety of reasons. The person who has had major surgery or the frail elderly person may not have the strength to care for their own health. The depressed or the alcoholic person may have lost the will to look after themselves. The mentally handicapped person may not have learned those skills necessary to lead an independent life. The most profoundly mentally and physically handicapped people will have neither the strength, will nor knowledge to live from day to day without skilled nursing care.

Gain Independence as Rapidly as Possible This is a concept which many mental handicap nurses find difficulty in understanding. It is perhaps natural for nurses to feel that they care so much for their charges that they will do everything for them. They derive great satisfaction from thinking that they are so incapable of 'looking after themselves' that they could not possibly exist without the constant attention of their nurses. This view of the nurse/patient relationship is incompatible with the best mental handicap nursing practice. The nurse must have a belief in the capacity of mentally handicapped people in her charge for improvement and assist them towards this goal.

This Aspect of her Work, this Part of her Function she Initiates and Controls: of this she is Master Here finally the image of the nurse as merely a doctor's handmaiden or 'washer, feeder and dresser' is destroyed. The nurse has a unique function to perform, the planning and giving of skilled nursing care 24 hours per day. She will certainly follow the doctor's instructions in matters of treatment and will work in close co-operation with many other professions in implementing treatment programmes, but it is the nurse who is responsible for the planning of the patients' day and ensuring that total nursing care of the highest standard is provided. From hereon the term 'patient' is used advisedly to imply a close specific relationship which we hope will be a temporary one.

TOTAL NURSING CARE

Henderson speaks of 'those activities contributing to health'. We shall examine these with particular reference to how they apply to the mentally handicapped. She lists 14 'components of basic nursing care'.

1. Helping patients with respiration.
2. Helping patients with eating and drinking.
3. Helping patients with elimination.
4. Helping patients maintain desirable posture (walking, sitting, lying) and changing from one position to another.
5. Helping patients with rest and sleep.
6. Helping patients select clothing, dress and undress.
7. Helping patients maintain body temperature within normal limits.
8. Helping patients keep their body clean and protect their skin.
9. Helping patients avoid dangers in the environment and protecting others from any potential danger from the patient such as violence or infection.
10. Helping patients communicate with others, to express their needs and feelings to others and to have these understood.

11. Helping patients to practise their religion or to conform to their concept of right and wrong.

12. Helping patients work at something that provides a sense of accomplishment.

13. Helping patients play or participate in recreational activities.

14. Helping patients learn, discover or satisfy the curiosity that leads to 'normal' development and health.

It is perhaps unfortunate that Henderson termed these components 'basic'. Some nurses take this to mean that they are menial tasks requiring little skill and that they can be left to the untrained or most junior staff on the ward while they carry out the supposedly more sophisticated and difficult tasks. This attitude is extremely damaging for both staff and patients.

The junior nurses feel that they are 'just a pair of hands' being used to do the most unpopular and, by implication, the least important, jobs. They are given no opportunity to regard patients as individuals with many different needs and problems since their only interaction with them is in performing seemingly unrelated and unimportant tasks upon them. They may also perform these badly, due to inadequate supervision and the lack of an example to follow. The senior nurses also suffer. By delegating such things as personal hygiene, management of incontinence and helping with dressing and undressing to the junior staff they deprive themselves of the opportunity of providing a definite service to the patient. They miss opportunities to assess, from close observation and direct handling, what a patient's needs may be. They also miss opportunities to have physical contact with patients, which is a very effective way of building a close, trusting relationship and which all nurses should take every opportunity to develop.

To adapt and tailor the components of 'basic' nursing care to the needs and problems of each individual patient is clearly a task which requires immense care and thoughtfulness and it is in this area that skilled nursing becomes the art of applying a science.

It is helpful, when considering a patient's proposed nursing care, to think of what particular problems he or she may have in each of the areas of basic nursing care before deciding on the nursing action to be taken.

Helping Patient with Respiration

A sound pattern of respiration with adequate exchange of gases is vital for everyone, but some mentally handicapped people are particularly prone to respiratory problems. People with Down's syndrome are prone to frequent respiratory infections. They also tend to be mouth breathers.

The person who is severely physically as well as mentally handicapped has special difficulties with respiration. The child with severe spasticity, for instance, may have a very shallow breathing pattern which again predisposes to frequent and perhaps fatal respiratory infections.

Many of these children also suffer from bulbar palsy, a paralysis of the lips, tongue and pharynx. These children can often develop an inhalation pneumonia as a result of inhaling food, secretions or vomit.

The nurse must therefore know the principles of oxygen administration and how to give naso–pharyngeal suction and postural drainage. She must also know the nursing measures which help to prevent respiratory infection in susceptible patients: the importance of correct positioning in maintaining a clear airway; the need for frequent position changes and activity to prevent stasis of secretions; and the use of correct feeding techniques to prevent inhalation of food.

Occasionally the nurse will have to cope with a respiratory crisis, most commonly a patient who is choking due to an epileptic attack or who has a piece of food lodged in the throat. She will therefore have to know the first aid treatments which will be necessary.

Nurses, as key health workers, also have a duty to discourage their patients from smoking. The mentally handicapped have problems enough without having to suffer needlessly from smoking-related diseases such as bronchitis, emphysema and cancer.

Helping Patient with Eating and Drinking

Few factors are as important to a person's overall health as an adequate nutritional state. However, many patients will require varying degrees of assistance in attaining this.

There are many feeding problems which the nurse will have to help her patient to overcome, but before dealing directly with these an overall plan for mealtimes should be established. The dining room atmosphere should be cheerful and home-like; conversation should be actively encouraged. Nurses should eat with the more capable residents. 'Administrative problems' should not be allowed to deprive the patients of an important good example when learning feeding and table etiquette.

As far as possible patients should be involved in choosing their meals from a varied menu. Dining room furniture, cutlery etc. should be as used in ordinary homes, except for the provision of special equipment for those patients learning to feed themselves— high-sided plates, non-slip mats etc. Mealtimes must never be rushed in order to 'get the work done', but must proceed at the speed of the patient. Bolted food can cause vomiting and other digestive disorders.

If nurses insist on feeding patients who, with training, could eventually feed themselves, they are simultaneously preventing the patient from gaining independence and also increasing their long term workload by creating a patient who will always require to be fed.

PROGRAMMES

Feeding   Self-feeding programmes will vary between hospitals and between individual patients, but the basic principles of training still apply. A child should be encouraged to finger-feed suitable foods as a first step but, depending on assessment of the degree of handicap, a child may begin self-feeding with a spoon or fork.

It seems that the most appropriate methods of teaching self-feeding skills are certain behaviour modification techniques called backward chaining, prompting and fading.

Backward chaining involves holding the spoon with the child and helping him scoop the food and lift it into his mouth. The nurse then releases her hold on the spoon at chin level and allows the patient to complete the activity by putting the spoonful of food into his mouth unaided. When this stage has been mastered she can then release her hand at chest level, gradually decreasing the degree of assistance needed until the patient can scoop the food and put it into his mouth unaided.

Prompting can take various forms, i.e. verbal praise and encouragement or physical contact, e.g. hugs and cuddles. *Fading* involves gradually reducing the level of prompting required until the desired behaviour occurs without the need for constant prompting.

VOMITING

This distressing problem can have a variety of causes, among them several gastric, renal, neurological and emotional disorders. Some severely handicapped patients may induce vomiting by mouthing their hands. Other simpler causes include over-feeding, air swallowing, and the gulping of food too quickly. The nurse, by close observation of the patient during vomiting and of the vomit itself, can provide important pointers to the possible causes of it.

REGURGITATION

Here the patient brings up a small amount of food as he brings up wind or between meals in an overflow action. It may be caused by simply over-feeding or it may occur in patients who suffer from paralysis of the pharynx or soft palate. It may also be present in patients suffering from a hiatus hernia.

RUMINATION

This is a very difficult condition to control. The patient is usually overactive and seems to enjoy the taste of the food which he chews for a while before spitting it out. If the problem is very persistent the patient may lose considerable nourishment. The patient should be encouraged to have a nap or quiet hour immediately after his meals and should be given toys or books to occupy him and hopefully distract him from the practice.

THE MOST SEVERELY HANDICAPPED

Common feeding problems in this group of patients include: the inability to chew—the patient may only have a primitive sucking reflex, and the persistence of infantile reflexes such as the extensor and Asymmetric Tonic Neck Reflex (ATNR), which can make a child extremely difficult to handle while feeding.

The Presence of a Bite Reflex   Normal children chew their fingers and mouth toys which desensitize the mouth area, but the severely physically handicapped child cannot do this, which leaves the mouth a very sensitive area. When, therefore, a cold spoon is placed in the child's mouth he reflexly clamps his jaws together.

Tongue Thrust   This is another infantile reflex whereby a spoonful of food placed on the child's tongue will simply be pushed out again.

Bulbar Palsy   Damage to the medulla oblongata causes this paralysis of the lips, tongue, pharynx and larynx.

In addition to these specific problems, the very severely handicapped person is totally dependent on his nurse for ensuring that his nutritional needs are met. It is the nurse's responsibility to assess the patient's appetite and ensure that the patients in her care have a balanced and varied diet.

These feeding problems require skilled nursing management and in this area the nurse should seek the practical help of a physiotherapist and speech therapist.

To inhibit the extensor and ATNR reflexes, the child should be sitting upright. Resist the temptation to 'gravity feed' by tilting the child's head backwards in the hope that the child will then swallow. This is very dangerous as the tongue will slip to the back of the throat and the child may choke, vomit, or inhale food into his lungs. Bite reflex can be inhibited by the use of an unbreakable plastic spoon.

The effects of tongue thrust can be minimized by placing a spoonful of food in alternate sides of the mouth where the food cannot be so easily pushed out by the tongue.

Feeding a child with a severe bulbar palsy can be extremely time consuming and messy and will require the nurse's utmost skill and patience. If the child's chewing and swallowing abilities are grossly impaired the nurse may have to manipulate the child's jaw in a chewing motion and lightly rub his throat in an attempt to assist him to swallow. The severely handicapped patients who are unable to chew solid foods should have their meals liquidized to an acceptable consistency.

SPECIAL DIETS

The mental handicap nurse may have to provide certain residents with special diets for a variety of reasons, e.g. for children having dietary treatment for any of the metabolic disorders, such as phenylketonuria or galactosaemia. Other special diets may be ordered for residents suffering from diabetes mellitus, coeliac disease etc. More commonly the nurse may be implementing a diet to reduce the weight of an obese resident or to try to increase the weight of a frail and underweight resident. In both of these cases it is important to keep an accurate weight chart in order that any progress can be observed.

Helping Patient with Elimination

In order to function properly the body must be able to rid itself of waste products. The main avenues of elimination are:
  1. Voiding of urine.
  2. Defaecation.
  3. Perspiration.
  4. Menstruation.
Many mentally handicapped patients have problems with elimination and require thoughtful and skilled nursing in what is regarded as an unglamorous and unpopular area of care.

URINARY INCONTINENCE

This is a major problem both for the patient and nursing staff. As a child grows older incontinence becomes increasingly socially unacceptable. He may find himself restricted in what he can do and where he can go, e.g. public transport, cinemas, swimming pools etc., frequently forbid incontinent people from using their facilities. Much physical work also is required from the nurse as she has to deal with the effects of the incontinence.

FAECAL INCONTINENCE

This is a most unpleasant problem for all concerned and its

consequences for the patient and staff are much more marked than in urinary incontinence. Clearly, overcoming the problems of incontinence will greatly increase the patient's level of social acceptability and personal independence.

NURSING MANAGEMENT OF INCONTINENCE

Considerable progress has been made in recent years in the establishment of successful toilet training programmes based on learning theories and behaviour modification principles for all but the most profoundly multiply handicapped people.

Details of programmes will vary between hospitals but the nurse should be conversant with the basic principles of toilet training and should appreciate the need for close co-operation with clinical psychology staff in order to ensure the success of a programme.

Basic Principles   A positive reinforcement in the form of a reward valued by that particular patient is used in conjunction with secondary reinforcers such as praise, hugs and smiles. A situation is deliberately contrived where the patient is given the maximum opportunity to show the desired behaviour, i.e. urinating into the toilet bowl, and then be appropriately rewarded for getting it right.

The task that we want the patient to perform, in this case using the toilet by himself, is broken down into small simple steps, e.g. taking down his trousers, and each step is rewarded when it is done correctly. The appropriate behaviour is thus built up step by step. When the patient has shown that he can perform the task over a certain period of time the rewards can be gradually withdrawn until he performs the task by himself unrewarded. Toilet accidents during the programme must be expected but should be discouraged without drawing undue attention towards the incident.

THE PROFOUNDLY MULTIPLY HANDICAPPED

Very careful nursing management of elimination in this most handicapped group of patients is vital.

Urinary incontinence   The nurse must carefully wash, dry and change the patient immediately after he has become wet or soiled. If urine is left on the skin the urea decomposes into ammonia which can cause severe skin burns.

The nurse must note any abnormality of the urine, e.g. if it has an extremely strong smell this could mean that the patient's fluid intake is insufficient, or that a urinary tract infection is present. The nurse must also be aware of any of her patients who have not passed urine for an unusually long period of time, as persistence of this condition can have serious renal consequences.

Faecal Incontinence   The nurse has two main priorities here; ensuring that a soft, formed stool is passed, and ensuring that the patient's bowels open regularly, approximately every third day. Many profoundly handicapped patients are unable to void their faeces due to the extent of the damage to their nervous systems. Therefore the danger of faecal impaction is ever present. It reflects poorly on a patient's nursing care when he is needlessly sent to a busy casualty department with a query 'acute abdomen' when in fact he is badly constipated. Nursing measures to combat this should form an integral part of the patient's daily routine.

1. *Exercise*: This is most important in assisting the passage of food through the intestines. The patient should have his position changed frequently. Formal excercises such as music and movement, hydrotherapy and passive movements will help. No patient should be left in bed or in a wheelchair for an entire day.

2. *Diet*: The nurse must ensure that her patients have adequate drinks with and in between meals. Dietary fibre is also useful in increasing the bulk of the stools and softening their consistency. Foods high in dietary fibre include green vegetables, dairy produce and whole grain cereals.

She should also ensure that her patients have some fresh fruit juice or fruit daily as this helps in forming a soft stool and also has a mild laxative effect. A stool softener such as Dioctyl may be prescribed if necessary. It is a harrowing experience to watch a helpless patient in extreme tenesmic pain passing a large hard faecal mass, and one which can be avoided by thoughtful nursing.

3. *Other measures*: With some profoundly handicapped patients these measures in themselves may be ineffective and they will require regular oral laxatives or evacuant enemas. Even more rarely this may not be successful and the nurse may have to empty the patient's bowel manually. With these patients it is important that a careful record is kept of their bowel movements.

Any procedure concerning rectal administration of drugs or rectal investigation demands the greatest care and thought on the part of the nurse who must try to cause the patient the minimum of pain, discomfort and indignity.

MENSTRUATION

What may be a frightening and traumatic experience for a normal adolescent girl can be much more so for the mentally handicapped girl who has much less understanding of the workings of her body Patients approaching puberty should be told in simple understandable terms about the sexual and biological changes that they are soon to undergo.

The nurse must also help the patient with the practical problems associated with menstruation. She must try to teach the girl how to use sanitary towels and ensure that she has an adequate supply of these to cover the period of menstruation. The nurse should also emphasize the importance of good personal hygiene during this time and ensure that the girl has every opportunity to bath as often as she wishes. The nurse should remember that the mentally handicapped girl can suffer just as much as a normal girl from dysmenorrhoea and pre-menstrual tension. A careful record of each girl's menstrual cycle should be kept.

Helping the Patient to Maintain Desirable Posture and Position in Sitting, Lying and Walking and Helping him Move from one Position to Another

Although this component primarily concerns the physically handicapped, it is relevant to all mentally handicapped people. Poor position and posture can constrict and pressurize vital organs and restrict the range of normal joint movements making optimal health impossible.

The observant nurse can tell a lot from a patient's posture and movements regarding his mood, e.g. the patient who is depressed may sit very still and hunched over. If a patient is in pain or discomfort and is unable to communicate the reason to his nurse she may notice vital clues from his position and posture, e.g. if the patient has severe abdominal pain he may lie with his knees drawn up to his chest and guard the area against being touched.

Dr Russell Barton in his book *Institutional Neurosis* describes a picture which will be all too familiar to mental handicap nurses; the posture and mobility of the institutionalized patient. 'The patient often adopts a characteristic posture, the hands held across the body or tucked behind an apron, the shoulders drooped and the head held forward. The gait has a shuffling quality, movements at the pelvis, hips and knees are restricted, although physical examination shows a full range of movements at these joints.' This is such a stigmatizing sign that nursing action to prevent and stop it is essential. A programme of adequate physical exercise and recreation will help a great deal here. What will *not* help at all is for groups of patients to be walked *ad nauseam* around the same well-trod path of the hospital grounds, or to be left sitting in a day room listening to endless Scottish country-dance music. The nurse is failing if she cannot think of more worthwhile and imaginative pastimes than these.

This component of nursing care assumes its greatest importance when caring for the physically as well as mentally handicapped patient. In planning the nursing care of these patients the nurse should work closely with the physiotherapist who can offer vital advice and expertise.

The aims in assisting the patient with posture, position and mobility are:

- i. To reduce spasticity where present and gain a full range of movement in every muscle group and joint.
- ii. To increase tone and postural control in athetosis and ataxia.
- iii. To train awareness of good position and movements of the body.

Specific nursing care involves paying close attention to the encouragement of good postures, positions and movements and the prevention of detrimental postures and movements 24 hours a day by giving careful attention to the patient's posture and movements while he is dressing, feeding, playing, sitting and sleeping. The nurse must ensure that her patients have suitable chairs, mobility aids, and body splints which will encourage optimal position and movement.

Group exercises should be organized, such as music and movement sessions. Individual physiotherapy will help many physically handicapped patients to improve their posture and mobility. Where patients are so severely brain damaged as to be totally dominated by abnormal reflexes, good positioning, especially at night, is of paramount importance in preventing positional deformities such as 'windswept' hips and scoliosis. The nurse must understand the rationale behind this treatment and carry it out always. (For this the reader should consult Chapter 6.)

The most severely handicapped patients will also benefit from 'patterned' passive movements such as Temple Fay (*see* Chapter 6), which should progress to active movements where possible. Nurses should carry these out with a physiotherapist or by themselves after instruction. These exercises are on the basis of overcoming tonic neck reflexes and are essential in helping to prevent muscle contractures.

Nurses often have to move patients from one position to another and it is a procedure which is rarely carried out properly. There are many different types of physical lift and mechanical aid which nurses may use depending on the ability of the patient to co-operate. The principles of good lifting are:

- i. That the patient be completely and decisively lifted.
- ii. That the nurses and the patient have total confidence that the lift will be done well.
- iii. That the lift be carried out in such a way that the nurse is not subjected to fatigue, muscle stress and unnecessary back strain.

Helping the Patient to Rest and Sleep

Sleep is the great restorer and rejuvenator which most of us take for granted. Those deprived of sleep due to pain or tension are extremely debilitated by this; indeed, so powerful is the need for sleep that forbidding a person to sleep is a very effective torture technique.

What problems may the mentally handicapped person have in sleeping and how may the nurse help her patients to have adequate rest and sleep? Sleep disturbances are among the commonest causes of stress that parents relate when requesting residential care for their mentally handicapped child. The effects of a teenager insisting on sleeping with his parents or a child bed-wetting or crying all night are not hard to imagine. Nursing management of this component should ensure that each patient has adequate rest and sleep according to his needs and particular sleep pattern.

Patients who have brain damage affecting the sleep centres in the pons and central core of the brainstem may have unusual sleep patterns, so it must never be assumed that because a patient is not fast asleep from 8 p.m. until 8 a.m. he presents a sleep problem.

Nursing measures to help the patient obtain adequate natural sleep should include ensuring that the patient's day has been interesting, active and stress-free and has generally given him a feeling of well-being which will promote natural sleep. The less busy hours before bedtime give the nurse the opportunity to play quiet games, read stories, or simply watch television with her patients. Patients should be allowed to stay up reasonably late and, as hunger interferes with sleep, a light supper and a hot drink should be made available shortly before bedtime. Patients must be encouraged to go to the toilet, wash and clean their teeth before going to bed. Incontinent patients must be clean and dry. Children should have a favourite soft toy to take to bed with them. The bedroom areas should be comfortable, warm and dimly lit. Also, since noises which are not noticed during the day can sound deafening at night, the nurse should wear soft soled shoes or even slippers.

The nurse should ensure that children in cots have the sides firmly fixed up and that where necessary any epileptic patients have protective padded cot sides in place. The nurse should quietly check on her patients approximately every hour unless a patient's condition merits more frequent observation.

Any duties which are to be carried out during the night should be done concurrently as far as possible. It does not assist the patient to sleep soundly if he is awakened three times during the night for perhaps medication, repositioning and changing or by nurses flashing inquiring torches into his face.

If a patient is very restless the nurse should sit with him and perhaps read a story or give him a warm drink. A child can be rocked gently on his nurse's knee until he falls asleep. All these nursing measures should be employed before resorting to sedative drugs.

Helping the Patient with Selection of Clothing, Dressing and Undressing

CLOTHING

The importance of clothing as both a protection against hot and cold environments and also as an indicator of a person's status, attitudes and peer group should be appreciated by mental handicap nurses. The lack of personal clothing is a characteristic of an institution—usually a penal one such as prison.

Although most mental handicap hospitals seem to have done away with the uniform of 'hospital grey' jackets, ill-fitting nylon shirts, and thin, elastic-waisted trousers, many have still to appreciate the great importance of proper clothing. The most important considerations for the nurse to bear in mind are:

i. That the clothes are ordinary clothes, as from a high street shop.

ii. Whenever possible, the patient should be taken to the shops and helped to choose his own clothing.

iii. The clothing should be appropriate to the environment. Warm clothes are required for winter and cooler ones for the summer.

iv. Special activities require special clothes, e.g. a track suit for sports and games.

Other considerations include practical ones: the clothes should be hard wearing and easy to launder. (This is particularly important where clothes are being chosen for incontinent patients.) Cotton/polyester is probably the best material to choose. Also, as dry cleaning is expensive, the nurse should try to avoid materials which require this.

Clothes should be appropriate in style for the patient's age: an elderly man looks just as institutionalized in multicoloured shirts and trousers as he would in an old institution uniform! Older patients should dress to look as dignified as the nurse would expect her parents to look.

The practice of giving patients old and worn clothes to wear while keeping a new set locked away in a cupboard for 'special occasions' cannot be justified as good nursing practice. Patients must have an adequate supply of clean personal clothing to enable them to appear smart always.

The nurse should always encourage the patient to take care of his clothes. He should have a personal locker or wardrobe to keep them in. If clothes are simply taken from and returned to a ward cupboard you cannot expect the patient to take a pride in 'his' clothes or appearance.

Special consideration should be given to the severely physically handicapped patient. The best type of clothing for him is probably the loose fitting type of sweatshirt which he can put on fairly easily, bearing in mind that he may have a limited range of limb movements which would make tight clothing unsuitable.

DRESSING AND UNDRESSING

Teaching the patient to dress and undress properly is an important part of the nurse's role in this area. The principles for teaching a patient to dress and undress are the same as for other activities. The nurse, by careful selection of clothing, will try to ensure that the patient has every chance of succeeding in the task. Clothes with very small buttons, awkwardly placed zips etc. create unnecessary difficulties for the patient. The training should be carried out slowly and one stage at a time, rewarding and praising where the patient does it right. Adequate privacy should be ensured for the patient when dressing and undressing.

Special care is needed when dressing the severely physically handicapped patient. The nurse should avoid the situation whereby the patient is laid on his bed and bundled into his clothes. Where possible the patient should be sat up in front of a mirror, with the nurse kneeling at his back, and dressed there, as this way he will *see* his clothes being put on. It is also important that the nurse uses this opportunity to put the patient's limbs through a range of passive movements to help prevent muscle contractures. The principle of putting the limbs into the clothes and not the clothes onto the limbs is a sound one.

Helping the Patient Maintain a Body Temperature within Normal Range

Nursing management of this component is mainly by helping the patient to select suitable clothing and by controlling the temperature of the patient's environment. Other measures involve the nurse observing her patients for any signs of pyrexia. This may be a sign of an infection being present. She must also ensure that her patients are not subjected to unnecessary chills, e.g. during dressing and undressing and at bathtimes. In patients with damage to the body's thermostat control centre in the hypothalamus the nurse may notice sudden unprovoked pyrexias. These should be treated by tepid sponging, fanning and offering lighter clothing. The attacks are usually transient.

Helping Keep the Body Clean and well Groomed and Protect the Skin

This is one of the most important components of total nursing care, especially in mental handicap nursing. Cleanliness is important physically, psychologically and socially. The patient whose personal hygiene, grooming and skin care is neglected may suffer physiologically from rashes, skin infections or pressure sores and psychologically and socially from the reduced social acceptance and interaction with others that this entails. Who would enjoy working with a patient who smelt strongly of body odour or halitosis?

Training in personal hygiene skills must therefore be a top priority for the nurse. Before this begins there must be adequate provision of facilities such as plentiful hot water, handbasins, baths and showers, with provision also for personal privacy. Patients should have their own toiletries where possible and be encouraged to use and look after them. The principles of personal hygiene training are basically the same as for teaching any other skills, although individual programmes may vary.

BATHTIME

Patients should be encouraged to bath at least three times per week. A daily bath for the severely physically handicapped and incontinent patient is not a luxury, it is essential. Bathtime should not be a dull chore which is performed like a human 'sheep dip'. This shows a lack of thought and imagination on the nurse's part. Less dependent patients should be able to have a bath or shower without a nurse hovering over them. When the nurse has to help the patient to have a bath she should use this opportunity for rapport with the patient and not simply to ensure his cleanliness. She should encourage the patient to wash as much of himself as he can and help only where he is unable. She will ensure that he is properly cleaned and dried, that ears and nostrils are clean and that hair is washed and nails trimmed as necessary.

Bathtime is a good opportunity for play and the nurse should ensure that the patient has toys to play with and time to enjoy this aspect of bathtime. It is perfectly acceptable for young children to be bathed together, where they have an ideal opportunity for social play and interaction; indeed this is normal practice in families with young children.

It is especially important when bathing the physically handicapped patient that the nurse pay special attention to cleaning inguinal areas, inside clenched fists, etc. It is also a good opportunity for the nurse to put the physically handicapped patient's limbs through a range of normal movements to help prevent muscle contractures. Bathtime is also the best opportunity to unobtrusively observe the patient's skin for any signs of rashes or bruises and for areas of redness caused by pressure.

The nurse must also observe some common sense safety rules at bathtime.

1. Run cold water first then top up to desired temperature with hot water.

2. Never add hot water when patient is in the bath.

3. Never leave the patient alone in the bath unless you are sure that he is capable of bathing alone.

4. Take special care when bathing patients prone to epileptic seizures.

5. Use a bath mat in the bath and put a large towel or blanket on the floor to prevent anyone from slipping.

ORAL HYGIENE

Good oral hygiene is essential for us all and the nurse must ensure that this aspect of personal hygiene is stressed in any training programme.

Patients must have toothbrushes and toothpaste and should be encouraged to clean their teeth after meals and before going to bed. The nurse must frequently clean the teeth and mouth of patients who are unable to do this for themselves. Special care should be given to any patient whose condition predisposes towards peridontal problems, such as mouth breathers, those who suffer from gingival hyperplasia due to phenytoin therapy and heavy smokers.

Patients should be seen by a dentist or dental hygienist at least every 6 months (*see Dental Care,* Chapter 6).

SKIN CARE

The skin must be kept clean and in good condition for it to perform its various functions. Patients who will require special skin care include those whose skin is excessively oily or dry (as in Down's syndrome); adolescents who may have acne; the severely physically handicapped and immobile patient; and patients suffering from certain rare clinical syndromes such as Sjögren–Larsson syndrome and Rud's syndrome, where ichthyosis, a congenital skin disease involving scaling and hyperkeratosis, is involved.

Various creams and ointments may be prescribed for oily or dry skins or acne, and the most meticulous nursing care will be needed if susceptible patients are not to succumb to pressure sores. Patients prone to pressure sores include those who are immobile, incontinent, thin and frail, and those who have sustained gross damage to the nervous system.

Pressure care should be 100 per cent prevented by:

i. Frequent changes of position for play and activities.

ii. Frequent changing of wet and soiled patients.

iii. Maintenance of good general health.

iv. Regular inspection of skin and immediate relief of pressure from any reddened area of skin.

Helping Patient Avoid Dangers in the Environment and Protecting others from Danger from the Patient such as Infection or Violence

ACCIDENT

The most vigilance here is needed when nursing ambulant patients who appear to have no sense of danger. Children may run quickly from the ward and onto a busy main road. The profoundly handicapped are also at risk as they may be unable to move themselves away from danger or to indicate any discomfort or pain. They are completely dependent on their nurse for protection.

It is extremely difficult to protect patients from accident or injury and simultaneously allow them to take an 'acceptable' amount of risks, which they must do if they are not to be cossetted and over-protected.

INFECTION

Protecting patients from infection is also difficult when large numbers of people are living closely together in a ward and often sharing communal facilities. In the event of the outbreak of a common institutional disease such as salmonella or dysentery, the nurse will have to employ special barrier nursing techniques.

VIOLENCE

Nursing care of the violent patient is a very skilled task. It is impossible for nurses to prevent every fight or argument that occurs in a mental handicap hospital, as she cannot be everywhere at once; but the observant nurse will often notice slight signs and subtle changes in behaviour which can indicate that a patient is about to become aggressive. She can then take action to try to defuse the situation.

There will also be occasions when the nurse will have to protect the patient from violence from himself.

Helping the Patient to Communicate, to Express his Needs and Feelings and to have these Understood

Although communication is dealt with in more detail in Chapter 8, its vital place in the fabric of nursing care merits its emphasis in a chapter called *Total Nursing Care*.

Impaired power of communication is probably the most crippling handicap from which the majority of mentally handicapped people suffer. The nurse's role in helping her patients to overcome this problem and to communicate more effectively will be considerable. Henderson stresses that 'Whatever the setting the nurse has an inescapable responsibility for helping the patient maintain and develop satisfying ways of expressing his needs, interests and desires'.

The normal child learns speech and language by interacting closely with his parents and peers. The patient in a mental handicap hospital is denied this close relationship. The quality of interaction is also lower in hospital as staff tend to use shorter sentences, make more commands, and to speak in sentences which demand at best only single word answers.

The nurse should think carefully about the quality of language which she uses. She should ask open-ended questions such as 'Tell me, what you did at school today?' rather than 'Did you have a good day at school today?' The former encourages a thought-out answer, the latter can be answered by a simple 'Yes' or 'No'.

The nurse must speak to her patients when working with them. It is both thoughtless and alienating for the patient if nurses fail to observe this simple courtesy. She should speak with the patient at the 'mother distance', and ensure that she has eye contact and the patient's attention. If he is not looking at her, the chances are that he is not listening to her.

The nurse must also realize that because a patient cannot talk it does not mean that he cannot communicate. Many patients unable to communicate verbally can be taught to use various forms of non-verbal communication such as Bliss or Makaton.

The profoundly handicapped who are unable to speak or to use a sign system also have a right to communicate and to have their attempts understood. In this area the nurse will require her most acute powers of observation. The indications that a profoundly handicapped patient is thirsty, uncomfortable or in pain may be only the slightest grimace, change in activity level or appetite. It is vital that the nurse act on these small signs in an attempt to discover what it is that the patient is trying to communicate. When it is remarked that a patient has a particular way of indicating a need or desire, it should be carefully noted so that others may be aware of it. The nurse must not give up trying if no immediate response is received. She must use all possible channels of communication, in order to establish a rapport with the patient.

Helping the Patient Practise his Religion or Conform to his Concept of Right and Wrong

Most mental handicap hospitals have a visiting chaplain from the various denominations. The nurse should co-operate with the chaplain to provide effective religious care for her patients. Some patients may wish to have individual interviews with the chaplain and many patients enjoy joining a congregational service.

Helping Patient with Work or Productive Occupation

This is a vital part of the mental handicap nurse's role. Failure to provide adequate stimulating occupation for patients encourages the hallmarks of institutionalization; boredom, apathy, lack of self-esteem and the exhibiting of institutional mannerisms such as body rocking, aimless pacing etc. The nurse must ensure that her patients are occupied by work which is *not* boring and repetitive, but which provides real challenge and self-satisfaction. This can be in occupational, industrial or arts and craft therapy units.

The nurse should not simply send her patients to these units but take a real interest in what they achieve there and, where possible, try to transfer the skills learned there to other activities. For example, the patient who has learned to weave a mat or basket should be able to learn how to tie a shoelace.

For patients unable to attend therapy units, activities should be provided in the ward which will usefully occupy the day. Some patients may be fortunate in obtaining employment outside the hospital in hotels etc. and the nurse must encourage them to function as well as possible, as this may be the first step towards that patient's eventual discharge.

Helping the Patient with Recreation

The ability to use leisure time constructively is lacking in most mentally handicapped people and, as they will have more leisure time than ordinary people, this facet of care assumes great importance for the mental handicap nurse.

No one would suggest that the patient's day should be crammed with organized activities from the moment that he rises until bedtime; however, the other extreme—of patients wandering aimlessly through hospital grounds or sitting body rocking in day rooms—is all too common. The nurse's aim should be to ensure that her patients have interesting ways in which to spend their leisure time and that the time for quiet rest periods is also recognized. The variety of recreational activities which are offered in a mental handicap hospital is numerous; swimming, horse riding, music and concerts, cinema shows, dances, coach trips etc. are all widely used and enjoyed.

PLAY

Play is an important part of every child's development and should be no less so for the mentally handicapped child. Play skills should therefore form an important part of the mental handicap nurse's repertoire. The nurse should know how to select and use suitable toys, depending on the extent of the child's handicaps. A well stocked toy library is a big asset here (*see* Chapter 8).

Play can take many forms. It can be imaginative, exploratory, symbolic, social, rough and tumble etc. It is important that play is not seen as a separate care entity to be performed at intervals throughout the day, but rather a tool to be used by the nurse to help improve a child's level of functioning.

The opportunities for play and stimulation must not be denied to those who are unable to play actively: these children should be placed in a variety of good positions throughout the day. They can be supported on foam wedges and bean bags and a variety of suitable soft and musical toys can be placed close by. With a little thought, the nurse can create a stimulating environment for these children which is infinitely preferable to an entire day spent sitting in a wheelchair or lying in bed.

Helping Patient Learn

The nurse's role in helping her patients to learn should permeate all of her interactions with them, operating on the principle which Henderson stated, that of 'assisting the individual in such a way as to help him gain independence as rapidly as possible'. Whether it be self-care, play, occupational or educational skills that the nurse is attempting to teach, there are certain basic tenets which the nurse should understand:

1. All those working with the patient should be aware of the training programme so that maximum consistency of approach can be obtained.

2. Be optimistic about what can be achieved, don't underestimate.

3. Do not accept the patient's present level of functioning, or the first few responses to training as an indication of the patient's potential ability.

4. Do not rely on simply supplying a stimulating environment: teach specific skills to specific patients.

5. The selection of objectives should arise from careful assessment from which clear needs become apparent.

6. Set precise, observable or measurable objectives.

7. Break tasks down to the simplest of steps; this gives the patient the greatest chance of achieving success.

8. Reward/reinforce desired behaviour immediately, consistently and appropriately.

9. Accept 'nearly right' behaviours and reward them. Gradually increase the difficulty of the task by very small steps.

10. Give maximum help at first and then gradually decrease the amount of assistance given.

11. Try to give the patients the chance to use the skill learned in a variety of different situations.

The problems of mental handicap are now viewed as primarily social and educational, rather than medical, and in this very wide field of helping the patient learn that the nurse should find one of the largest areas of her role.

CHAPTER 14

Ward Management and the Planning of Nursing Care

IT WILL BE OBVIOUS that planning for the many and varied needs of each individual patient requires a methodical approach and much thought.

THE NURSING PROCESS

For several years now many nurses have been using a system of organizing and giving nursing care called the *Nursing Process*. The Nursing Process is not an academic exercise for nursing theorists, nor is it an instant panacea which will revolutionize nursing care overnight: it is a method of organizing nursing care which demands that nurses take into account the specific needs of individual patients. At first it may seem impossible to plan and provide such individual care for large numbers of patients, but these skills should develop as nurses gain experience and a greater insight into the relevance of the nursing process to the provision of improved nursing care.

The 'stages' of the nursing process are:
1. Assessment.
2. Planning.
3. Giving nursing care.
4. Evaluating the care given and adapting as necessary.

We shall examine these with particular reference to mental handicap nursing.

Assessment:

Assessment should involve the gathering of information by close observation so that from this definite nursing problems may be identified for subsequent care. Care must be taken that assessment is not done simply for its own sake; assessment must be a basis for action.

As there will be other professionals involved in the mentally handicapped person's care, it is important that those workers supply accurate and up-to-date assessments and relevant progress reports for inclusion in that person's notes so that nurses and other co-workers can find, at a glance, his problems and progress in any particular area.

Planning

Planning should involve the formulation of an individual nursing-care plan for each mentally handicapped person. The format of these care plans will vary between hospitals and units but basically they should include the main areas of care and nursing actions to be taken.

The nursing care plan must be kept up to date by the nurse(s) responsible for the care of that particular mentally handicapped person or it will be of no use. The care plan should give a concise picture of that person and his individual needs and proposed care; it should also do away with the profusion of bathing books, etc. which are still to be found in many wards, as all this information will be on the care plan.

It would be naïve to imagine that the nursing staff will be able to carry out total nursing care for each mentally handicapped person every day of the week. The mentally handicapped person may simply have too many problems or, more probably, wards will have too few staff and too many occupants. The nurse must therefore determine the mentally handicapped person's most pressing problems and those which can realistically be tackled.

Implementing Care

There has been a growing belief within the nursing profession that the traditional 'task-centred' approach to patient care is incapable of providing for the needs of patients as individuals. This system involves nurses being allocated various tasks such as 'bathing duties', 'shaving patients' etc. For the nurse this means that she sees nursing care as being a series of unrelated tasks to be performed on, rather than with, a patient. For the patient, it means that he can be attended to by various nurses throughout the day, none of whom may have an overall picture of his needs and care.

The concept of patient-centred nursing care is especially important within mental handicap nursing where a vital part of the nurse's role will be establishing a rapport and good relationship with the mentally handicapped people.

The nurse, when taking charge of a group of mentally handicapped people has the opportunity to see each as an individual and to have an overall view of his needs and problems and so to plan and give her nursing care accordingly. For the mentally handicapped person it means that he is being cared for by a familiar nurse who will, by her closer contact, develop a deeper knowledge and greater understanding of him.

Evaluating Care

It is essential to have a system of evaluating the nursing care which has been given in order that successful patterns of care are continued and built upon and that nursing action which has not resulted in the desired aim can be modified. This evaluation is best carried out at regular multi-disciplinary conferences where a particular mentally handicapped person's problems and care can be discussed by the various professionals involved. As with assessment, evaluation must be directed towards improving the standard of patient care.

Many nurses regard the nursing process with suspicion, as they feel that it implies a criticism of present nursing practice, or else they say in reply that 'We already do that' or that 'We don't have time.' Neither of these is acceptable as a reason for non-implementation of the nursing process and for continuing with 'task-centred' patterns of care. Sufficient research has been done to show that many hospitals and units are very pleased with the improvements in patient care and staff morale which has come about as a result of implementing the nursing process. The 'We already do this' argument is also unconvincing. The nursing process is not simply a set of new forms to complete, nor is it patient-allocation alone; it is a new way of looking at patient care, and of thinking of how one can modify the basic principles of nursing care to suit each individual patient.

IMPORTANT QUALITIES OF A MENTAL HANDICAP NURSE

Friendliness

The nurse's relationship with the mentally handicapped people in her care should be a partnership. She is there to help them to achieve aims, not simply to carry out tasks upon them. Most nurses in mental handicap know how much the mentally handicapped people value gestures of friendship—much more so than do others.

The nurse must use her discretion as regards just how friendly to become. The old adage that nurses must never become 'emotionally involved' with their patients is a nonsense. How can you work in a close, committed way over a long period of time with people and *not* become emotionally involved? The advice here is for the nurse not to allow her involvement with the mentally handicapped people to impair her clinical judgment or working relationship with them.

Dependability

The mentally handicapped person living in a mental handicap hospital sees a great many nurses come and go and has few chances to establish any long-term friendships and relationships. This is one reason why he must see his nurse as being totally dependable. If a nurse promises a mentally handicapped person a present or special treat she must fulfil this promise. She herself may forget all about it, but he certainly will not! When the mentally handicapped person senses dependability in his nurse he experiences security as a result of this.

The quality of dependability is also important to the nurse's co-professionals. They must know that treatment programmes, once agreed upon, are being carried out. The ward sister must be able to depend on her staff to carry out the nursing care which has been delegated to them: having to check constantly that a satisfactory standard of care has been given is annoying for all concerned and, of more importance, it is a waste of nurse's time.

Acceptance of Responsibility

Mental handicap nurses have for a long time demanded to be accepted and treated as professionals in their own right. With this acknowledgement comes an inescapable responsibility for total patient care.

The nurse in charge of a group of mentally handicapped people must ensure that all agreed treatment and training programmes have been carried out to the best of her ability and that any significant physical or psychological changes in her charges are reported accurately to the appropriate person.

Self-discipline

This is of vital importance when working with the mentally handicapped, many of whom can exhibit extremely trying behaviour. Nurses may be insulted, cursed at, accused of mistreatment or even physically assaulted. It takes great self-discipline to keep calm and to react professionally in situations such as these. The skilled nurse will try to defuse such situations by calm reasoning and not by becoming involved in heated arguments. She will try to anticipate aggressive outbursts and ensure that the maximum number of staff are on hand to handle the situation with the minimum of physical force. She will try to give the same standards of care and attention to unco-operative as well as the popular mentally handicapped person.

Observation

The mental handicap nurse must develop acute powers of observation. She must know how to observe and what to look for. She will need to be able to detect significant physical changes in, for instance, the mentally handicapped person's colour, toilet habits, appetite and activity level. She will also have to be aware of equally significant mental changes, e.g. increased apathy, depression, loss of interest and deterioration or improvement in concentration ability.

This quality is of greatest importance in the nursing care of the profoundly multiply handicapped. A child who is deaf, blind, immobile, unable to speak and profoundly mentally handicapped is utterly dependent on his nurse to realize when he is hungry or thirsty, uncomfortable or in pain and discomfort. The signs which these people can give are very subtle, e.g. slight restlessness, increased chewing movements, or a fleeting grimace. It is essential that the nurse learns to recognize these signs and acts upon them if the mentally handicapped people are to have important needs met, and discomfort alleviated.

Adaptability

No single profession has a pre-ordained right to care for the mentally handicapped. Their needs and problems are so diverse as to require the help of many different professions. If these professions decree rigid guidelines as to what is their work and what is not, then there will inevitably be inter-professional squabbles and demarcation disputes.

The approach to care must be an adaptable one and the attitude that certain tasks are the definite province of nurses, teachers, physiotherapists etc. must not be taken.

Sense of Humour

Many people think that mental handicap is such a sad condition that humour has no place in a mental handicap hospital and that somehow all laughter is directed *at* the unfortunate patients. This attitude would lead to a very depressing living and working environment for both staff and mentally handicapped people.

In a ward where the nurses are cheerful and enjoy laughter the mentally handicapped people are almost certain to be much happier. The nurse should know intuitively when to laugh at something which is amusing and when not to laugh at an unfortunate incident or at someone's disabilities. The mentally handicapped can often have a sense of humour and will readily share in a joke!

A Creative Imagination and Enthusiasm

The famous American nurse Annie Goodrich talked of the three phases in a nurse's development being the emotional, the technical and the creative.

The junior nurse will have an emotional response of wanting to help people; as she progresses in training she then thinks of good nursing in terms of technical skills, i.e. the setting up of infusions and learning complicated procedures. The mental handicap nursing equivalent of this phase is probably the nurse who delights in rhyming off vast numbers of obscure clinical syndromes or who relishes doing a medicine round.

Eventually it is to be hoped that the nurse reaches the creative phase, where she combines her emotional commitment, her technical skills and her realization of what the essence of good nursing is in order to plan and provide total nursing care for individual patients. This is the true art of nursing. This is where the mental handicap nurse must be especially creative in tailoring her nursing care to suit the many needs and differing personalities of the mentally handicapped people. This calls for ingenuity and an ability to adopt methods to suit individuals even in the face of opposition and apathy from patients or colleagues.

Empathy

This is probably the most important attribute that a nurse can possess. It is the ability to put yourself in another person's place at a particular moment and accurately to perceive his feelings and their meaning. An acute sense of empathy should be cultivated by every nurse.

It is a sobering exercise for a nurse, when carrying out part of a patient's nursing care, to stop and ask 'Is this how I would like this to be done if I were the patient?' In a great many cases the answer would be 'No', which means that the procedure could be done much more thoughtfully. The nurse should ask this question every time that she approaches a patient in order to perform a task.

Leadership and Supervision

Every nurse should be a leader to some degree. Leadership involves getting people to work for you to the best of their abilities and developing their various nursing skills. Leadership is usually one of three main types: autocratic; laissez-faire and democratic or creative.

AUTOCRATIC

Here the leader is all-powerful and expects her subordinates to respect her and obey her instructions. A questioning attitude is *not* encouraged by this type of leader. This form of leadership can be of use in, for instance, an accident or emergency area or an intensive-care unit, where there is no time for group decisions and where the leader is usually highly trained and experienced and is perhaps the only person in such a unit with the necessary skill and knowledge. This form of leadership has no place in mental handicap nursing.

LAISSEZ-FAIRE

This style of leadership involves minimal direction and instruction from the leader and people are left very much to their own devices. The effects of this style of 'leadership' are usually chaotic and it has no place at all in nursing.

DEMOCRATIC OR CREATIVE

This style of leadership is widely held to be the most effective and satisfactory. The democratic leader tries to instil a unity of purpose among her co-workers. She frequently asks others' opinions and values them. She makes sure that her co-workers are fully aware of what is going on within her unit. She discusses aims and plans with her staff and helps to guide them towards acceptable goals. She delegates responsibility to her staff and praises them on work well done. She gives her staff a degree of automony, allowing them to make decisions for themselves within the limits of their capabilities and experience. She plans and organizes so that things are done at the right time and in the proper way. She provides guidance to her staff and always criticizes constructively. She co-operates with other professionals, not behaving as a simple handmaiden; nor does she think that she has exclusive knowledge of her patients.

She appreciates that her staff work with her, not for her or under her. She does not ask her staff to do things which she herself would not do. She does not spend her entire day in the ward office but works with her staff and patients. She is constantly appraising her performance and that of her staff in order to see where improvements can be made.

Communication

Communication involves the exchange of ideas and information and the understanding of these by the people concerned. In a mental handicap hospital the nurse will have to be able to communicate effectively with her nursing colleagues and many different professional groups, e.g. social workers, doctors, speech therapists etc. If an effective method of communication does not exist between these co-professionals then there will be no real multi-disciplinary team effort on behalf of the mentally handicapped person. Professional isolation and inter-professional squabbles over status and role will be much more likely to occur.

What, then, are the major problems in communication that the nurse must try to overcome? They include: the limitations of the person receiving the communication; distraction of the receiver's attention, both external and internal; the unstated assumption that the receiver already knows some of what is being said; the communicator and the receiver's attitudes, beliefs and prejudices; poor presentation of the communication, i.e. incoherent delivery, unfamiliar abbreviations and the use of jargon; and the absence of channels of communication.

COMMUNICATION WITHIN THE NURSING TEAM

Written communication: clear and effective written policies and nursing instructions are of immense help in ensuring that each member of the nursing team knows the problems and agreed nursing care for the mentally handicapped people. If nursing care plans etc. are kept up to date, a new nurse should be able to come on to the ward and quickly find out each individual mentally handicapped person's problems and current nursing care.

When writing reports, assessment and nursing orders, clear simple English should be used, and the temptation avoided to embellish writing with jargon and abbreviations—it impresses no one and detracts from the comprehensibility of the work.

It is also important to be specific and to avoid vague or abstract instructions. What for instance, does: 'Push fluids' mean? 10 ml or 100 ml? It is over one hour or over 24 hours? This is really meaningless. 'Encourage socially acceptable behaviour.' What exactly *is* this 'socially acceptable behaviour'? It may mean two different things to two different nurses with the mentally handicapped person becoming confused as a result. So it is always important to try to make sure that all instructions are precise and not open to misinterpretation.

Other professionals in the ward team can help improve communication within the ward by submitting accurate assessments and descriptions of their work with mentally handicapped people for inclusion in the nursing notes. This means that the nursing staff will know exactly what their co-professionals are doing with the patients and can see how this contributes to the practice of total patient care.

EFFECTIVE COMMUNICATION

How can communication be more effective? First, it is most important to learn to be an attentive listener. The old adage that God gave us one mouth but two ears makes great sense. Few things are as infuriating as speaking to someone who is not listening or who constantly interrupts with their point of view. No matter how good someone's ideas and opinions are, they will almost certainly be disregarded or disagreed with as a reaction to their rudeness.

Think carefully before speaking. Words must be chosen carefully to minimize the chance of being misunderstood. Speak clearly and confidently; do not mumble into a book or Kardex or listeners will lose interest. Speak in language that listeners will understand. Avoid transient, trendy phrases: do not let the language used plumb the depths of 'ward situations', 'on-going situations', 'at this point in time', 'forward planning', 'feedback', or any of the host of other glib phrases intended to confer a sense of understanding and knowledge of the subject on their user—they show only a laziness in the use of language and superficiality of knowledge.

Try to be objective and avoid communicating personal prejudices to listeners. The importance of non-verbal communication must be remembered: how words are spoken, the tone of voice used, body posture, gestures and facial expressions are all very powerful channels of communication. Think of how, in *Julius Caesar,* Mark Antony stressed that Caesar was an honourable man but managed to convey the exactly opposite meaning to the crowd! How something is said is as important as what is said.

WARD MEETINGS/CASE CONFERENCES

These should be held regularly to provide an opportunity for all members of the ward team to discuss the problems and progress of particular mentally handicapped people. Any major changes in a person's care or training should be made here, when all the various professionals concerned will know about it and have the opportunity to discuss it.

The case conference also provides a good opportunity for learner nurses to present a nursing-care study at the meeting, giving full background/historical details, the various problems which the mentally handicapped person has, and detailing what specific nursing care and training he is receiving. This is a good starting point for discussion.

NURSING CARE PLANNING CONFERENCE

This should take place at the changeover of every shift. The nurse in charge of her group of mentally handicapped people should give an up-to-date report on their care and progress, mentioning any specific problems that have occurred during her shift. With the nurses on the oncoming shift, she can plan any necessary changes in nursing care and management. At this changeover the nurse in charge of the ward should give any special instructions to her staff regarding the mentally handicapped people and assign any special duties to her staff.

BUILDING GOOD INTER-PERSONAL RELATIONSHIPS

Because of their many and varied problems, the mentally handi-capped need the skills and attention of many professional groups. If these groups cannot co-operate and work in harmony with each other, then the patient ultimately suffers.

There is an abundance of prejudice within mental handicap care which would have us believe the following. Social workers are all idealistic do-gooders who are always at meetings and have no idea of the harsh realities of life for the mentally handicapped. Psychologists are people who go to university to come and tell nurses how to care for mentally handicapped people, propose endless impractical schemes, then vanish. Doctors think that they are Gods and overrule everyone's ideas and proposals. Mental handicap nurses are not really nurses, but just custodians, who have no social or educational perspectives on the problems of mental handicap. All staff in mental handicap hospitals will have heard such views as these expressed about various groups at some time or other!

How can nurses begin to establish genuinely good working relationships with fellow nurses and co-professionals? They must interact with others as they would like them to interact with them. To obtain co-operation, respect, advice or information then they must be given in equal amounts. They can try to gain the respect of fellow professionals by their demonstrations of skilled nursing and try to show that nursing involves total patient care and is not simply the practising of few skills upon an anonymous group of people. Showing a genuine interest in the work of other professionals will help, the nurse trying to tie their work in with her concepts of total nursing care, for example the way a speech therapist helps a mentally handicapped person to communicate or the way a physiotherapist helps the mentally handicapped person maintain desirable position and posture. The attitude of 'That's not my job, it's theirs' from any professional group has no place in mental handicap care and is destructive to good working relationships.

The nurse should have a cheerful, friendly approach to other professionals, and not react to them as nuisances who come to 'upset the ward routine'. Trouble should be taken to thank them for their work on the mentally handicapped person's behalf; a little gratitude and praise is a great morale booster for us all.

Finally, as Virginia Henderson said, 'No professional should make such demands of another professional that he or she is unable to fulfil his or her unique function'.

DEATH AND CARE OF THE DYING

The mental handicap hospital will be the home for many people for their entire lives and the nurse will probably have to deal with death at some point in her career.

Death is life's only certainty—Henderson reminds us that the nurse has an important role to play in helping the dying patient so that death, when it comes, is as peaceful, pain-free and dignified as possible. To do this for a dying person is not an admission of defeat but rather the end result of much thoughtful, skilled nursing care.

There is no reason to imagine that dying will be any less of a fearful and anxious occurrence for the mentally handicapped than for anyone else and the dying person will require a lot of comfort and personal attention from his nurse. If someone has lived in a ward or unit for many years, it is best if he is cared for by nurses that he knows well and with whom he has established a relationship. For the same reason the author considers it bad policy to send dying patients to an infirmary-type ward or to a general hospital unless acute general medical services are urgently required. It is far better that someone should die in familiar surroundings, being cared for by nurses that he knows well.

The mentally handicapped person's parents or relatives should be informed when death is imminent as they may well wish to be with their relative. They should be treated with tact and sympathy and offered courtesy facilities, such as meals and overnight accommodation, should they require it.

After death, the last offices and funeral arrangements should be carried out according to the hospital's policy.

The other mentally handicapped people who realize that a death has occurred should be given a simple, truthful explanation of it: death is not something to be concealed.

FIRE PREVENTION

1. Smoking is the cause either directly or indirectly of many fires in hospitals and one should ask the question: how can mentally handicapped people be protected from the careless action of individuals?

It may be necessary to withhold the right of certain mentally handicapped people to control their own cigarettes and matches, but only in extreme cases will it be necessary to stop them from smoking. However, controlled smoking is necessary if the risk of fire is to be reduced.

Designated smoking areas should be made available. Care should be taken in furnishing and equipping such a room: it may, for instance, be unwise to have fitted carpets; curtains will need to be fire resistant; and chairs should be such that it is impossible for smouldering cigarettes and matches to be caught up in the folds.

An external emergency exit, clearly marked, fire-fighting equipment and a fire-alarm should be available. Smoking should be totally banned in areas which are visited only infrequently. Those confined to bed should only be allowed to smoke when nurses are available to supervise them. There is less risk of a serious outbreak of fire in areas which are frequently visited.

Mentally handicapped people who have free access to smoking should be made regularly aware of the risks of fire, of how accidents can be avoided and of what to do if a fire does occur.

2. All electrical equipment should be periodically inspected to test its efficiency and to correct any flaws. Also, any defect noted during daily work should be reported to the engineer's department and the fire officer. The insulation around electric wiring does not last for ever, and though service may be good, it is easy to be lulled into a false sense of security. It should be mandatory that only an electrician should add extra wiring and plugs to already existing circuits and repair fuses. Proper earthing of electrical equipment is also essential.

3. There should be proper maintenance of all types of equipment, especially those worked by gas and electricity.

4. Suitable storage for all combustible materials, such as floor polish, cleaning fluids, paint, paraffin and waste paper, should be provided. Metal cupboards will be more suitable and safer than the usual wooden ones.

5. Frequent cleaning and inspection of all linen cupbords, attics, basements and storage cupboards to see that they are being properly used, and that no unauthorized storing takes place, should be undertaken.

6. Periodic fire-fighting practice should be held within the hospital so that the Fire Brigade may become familiar with the hospital, the types of ward and the equipment and its location.

7. Preparedness for an emergency is helped by regular fire drill, both for mentally handicapped people and all the hospital staff. Instructions dealing with each member on every ward must be set out so that no confusion occurs when the need arises.

8. Maintenance of escape routes is equally vital. It is also essential that they should be kept completely free from obstruction of any kind. Stair landings have a habit of becoming dumping grounds for cupboards and for sacks of soiled laundry awaiting collection.

The rooms abutting onto a corridor which is an escape route should have fire resistant doors to contain any fire which may arise inside the room in order that it will not prejudice the passage outside the door.

9. Oxygen is used in most hospitals. In the wards or departments where it is being used the following rules should be strictly adhered to:

a Smoking or naked lights should not be allowed.

b Electrical equipment, because of the possibility of sparking, may be banned.

c Metal trolleys should be earthed by a piece of metal chain trailing on the floor.

d Oil should never be used on this equipment.

e Inflammable material should not be in close proximity to it.

10. Fire-fighting equipment in the shape of portable extinguishers of a kind suited to the immediate risk should be in sufficient quantity and in suitable locations to make them readily available when required. Training in the use of such equipment must be regular and 'Fire Points' should be established where one could expect to find a fire-alarm point, a fire instruction board and-fire fighting equipment, preferably in an easily accessible and public area.

All fire-fighting equipment should be checked at least twice every year.

11. A fool-proof method of notification of an outbreak of fire, speed of notification and response to the fire-alarm are essential precautions and may render a fire harmless.

Careful Use of Fire-guards All ward fires, whether coal, gas or electric, are a potential danger and must be treated as such. Every fire in use must be shielded by a securely attached guard which must be kept locked. At times when the fire needs attention the nurse must first gather together all the requirements for the job before unlocking and removing the guard, and before leaving the fire must replace the guard and lock it in position. Attending to fires on the wards should be the responsibility of the nurse.

IF FIRE OCCURS

Evacuation The method of evacuation will depend upon the type of mentally handicapped person to be evacuated. Ambulant people can be told to leave immediately by the nearest exit and escape route. Semi-ambulant people may require some physical assistance which could be given by the more mobile patients.

The real problem arises with the non-ambulant, the removal of whom can be time consuming and physically exhausting for one person. There is no satisfactory method for quick evacuation for such patients. Every effort must therefore be made to flood the ward with staff immediately the alarm sounds in order to facilitate rapid evacuation.

Those hospitals which are situated in isolated areas and some distance from a fire service unit may find it necessary to maintain some form of hospital fire service whose members could include staff and patients. The risk of fire is ever present; it will never depart, and it is the clear duty of every member of staff to be alert to the danger of fire, to observe and anticipate danger, and to do their best to reduce or eliminate it. It is equally their duty to attend training periods so that they are fitted, as far as is practicable, to deal with any fire emergency which may arise in the course of their activities.

Fire-fighting Procedures   In the event of a fire occurring, the following routine should be observed in that section of the building affected:

1. Give the alarm.

2. Remove all mentally handicapped people from immediate danger.

3. Close all doors and windows to prevent the spread. This applies also to the exits, though they must not be locked.

4. All available staff not required to attend to the mentally handicapped people should use the fire-fighting equipment in an attempt to localize the outbreak until extra help is available.

5. Avoid panic. This can cause more danger to the mentally handicapped people than the actual fire.

CHAPTER 15

Epilepsy

INTRODUCTION

THE CARE OF THE mentally handicapped demands close attention to the problems of epilepsy. Precise figures are difficult to come by, but the incidence increases with the severity of the mental and physical handicap. In the wards of a hospital caring for the severely and profoundly mentally handicapped it is likely that at least one third will suffer from epilepsy.

The occurrence of epilepsy varies considerably in the various syndromes associated with mental handicap. In the early months of life the syndrome of infantile spasms brings the two conditions together. The majority of children who suffer from these so-called 'salaam attacks' subsequently become severely retarded, the cause being ascribed to various cerebral conditions such as malformations and brain damage, although in those children who develop normally prior to the attacks the aetiology is often unknown. From the ages of 1–6 years the two conditions are again associated in 'the Lennox syndrome', perhaps better known by the general title 'myoclonic epilepsies of early childhood'. This condition is characterized by a variety of seizures which are often extremely difficult to treat, and frequently associated with mental handicap. Epilepsy is very common in tuberous sclerosis and frequent in those suffering from cerebral palsy. It occurrs in about one third of patients with phenylketonuria and similar metabolic disorders, and in cases of localized brain damage partial seizures of focal origin are frequent.

The problems of diagnosis and treatment of epilepsy in the mentally handicapped are compounded by the difficulties they have in communicating: in addition, E.E.G. recordings are often much more difficult to obtain and may be spoiled by movement artefacts. The prodromal symptoms prior to a seizure may pass unnoticed and inability to describe sensations and feelings may make the diagnosis of temporal lobe epilepsy more difficult. The mentally handicapped child may be quite unable to convey to caring staff his discomfort and misery, caused by the side-effects or over-dosage of drugs, and runs the risk of receiving additional medication for a 'behavioural problem'. Intelligent observation and recording are the most important requisites for the proper management of epilepsy in the mentally handicapped.

CAUSATION

Epilepsy is sometimes separated into two categories—primary or *'idiopathic'*, and secondary or *'symptomatic'*. The distinction is simply between those in which no cause can be found for the seizures and those in which a probable aetiological factor is discovered. Such factors can be divided into three categories—those where they exert their effect before birth, around the time of confinement, and in early infancy. Some of the post-natal factors may of course be responsible for the development of epilepsy at a much later stage in life.

Pre-natal factors include the effects of X-rays and of teratogenic drugs. Virus infections such as rubella, cytomegalo-virus and toxoplasmosis can cause cerebral abnormalities which give rise to seizures. Genetic factors including some of the chromosome abnormalities may also be associated with epilepsy. Around the time of birth obstetric complications may lead to anoxia and physical trauma to the soft cranium, and again epilepsy may result. Post-natal factors include metabolic disturbance such as hypoglycaemia and hypocalcaemia and infections such as meningitis or encephalitis. Accidental injury may result in a subdural haematoma and of course one must also keep in mind the possibility of non-accidental injury. Vascular abnormalities such as aneurysm may lead to haemorrhage. Poisons such as lead, and intra-cerebral-space-occupying lesions also have their place in this group.

In addition to the underlying aetiology it would appear that some kind of trigger is necessary to provoke a seizure. In photosensitive epilepsy, seizures are caused by flickering light within a certain frequency and the 25 Hz and 50 Hz flicker of TV is distinctly epileptogenic. Children should be kept 4 m back from TV; susceptible individuals can view safely if one eye is covered.

In other kinds of epilepsy the trigger is less specific. Emotional stress or excitement or a sudden noise may precipitate a seizure, and infections, metabolic disturbances or fluctuating hormone levels may become triggering influences. Some drugs, notably the phenothiazines, will precipitate fits and the withdrawal of drugs can also be accompanied by an increase in the occurrence of seizures.

INVESTIGATION

It is of the utmost importance that a correct diagnosis be made in patients who are apparently suffering from epileptiform seizures. To label a patient 'epileptic' erroneously and commence appropriate long-term therapy is a clinical and social catastrophe and true epilepsy must be distinguished from such conditions as benign paroxysmal vertigo, breath-holding attacks, syncope of various causations and from manifestations of psychiatric disturbance.

While the diagnosis is largely based on a careful history involving a precise eye witness description of the events preceding the 'fit' and a detailed description of the sequence of the fit itself and of subsequent events until the patient has recovered fully, there are certain investigations which may help with the diagnosis and with the identification of the underlying cause. Routine blood and urine testing should be done, as should X-rays of skull and chest. An EEG is an essential investigation but it must be remembered that a normal EEG does not exclude the diagnosis of epilepsy. An EEG demonstrating the stigmata of epilepsy does not mean that the patient is epileptic, as a percentage of adults who never have seizures may show typical EEG abnormalities. There are also a number of other sophisticated techniques such as CAT and isotope brain scans, cerebral angiography and occasionally a lumbar puncture for CSF examination.

It cannot, however, be emphasized too strongly that the diagnosis of epilepsy is largely a clinical one, resting upon a very close observation of the patient's 'turns', and not solely upon the results of laboratory investigations.

CLASSIFICATION

The latest classification was the revision in 1980 of the Classification of the International League against Epilepsy. It distinguishes broadly between generalized seizures which are more or less symmetrical with no evidence of a focal onset, and partial seizures which start by activation of a group of neurones limited to a part of a single hemisphere of the brain. A summary of the classification is given in *Table 6*.

Table 6. Classification of seizures

Generalized Seizures
  1. Absence Seizures   —typical or atypical
  2. Myoclonic Seizures   —myoclonic jerks or clonic seizures
  3. Tonic-clonic Seizures   *—grand mal*
  4. Tonic Seizures
  5. Atonic or Akinetic   —'drop attacks'
     seizures

Partial Seizures
  1. Simple partial   —includes Jacksonian and TLE
  2. Complex partial   —impairment of consciousness
  3. Partial seizures either simple or complex evolving to generalized tonic-clonic seizures

  4. Generalized tonic-clonic seizures with EEG but no clinical evidence of focal onset

Unclassified Seizures
  (Based upon provisional 1980 Revision of Classification of the International League Against Epilepsy)

Generalized Seizures

1. ABSENCE SEIZURES

These are known in previous classifications as *petit mal*. They consist typically of abrupt onset and cessation of periods of impaired consciousness, perhaps accompanied by automatisms or some rhythmic muscle jerking. The patient does not fall to the ground or convulse in any way. An EEG taken during this attack will usually show 3 Hz 'spike and wave' discharge pattern. Some atypical absences may have a less abrupt onset and cessation and involve more change in postural tone.

2. TONIC-CLONIC SEIZURES

These are the classical *grand mal* seizures, following a typical pattern which warrants detailed description:

Prodromal Period The seizure may be preceded by vague symptoms lasting as long as 24 h which to the experienced nurse may indicate the approach of a seizure.

Aura As the seizure commences the patient may be aware of some physical or psychological sensation, often highly unpleasant, which heralds the onset and may cry out or show sudden distress or alarm before being engulfed in the seizure itself. The occurrence of an aura suggests a focal origin.

Tonic Phase The patient becomes rapidly unconscious and falls. Extensive strong muscle contraction may lead to injury to the tongue from clamping of the jaws, and cyanosis is the result of restricted breathing. This phase lasts around 15–30 s.

Clonic Phase Lasting 30–60 s or longer consists of clonic or repetitive jerking movements of the head and limbs. There may be urinary or even faecal incontinence.

After the convulsion there is a stage of unconsciousness which may last for several minutes during which the patient cannot be roused, and a period of sleep may then follow. Alternatively, he may show confusion, possibly with automatism. Transient paresis of a limb or limbs may occur (Todd's paresis) particularly if the attack has commenced focally.

Occasionally the clonic phase of a *grand mal* seizure will be followed immediately by another tonic phase and the cycle will repeat itself in a continuous convulsive state known as *status epilepticus*. It is a serious condition liable to lead to brain damage if allowed to continue for much more than 30 min, and can be life threatening. It calls for very urgent treatment.

3. MYOCLONIC SEIZURES

These consist of sudden spasmodic contraction of muscle and are commonest in infants. The sudden extension of the arms and flexion of the body inspired the term 'salaam' attacks and they may occur singly or as multiple events.

4. TONIC SEIZURES

These are *grand mal* seizures in which only the tonic phase occurs, without spasmodic jerking.

5. ATONIC OR AKINETIC SEIZURES

In these the patient becomes suddenly unconscious with loss of postural tone and falls to the ground. Consciousness usually returns within seconds and he almost immediately gets to his feet again. The suddenness of a fall can lead to injuries, often to face and head.

Partial Seizures

Seizures which commence in a localized part of the brain are described as partial seizures. They are sub-divided into simple and complex groups.

1. SIMPLE PARTIAL SEIZURES

This group includes Jacksonian or focal epilepsy which may begin distally in one limb, and temporal lobe or psychomotor seizures which provide a range of motor and sensory effects including speech difficulties, problems with recognition and understanding and sometimes a mixture of sights, sounds and smells, the total experience being on the whole usually rather frightening to the patient. Temporal lobe seizures are often accompanied by repetitive sucking or chewing movements of the mouth, or stereotypic movements of hands and head.

2. COMPLEX PARTIAL SEIZURES

These seizures involve some impairment of consciousness.

Partial seizures, whether simple or complex, may evolve gradually to a full *grand mal* or tonic-clonic seizure. The occurrence of an aura immediately before a *grand mal* suggests that the onset may have been focal and the presence of a residual paresis following the seizure may also suggest a focal origin.

Unclassified Seizures

The presence of this category indicates that there are many seizures which do not appear to fit into the classification, and a precise description of the series of events in the course of a seizure may often be of much greater value than a diagnostic label.

THE NURSING ASPECTS OF EPILEPSY

The nurse is in a unique position to make a major contribution to the care and treatment of epilepsy in the mentally handicapped. She is the one present at the onset, during its development, and after the seizure is over and her detailed observations will enable a precise diagnosis to be made and the correct treatment regime to be selected.

Questions a nurse may be able to answer include the following: Was there any precipitating factor such as previous malaise or constipation, or a fall, or perhaps a sudden fright? Immediately prior to the seizure was there any warning such as a cry? In the case of a *grand mal* seizure, how long was the tonic phase, and was there cyanosis or incontinence? Did the seizure have a focal onset and, during the clonic phase, which parts of the body were moving? How long did this last and was the person injured and did he vomit? How deeply unconscious was he during the phase of muscular relaxation and was there any evidence of post-ictal automatism or a Todd's paralysis? If he slept, for how long did he sleep and did he seem fully recovered when he awoke?

Precise answers to these questions will be of much more value than a general statement such as '*grand-mal* seizure, slow recovery.' Description of an absence, in terms of its length, and associated movements or loss of postural tone, and a description of a psychomotor attack in as precise terms as possible, will be most helpful in planning treatment.

During the seizure itself there is little indication for active intervention other than to protect the patient from self-injury, making sure that he is in a position least likely to lead to airway obstruction, especially should he vomit. The traditional technique of placing a hard object between the teeth to prevent injury to the tongue is liable to cause severe dental injury, and is therefore not now advised. Emergency treatment such as diazepam rectally will be given according to instructions and should the seizures recur or proceed to status epilepticus immediate medical advice must be sought. Continuous convulsion can lead to serious cerebral injury.

Carefully kept charts of the occurrence of seizures can be of great value, and bar-graph type of charting, showing the number of seizures occurring per week and the current drug therapy, can assist greatly in the planning of a treatment regime.

THERAPEUTIC MANAGEMENT.

The use of specific anticonvulsant drugs is a major part of the management of epilepsy and once the diagnosis is clearly established most epileptics will require long-term drug treatment. Because of this long-term feature, it is extremely important that the correct drugs should be prescribed and that the minimum number of drugs should be used to control seizures. Prior to the availability of techniques for measuring blood levels of anticonvulsants, one drug tended to be added to another in an attempt to control seizures until the patient was taking four or five drugs concurrently. Now that drug levels can readily be obtained the aim is to use the smallest number of drugs and to prescribe these in dosage which will maintain therapeutic levels.

It has recently been shown that the majority of new cases of epilepsy not associated with major neurological abnormality can be controlled by one drug. In the mentally handicapped more severe and intractable types of epilepsy are likely to be met with, and more than one anticonvulsant may be required in these cases. It should also be borne in mind that the addition of drugs to the treatment regime may not in the long run improve the seizure rate greatly, but may add the additional burden of toxic side effects. Some of the psychiatric features of the so-called 'epileptic personality' are now considered to be due to the untoward effect of long term drug therapy.

The frequency of dosage of anticonvulsants is of some importance. Those drugs which have a long 'half-life' (a term from the science of pharmacokinetics, measuring the length of time the drug persists in the blood-stream after a single dose) may only require to be given once daily, and while more frequent dosage will not be harmful a single daily dose regime is more convenient for patients on self-medication and may assist compliance where a more frequent dosage may result in omissions due to inconvenience or forgetfulness. In the case of patients taking a number of drugs a single daily dose may assist simplification and consistent medication.

The main anticonvulsant drugs in current use are:

Phenytoin (Epanutin)
Sodium valproate (Epilim)
Carbamazepine (Tegretol)
Ethosuximide (Zarontin)
Clonazepam (Rivotril)
Nitrazepam (Mogadon)
Phenobarbitone
Primidone (Mysoline)
In the treatment of status epilepticus:
Diazepam (Valium)

Lorazepam (Ativan)
Paraldehyde
Phenytoin
Chlormethiazole (Heminevrin)
ACTH

Phenytoin (diphenylhydantoin, Epanutin) is an excellent anticonvulsant for all forms of epilepsy other than *petit mal* absences and myoclonic epilepsy. It is also one of the most difficult to maintain at correct level and requires careful monitoring by blood level measurement. A dose of around 5 mg kg daily is used, to produce a serum level in the region of 40–80 µmol l. Since the drug has a long half-life the dose need normally only be given once daily. The signs of toxicity include nystagmus, ataxia, excessive salivation, vomiting and often an increase of seizure frequency. This last feature illustrates the pitfalls of dose adjustment on purely clinical grounds.

Phenytoin should be avoided where possible in young females as it has a tendency to cause increase of hair on the body and a coarsening of the features and, in addition, may produce unsightly hypertrophy of the gums.

Sodium valproate (Epilim) is of use in all forms of epilepsy, perhaps with the exception of psychomotor seizures. It is highly effective in simple absences (*petit mal*) with 3 Hz 'spike and wave' patterns in the EEG; also in *grand mal* and partial seizures other than temporal lobe epilepsy.

It should be introduced gradually and preferably given at a mealtime as it can cause gastric symptoms. It is given in a dose of 20–50 mg kg, and the dose is usually divided between morning and evening. The use of the 500 mg enteric-coated tablet may make a single daily dose feasible. Temporary thinning of the hair may occur and some patients show increase of appetite and weight gain. More serious side effects such as thrombocytopenia are rare.

Carbamazepine (Tegretol) was originally developed for the control of trigeminal neuralgia and subsequently found to have antiepileptic activity. Its particular value is in psychomotor epilepsy although it is also effective in other partial epilepsies and in generalized tonic-clonic seizures.

Its shorter half-life requires it to be given two or three times daily and it is important to start slowly, building up the dose over one or two weeks. The effective dose lies usually between 600 and 1200 mg daily and therapeutic levels are considered to be around 17–42 µmol l.

Side effects include nystagmus, inco-ordination, ataxia and drowsiness, and these are an indication for rapid reduction in the dosage.

Ethosuximide (Zarontin) is considered widely to be the first choice in the treatment of typical absences (*petit mal*) and due to its long half-life need only be administered once daily. The maximum dosage in children up to the age of six is around 500 mg daily and from 750 to 1000 mg per day in the adult. The use of this drug should be confined to those who suffer from typical absences and show the classical spike and wave EEG pattern, being rarely of value in other forms of epilepsy. Ethosuximide can cause side effects such as nausea, headache and drowsiness, and possibly behavioural disturbances. As with other drugs it should be introduced slowly to minimize these effects.

Clonazepam (Rivotril) and nitrazepam (Mogadon) are both of value in the treatment of infantile spasms (myoclonic seizures) but carry the troublesome side effects of sedation and hyper-secretion. They are rarely of use in adult forms of epilepsy.

Phenobarbitone has held a prime place in the treatment of epilepsy for many years and is an extremely effective anticonvulsant, particularly for generalised tonic-clonic seizures (*grand mal*). Despite its familiarity and relative cheapness it is rapidly losing its dominant place in the light of increasing awareness of its side effects, particularly hyperactivity, behaviour disorder, and impaired learning in children, and the tendency to depression and over-sedation in adults.

Primidone (Mysoline) is broken down in the body to phenobarbitone and phenylethylmalonamide (PEMA) and probably acts mainly by virtue of the former metabolite. It carries the same problems as phenobarbitone and if serum levels are required then it is the level of phenobarbitone in the blood that is usually measured. Owing to the shorter half-life of PEMA it may have to be given twice or three times daily.

Status Epilepticus

Diazepam (Valium) is probably the drug of first choice currently in the treatment of status epilepticus. This drug is surprisingly ineffective in controlling convulsions when given by the intramuscular route and intravenous injection carries a slight risk of temporary apnoea which could be life-threatening in the absence of the appropriate specialized facilities. For these reasons diazepam is now being used extensively by the rectal route in a dose of 0·5 mg kg in children and a single dose in adults, usually being limited to no more than 20 mg. The intravenous preparation can be injected directly into the rectum using a small plastic syringe with or without a special adaptor. A needle of course must not be used.

Effective blood levels can be obtained within ten minutes and apnoea is much less likely by this route.

Lorazepam (Ativan) is a possible alternative to diazepam for intravenous use, being less likely to cause respiratory problems.

Paraldehyde injected intrumuscularly using a glass syringe is a safe and effective agent for the control of persistent convulsions.

Phenytoin can be administered by the intravenous route, but specialized monitoring is required to deal with side effects such as cardiac arrhythmias.

Chlormethiazole (Heminerin) can also be employed as a continuous intravenous infusion, and *ACTH* may be a useful adjunct to the reduction of cerebral oedema.

General Management

Folate deficiency frequently occurs in patients on anticonvulsants, particularly phenytoin, phenobarbitone and primidone. Folate levels should be investigated at intervals and, if low, cautious replacement therapy instituted. It is thought that the effect on folic acid may be associated with the anticonvulsant action of these drugs and therefore over-enthusiastic replacement may lead to an increase in seizures, although evidence for this view is not conclusive.

Deficiency of Vitamin D may also occur in long term anticonvulsant therapy and again phenytoin, phenobarbitone and primidone have been thought to be the drugs mainly responsible. The more severely handicapped may be less exposed to sunlight and the insidious development of metabolic bone disease may be missed. The prophylactic use of Vitamin D has not been recommended but blood levels of calcium, phosphate and alkaline phosphatase should be checked from time to time and X-rays of bone structure carried out if suspicion arises.

The epileptic who is having seizures daily may require some form of protective headgear to prevent recurrent injury. Further efforts are needed to design models which will be functional, comfortable and presentable.

As regards work and leisure it will be tempting for the conscientious carer to provide safeguards against injury, but such safeguards are inevitably confining and can be a serious barrier to the individual's enjoyment of a reasonable life-style. Some balance must be found between the obvious risks of injury and the enjoyment of a free and happy life and where seizures are well controlled few restrictions need be imposed.

In the area of mental handicap the issue of driving may not often arise, but it is important to remember that an epileptic who has been free of daytime seizures for a period of three years is not debarred from holding a driving licence. This kind of enlightened legislation accepts a certain degree of risk, and in the care of the mentally handicapped epileptic a certain degree of risk must also be accepted in an attempt to ensure a reasonable quality of living.

CHAPTER 16

Drugs and their Indications

IT IS IMPORTANT for nurses to have a knowledge of the commoner drugs in use today. The list given here is by no means complete since the wide variety of compounds nowadays available includes many examples of groups of drugs where usefulness, advantages and disadvantages overlap to a very considerable degree and the ultimate choice by the clinician of a particular preparation is determined largely by fashion and personal preference. The major tranquillizers are a striking example of a group where such duplication occurs.

It is also important to be aware that advances are being made and that certain newer drugs are found to be better than their predecessors in some way or another. Here an example can be found among the antidepressants where mianserin has been found to have fewer unwanted effects. For this reason prescribing policy must never be static, but instead it must be kept under constant review as new compounds become available.

Drugs in common use are divided for convenience into certain classes according to the prominent action produced by them. The drugs included here are listed according to this system of classification and set out in tabular form as follows:

1. *Sedatives* (*Table 7*). These are drugs mainly used to help sleep.

2. *Anticonvulsants* (*Table 8*). These are drugs used to treat the various forms of epilepsy. Current opinion favours the use of one anticonvulsant only rather than the use of combinations of two, three or more drugs as has been employed in the past.

3. *Antispasmodics* (*Table 9*). These are drugs which are used in psychiatric practice to control the disorders of movement and muscle tone which can occur as an unwanted effect of the major tranquillizers.

4. *Tranquillizers* (*Table 10*). These are drugs which calm the patient and reduce tension, agitation and anxiety. Major tranquillizers are used mainly when there is a psychotic background and they have a specific antipsychotic effect, but they can also be given to non-psychotic patients to control anxiety symptoms. Minor tranquillizers are for use in non-psychotic patients.

5. *Antidepressant drugs* (*Table 11*). These can be used to elevate mood in all kinds of psychiatric illness, but are less effective when the mood change is an understandable response to definite environmental factors.

6. *Miscellaneous* (*Table 12*). In the miscellaneous group lithium is used to reduce mood fluctuation in affective illnesses while ECT continues to have a unique and invaluable role in the treatment of severe depression.

Table 7. Sedatives

Drug (barbiturate)	Trade name	Average daily dose	Indications	Side-reactions	Nursing care
Amylobarbitone	Amytal	100–200 mg	Sleeplessness	Physical addiction with delirium tremens or epilepsy on sudden withdrawal	Treatment for over-dosage. Aim to maintain respiration and eliminate the drug by stomach lavage and i.v. fluids
Chloral hydrate		0·3–2 g	Sleeplessness	Dyspepsia and gastric irritation	Must be given as a mixture well diluted; withdrawn from patient gradually
Dichloral phenazone	Welldorm	650 mg–1·3 g	Sleeplessness	Skin rashes, nausea	Avoid administration over long periods because of dependency. For over-dosage: gastric lavage or emetic strychnine 8 mg hypodermically. Artificial respiration
Paraldehyde		10–20 ml	To quieten and induce sleep in the mentally disordered. Status epilepticus	Erythematous rash, gastric irritation, toxic hepatitis. May cause abscesses by i.m. use. Plastic syringes contra-indicated	
Nitrazepam	Mogadon	5–10 mg	Sleeplessness	Morning drowsiness	
Glutethimide	Doriden	250–500 mg	Sleeplessness	Nausea, skin rashes	
Temazepam	Normison	10–30 mg at bed-time	Sleeplessness	Morning drowsiness	
Flurazepam	Dalmane	15–30 mg at bed-time	Sleeplessness	Morning drowsiness	

Table 8. Anticonvulsants

Drug	Trade name	Average daily dose	Indications	Side-reactions	Nursing care
Ethosuximide	Zarontin	500–1500 mg	Epilepsy—*petit mal*	Gastro-intestinal disturbance, agranulocytosis	Frequent blood-count
Phenytoin sodium	Epanutin Epitoin	200–600 mg	Epilepsy—*grand mal* and focal	Gum hyperplasia, ataxia, nystagmus, tremors, rashes, headache, blood disorders including megaloblastic anaemia	15 mg folic acid daily for megaloblastic anaemia
Primidone	Mysoline	Adults: 0·5–2 g Children: 0·25–1·0 g in divided doses	Epilepsy—*grand mal* and focal	Mild and transitory giddiness, nausea and vomiting. Occasionally megaloblastic anaemia	15 mg folic acid daily for megaloblastic anaemia
Sulthiame	Ospolot	200–600 mg	*Grand mal* and focal epilepsy, particularly when associated with behaviour disorder	Paraesthesia of the face and extremities, tachypnoea, dyspnoea, headache, giddiness, ataxia, anorexia, nausea, loss of weight	
Carbamazepine	Tegretol	Initially 100 mg once or twice a day. 800–1200 mg daily for adults	*Grand mal* and focal epilepsy. Trigeminal neuralgia	Drowsiness, dizziness rashes, dermatitis, aplastic anaemia, jaundice. Do not give in early pregnancy. Do not give with MAOI therapy	Regular blood-counts
Clonazepam	Rivotril	4–9 mg daily in adults. Infants (0–1 year) 0·5–1 mg daily. Ampoules for status	All clinical forms of epilepsy in infants, children or adults, especially typical or atypical *petit mal*	Fatigue, somnolence, co-ordination disturbances, salivary hypersecretion, bronchial hypersecretion	Avoid alcohol and driving. Do not give in pregnancy

Drug	Name	Dose	Indications		
Diazepam	Valium	15–30 mg daily for adults. Ampoules for rectal i.v. or i.m. use in status. 0·15–0·25 mg/kg of body weight. Can be repeated 1 hour later; may be put in a drip	Status epilepticus	Ataxia with big doses: i.v. injection rarely causes collapse, hypotension and apnoea	With i.v. injection have facilities for resuscitation available (Lorazepam can be given rapidly i.v.)
Sodium valproate	Epilim	600–1600 mg daily in adults	All types of epilepsy including *petit mal*. In women of child-bearing age use only in severe cases or resistance to other drugs	Minor gastric irritation with nausea. Partially excreted in the urine in the form of ketone bodies, hence false positives when testing the urine of possible diabetics	Well tolerated with other anticonvulsant drugs. May potentiate MAOI. Teratogenic in animals, therefore avoid in pregnancy unless essential
Phenobarbitone	Gardenal Luminal	30–120 mg	*Grand mal* and focal epilepsy	As for amylobarbitone sodium. Paradoxically may cause hyperkinetic behaviour in children and confusion in the elderly	As for amylobarbitone sodium. Sudden withdrawal from epileptic patient may lead to further seizures

Table 9. Antispasmodics

Drug	Trade name	Average daily dose	Indications	Side-reactions	Nursing care
Benzhexol	Artane	5–20 mg in divided doses	Drug-induced, Parkinsonism	Drowsiness, dryness of mouth, nausea and vomiting. Delusions and confusion	May precipitate acute glaucoma
Orphenadrine	Disipal	50–150 mg	As for benzhexol	As for benzhexol	As for benzhexol
Benztropine	Cogentin	0·5–6 mg	As for benzhexol	As for benzhexol	As for benzhexol
Procyclidine hydrochloride	Kemadrin	Oral 7·5–30 mg in divided dose, i.m. 10–20 mg	As for benzhexol	As for benzhexol	As for benzhexol
Tetrabenazine	Nitoman	75–200 mg in divided doses	Tardive dyskinesia. Abnormal movement in Huntingdon's chorea	Drowsiness, dyspepsia, hypertension, Parkinsonism in high dosage	Should not be given with MAOI drugs

Table 10. Tranquillizers

Drug	Trade name	Average daily dose	Indications	Side-reactions	Nursing care	Remarks
a. Major Tranquillizers (Oral)						
Chlorpromazine	Largactil	75–800 mg orally daily. 25–100 mg by injection, repeated as required three or four times in 24 hours	Excitement or extreme agitation in psychoses, mental tension, excitable states in the mentally handicapped person	Drowsiness, hypotension, Parkinsonism, dry mouth, jaundice, light sensitivity, blurred vision. May precipitate or potentiate epilepsy Dystonia	Observe for the appearance of any side-reactions and for the appearance of skin disorders. The nurse must take precautions and not handle the drug unless she is wearing rubber gloves	Patients have to be kept in a supine position for at least 1 hour after injection
Thioridazine	Melleril	30–600 mg daily	Neurosis and psychosis	Drowsiness, dizziness, hypotension, dryness of mouth, transient oedema		Does not cause skin reaction in sunlight
Haloperidol	Seranace Haldol	1·5–40 mg daily	Psychotic disorders especially mania	Parkinsonism may be prominent		(Not for severely depressed patients.) Useful for extreme and rapid action
Droperidol	Droleptan	5–15 mg i.v. Up to 10 mg i.m. 5–20 mg oral	Psychotic disorders especially mania— for rapid calming. In anaesthetics			

Table 10. Tranquillizers (cont.)

Drug	Trade name	Average daily dose	Indications	Side-reactions	Nursing care	Remarks
Pimozide	Orap	2–8 mg once daily	Schizophrenia, chronic anxiety, monosymptomatic hypochondriacal psychosis	Extrapyramidal effects less common		Once daily dosage an advantage
Perphenazine	Fentazin Trilofon	8–24 mg	Anxiety and agitated and excited patients	Dystonic reaction may be severe		More potent and less toxic than Largactil
Trifluoperazine	Stelazine	Mild cases 2–4 mg daily chronic or acute cases 15–30 mg daily	Less sedative than chlorpromazine	Restlessness and akathisia		
b. Major Tranquillizers (Depot)						
Fluphenazine enanthate injection	Moditen enanthate	25 mg every 2 or 3 weeks i.m.	As for chlorpromazine. Chronic schizophrenia	As for chlorpromazine	Watch for extra pyramidal symptoms which respond well to antispasmodics	Give small test dose before starting treatment
Fluphenazine decanoate injection	Modicate	25–50 mg every 1–3 weeks i.m.	As for chlorpromazine. Chronic schizophrenia	As for chlorpromazine	As above	As above
Flupenthixol decanoate injection	Depixol	20–40 mg every 2–4 weeks i.m. depot injections	Schizophrenia. Its alerting reaction is particularly useful in the withdrawn, apathetic or depressed patient	Extrapyramidal reactions less common	May cause overactivity	As above

Flupenthixol	Fluanxol	See later			Drowsiness can occur and thus care should be taken with patients who drive or operate machinery
Cis-flupenthixol decanoate	Clopixol	100–400 mg every 2–4 weeks i.m.	Psychosis associated with aggression		
Fluspirilene	Redeptin	2 mg/solution for injection. Given weekly up to 20 mg	Schizophrenia	Extrapyramidal reaction less common, Fatigue and upper gastro-intestinal symptoms such as nausea and vomiting can occur. May potentiate epilepsy	
c. Minor Tranquillizers					
Diazepam	Valium	8 mg–40 mg in divided doses	Anxiety and tension in the absence of psychosis	Drowsiness, disinhibition, constipation	Dependency can occur with prolonged use. Abrupt withdrawal can precipitate epilepsy. Avoid alcohol
Chlordiaze-poxide	Librium	15–100 mg	As for diazepam	As for diazepam	As for diazepam

Table 10. Tranquillizers (cont.)

Drug	Trade name	Average daily dose	Indications	Side-reactions	Nursing care	Remarks
Oxazepam	Serenid-D	45–90 mg daily	As for diazepam	As for diazepam		As for diazepam
Lorazepam	Ativan	3–7·5 mg daily in divided doses	As for diazepam	As for diazepam		As for diazepam
Chlormethiozole edisylate	Heminevrin	1–4 g	Agitation and restlessness, delirium tremens and drug withdrawal states	Sneezing, conjunctivitis, nausea, hypotension		As useful sedative with anticonvulsant properties. Can lead to dependency with prolonged administration
Potassium clorazepate	Tranxene	15 mg	As for diazepam	As for diazepam		

Table 11. Antidepressants

Drug	Trade name	Average daily dose	Indications	Side-reactions	Remarks
Monoamine oxidase inhibitors					
Phenelzine	Nardil	45 mg	Depression	Oedema, hypotension nausea	All MAOI drugs produce profound hypertension when taken with certain drugs (amphetamines, opiates, tricyclic antidepressants, barbiturates, tranquillizers) and foods containing tyramine (cheese, yeast, marmite, broad beans)
Isocarboxazid	Marplan	40 mg	Depression	Coryza-like symptoms, oedema, hypotension vertigo	
Tranylcypromine	Parnate	20 mg	Depression	Restlessness, dizziness, dry mouth, headache, agitation	
Tricyclic and related compounds					
Trimipramine	Surmontil	Up to 150 mg	Depression	Dry mouth, oedema, pruritus, hypotension, blurred vision, retention of urine, drowsiness, should not be given at the same time as or within 14 days of patient having an MAOI	Sedating. Tricyclic and related drugs should be given only with extreme caution when antihypertensive medication is already being prescribed
Amitriptyline	Tryptizol	Up to 150 mg	Depression	Dry mouth, oedema, pruritus, hypotension, blurred vision, retention of urine, drowsiness, should not be given at the same time as or within 14 days of patient having an MAOI	Sedating. As above

Table 11. Antidepressants (*cont.*)

Drug	Trade name	Average daily dose	Indications	Side-reactions	Remarks
Doxepin	Sinequan	30–150 mg	Depression		An effective anxiolytic
Imipramine	Tofranil	Up to 150 mg	Depression	Dry mouth, oedema, pruritus, hypotension, blurred vision, retention of urine, drowsiness, should not be given at the same time as or within 14 days of patient having an MAOI	Less sedating
Dothiepin	Prothiaden	Up to 150 mg	Depression		Elderly patients may tolerate this tricyclic better. Sedating
Mianserin	Bolvidon, Norval	Up to 120 mg	Depression		Causes fewer anticholinergic side effects such as dry mouth, blurred vision and retention

Maprotiline	Ludiomil	Up to 150 mg	Depression		Useful if there is co-existing cardiac disease. Antiaggressive
Nomifensine	Merital	Up to 150 mg	Depression	Dry mouth, oedema, pruritus, hypotension, blurred vision, retention of urine, drowsiness, should not be given at the same time as or within 14 days of patient having an MAOI	
Clomipramine	Anafranil	Up to 150 mg	Depression		Sedating useful when phobic or obsessive/compulsive features are present. May be more rapid if given i.v.
Trytophan	Pacitron	Up to 6 g	Depression	When given along with MAOI it may provoke a reaction resembling alcohol intoxication	Has a different mode of action from all other antidepressants in that it is a precursor of one of the neurotransmitters. May be more rapid in action
Flupenthixol	Fluanxol	Up to 3 mg	Depression	Not recommended for over-active, agitated patients. May cause restlessness or Parkinsonism	
Trazodone	Molipaxin	Single dose up to 100 mg	Depression	Sedating	Useful when there is co-existing heart disease

Table 12. Miscellaneous group

Drug	Trade name	Average daily dose	Indications	Side-reactions	Nursing care
Benperidol	Anquil	0·25–1·5 mg in divided doses	Control of deviant and antisocial sexual behaviour. Adults only	May potentiate the action of opiates, barbiturates and other neuroleptics	Regular blood counts and liver function tests during prolonged therapy
Cyproterone acetate	Androcur	Up to 200 mg	Excessive sexual drive in males when associated with deviance or violence	Tiredness, irreversible gynaecomastia, reversible infertility	Regular checks of liver function are required
Lithium compounds Lithium carbonate	Camcolit	250–1500 mg in divided doses	Manic states and to prevent mood swings in relapsing affective psychoses	Vomiting, ataxia, drowsiness, coarse tremor, dysarthria, confusion and coma	Patient's dose controlled by regular blood tests to assess serum level
Lithium carbonate	Priadel Phasal				
Baclofen	Lioresal	Up to 60 mg for adults	For spasticity. May reduce self-mutilation	Confusion, drowsiness, hypotonia	

CHAPTER 17

The Disturbed Mentally Handicapped Child

MENTAL ILLNESS OR UNCOMPLICATED DELAY?

ALTHOUGH MENTALLY HANDICAPPED children sometimes seem to behave strangely, or inexplicably, this does not necessarily mean that they are mentally ill. Mental handicap and mental illness are two very distinct conditions. Both people of average intelligence and of defective intelligence can be either mentally ill or mentally healthy.

Severe delay in mental development, for instance, often causes apparent detachment, bizarre mannerisms and repetitive movements of the body. If the mentally handicapped person has a mental age of less than one, he is not mentally ill because he shows such behaviour. The normal child in infancy is often to be seen holding up one hand close to his face, and intently looking at it, clasping hands together or rubbing them, playing with his fingers, opening or closing his fists. The normal infant may not make any response when a strange object, or person, goes out of his immediate field of interest. The baby in a pram often spends his time reproducing movements that he made first of all by chance, spinning or throwing objects, repeatedly turning over objects to examine them.

We have to ask about such mannerisms—are they what we would normally expect of a child of that mental age or are they *out of step*? The extended infancy and toddlerhood of the mentally handicapped child will mean that there are many times that we have to ask this type of question, in particular again when sexual curiosity arises. Underclothes exert a common fascination for the normal 4-year-old and so also for the mentally handicapped child of 9 with a mental age of 4.

The mannerisms of infancy tend to be rather persistent in the mentally handicapped child. This is to some extent because the mentally handicapped child does find language a bewildering and difficult barrier often, and resorts to the easiest ways out, which are mannerisms and gestures which he knows to be safe and comforting and often quite communicative. We all know the mother who is always complaining that her mentally handicapped child is imitating all the mannerisms at special school and none of the language! Mentally handicapped children often revert to the gesture of vacuous smiling as being socially the next best thing to the tiresome tactic of speaking. They are impulsive and so resort to the easiest strategy.

ILLNESSES STEMMING FROM THE ENVIRONMENT

When the child's behaviour cannot be just ascribed to developmental delay, if, for example, his mannerisms are excessive—excessive headbanging, self-mutilation or excessive anxiety or aggressive behaviour—then we should consider whether the child is *mentally ill* and look for causes and cures. The first place to look is in the immediate environment; that means the child's home, his family, the people who are close to him, at home or in the ward or school.

This search is still likely to find that the child is not ill at all. He may be showing 'disturbed' behaviour as a *healthy response!* The child's unhappiness may be reasonable grief at the loss of a room-mate, reasonable anger at the loss of a privilege, or reasonable apathy at the lack of stimulation in his environment.

The hospital ward is often accused of being the chief culprit in an unstimulating environment, but the mother of the mentally handi-capped child can equally be a poor stimulator by leaving him for prolonged periods in a pram, or else, out of her own feelings of rejection, finding herself unable to communicate with the child.

The environment may conversely be too overstimulating; as in a home chaotic with mother–father dissension, drunkenness, infidelity and uncertainty. At school, too, insecurity is demoralizing and unsettling to any child, mentally handicapped or not. Factors such as a work level much above the child's apparent capabilities, or a special school, training centre, or remedial class which is over-crowded or where there are frequent teacher/pupil changes, will result in inattentiveness and distractibility—*a reactive behaviour disorder*. The occurrence of any environmentally determined behaviour depends on the setting and the consequences of the behaviour. Change either and the behaviour will change.

Case 1

Bridget is 10. She suffers from severe mental handicap and epilepsy. She was admitted for assessment and to give her mother relief. Her mother also has another daughter, a 7-year-old, Barbara, also mentally handicapped (mildly) and more of a behaviour problem. Bridget was talking and was in a walkie pen at 10 months when she had a stroke—febrile cerebral throm-bosis, which resulted in her being paralysed on the right-hand side.

On examination, she was a pretty child, who soon showed her determined personality—flapping her good arm when she was frustrated and using single words at the 1-year level effectively. Her motor output was appro-priate for a $1\frac{1}{2}$-year-old. She was also found to have a hemianopia (blindness on the left side of her vision) by developmental screening (Sheridan method). Her hearing was intact (Stycar method). Her play was at the $1\frac{1}{2}$-year level and she performed at 1 year 6 months on the Vineland and Progressive Assessment Charts. She could use her spastic arm as an effective weapon. She could build a tower of four bricks and could scribble. She was not fully toilet trained. By Woodward's tests she was shown to be at the infantile stage of acting on objects to reproduce, repetitively, pleasurable effects. She was prone to reach out clumsily with clawing movements on her blind side, and enjoyed precipitating photic fits by pulling at venetian blinds, looking sideways at windows and tugging at curtains.

Impression A severely retarded child—developmental delay—healthy response in organically handicapped child. Maladaptive behaviour likely to increase in response to rewarding consequences.

Management Taking her sister's interests into account, as well as Bridget's training needs—which include a behavioural analysis and modifying her environment—admission to residential care on a 5-day-week basis was arranged. Medication for epilepsy reviewed.

Case 2

Barbara, her sister, is 7. She had few toys in early childhood. Mother said, 'It wouldn't have been possible. Bridget would take everything away from her and she quite early started to knock Barbara about. I never got peace to feed Barbara.' At school entry she was found by the Educational Psychologist to have an IQ of 60 and placed in a special school, which she found boring. At home she showed considerable behavioural problems: babyish poking and nipping and imitating her older sister. She showed a poorly veiled hostility towards her mother's martyred behaviour. The home was geared for the profoundly handicapped older sister. There were no curtains, no sharp edges lest Bridget fall against them. When Bridget was admitted to hospital Mother said that for the first time the family had been able to go out for a walk. Barbara related quite well with her elder damaged sister. Bridget would sit gravely and appear to listen to what her younger sister would say and then make her own contact, partly by speech and partly by poking. Following the admission of her elder sister, the relationship between Barbara and her mother steadily improved and her intelligence quotient at the last testing was 72.

Impression Reactive behaviour disorder. Understandable resentment at her mother's overprotectiveness of her elder sister.

Management No specific treatment as the admission of her sister resolved the problems. Transfer to remedial classes in ordinary school under consideration.

A traumatic event—for example taking a child unsedated for a lumbar puncture—may lead to a psychoneurosis, such as a phobia for white coats. Prolonged thoughtlessness in the environment can have similar results:

Case 3

Katrina is 12. Her parents are professional people and her mild brain damage is attributed to prematurity. She caused little problems in infancy or early school and was able to go to the ordinary school as her IQ was 71. When it came to secondary school she became very different—disobedient and aggressive, leaving the classroom, tearing up her school-books and eventually refused altogether to go to school. The very word 'school' would make her flap her arms and stutter. The environmental change to having several teachers and having to move from one classroom to another, away from the cosiness of the normal primary class, was overwhelming. She found it difficult to adjust to more than one teacher and she could not often find the way from class to class in the large school. Katrina did not receive understanding at home and was forced, for several months, wretchedly to continue baffled and demoralized. She then became phobic and refused completely to go to school.

Impression   Psychoneurotic disorder.

Management   Counselling parents to accepting their daughter's limitations, transfer to special school.

If these factors are not changed, if uncertainty or insecurity is prolonged in the house or in the hospital, more lasting disorders, difficult to eradicate, may arise. The child may develop *childhood depression* or a *psychosomatic illness*, i.e. an illness such as asthma or cyclical vomiting. 'Depression' in itself may appear as weeping or tantrums, but equally commonly may disguise itself as a psychosomatic illness, or as an aggressive or acting-out one.

Case 4

Robert is 12. He was referred with nervous tics, stammering and a skin rash. He is a mildly handicapped boy of IQ 65. He had a history of minor epilepsy since the age of 2 months. The onset of the nervous symptoms had been directly following the death of his 13-year-old brother from leukaemia the year before. On examination he had a facial tic and a vocal tic, was generally very excitable and cried easily. He had an urticarial rash which got much worse during the excitement of the examination.

Valium, a minor tranquillizer, helped the boy to settle at school, but it was only after intensive work with his mother that it was found that she was suffering from a depression. She had been unable to grieve for the death of her son and, by working hard and shutting herself off from the thought of her son and from discussing it with her husband, continued in a state of bereavement which was affecting her live son.

Impression   Psychosomatic symptoms resulting from anxiety and grief about his mother's emotional ill health.

Management   Continuation of medication, combined with treatment of mother's depression.

If between the ages of 6 months and 5 years, emotional bonds are thoroughly disrupted and the child does not develop a basic trust with a single loved figure in the home, or foster home, then permanent damage, irremediable scarring, is likely to occur to his personality and he may then develop a *personality disorder* with shallowness in affections, difficulty in personal relationships and preference for immediate satisfaction of his own desires without real care for others.

Case 5

Tommy is 14. He was referred by the Children's Panel because he had been found strangling rare birds in the park's aviary. He was also soiling. He showed persistent vomiting in infancy. The home broke up when he was 2 after 6 months of considerable disharmony. He was soiling, smearing and biting himself prior to the parents' separation. At that time also he was showing general slow psychomotor development. Thereafter he had been cared for in the local authority children's home and with two different foster parents, who had to give up through their own ill health. When tested at age 4, Tommy was found to be only at the 2-year-old level mentally and was also only 94 cm tall, two standard deviations below normal. He had only a few words and no grammar and, at that time, was seen to be indiscriminate in his friendships, to run readily to anybody and not to be indicating his toilet needs. In school he was aggressive and uncaring about the results of his aggression upon others. He truanted frequently and was heedless of sanctions. Tommy could give no reason why he strangled the birds with his bare hands. He could not play at all in the playroom to give us any hint as to why he had acted in this way. All the social workers and doctors and nurses who have ever dealt with him have stated sadly, 'We have never been able to get to know Tommy.'

Impression Personality disorder following severe loss and lack of emotional bonds at a critical time in the development of personality.

Management Admission to a hospital unit which is organized as a therapeutic community. If such a concrete object lesson in living and working with others does not improve his interpersonal relationships after 2–3 years, transfer to a unit run on token economy system will be considered.

These illnesses, which all can be said to stem from the environment, are a continuum—they merge into each other as the degree of illness increases. If a reactive behaviour disorder goes on long enough it becomes a psychoneurotic disorder, or a psychosomatic disorder and then can become engrained into a personality disorder.

These disorders are eminently treatable in their early stages and this depends on the psychiatric and social worker team's ability to effect environmental change. This will be by working with the mother, if the child is at home. The team tries to mend the dislocation that has occurred between her and her mentally handicapped child, whether this is due to overprotectiveness or rejection, and likewise also in the ward or the children's home by finding what has caused the dislocation there. Sometimes satisfactory change cannot be managed in the home or ward and it may be then that the child has to be transferred. It is occasionally found that the child who is aggressive and acting-out in one living unit becomes calm and biddable in another. Such changes should not be contemplated lightly when an environmental cause has not been identified, but can be justifiable in the last resort.

ILLNESSES STEMMING FROM THE CHILD'S DISORDER

Overactivity

This is one of the severest problems with which the mentally handicapped present and also one of the most resistant to treatment. If the child is very young it is important to make sure that the activity is excessive and not just the bustling rummaging of a toddler. Hyperkinesis is an excessive amount of mobility, which is inappropriate in a given environmental situation. It is continuous, fragmentary, irritating. If you restrain the child he will become overactive. An environment with plenty of space does decrease it. Hyperkinesis generally gets less as the child grows older and, particularly if the child is of normal or approaching normal intelligence, then we can offer some hope to the parents that it will decrease. With profoundly handicapped children we simply do not know whether the hyperkinesis will resolve with age. The response of hyperkinesis to drugs is unpredictable. Sometimes hyperkinesis is due to epileptic discharges. If an ECG shows that the overactive child has a 'spike and wave' discharge, i.e. *petit mal*, then ethosuxamide or sodium valproate helps. If the child has a temporal lobe discharge, the drug of choice is carbamazepine.

It is important not to use phenobarbitone as this has a disinhibiting 'intoxicating' effect on children and can make them very overactive.

For those without abnormal signs on their ECG amphetamine (the same drug that causes restlessness and wakefulness in adults) paradoxically produces calmness in the overactive brain-damaged child. Medication should start at 5 mg and then increase to quite large doses of 30–40 mg per day, given in the morning, so as not to cause any sleeplessness at night. Chlorpromazine is the choice if amphetamines fail. There is no evidence that other major tranquillizers are significantly better.

Case 6

Marjory is 9 and her overactivity is becoming less marked now. Her birth was normal although she weighed 5 kg She was sitting up at 6 months and walking at $1\frac{1}{2}$ years. She was babbling normally at 1 year and her speech appeared to be developing well until she was 21 months when she developed a measles-like skin rash and a high temperature, which lasted a few days, faded and then returned. After that she made no further developmental progress. Her father was in the Air Force and the family left for Singapore, so she received only discontinuous medical and educational advice. Tranquillizers certainly did not work; if anything they seemed to make her more active. She would remain awake for most of the night. Her parents often had to take it in shifts to look after her. On examination, Marjory's motor output was very high; she was extremely distractible. Although her mental age was that of a 4-year-old, she had the distractibility of a $1\frac{1}{2}$-year-old. Neurologically she did not show any gross neurological signs, but did show generally poor posture and balance. When excited, she would jump up on her toes like a bird, flapping her hands.

Impression   Brain damage: hyperkinesis.

Treatment   Amphetamines prescribed. They made her much more calm but, eventually after some four weeks, the effects wore off. Nurses stopped her cat-napping during the day to avoid nocturnal wakefulness and she was transferred to an open-plan ward where there was much more space for her to run around and fewer small children around to make the nurses anxious that she might accidentally strike.

Stereotypes

Mannerisms are of developmental origin but often remain in an inappropriate manner in people who have developed beyond the developmental stage of mannerisms. They are then called stereotypes and we attribute their continuation to the relief of anxiety they provide, by regression to a routine which is pleasurable and which insulates the child from a confusing or boring world.

If the stereotype behaviour is so excessive that it is tiring to the profoundly handicapped person, then behaviour therapy (that is positive and negative rewards for reduction or increase respectively in stereotype behaviour) can be helpful.

Territoriality

This is a developmental feature found in the profoundly handicapped child who is inconsiderately moved from his favourite seat in one part of the ward or occupation centre, and becomes inordinately disturbed. Territoriality may be a crucially adaptive primitive form of social organization, human as with many simpler species and, if upset, the results are as catastrophic as putting a canary in the territory of a bunch of sparrows. There will be apparently inexplicable behaviour disturbances and the risk of injury to the hapless intruder.

Soiling (Encopresis) and Bedwetting (Enuresis)

These can be a symptom of psychoneurosis, physical illness or developmental delay. Developmental delay, although the simplest to understand, is perhaps the most difficult to treat because training can be achieved—though it seems trite to say so—only by persistence and genuine pleasure at the child's efforts. Irritability, hurriedness and disgust will result in failure. The commonest cause of a child's failure to become dry at night is anxiety. He fears a vicious circle of escalating consequences of repeated wetness. Sometimes, of course, bedwetting can be a protest and used as a weapon by the child against his parents. For both causes, however, an antidepressant (Tryptizol), in doses of 25 mg per night, both relaxes the child and tightens the sphincter at the bladder outlet. If this does not work in children over 7 years, training can be accelerated by behavioural techniques in the form of a wet alarm pad. The fluid intake is supplemented to increase the frequency of urinations during the night and make training take less time. The alarm rings when the pad becomes wet and this unpleasant noise is eventually avoided when the bladder is full by the child rising to go to the toilet. This avoidance conditioning is usually achieved, if applied conscientiously, in about four nights. The child should not be left lying on the wet pad as burning can result, particularly if the pad is not adequately covered with a sheet. This treatment is effective with children so low in intelligence as to be untestable and children without even any language and adults with long histories of incontinence—almost everyone can be toilet trained!

Epilepsy

This is sometimes a cause of inexplicable unprovoked aggression or moodiness. The treatment of epilepsy in children places major and correct emphasis on preventing fits. This is of critical importance in avoiding the deterioration in intelligence. The more fits a child has, the more he falls, the more he bangs his head, the more absences he has from the world, the more he is likely to starve his brain of oxygen and, eventually, the more his IQ falls.

Drug treatment on the other hand does not appear to affect intelligence. Mother or nurse will soon know for the individual child what are that child's individual common precipitants. These are likely to be in the following order: emotional activity, fatigue, sleep itself. Abrupt withdrawal or reduction of anticonvulsant medication, certain drugs such as the phenothiazine drugs (Largactil) and the tricyclics (the antidepressants, such as Tofranil or Tryptizol) can also make fits more likely. The professional also has to be on the lookout for the unusual precipitants and to *ask* about them. The flicker of television, sunshine filtering through venetian blinds, even the reading of specific words and the hearing of specific sounds can fire off fits and status epilepticus (continuous seizures). Severe brain damage will result if the seizures are prolonged and even death can occur.

The prevention of fits has its problems—drowsiness through change in the child's tolerance, and unsteadiness through the toxic effects of certain of the anticonvulsants (notably Mysoline) on the balance area of the brain (cerebellum). If a known epileptic child does not have the occasional fit, there is some basis for the belief that he will become moody and irritable (epileptic dysthymia) so that occasional fits are even encouraged by lowering the anticonvulsant dose or even more occasionally ECT is instituted. The term 'temporal lobe epilepsy' refers to fits, seizures arising in the temporal lobe, and associated with an aura, a smell, an unusual taste or an unusual feeling in the epigastrium and followed by a period of altered consciousness and occasionally aggressive behaviour but not usually actual unconsciousness. Attempts to ascribe epileptic behaviour disturbances of the mentally handicapped to temporal lobe epilepsy without firm EEG evidence should be resisted. In general, the more normally the handicapped epileptic child is treated the fewer behaviour disturbances he shows and also there is better overall control of his fits.

CHILDHOOD PSYCHOSES

The reason for giving particular attention to the childhood psychoses is not their commonness (early infantile autism only affects about 4 in every 10 000 schoolchildren, for instance) but because, by the signs and symptoms they show, these illnesses are particularly graphic in helping us to understand the symptoms and signs and the seemingly strange clinical features that we see in other mentally handicapped children.

Early Childhood Autism
Early childhood autism is commonly defined as a disorder evident before 30 months of age in which there is a profound failure to develop normal social relationships together with delayed and deviant language development and the presence of compulsive

phenomena. Many autistic children are intellectually retarded. These tend to show more resistance to change than the smaller numbers who are of normal non-verbal intelligence. Those of normal intelligence show a greater variety of rituals. Almost all show retarded language development

Psychosis of early onset (early infantile autism) is now known to be a *different* entity from late onset psychosis (LOP) in childhood. Early infantile autism starts in the first three years of life. In fact, most patients seem abnormal from birth. Mother commonly reports, 'He didn't seem to want to live. He just lay there. He was so quiet. He would have died if I hadn't fed him.' More seem to be first-born boys and more seem to be from higher social classes. Some autistic children are normal at birth and develop normally for many months even to the stage of speech acquisition. Then there occurs an infectious illness, usually mild and viral in origin. The child's progress stops and autistic features appear. In such 'secondary autistics' neurological signs of deficit may be detected.

In recent years the numbers of autistic children seem to have started to diminish, possibly due to the improved neonatal paediatric techniques, so that fewer babies are anoxic in the neonatal period, and due also to better herd resistance to viruses in the early years.

There are nine main diagnostic points, which a recent study has shown to be in the following order of importance.

1. ABSENT OR DELAYED SPEECH DEVELOPMENT

The child may have no speech, or if he has speech it may seem delayed at the vocalization, the one-word, the two-word utterance or the telegrammatic stages of speech development. He may show echolalia (repeating the last bit of a sentence back without understanding its meaning) and there may be particular confusion over personal pronouns. This happens also in ordinary children temporarily as part of their development. It seems that the autistic child's peculiar difficulty is in extracting sense from the strings of words that he hears people say. He does not get the 'gist' of the sentence and he just repeats back the end of the sentence in an 'echobox' manner.

2. A TENDENCY TO IMPOSE EXCESSIVE STRUCTURE ON MATERIAL

That is, striving to maintain or restore sameness; a resistance to change in environment. The child may become very anxious if the playroom has not all its toys in the same position as during the previous session. He may insist on always going the same walk along the same streets. He has a droll preference for monotony. This may be because monotony reduces change, which reduces anxiety.

3. IMPAIRED RELATIONSHIPS WITH PEOPLE

The child seems aloof. He seems to have an empty distaste for other people, regarding them often more as objects than as persons. Even with treatment, poor mixing usually persists into adulthood. Eye avoidance is characteristic, but this seems to vanish about the age of 5 or 6.

4. PATHOLOGICAL PREOCCUPATION WITH CERTAIN OBJECTS OR PARTS OF OBJECTS, WITHOUT REGARD TO THEIR NORMAL FUNCTIONS

The child may spend much time spinning or looking at a mirror or a piece of cloth, much in the way that an infant does, as was described earlier.

5. DISORDER IN MOTILITY PATTERNS

Rocking, spinning, holding objects close to him, excessive over-activity and unusual postures are all seen. Again these are features from the first year of infancy which have been previously described, but they occur in the autistic child even when he has the mental ability to have put such mannerisms aside and to utilize objects appropriately.

6. APPARENT UNCONCERN OR UNAWARENESS OF HIS PERSONAL IDENTITY

Self-aggression and self-mutilation, the continued confusion over personal pronouns, calling himself, 'you' and Mother 'them' or 'me'.

7. ABNORMAL PERCEPTUAL EXPERIENCE

The child may often hold his hands over his ears to avoid an ordinary sound input, as if there were a terrible cacophony of noise. Perhaps he is picking up the noise in the system, as a microphone does? The child may be insensitive to pain and temperature or may spend a lot of time scrutinizing his hands from the peripheries of his vision, out of the corners of his eyes.

8. ACUTE, EXCESSIVE AND SEEMINGLY ILLOGICAL ANXIETY

Often this is caused by a sudden change in routine or in the environment. A child may then appear terrified or he may, on the other hand, show paradoxically a lack of fear when it would be appropriate. He may look down precariously from great heights, on the one hand, but be quite unwilling to jump off a single step.

9. A BACKGROUND OF MARKED MENTAL RETARDATION IN WHICH
THERE ARE ISLETS OF NORMAL OR NEARLY NORMAL OR EVEN QUITE
EXCEPTIONAL ABILITIES

The authors once treated a patient who never spoke during his first years of life nor showed any mental development beyond that of a 1-year-old until he was 4 and then suddenly wrote, with both hands at once, from the outsides in, 'British Constitution'!

It seems that the autistic's central problem is one of extracting meaning from his surroundings and imposing meaning upon surroundings. He does not seem to have an adequate 'deep memory store' to arrange the meaning that he has tried to extract from what people have said and done. The autistic child is often overactive and this is made worse by excitement (unlike the uncomplicated handicapped child who generally becomes less overactive if interesting things are happening around him). Nine per cent of early childhood autistics develop seizures in adolescence. More than half the early childhood autistic children have defective intelligence and about half require institutional care. A quarter can manage special school and then sheltered employment. Our best guess now is that this is an illness due to brain damage and not due to psychological causes. Recent work indicates that while microscopic examinations of their brain show that they should be processing normally, a closer examination reveals cystic degeneration of nerves. If oxygen lack occurs in severe but not catastrophic degree to a mature, full term neonate, the 'watershed' areas of cortex—where the blood supply is frugal anyway—may be denuded of oxygen and damaged. These areas subsume visuospatial, linguistic and memory functions. Brain damage 'extroverts' the adult mammal, 'introverts' the immature mammal; we know this from studies of cats and primates. *Ergo*, given crucial timing and location of brain damage, the profile of autism results.

Late Onset Psychosis

If a psychosis occurs in a schoolchild this will not be at all like early childhood autism. The older the child the more likely it is to resemble adult schizophrenia. Late onset psychosis (LOP) is a very different illness from early childhood autism. The children are hallucinated or deluded or perplexed or at least seem to be suffering. The hallucinated child may not clearly report his hallucination but he gives the feeling of 'someone else being in the room as well'. Such children have a high rate of schizophrenia in their parents, unlike the early childhood autistics. Neurological examination does not show signs of cerebral disease. Their IQs are much higher than those of the other childhood autistics, on average, and when they come to adolescence they show classic schizophrenia. Their treatment, therefore, will consist of psychotherapy and the phenothiazine drugs, such as Largactil.

Case 7

Andrew is 5. He was referred from the local nursery school because of his odd behaviour. He was a forceps delivery baby and required oxygen. His mother found him difficult to wean and later he resisted any change in this diet. He was also difficult to toilet train, but by 4 he was dry. He showed marked delay in speech, with little normal babble. He would often substitute his hands for toys and play with his hands instead. The parents were loving sensible people, particularly disturbed by his obsessionality. He liked playing with cigarette packets and, if there was even a slight fault in the cigarette packet, he would notice it and become dissatisfied, saying, 'That bloken'. He liked to have blocks perfectly aligned and loved water play. The parents noticed that he had islets of intellect and could plan, for example, to secrete desired objects upstairs to his bedroom. On examination in the playroom Andrew showed eye avoidance and wandered solitarily about. He showed end-of-sentence echolalia and did not use any pronouns, such as 'I' or 'me'. He was able to make a stair of six bricks very quickly and accurately at the $4\frac{1}{2}$-year level, but only speaking at the 2-year level. Physical examination showed no abnormality. An EEG showed minor general abnormalities, but no sign of fits. The Terman–Merril intelligence test showed him to have an IQ of 58, but this was not felt to be an accurate estimate.

Impression Early childhood autism.
Treatment Transfer to Rudolf Steiner School at age of 7.

THE 'BLIND DEAF'

Blindness is a relatively common affliction in the mentally handicapped population. Its causative factor is usually that which has caused the mental handicap. It is not unusual for the blind child often to be also deaf. This double handicap is particularly likely to be due to rubella in the first 3 months of the mother's pregnancy.

Though a blind child smiles at six weeks, he does so less frequently and in response to touch rather than sight. He cannot reach out and use his hand to locate objects, but has to wait to be touched by them. As a result, understanding of the world, and particularly the definition of the self from not self, cannot be reached through normal integration of sensations coming from hand, eye and mouth. Such difficulties mean that the blind child may prefer to rely on body stimulation and movement for pleasure—rocking, twisting, thumb sucking—rather than through manipulation of objects, essential to the sort of play which leads to adaptation, control, symbolization and learning about the world. To him the unknown is dangerous.

For the child with some sensory component missing, e.g. sight, there may be no relief from mother's angry word by the sight of her smile afterwards. Thus blind children do not maintain the idea of their parents as a constant object in their minds until a later period than normal (Bentovin, 1972).

The blind-deaf child is rather like the autistic child in the secondary emotional handicaps that he may show: *viz*. 'Isolation Syndrome', the obsessionality, the preference for sameness, the inexplicable tantrums and also self-mutilation. Self-mutilation is commonly an attention-seeking behaviour. One thing that normal humans cannot stand is seeing a child harm himself. The blind-deaf child in particular enjoys the flashes he gets from stimulating the optic nerve, and readily learns that immediate attention is forthcoming. The anxiety tolerance of the staff is generally too low to allow the child to harm himself and therefore extinguish this unpleasant and dangerous behaviour spontaneously. So everyone tends to reinforce it by rushing to the child and stopping him mutilate himself. Behaviour therapy is the best treatment, although tranquillizers can, by drugging the child, make him less active in his self-mutilation. A psychologist should be consulted and attention should be given to the child at moments when he is not harming himself and also, if he starts harming himself, attention which is at that time being given should be immediately removed. This can be hard for the nurse to do and sometimes toy rubber boxing gloves or similar padding have to be fastened to allow such treatment to be undertaken. Alternatively, another form of less harmful habitual behaviour can be thoroughly rewarded and reinforced, and the child may take to that instead, abandoning his previous attention-seeking mutilation, i.e. differential reinforcement of other behaviour (DRO). In other words, self-mutilation should be looked at as a primitive form of communication and the child should be helped to use a better channel, by such strategies as *time out* (*see* Chapter 20) of the reinforcing situation or diversion. Thus the behaviour should be thoroughly described including its setting and consequences, and either or both changed.

Very rarely, self-mutilation is associated with a syndrome with a high blood uric acid, and in all cases in which this occurs, the doctor should investigate the patient to see if he has tophi, such as are found in gout, where high uric acid is responsible. This is called 'Lesch Nyhan Syndrome'. Other disorders which are prone to involve self abuse are Norrie's Disease, and de Lange Amsterdam dwarfs.

Blindness itself will not limit the learning capacity of the child. In fact, it is less harmful to the child's intellectual development than deafness alone, as the child's most important communication channel—speech and hearing—is available in the former. It is possible for the uncomplicated blind child to develop a satisfying life and, provided the contents of the environment are not changed in a bewilderingly frequent manner, his mobility and independence will develop satisfactorily.

As with all handicaps, with blindness excessive sympathy is both smothering and irritating to the growing child. He will become increasingly demanding and dependent and this will, in turn, prolong his habilitation.

Thus we have the concept of behaviour disturbances and mental illnesses superimposed on mental handicap and these disturbances can be grouped into the categories of (1) healthy responses; (2) reactive behaviour disturbances; (3) psychoneurosis; (4) psychosomatic illness; (5) character disorder—in these disturbances in children, drugs are generally of little value; (6) developmental deviation and brain damage; and (7) psychoses—with these disorders, stemming from disorders in the child primarily, drugs may have a major place, as for example the anticonvulsants, but our main treatments will be more structured environments, and more educational techniques, particularly language learning strategies, for language liberates the individual: it enables the child to feel he has entered the human race.

CHAPTER 18

Mental Illness in the Adult Mentally Handicapped

MOST MENTAL ILLNESSES do not show themselves until after the adolescent stage has been reached, compared with mental handicap which occurs with the beginning of life or soon after. Any of the forms of mental illness which may occur in the fully developed mind may also occur in the mentally handicapped; however, the lower the IQ, the more difficult it is to recognize mental illness in the mentally handicapped as the diagnosis of mental illness is largely dependent on verbal communication: thus the diagnosis of mental illness in the mentally handicapped is made more often in those whose intelligence is towards the upper end of the defective range.

Mental illness is principally divided into *psychosis* and *psychoneurosis*. Psychosis corresponds to the lay term 'madness' and psychoneurosis to the lay term 'nerves'. A person suffering from a psychotic illness loses contact with reality, whereas in neurotic illness, contact with reality is maintained.

Psychoses are divided into *functional* and *organic* psychoses. Functional psychoses are those in which function is disturbed but there is as yet no demonstrable physical cause to explain the symptoms. Organic psychoses are those in which there is a demonstrable physical cause, i.e. tumour, infection, change in blood vessels, etc.

The more common types of mental illness may be classified as is shown in the plan below.

FUNCTIONAL PSYCHOSIS

1a. Schizophrenia

This illness is characterized by symptoms which interfere with the patient's thinking, emotions, drive and motor activity and may result in a gradual deterioration of personality. The incidence in the general population is 0·85 per cent: it is higher in the relatives of schizophrenics. In most cases, the illness begins between the ages of 15 and 25; the predisposing personality is often introverted or 'schizoid'. Typically the schizophrenic is of asthenic build. Recently there is some evidence to suggest that the condition may be due to biochemical abnormality. The prognosis is better in atypical forms of the illness, i.e. where it has an acute onset, a precipitating factor,

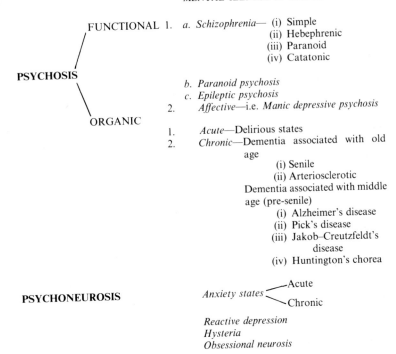

FUNCTIONAL 1.   *a. Schizophrenia*— (i) Simple
(ii) Hebephrenic
(iii) Paranoid
(iv) Catatonic

b. Paranoid psychosis
c. Epileptic psychosis
2.   *Affective*—i.e. *Manic depressive psychosis*

PSYCHOSIS

ORGANIC

1.   *Acute*—Delirious states
2.   *Chronic*—Dementia associated with old age
(i) Senile
(ii) Arteriosclerotic
Dementia associated with middle age (pre-senile)
(i) Alzheimer's disease
(ii) Pick's disease
(iii) Jakob–Creutzfeldt's disease
(iv) Huntington's chorea

PSYCHONEUROSIS   *Anxiety states* ⟨ Acute / Chronic

Reactive depression
Hysteria
Obsessional neurosis

where the personality is extrovert and the build pyknic, where the patient is realistically disturbed by his symptoms and where there is no marked family history.

Schizophrenic illnesses are classified into four types and all four may show the characteristics of each other. Schizophrenic means 'split mind' and in the schizophrenic there is dissociation between thinking and feeling. The major features of the illness are:

Disturbance of Thinking   There is loosening of associations and disconnection of thoughts ranging in severity from vagueness in thinking to a stage where the patient's utterances cannot be understood at all.

Disturbance of Emotions   The patient's expression of emotions is not in step with his conversation; he may sit with a rather fixed smile on his face even if being asked about a recent bereavement of a close relative.

Disturbance of Drive or Volition   The patient is lacking in the will to do anything constructive and may spend time in bed or sitting staring into space often without realizing that he is so inactive.

Disturbance of Motor Activity This may range from stupor to wild excitement and overactivity. Patients may allow their bodies and limbs to be placed in unusual positions which are maintained indefinitely.

Primary Delusions A delusion is a false belief with no basis in reality. A delusion which appears out of the blue in fully developed form in the setting of clear consciousness and which is immediately accepted as valid by the patient is a primary delusion and is characteristic of schizophrenia: for example, a patient who has gone to a party may suddenly feel that everyone is hostile to him and wants to kill him.

Hallucinations A hallucination is a perception which has no basis in reality. Hallucinations may also occur in other mental illnesses. Auditory hallucinations are the most common in schizophrenia; the patient may hear voices commenting on his every action. Visual hallucinations as well as hallucinations of touch, taste and smell may occur.

(i) SIMPLE SCHIZOPHRENIA

This disorder usually develops during adolescence or early adulthood, and is characterized by its insidious onset. There is a gradual withdrawal of interest, a lack of attention and concentration causing inability to hold a conversation and eventual incoherence. There is disharmony between mood and thought. Simple schizophrenics do not manage to hold responsible jobs and may have anti-social tendencies. They never fulfil the promise of their earlier years. It would be difficult to diagnose simple schizophrenia in the mentally handicapped, particularly in those in hospital as there are few features which would distinguish it from the effects of prolonged hospitalization.

(ii) HEBEPHRENIC SCHIZOPHRENIA

This disorder begins insidiously in adolescence or early adulthood. Typically those who develop it have been emotionally shallow and idealistic, tending to dwell on obscure topics. There may be periods of excitement alternating with depression. A depressive reaction may herald the onset of the illness. There is marked disturbance of thought. Hallucinations are common especially in the later stages. Senseless, impulsive, erratic behaviour is common. Hebephrenic schizophrenia can be recognized in the mentally handicapped.

(iii) PARANOID SCHIZOPHRENIA

This disorder begins later in life, usually between 30 and 40 years of age. The main symptoms are primary delusions, secondary delusional interpretations and hallucinations of a persecutory nature. The patient may claim that his mind is being controlled by radio waves, his thoughts can be read by others or that he is being sexually assaulted. The symptoms which lead to personality deterioration are less in evidence. Paranoid schizophrenia can be diagnosed in the mentally handicapped.

(iv) CATATONIC SCHIZOPHRENIA

This type is more likely to have an acute onset than other types. The most frequent type of catatonic symptom is stupor, the patient being completely immobilized in a fixed posture. Lesser degrees of immobilization may occur with transient blocking of movement only occurring. There may be negativism in the form of food refusal, soiling of clothes with urine and faeces: the patient may not reply when spoken to until the questioner has turned away. Muscular rigidity may appear when the patient is touched and disappear when he is left to himself. Stupor may alternate with over-activity and excitement and the patient may change very suddenly from one to the other. During the excited phase, the patient may be very impulsive and aggressive. He may be hallucinated and delusional. Catatonic schizophrenia can be recognized in defectives. Mentally handicapped persons who develop schizophrenia tend to have less complex delusional systems than would be found in schizophrenics of normal intelligence. Between acute episodes, there may be less evidence of personality deterioration, the personality of the mentally handicapped individual being less complex originally. The more severe the mental handicap the less can 'types' of schizophrenia be distinguished. In the profoundly handicapped only blurred over-active or underactive states, determined 'larval psychosis' by MacGillivray (1956), can usually be distinguished.

TREATMENT

Schizophrenic symptoms can be modified by the phenothiazine and butyrophenone groups of drugs and by ECT. In the acutely disturbed patient chlorpromazine (the best known of the phenothiazine group) or haloperidol (the proto-type of the butyrophenone group), would be used; where the patient is withdrawn and uncommunicative, a less sedative phenothiazine such as trifluoperazine would be used. In both very overactive and very withdrawn patients where the condition is acute ECT may be used. Relapse can to some extent be prevented by injections of long-acting phenothiazines, given at 2-, 3-, or 4-weekly intervals. A community psychiatric nursing service can play a vital part in rehabilitation by ensuring that patients, released from hospital, receive maintenance therapy and in advising relatives on further management.

1b. Paranoid Psychosis

This can be recognized in the mildly mentally handicapped; it is usually a phenomenon of middle and old age, and there is a high incidence of impairment of vision and hearing in patients who develop paranoid delusions in later life, just as there is in normally intelligent adults who develop paranoid illnesses at a late age.

1c. Epileptic Psychosis

There is a higher incidence of schizophreniform psychosis occurring in association with epilepsy than could be expected by chance, the psychotic experiences growing out of the personality change and semi-confusional epileptic phenomena.

DIAGNOSIS

Schizophrenic and paranoid psychosis would be difficult to diagnose in patients with an IQ much below the upper end of the moderate range of mental retardation. A schizophrenic or paranoid psychosis may produce an apparent drop in the level of intellectual functioning as assessed on intelligence testing, but the pre-morbid level of intelligence is a more accurate indication of the patient's intellectual potential.

2. Affective Psychosis

MANIC DEPRESSIVE PSYCHOSIS

This illness is characterized by mood swings from elation to depression; it is predominantly an illness of middle life, though the first attack may be earlier. Between attacks, the patient returns to his normal personality. It may present as mania or depression or a mixture of both. The patient may have one or two attacks only in a life-time, or repeated illnesses. Chronic depression and chronic mania can occur, and more rarely there may be continuous alteration from mania to depression. The predisposing personality is typically extrovert and subject to mild mood swings. Twelve per cent of the children of an affected parent are affected. Again there is recent evidence to suggest that the biochemical factors may be involved in its causation. Women are affected more than men. Prognosis is best where the attack is typical (opposite to schizophrenia), worse where there are manic episodes, and worst of all if there are episodes of mania and depression.

Depression The onset may be sudden or insidious. Typically, the patient feels at his worst in the mornings and mood improves towards evening. The highest incidence of suicide is in the early morning. The depressed patient feels hopeless, unworthy, guilty and possibly hypochondriacal. If delusions are present they are depressive in content; the patient believes that he has cancer or that he is infecting everyone around him. Hallucinations are rare but, if they occur, take the form of voices making insulting remarks or of horrible scenes being enacted, i.e. they are depressive in content. The depressed patient is slowed in all his functions, and may become stuporous; appetite is poor, sleep is disturbed and there is early morning wakening with inability to return to sleep.

Rarely the depressive may be violent towards others, i.e. may kill other members of the family, rather than leave them in an evil world.

Treatment In a severely depressed patient, ECT is the treatment of choice. Where the illness is less severe, one of the tetracyclic or tricyclic antidepressant drugs would be used.

Mania Mania is rarer than depression. The patient is hyperactive. Prior to modern treatment, death from exhaustion was not uncommon. Ideas flash through the patient's mind, he is grandiose and may feel he has great powers. Mood is one of infectious gaiety but at times the patient may be very irritable and require great tact and patience on the part of the nursing staff.

Treatment Mania can be treated successfully with haloperidol, droperidol, with phenothiazines in addition if necessary. ECT is sometimes useful. Where the patient is having frequent mood swings, lithium is used as a maintenance therapy.

DIAGNOSIS

Affective disorders can be recognized in the mentally handicapped, mood change tending to be poorly sustained and in the manic lacking in the quality of infectious gaiety typical of the normally intelligent manic. Associated delusions tend to be naïve. Affective disorders can occur in severely mentally handicapped adult patients, but diagnosis can be difficult the more severely handicapped the patient and may need to be based on a prolonged study of behaviour, weight and sleep patterns by observers who know the patient well, supplemented by a knowledge of mental illness patterns in the family.

ORGANIC PSYCHOSIS

The effects of organic cerebral disease are more marked in the mentally handicapped than in the normal population. The normal mental changes which occur in old age and those associated with senile dementia appear much earlier and progress more rapidly in the mentally handicapped.

Organic mental illnesses are caused by anatomical or physiological disturbance in the brain or result from physical illness elsewhere in the body. The nature of the symptoms depends on the rate of development of the disease process. The most important symptom which distinguishes the organic psychosis from the functional is clouding of consciousness. This is a state of disturbed awareness which may vary from mild disorientation in time and place to coma.

Organic mental states may be acute or chronic.

1. *Acute Organic Psychosis or Delirious States*

These may occur in association with physical illness such as pneumonia; the delirious patient is restless, has a poor attention span, his thinking is concerned with imaginary experiences and there may be hallucinations; he is disorientated in time and place. Sleep is disturbed.

Delirium may be drug induced; barbiturates taken in excess may give rise to confusion, ataxic gait, constipation, foul breath, acneiform skin eruptions and coma. It has to be remembered that delirium in the mentally handicapped may be caused by the toxic effects of anticonvulsants and dose levels should be kept under review; in this context it should be remembered that the mentally handicapped are now susceptible to the toxic effects of not only barbiturates and anticonvulsants but also antidepressants and tranquillizers. Patients who have been on tranquillizers for some time should be advised to discontinue them gradually over a period of weeks rather than stop them suddenly, which may lead to unpleasant withdrawal effects and sometimes delirium. Similarly, alcohol withdrawal may be a cause of delirium.

Delirium may be caused by chemicals, e.g. those containing lead: where lead poisoning is acute, there is delirium, aphasia, convulsions and coma if untreated; in chronic lead poisoning there is failure of concentration and memory, headache, deafness, transient speech defect and visual disturbance.

2. *Chronic Organic Psychosis*

The irreversible decline of mental functions produced by organic brain disease is termed dementia. The process begins with failure of recent memory, attention and slow, vague thinking. Mood is labile and shallow, judgement is impaired. There is progressive intellectual failure until at the end stage, at which the patient leads a vegetative existence requiring everything to be done for him. The dementias are divided into the senile and pre-senile groups as follows.

DEMENTIA ASSOCIATED WITH OLD AGE

(i) *Senile Dementia*   Senile dementia occurs at about the age of 70, is more common in females and there is an increased incidence in the families of those afflicted. The onset is insidious and there is steady and rapid deterioration of all aspects of intellectual functioning. Delusions and hallucinations may occur.

(ii) *Arteriosclerotic Dementia*   There is degeneration of the cerebral blood vessels with secondary degeneration of brain tissue. There is patchy failure of brain function. Personality is preserved to a later stage than in senile dementia. There may be associated hypertension, cerebro-vascular accidents, neurological signs and epileptiform fits.

The diagnosis of dementia in the mentally handicapped is difficult and would depend on a knowledge of pre-morbid level of functioning.

DEMENTIA ASSOCIATED WITH MIDDLE AGE—PRE-SENILE DEMENTIA

(i) *Alzheimer's Disease*   This condition begins in middle life with impairment of memory and loss of efficiency, accompanied by emotional disturbances and change in muscle tone. There is generalized atrophy of the cerebral cortex with the temporo–parietal region being particularly affected causing difficulty in speaking and senseless repetition of words or sentences, echoing of phrases and repetition of last words or parts of words of a sentence. There is loss of sense of position in space. The patient's gait becomes stiff and awkward. There may be convulsions, and in the terminal stage the patient leads a vegetative existence. More females than males are affected. Cases of Down's Syndrome are prone to develop this disease.

(ii) *Pick's Disease*   In this condition the atrophic change affects the three outer layers of the cortex and, in particular, the frontal and temporal areas. Personality change occurs first, and the first indication may be uninhibited behaviour; speech defects occur, the patient omitting words or using them in a peculiar fashion. There may be increased sensitivity to pain. Epilepsy and disturbances of gait are less common than in Alzheimer's. The terminal stage is identical in both. Familial incidence is more common than in Alzheimer's. The atrophic changes of Pick's disease are commonly seen in dementing mongols from their fortieth year onwards.

(iii) *Jakob–Creutzfeldt's Disease* This is a rare disease of middle life which begins with memory impairment and widespread neurological disturbance, causing tremors and spasticity of the limbs and disturbance of gait.

(iv) *Huntington's Chorea* This disease is transmitted by a single autosomal dominant gene and about half the offspring of an affected person can, therefore, be expected to develop it. In the majority of cases, the illness begins between 25 and 35, but it may be as early as 3 or as late as 70. It may thus be a cause of mental handicap where there is early onset.

Neurological symptoms may be preceded by mood change; the involuntary movements usually commence in the face, hands and shoulders, but an abnormality of gait may be the first sign. Memory may be surprisingly well retained even when the disease is well established. Depression is common, and there is a high incidence of suicide. The average duration of the illness is 10–15 years, with death taking place before the age of 60, but in some cases the disease is more slowly progressive.

PSYCHONEUROSIS

Anxiety States

All individuals experience anxiety at some time in their lives, i.e. prior to an interview or examination. In response to stress in the normal individual, there is an increase in the concentration of adrenaline in the blood, an increase in blood sugar, a rise in blood pressure and pulse rate, skin becomes pale and sweats, mouth becomes dry; respiration becomes deeper and more frequent; there is generalized trembling. There may be frequency of micturition, diarrhoea, nausea and vomiting. In prolonged anxiety states, there may be increased muscle tone, tension, restlessness, sleep and appetite disturbance, causing deterioration in general health. In psychoneurosis anxiety appears inappropriate to the situation or excessive in degree.

ACUTE ANXIETY STATES

An acute anxiety state may appear in the mentally handicapped as a response to stress in the same way as in the normally intelligent individual.

CHRONIC ANXIETY STATES

Chronic anxiety states may occur in the mentally handicapped in the higher ranges of defective intelligence. There is generally an inherited pre-disposition, or history of insecurity in early life caused by loss of a parent by death or divorce. Stressful situations of many kinds, instead of producing a constructive response, may induce a state of continuing conflict in those individuals predisposed to the development of neurotic illness.

TREATMENT

Treatment is by mild tranquillizers such as valium or librium and manipulation of the environment so that where possible stressful situations are avoided.

Neurotic or Reactive Depression

Neurotic or reactive depression is a reaction to some external cause, e.g. death of a close relative, but is more intense than one would expect. It is distinguished from endogenous depression by the fact that there is a definite precipitating factor, a tendency for mood to worsen towards evening, inability to get off to sleep and frequent waking throughout the night.

In practice there is overlap between endogenous and reactive depression, many patients having features of both.

TREATMENT

Mild tranquillizers may be helpful as there are often associated anxiety symptoms. The patient has to be helped to come to terms with whatever has been the precipitating factor.

Hysteria

Hysterical symptoms have a motivation which is unrecognized by the patient and there is often gain from the symptom. Hysterical symptoms may occur in any personality type in a setting of mounting emotional strain, e.g. marital strife may have caused strain for some time, when an argument, no more serious in itself than previous arguments, may precipitate dissociative symptoms, i.e. complete loss of memory or regression to the age before the marriage took place.

In conversion hysteria, the patient solves a conflict by producing a symptom such as paralysis of a limb, or blindness or symptoms of any other physical illness. People of dull intelligence are more likely to develop dissociative symptoms than those of superior intelligence.

Obsessional Neurosis

An obsession exists when a person cannot exclude thoughts from consciousness, distinguishes them as unreasonable, and attempts to resist them but cannot do so. Obsessions with sex and violence, death, dirt and germs are typical. *Rumination* is the term applied to repetitive obsessional thinking; *compulsions* are acts which the patient feels compelled to carry out.

The overall incidence of obsessional illness is low. Obsessional ruminations may appear secondarily in anxiety states, but true obsessional neurosis is a rare occurrence in mental handicap of any degree.

DIAGNOSIS AND TREATMENT

Mildly mentally handicapped people who are floridly psychotic are most likely to be admitted to mental hospitals for treatment in the same way as normally intelligent patients who become psychotic. Diagnosis of mental illness in the mentally handicapped is more difficult where the illness is less florid and where the patient is more severely handicapped. Reid et al. (1978), in a cluster analysis of the behaviour problems of profoundly retarded people, were able to identify autism, disintegrative psychosis, hypsokinesic syndrome and multiple problem (eg. noisy, regurgitation) groups. Such problems may be seen in the severely mentally handicapped whether they are looked after at home or in a residential setting. Where such problems occur in the mentally handicapped who are kept within the family, they may become inextricably entwined with the family psycho-dynamics. Such problems may, or may not, subside following admission to a residential setting. The possibility of superimposed psychiatric illness in the severely mentally handicapped should be kept in mind where there is a family history of mental illness, where there is a deterioration in level of functioning or where there seems to be a definite pattern to the behaviour disorder, as the making of a psychiatric diagnosis has treatment implications, and if acceptable psychiatric diagnostic categories can be established, then it becomes possible to prescribe, or withhold, drugs on a more rational basis.

CHAPTER 19

Personality and Character Disorders (including Psychopathy)

INTELLIGENCE, PERSONALITY AND MENTAL ILLNESS have each to be regarded separately. People of the same intelligence have very different personalities. Intelligence and personality are distinct but interdependent, for severely limited intelligence does limit the personalities of the more severely handicapped. A mental illness is a condition that is superimposed on a personality.

What do we mean by the terms 'personality', 'character', 'temperament' and 'trait'? *Personality* (Allport) 'is the dynamic organization within the individual of those psycho-physical systems which determine his unique adjustment to his environment'. *Character* is the moral, ethical or will aspect of personality—his fibre, courage and goodness. This aspect is largely acquired. *Temperament* is the mood aspect of personality: the predominance of cheerfulness or sadness; the ease with which he is aroused to anger or reduced to distress. These terms, 'personality', 'character' and 'temperament' are roughly analogous to the Freudian 'ego', 'super ego', and 'id', respectively. *Traits* are the superficial characteristics which we describe in a person, such as 'sociability' or 'impulsiveness'.

Just as we cannot really talk about an infant's 'personality', 'traits' or 'character', as these have not yet developed, but can state what his temperament is, so we can describe the profoundly handicapped only in terms of temperament: is the child or profoundly handicapped person calm or irritable? The only adjectives that apply to the low grades are ones such as 'excitable' and 'apathetic'.

As we move up the intellectual grades, we can, in moderately handicapped people, distinguish considerable personality differences. The commonest dimension is that of the extraversion and introversion, which has been used by many psychiatrists and psychologists from Jung to Eysenck. The extravert is the outgoing, predominantly cheerful, active, easy-in-personal-relationships person, whilst the introvert is the shy, speculative, easily tired individual. These personality types are related to body types; fat (pyknic) and thin (leptosomatic) body types respectively. The extravert tends to be hard to 'condition'. He learns lessons with difficulty and is less inhibited.

The state of mild brain damage common in the mentally handicapped, known as minimal cerebral dysfunction (MCD), is characterized by fluctuation of attention, distractability and extraversion.

267

It is considered to be an important component in delinquency, accounting for the disinhibition, impulsiveness, the learning difficulties and the aggression. Therefore brain damage can cloud the basic personality, with 'extraverting' or 'disinhibiting' attributes.

A survey of behavioural patterns in a severely and profoundly mentally retarded hospital adult population was carried out by cluster analysis (Reid, 1980). Eight clusters were identified. Most patterns seemed related to underlying brain pathology.

Reid and his co-workers confirmed that there was a great variability in outcome for children who had hyperkinetic syndromes. Some of the patients had become slow and lethargic adults where others had become persistently aggressive and a few severely hyperkinetic. Reid and his colleagues also identified a small group of mentally handicapped people who showed a package of behaviour problems including feeding disorder, irritability state, stereotypic-stripping, self-injury, overactivity and noisiness. They considered that the behaviour problem might be related to either brain damage or dysfunction of the limbic areas of the brain. One of these had an associated disturbance of body temperature.

They also identified a group of mentally handicapped people who showed severe and persistent stereotypic and ritualistic behaviour along with social withdrawal and absent or distorted language. The impression was of a spectrum of autistic disorders ranging from a few people with a nucleus early childhood syndrome to a larger group with isolated autistic features.

Some of those were, undoubtedly, a mixture of brain damage and family psychodynamics.

Thus we can see that heredity (in the form of basic extraversion–introversion) and environment (the character and traits that we acquire from our childhood experience and perhaps from the accidents that may damage our brain) both play a part in the composition of the personality.

INHERITED ASPECTS OF PERSONALITY

Several mental handicap conditions appear to be accompanied by a placid or cheerful temperament. Retarded children, as a group, do laugh more than normal children. Retarded children laugh more at home than in hospitals. It is likely, however, that this laughter is not so much a sign of temperament as a compensatory system of language.

Mongols cry less than other children. There is a long tradition of mongols being thought of as of a cheerful and happy disposition, affectionate, and good tempered. One interesting study concluded that, among 140 mongols admitted to a mental deficiency hospital, there were no personal qualities by which they differed from non-mongols. Gibson (1980) in his textbook on this anomaly points out that it is now possible to draw a crude but informed caricature. Firstly, there is a characteristic development of the Down's personality. The Down's individual typically starts as the placid, sensorily insufficient infant who becomes an emotionally outgoing child who turns into a sullen adolescent and finally prematurely ages and shows marked behavioural deterioration in early adult life: but not always and perhaps not even in most cases. Gibson considers that we need to know much more about the reliability of the stereotype of the biddable mongol and the sensory metabolic and nervous system changes which appear to accompany it. Murdoch (1981) has proposed that many of the features of deterioration and performance in Down's are due to target endocrine organ failure—that the Down's are more prone to diabetes, hypothyroidism, gonadal insufficiency and adrenal insufficiency. They get more infections and are less likely to suffer from coronary artery disease. Hypothyroidism is difficult to detect. Cunningham (1979) has shown how Down's anomaly people go through with their parents in the first 8 months a honeymoon phase of almost normal child development; then they experience, possibly because of a small cerebellum, difficulty in grasping and holding, and eventually become resigned to their deficits. Their speech, Dodd (1972) has shown, is normal with regard to babble until about a year, and only thereafter deteriorates, showing signs of 'cerebellar speech' with consonant imbalance and inconsistent errors.

Behaviour difficulties in younger Down's anomaly people are less common and less acute than for other mental retardates. The particulars of minor behavioural deviation are not much different from other imbecile groups—for example, the hyperactivity and attention deficit—but the autistic 'isolation syndrome' patterns are rare in Down's syndrome. The later primitive catatonic states, depression and senile dementia appear to be based on a progressive neuropathology. Reid et al. (1978) have noted that Alzheimer's disease, which is present and is almost universal in mongols over the age of 35, can be diagnosed clinically in a substantial number of these cases.

Thus factors which complicate the personality stereotype in Down's syndrome appear to be age, intelligence levels, communication facility, a variety of abnormal karotypes and sex. The characteristic biddable stereotype is most commonly seen between 6 and 12 years, and is dependent on the above variables, particularly IQ and sex. The less attractive behaviours, Gibson suggests, accelerate with developing neuropathology and other somatic processes such as hypothyroidism.

Of the other chromosome disorders, Turner's syndrome, which is usually associated with normal intelligence, appears to have no definite personality type, but there is some association with anorexia nervosa (refusal to eat). Children with Klinefelter's syndrome have immature and passive personalities. They are easy to handle as babies and have no negativistic period and are over-dependent, lack initiative, concentration and perseverance, and have school difficulties. As adults, such males are frequently mentally handicapped and prone to mental illness, epilepsy and antisocial conduct.

Males with extra Y chromosome are characteristically very tall (over 1·8 m) and have particularly large male features, such as genitalia and heart size. They are considered to suffer from a severe disorder of personality associated with mild intellectual impairment. They have been described as being extremely unstable and irresponsible, without depth of affection. They have difficulty in social adjustment, arising from their emotional instability, but rarely display violent reactions, criminal behaviour being minor in character. Some people with this syndrome may have normal intelligence; antisocial conduct cannot be simply explained by low intelligence. As males with extra Y chromosome and the extra X chromosome are both more liable to mental illness and to antisocial conduct, the best guess is that the mental troubles of the sex chromosome disorders stem from, again, minimal cerebral dysfunction.

ACQUIRED ASPECTS OF PERSONALITY— THE DISORDERED CHARACTER: AN ENVIRONMENTAL DISORDER

When we are examining the subject of crime, we are concerned more with moral and ethical aspects of personality development and, therefore, with character development.

Bowlby (1969), at the Tavistock Clinic, showed that maternal deprivation resulted in emotionally unresponsive children, particularly in those who had not developed emotional bonds between the age of 6 months and 3 years. In the case of the male, often he became the affectionless, crime-prone 'psychopath', and in the case of the female, the inadequate, feckless and uncaring mother.

Inadequate mothering, and poor child-rearing patterns in bad environments, demonstrably cause crime. Of the hereditary factors, only the chromosome disorders are doubtfully associated with crime. Is there any real evidence that low intelligence causes crime? One has the sort of feeling that the unintelligent are prone to offend, but does the evidence bear this out?

The weight of current opinion is that intelligence plays very little part in causing crime. This was certainly not the view earlier in the century. Fernald, in 1912, stated: 'Every feeble-minded person, especially the high grade imbecile, is a potential criminal. It has been truly said that feeble-mindedness is the mother of crime, pauperism, and degeneracy.' Goddard, in 1919, pronounced: 'The so-called criminal-type is merely a type of feeble-mindedness.' In America at least the term 'moron' was synonymous at that time with criminal.

In Britain, antisocial conduct was, even at that time, and increasingly since, considered largely the outcome of poor environment. As intelligence tests became more precise, it was shown that many people whom we considered mentally defective at the beginning of the century were not true defectives, and the proportion of criminals considered defective was falling. Only 3·5 per cent of criminals in prison are potentially certifiable subnormals.

It is useful to regard the mentally handicapped as constituting two main groups: those who are subnormals due to organic defects (e.g. brain damage) and those who are described as 'subculturally' subnormal (due to normal genetic variation). The former group is unlikely to be involved in criminal activities by reason of the severe social restrictions stemming from severe mental and, commonly also, physical handicap. The low intelligence in 'subcultural' subnormals is attributable not only to genetic variation but also to such factors as deprived social intercourse, inadequate home background and poor stimulation. These are the very factors which are commonly associated with antisocial behaviour—with 'psychopathic' disorders. The major causes of delinquency in the mentally handicapped appear to stem from the home background—deprivation—not from intelligence, as is the case with delinquents of normal intelligence.

When mentally handicapped do offend, sexual offences are particularly prevalent. Recent studies have shown that perception of sex is distinctly influenced by intelligence. A common unhappy combination is an adult sex drive with a naïve morality, imposing on the handicapped a harsh, guilt-ridden attitude towards his normal feelings and an inability to distinguish the degrees of sexual behaviour that are permissible. Therefore sex education for the mentally handicapped as part of education in human relationships is particularly important in preventing offences. Such counselling is part of the psychiatric nurse's role (see Chapter 12).

An adverse environment stultifies character development so that an 'affectionless', impulsive, self-centred individual can arise. When such a condition is complicated by low intelligence, the hospital nurse is often called upon to treat at the request of the Courts. The following principles underlie treatment.

The Fostering of Morality

The child begins by attributing moral perfection to his parents and does not begin to see their natural imperfections until he is about 6 years old. The 2- or 3-year-old mind cannot distinguish 'justice' from 'authority'—what is 'fair' from what 'they' (adults) order or require. There is no idea of fairness. Little children and the severely handicapped consider the most severe punishment the most just. They emphasize the necessity of the punishment itself. Older children emphasize that things must be 'put right'. With growth, blind, total respect for the adult decreases and is replaced by fairness and mutual respect (the feeling that the adult respects the child, too). If the adult is inconsistent even this dwindles.

Most children between 6 and 8 condemn stealing because it is not allowed, and because of what will ensue in terms of punishment. Motives and mitigating circumstances are ignored.

The effects of mutual respect leads to the development of the equality ethic. The 9-year-old mind can appreciate the idea of justice, fair shares and rigid adherence to rules, but still ignores mitigating circumstances. When children learn to allow for the circumstances of the particular case, equality is superseded by *equity*. Ninety-five per cent of 13-year-olds have achieved the equity concept.

The character-disordered child has, during the 'sensitive period', up to the age of 5, not developed firm emotional bonds with respect for, and basic trust in, a caring adult. This deficit the care-worker or therapist must try to replace by consistency, personal stability and fairness.

The Fostering of Communication

Behaviour disturbance is often an 'acting-out' of problems the young offender cannot communicate. Group therapy promotes action in words rather than in deeds, listening to other's opinions, and provides the chance to achieve respect in the group. He learns to see himself from another's point of view.

Sanctions, too, are more effective if they are verbal and explanatory; the imperative sanction—a slap or a simple 'Don't do it'—becomes, if the misdemeanour is repeated, a challenge to authority. A propositional appeal—'Don't do it—because it hurts others and the result is "expensive" damage'—means that a further challenge is against the principle—not the advocate of the principle. Similarly, higher authority should seldom be invoked—'I'll bring down the doctor,' has often the same result as, 'I'll bring in the police,'—the confirmation of contempt for all authority.

Abstract morality—altruistic motives—can be encouraged by the young person working with the more handicapped in the unit and his loyalty and efforts with them being rewarded by verbal praise rather than extra pocket money.

The Fostering of Success

In one recent study in Scotland of a therapeutic community for delinquent defectives, who had subsequently a particularly high rate of recidivism, one of the major criticisms was that the hospital had not geared these mentally handicapped boys for life in the subcultural ghettoes to which they were returning. There was too much emphasis on traditional psychodynamic theory and traditional education and too little training in work practice and social competence and little or no social support after discharge. The young offender is the way he is partly because he is demoralized. He ought to have success opportunities and these will raise his morale and self-respect most if they are related to the successes he sees in his peers of normal intelligence. Therefore educational successes should be arranged in school, in physical and artistic recreation, and in the industrial workshops of the hospital or centre. He should never be allowed to become so low in self-regard that he has 'nothing to lose'.

The Fostering of Interests and Involvement

Young offenders commonly say: 'I'm a loner, "an outsider".' 'I don't seem to fit.' 'I've nothing to lose.' In the search for success opportunities and interests, the nurse or social worker is trying to write a diversity of scenarios in which the young handicapped offender can hopefully develop a repertoire of acceptable behaviours rather than one or two habitual responses such as stealing, aggression or misdirected sex. Most normal people play several roles—father, colleague, partner, friend, boss, son, etc.—the handicapped person often plays only the role of a child.

Boredom—a contributory factor in most delinquency—is often a predominant feature in sexual offences. Sexual energy (libido) can be canalized into physical and mental pursuits. The backward youth has often few outlets, and is aware of this and anxious about it. Frequent masturbation is pleasurable, readily available and immediately anxiety-reducing. Such preoccupation is, however, also guilt ridden and only one step removed, in his concrete morality, from indecent exposure or assault.

There is the problem of finding an appropriate sexual identity. Long standing contact with mother, involving close body-care over a prolonged period, may mean that the boy may tend to adopt a feminine role rather than an assertive masculine one. The rigid, passive attitude also favours a feminine identification. Frequent surgical or medical procedures or the use of appliances, calipers, urinary bags—may also provoke feelings of being damaged or mutilated and this too may emphasize feelings of being different. The 'passing' problem has to be dealt with first.

The practical problems of everyday life have to be solved, not simply in order to get along, to live successfully, but also because as every mentally handicapped person sees it, failure would lead to forcible return to the hospital. But the demands of everyday life also have to be coped with in order to 'pass', simply because no ex-patient is willing to seem to others to be mentally handicapped (Boswell and Wingrove, 1974).

Some Scandinavian authorities advocate sex manuals and pornography. At present evidence as to whether this material provides sexual relief or increases sexual drive and weakens judgement is controversial; evidence is gathering in favour of the latter. Sexual problems in the mentally handicapped fall fairly far down their list of problems. The medical and nursing standpoint on this must be clear: no rules—simply guidelines; each individual person or couple should be considered as ordinary people, taking their own circumstances and privacy into account. Sex education programmes require simple language and contraceptive advice is an essential ingredient of all recognized programmes, e.g. The Elementary Adult Sex Education (EASE) Curriculum.

PHYSICAL TREATMENT

Drugs play a small but significant part in the treatment of the psychotic, neurotic and epileptic illnesses which are often super-added to the personality disorder. Major, minor and anticonvulsant medication are then, respectively, necessary. Inexplicable violence is particularly associated with epilepsy due to disorders of the temporal lobe. Sometimes in such a case stereotactic surgery is helpful. Amphetamines occasionally help in the socialization training of young delinquent 'extraverts'.

At the time of writing droperidol (i.m.) remains the drug of choice for the immediate control of severe violent outbursts when reasoning fails. This ultimate measure requires not only sufficient senior authority but also sufficient staff present to prevent injury to staff and patient during the restraint necessary to administer the drug.

Sexual disorders may require psychotherapy and also may, with the patient's co-operation, be cured by aversion treatment by a psychologist. This involves associating pictures of the previously pleasurable and offending act with unpleasant stimuli, such as emetics or electric shocks. Stilboestrol (1 mg daily)—a female hormone derivative—may very occasionally reduce libido to tolerable levels in sufficiently motivated subjects. This drug has undesirable feministic effects and Benperidol does not appear to possess these side-effects. Cyprosterone-acetate (Androcur) is used for the treatment of severe hypersexuality in the male. It has considerable side effects such as disturbances of liver and bone function and it should not be given to immature youths without stringent medico-legal consideration.

The return to the community should be phased either by the young person initially going out to work from the hospital or by his transfer to a staff-intensive local authority hostel, and suitable daytime occupation must be found. He should always be encouraged and welcomed back at the unit for recreation, advice, and the praise of staff and of those not yet ready for return to the community. For many reasons, it is imperative that the ex-patient finds a benefactor or mate. Ideally, this mate should be a normal person.

CHAPTER 20

Training the Mentally Handicapped— A Behavioural Approach

THE BEHAVIOURAL APPROACH TO TRAINING the mentally handicapped is often termed 'behaviour modification'. Many people confuse behaviour modification and behaviour therapy. The latter refers to more traditional one-to-one psychiatric therapy, based generally on Pavlov's classical conditioning and the learning theories of psychologist Clark Hull. It involves such techniques as *desensitization, assertive training* and *aversion therapy*. It is the former, behaviour modification that we are concerned with here. Behaviour modification is the name popularly given to the practical application of the branch of psychology known as the 'experimental analysis of behaviour'. This came into being during the early 1930s, largely through the work of B. F. Skinner with animals. Later, behaviour analysts moved into applied areas and tackled problems in hospitals, schools and other institutions. More recently, this branch of psychology (more properly termed *applied behaviour analysis*) has been employed in the 'open community', tackling social problems, such as delinquency and disadvantaged children. Throughout its history, applied behaviour analysis has been successfully used with the mentally handicapped, and a large body of literature has built up. Here we shall first consider the principles of behaviour analysis, and then some of the techniques arising from this, together with examples drawn from mental handicap and nursing practice.

PRINCIPLES OF BEHAVIOUR ANALYSIS

As the title says, we are concerned here with behaviour. This is what a person is actually seen to do, rather than what we think he is doing. As J. B. Watson (1900) said, 'Let us limit ourselves to things that can be observed, and formulate laws concerning only these things'. Using behaviour as a unit of study, it is possible to be objective. Many people still talk of human events in terms of internal 'drives', 'motives' or 'states of mind'. Here we are concerned only with the events themselves and the observable laws that govern them. More particularly, here we are concerned with *Operant Behaviour*. This is behaviour that operates on the environment, producing a consequence or 'pay off'.

A general behaviourist approach assumes that man is a creature of his environment and is thus influenced by what goes on around him. The operant approach stresses man's interaction with his environment and how this modifies his behaviour. If we take this a step further, we start to look at how these relationships and interactions influence behaviour. This is the subject matter of behaviour analysis.

Obviously we first have to know what we are looking for—i.e. we must describe the behaviour we are interested in. This is done in objective terms. For example, instead of saying, 'I want to observe Bill's ability to discriminate colours', we say, 'I want to observe the number of times Bill correctly discriminates red from yellow'. The first example is not directly observable; the second is. The complexity of human behaviour is such that this definition phase is very important and the description should be as clear as possible, otherwise great difficulties in observation will be encountered.

Having described our behaviour, we have to know how to quantify it. Just as length is measured in metres and centimetres, weight in grammes and kilogrammes, so behaviour is measured by its frequency. In other words, how often it occurs in a given time period. So if Jim swears 50 times a day, the frequency of his swearing behaviour is 50 per day. All behaviour is measured in terms of its frequency.

A behavioural (sometimes termed 'functional') analysis involves careful observation of the previously defined behaviour in the person's normal environment (ward, classroom, home, etc.). From this should come the information upon which the analysis is based. It should include the setting, antecedent events (what happens before the behaviour), frequency and consequent events (what happens after). It should then be possible to identify or analyse how the particular behaviour in question is related to the environment, i.e. isolate the events which act as a stimulus or cue to it, and the events which follow to reinforce it. If the behaviour is to be changed, behaviour analysis continues with an alteration of these cues and consequences.

Reinforcement and Extinction

It is precisely these effects mentioned above that we are concerned with in this section. It was mentioned earlier that Operant Behaviour is maintained by some sort of 'pay off'. This is technically termed *reinforcement*. The basic principle of behaviour analysis is that the consequence of a behaviour has an effect on the chances of that behaviour occurring again.

In simple terms, pleasant consequences will make the chances of it happening again more likely, whereas unpleasant consequences will make them less likely. If nothing at all happens, particularly if before there were reinforcing consequences, then the behaviour is likely to 'extinguish' or die away. Let us consider some of the ways that reinforcement can occur.

1. Positive reinforcement

A positive reinforcer is something which, when following behaviour, increases the frequency of that behaviour.

2. Negative reinforcement

A negative reinforcer also increases the frequency of behaviour. This is when a behaviour ends something unpleasant—the 'relief' may be the reinforcer, as it is a pleasant consequence. Taking a bath to avoid disparaging comments about lack of cleanliness is an example.

3. Punishment

If a behaviour is followed by unpleasant things, then it is less likely to occur again. Many common behaviour control methods are unfortunately based on punishment rather than reward.

Of course, what reinforces one person in one situation will not hold for other people: 'One man's meat is another man's poison', as the saying goes. All sorts of things can act as reinforcers, however, and they fall generally into two classes: primary (food, drink, warmth, sex, etc.) and secondary (money, success, praise and attention, etc.). It is important to know what is reinforcing to a person before trying to change his or her behaviour. Using re-inforcers of a type that is mentioned above, it is possible to increase, decrease or eliminate behaviour. In the next section, we will discuss some of the techniques that enable this to be done.

Before moving on to this, however, it is worthwhile considering the role of stimuli in maintaining behaviour. A stimulus is something that acts as a cue to behaviour. It may be anything that occurs in the environment. A sign saying 'Bargain Sale' may be a cue for certain types of behaviour in a shop for example. Likewise a red traffic light means 'Stop'. Much of human behaviour is under 'stimulus control'. It is possible to teach this by a process called *discrimination learning*. Here a reinforcer is given for responding to one type of stimulus and not to another. For example, a child giving the correct word for a picture is rewarded; the wrong word is not. This type of learning is important for teaching many things to the mentally handi-capped.

TECHNIQUES OF BEHAVIOUR CHANGE

Lindsley (1964) wrote, 'Children are not retarded; only their behaviour in average environments is retarded'. This quotation enshrines the radical behaviourist view of mental handicap, i.e. as a condition where people have failed to learn adaptive skills. Behaviour modification is one way in which this can be overcome. Often their failure to learn adaptive skills is accompanied by successful learning of useless, often harmful behaviours, such as self-injury, stereotyped mannerisms and rocking. These must be eliminated before the learning of more adaptive behaviour can take place. As a result, the techniques available to nurses are of two types: those used to establish a new or more *adaptive* behaviour and those used to eliminate a non-functional or *maladaptive* behaviour. They are often used together. The use of these techniques should stem from a thorough analysis of the individual's behaviour and environment and they are not put forward as a 'cookbook' of teaching methods.

Teaching Adaptive Skills

There are a number of specific teaching techniques that have been developed to establish new adaptive behaviour. They represent ways of using positive reinforcers to increase behaviour and, particularly, to teach behaviours that are not already existent in a person's behaviour repertoire.

SHAPING

Perhaps the most widely used set of techniques for establishing behaviour comes under the heading of 'shaping'. Most severely and profoundly mentally handicapped people have very limited repertoires of behaviour, so to teach these skills means that existing responses, such as they are, must be built on and expanded. This is what is implied by 'shaping'. Initially a response similar to a desired one is selected and reinforced so that it occurs frequently. The next stage is to select a variation of the original response and reinforce it. The criterion for reinforcement is changed each time, making the trainee go a step further towards the target before being reinforced. A skilful therapist can, using this technique, develop target responses easily, by gradually working towards it in small steps that are within the trainee's capability. For example, a resident may not like going upstairs. In order to shape this we might start with a response which he already has, such as walking. He would be reinforced firstly for walking towards stairs. Then the target would be changed to walking towards the stairs and up one step. The next stage would be to include another step in this chain of behaviour.

This way the target behaviour of climbing stairs is reached by starting with an existing response and extending it by 'small steps'.

PROMPTING

It may be that a response is just not in the resident's repertoire at all, and so 'shaping' in the above way would be difficult and time consuming. This is where the technique of 'prompting' is useful. Prompting means giving the patient as much help as is necessary for him to accomplish the target behaviour. There are generally three kinds of prompt, which may be used separately or together. Physical prompts may involve physically guiding a patient's hand through the motions of the target response. Gestural prompts is the term for 'miming' or demonstrating the action (without necessarily having physical contact with the trainee). Verbal prompts correspond to instructions and directions (e.g. 'Put your shoes on'). It is often better to start by using all three types, gradually working through to none at all.

FADING

Prompts are useful to start a response which can then be rewarded, but in order for learning to take place, they must be removed. This is done by a process called 'fading', which involves gradually removing prompts until they are finished with. In teaching a sight vocabulary, for example, a word might be matched to the picture. The picture is then made fainter and fainter as the patient responds with a word, until he is eventually responding only to the word which is still clearly visible. Slide projectors which do this are now available.

CHAINING

Human behaviour often occurs in set sequences—or chains—composed of many small behavioural links. Many activities are like this, including washing, dressing, toothbrushing, cooking, making jig-saws and many work activities. When a complex behaviour like this is tackled, the large chain is broken into its small links, and put together. The trainee is required gradually to put more links together before gaining reward.

Quite often it is better to put the links into the chain *backwards*. This is because the last step, when taught first, is the end product, so the trainee knows what he has to aim for, and is reinforced quickly. As training proceeds, more and more links are required to finish the tasks. A good example of this is teaching dressing. Here the technique of backward chaining dictates that the patient starts off fully clothed, apart from perhaps his jumper, which is around his armpits. He is then prompted to pull this to his waist and reinforced. He has, in effect, completed the full dressing procedure. Training then proceeds backwards, through small steps with each garment until the trainee, unclothed, can pick up and put on each garment before being rewarded. Backward chaining can be very useful training to teach a lot of adaptive skills needed by most severely and profoundly handicapped people.

MODELLING AND IMITATION

Normal children learn much through imitation, particularly of their parents or playmates. Often mentally handicapped people do not imitate spontaneously, and so do not learn things as normal children would. As a result it is necessary to teach them to imitate. This can be done by reinforcing an attempt to copy the trainer's response, gradually shaping it until it corresponds. This is often done in speech training, where firstly motor responses, such as arm raising, are imitated before speech sounds are treated likewise. Once imitation has been taught, it can be an important technique for teaching new behaviours. The trainer (or even other residents) can model the response required and the trainee can be reinforced for imitating it [notice that gestural prompts (*q.v.*) are examples of models].

The above are the main behaviour techniques that have so far been developed for teaching the mentally handicapped. New ones are developed and old ones utilized, as a direct result of experimental (or functional) analysis of a resident's behaviour.

ELIMINATING MALADAPTIVE BEHAVIOUR

The word 'maladaptive' is often used to describe some of the undesirable ways in which mentally handicapped people behave. Such behaviour causes concern and distress to staff, to other patients and, much more importantly, hinders the learning of adaptive skills. Examples of maladaptive behaviour are: self-injurious behaviour, physically and verbally aggressive behaviour, stereotyped mannerisms and other 'unacceptable' behaviour. Obviously what is considered maladaptive will vary according to the standards of society as a whole, the local community and, unfortunately, the tolerance of nursing staff. Generally speaking, maladaptive behaviour is of no functional value in the person's environment and interferes with the learning of the adaptive skills already discussed. A decision to eliminate such behaviour often involves ethical and legal considerations. Most traditional methods of elimination are punitive—restraint, bed-rest or drugs—and do not re-educate the patient in more adaptive behaviour. Some of the techniques developed for applied behaviour analysis involve punishment, although they are based on proven effectiveness and strictly controlled conditions. Here again the matter becomes an ethical one and practice varies according to the policy of institutions.

When dealing with maladaptive behaviour, a behavioural view dictates that much maladaptive behaviour, like adaptive behaviour, is the result of the interaction of a person and his environment. Therefore, if some aspect of this relationship is changed, the behaviour should be altered. A functional analysis of the behaviour is therefore essential, as this determines which technique of behaviour elimination is to be used. If a maladaptive response is being maintained by reinforcing schedules operating in that mentally handicapped person's environment, then these must be changed in order to effect response elimination. For example, consider a mentally handicapped person who continually strips his clothes off and is then redressed by a nurse. It is likely that the stripping is maintained by the reward of nurse's attention that continually follows it. Elimination of the stripping behaviour would be achieved by withdrawing this reward, thus, in technical terms, extinguishing it. Practically this would mean that the nurse would ignore the stripping and give the person attention only when he was dressed. Notice the method of eliminating the maladaptive behaviour was a *direct result* of a functional analysis of the problem. Ignoring the problem behaviour would not have much effect if attention were *not* the maintaining factor.

This analysis may result in the implementation of many methods of behaviour elimination, some of them more common than others. The above example showed how extinction of a response might be carried out, where this is relevant to the characteristics of the mentally handicapped person–environment interaction. Another technique, often misused, is *time-out* (from Positive Reinforcement). This works on the principle that being out of a rewarding situation for a short time has a punishing effect. The usual time-out programme involves the use of a small, stimulus-free room, in which the patient is placed for a pre-set period of time (usually about 10 minutes), immediately following a maladaptive response. The time-out room, although useful, is not necessary as long as removal from reinforcers is possible. Time-out has been shown in many studies to be an efficient method of eliminating behaviour. Obviously to be effective, there needs to be a rewarding 'time-in' situation to accompany it. Time-out contains elements of extinction, but probably is best considered a punishment technique, the use of which will be discussed later.

It is also possible to eliminate behaviour with reinforcement. One way of doing this is to reinforce a response only when it has occurred *after* a set period of time has occurred since the last response. In this way a low rate of response is produced. (The technical name for this schedule is *differential reinforcement of low rate*.) It has proved useful in reducing less serious maladaptive behaviour in classroom settings. Another method of eliminating behaviour by reinforcement is termed *differential reinforcement of other behaviour*. This means that, in effect, any behaviour occurring within a specified time is rewarded, *except* the problem behaviour. Typically, this involves the use of a timer, which rings off a time limit. If the target maladaptive response, e.g. self-injurious behaviour or coprophagia, has not occurred, reward is given. If response has occurred, then the timer is reset and no reward is given. The 'other' behaviour rewarded strengthens, while the problem behaviour falls off. It is also often possible to reward behaviour that is directly incompatible with the target maladaptive behaviour, so preventing this latter from occurring.

Despite the fact that it is not solely part of the applied behaviour analyst's techniques, punishment must be mentioned as a means of eliminating maladaptive behaviour. As stated previously, time-out is a punishment method as it occurs following a response and provides unpleasant consequences which reduce the frequency of responding.

Other methods used include aversive stimulation (electric shock, high intensity noise or physical punishment); over-correction, where a response is followed by an unpleasant consequence, such as being forced to work, or repetitive tasks; and response cost, where the reward previously given, particularly tokens in a token economy programme, is taken away as a result of maladaptive behaviour (like a fine). Many studies exist to show the effectiveness of these procedures, particularly in severe cases of, for example, self-injurious behaviour, but ethical doubts by many workers restricts their usage (despite the control that is possible over them). Often they involve an unacceptable level of severity, many have adverse effects and recently have been legally restricted, particularly in the United States.

Much research remains to be done into methods of eliminating behaviour using educative and reinforcement techniques. The importance of a thorough functional analysis of the problem cannot be stressed enough, as this type of behaviour is most often the result of the institutional environment, and is maintained by rewarding situations that occur in it. The identification of these, and their withdrawal, should lead to the elimination of much maladaptive behaviour. *It should be remembered that nurse attention is a potent source of reinforcement for institutionalized people—especially for bad behaviour.*

BEHAVIOUR PRINCIPLES IN THE CARE OF THE MENTALLY HANDICAPPED

The final part of this chapter will attempt to deal with some of the implications of the behavioural principles described above for the care (particularly nursing care) of the mentally handicapped.

There are many misconceptions about the behavioural approach to teaching the mentally handicapped. One of the most prominent of these is that it is really only 'a bag of tricks', with only the techniques important. This can be seen reflected in the way many attempt to use these techniques to alter behaviour without first experimentally analysing it to find out the relationship between responses and environment. The applied behavioural analysis approach, however, is a philosophy and a way of looking at all behaviour. This philosophy affects all aspects of care of the mentally handicapped, and a behavioural approach should not just be confined to 'projects' or 'programmes' as it so often is.

In his novel *Walden Two* (1976), B. F. Skinner outlined how a behavioural approach to life could bring about social and cultural change. Likewise if behavioural principles were known and understood by all who work with retarded people, then a fundamental change in the philosophy and practice of care would occur. Special psychologist-originated projects would not be necessary, as mentally handicapped people would be in a continuous teaching situation, with rewards rearranged so that care staff helped them to help themselves. This is, of course, at present only an ideal, but the continuing success of behaviourally-based programmes and institutions shows how much could be achieved for the retarded if it were a reality.

Another misconception is that behaviour principles are the province of psychologists exclusively. Nothing could be further from the truth, as the many training courses for parents, social workers, care staff and teachers show. In June, 1973, the Joint Board of Clinical Nursing Studies outlined a curriculum for teaching behaviour principles to nurses. This has since been adopted in approved centres, with many others running similar courses based on the same syllabus. If the reordering of reinforcement contingencies in an institution is to work to 100 per cent efficiency, it is important that the principles are understood by everyone from the psychiatrist to the domestic staff. This is not to say, however, that the guidance of a skilled psychologist is not important in establishing and maintaining programmes.

Lastly, some people raise doubts about the 'humanity' of the behavioural approach, saying it treats humans as machines. Often these criticisms stem from ignorance of what applied behaviour analysis entails. In fact, applied behaviour analysts are motivated by a desire to see positive, constructive things being done with the mentally handicapped. Applied behaviour analysis provides not only a clear outline of the objectives being taught, but also how to teach them most effectively. Its structured approach provides a concrete basis for action for an individual rather than a 'fuzzy' set of vague concepts. More importantly, it provides successful learning opportunities for the mentally handicapped, who have usually a history of continual failure. If a programme does not work, the mentally handicapped person is not 'stupid' or 'untrainable'; the programme is wrong and has not been effective in producing behaviour change. It is difficult to see how such an approach can be termed 'inhumane'.

In conclusion, it can be seen that the behavioural approach to training the mentally handicapped is much more than a set of techniques. It is a philosophy of care, and of viewing people. It also provides a basis for constructive action in teaching the mentally handicapped. As Skinner has said: 'It is important to make clear that caring is first of all a matter of acting, and only secondarily a matter of feeling' (1972).

A Footnote on Token Economies

In token economy programmes, target behaviour (usually self-help skills) is reinforced not with primary reinforcers such as food, but with tokens, a type of secondary reinforcer. They may be in any form—washers, counters or paper stars. Tokens are exchanged later for a wide variety of reinforcers, each with a particular value. The advantage of tokens is that they are portable, durable and inexhaustible. They also allow a behaviour chain to be rewarded, without interrupting it (imagine recording each step of a tooth-brushing programming with sweets!) Many hospitals now have token economy programmes, and have shown improvements in target behaviours. Some researchers, however, have doubts as to the usefulness of these programmes, as often they are complex to run, and open to the influence of many disturbing factors. The time taken to teach a resident the value and usage of a token might be better spent teaching the value of social reinforcement, which operates in all human behaviour.

PRACTICAL NOTES ON BEHAVIOURAL NURSING

1. Ensure that reinforcement follows the desired response immediately. It is better to omit than delay a reinforcer.

2. Make clear to the person what the reward is for, always using the same words. This way they will associate words with behaviour and reward.

3. If using primary reinforcers, always add verbal and social reward as well. Eventually the primary reinforcers can then be faded out, and the behaviour maintained by natural reinforcers.

4. Ignore maladaptive behaviour completely. To attend to it (even by telling someone off) is likely to reinforce it.

5. On the other hand reward adaptive behaviour wherever it occurs.

6. When rewarding, be dynamic! Make a big event of it and show the individual that you are really pleased. No mumbling, muttering or half-hearted praise.

7. When teaching new skills, always specify the target behaviour in clear objective terms and break it into small steps. Do not move onto another step until the one before it is mastered.

8. Do not do anything for a person that he is capable of doing himself, so as to encourage independence and create a teaching situation.

9. Do not encourage psychotic or maladaptive behaviour (even for demonstration) as you will reward it.

10. Mentally handicapped people are not sick; they have merely not learnt. Be careful not to pre-judge them ('He'll never learn to do that!') and their capabilities.

Goal Planning

One way in which the behavioural approach to teaching the mentally handicapped can be put into practice is through the idea of 'Goal Planning'. This method is basically a means of providing an individual *specific* behavioural target for any handicapped person. There are many types of these in use, but they all have certain features in common. These are:

1. They are based on an initial assessment of a person's skills, problems and needs.

2. A person's strengths or skills are used to set targets or goals which help tackle their needs or problems.

3. The goal is split into small steps that are easily attainable.

4. The goal plan is written down and states clearly who will do what and when.

5. Goals are set for specific items of behaviour.

6. Goals are reviewed at regular intervals and new ones set as a result of the review.

7. Goal planning meetings involve all people concerned with a mentally handicapped person. This would include staff of all disciplines, the patients and the mentally handicapped person.

In any system of goal planning the writing and recording of goals set is very important, especially if more than one person might be teaching the goal to the client. The records should be clear and brief and should take the form of a description of what the person would be doing when the goal is achieved. Here is an example:

Goal—John will travel independently on a bus.

Steps—1. John will learn to differentiate between 10p and 50p pieces.
       2. John will learn to identify numbers of buses.
       3. John will travel into town on a bus with an escort.
       4. John will travel one stop independently and be collected by an escort.
       5. John will travel to town and be met by an escort.
       6. John will travel to town and back independently.

Action—Mrs Black will teach John Step 1 by 12th September.

The above example could have many more steps (or 'sub-goals') if necessary. For example, step 3 could be divided into many more. Similarly, for a very severely handicapped client the goals set would reflect their immediate needs, and the sub-goals would probably need to be a lot more simple.

There are many types of goal planning systems in use. Perhaps one of the best known is the 'Portage System', which is designed for parents and pre-school handicapped children living at home. Individual programmes such as are provided by goal planning procedures are a feature of many modern service provisions (e.g. the ENCOR Service in the USA). They are likely to become a feature of most forms of care for the mentally handicapped over the next few years.

CHAPTER 21

Intelligence and Intelligence Testing

THE CONCEPT OF INTELLIGENCE is one which tends to provoke much debate and controversy. There is, for example, no one wholly acceptable definition of intelligence. Also, the factors which contribute to intelligence, and their relative importance in terms of the individual differences which occur, are not altogether clear, and the various standard tests devised to measure intelligence are viewed with doubt and suspicion by many. However, in spite of the difficulties of definition and measurement, it remains a useful concept for those involved in education and training, since knowledge of an individual's intellectual level can enable predictions to be made about that person's potential and behaviour in different situations.

DEFINITION OF INTELLIGENCE

It has been said that intelligence, like electricity, is easier to talk about than to define. This is borne out by the variety of definitions which have been put forward, such as 'the ability to carry on abstract thinking', 'the ability to solve problems', and 'general innate cognitive ability'. Some have avoided the issue by suggesting that intelligence is 'what intelligence tests measure'.

However, the problem might be tackled more fruitfully from a different angle. Rather than attempting to define intelligence in terms of an abstract concept, it may be more meaningful to state what is meant when an individual is described as being intelligent. This would usually be taken to mean that the person tends to adopt an intelligent mode of response in most of the things he undertakes, by, for example, being aware of the consequences of his actions, by being able to adapt to changes in the situation, by applying previously learned principles to new problems, and by acting appropriately to obtain the desired goal.

Thus, while definition of the concept of intelligence is difficult, the characteristics of intelligent behaviour are more easily identified and described.

STRUCTURE OF INTELLIGENCE

When an individual is described as being intelligent, an over-riding capacity or ability is implied which has a fundamental influence on his performance on all intellectual tasks, irrespective of the specific nature of these tasks. There is ample evidence from studies to support this idea of an over-riding intellectual capacity. When a variety of tests involving different types of mental ability are given to a large representative sample of the population, a common factor appears to affect their performance in that individuals tend to perform at approximately the same level on most, or all, of the tests. The importance of this common factor of intellectual ability has been stressed by various workers in the field of intelligence, such as Spearman and Burt, and it is often referred to as general intelligence or 'g'.

While 'g' is the dominant influence on performance of mental tasks, some contribution is also made by abilities and skills which are specific to a particular task or group of tasks.

According to Burt, who studied the structure of human abilities for over half a century, intelligence is arranged in a hierarchical fashion (as shown in Fig. 15). After 'g', the next most important factor is one which distinguishes verbal and non-verbal abilities (major group factors). These further sub-divide into 'minor group factors', which in turn are composed of skills which are entirely specific to a particular task.

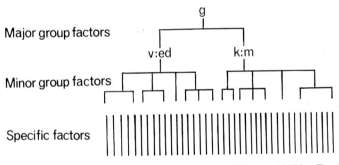

Fig. 15. Diagram illustrating Hierarchical Structure of Human Abilities. From Vernon (1950).

While Burt's hierarchical view of the structure of intelligence has obtained a lot of support, particularly in Britain, an alternative explanation was put forward by Thurstone (1938). Thurstone, an American psychologist, carried out a number of large-scale studies in which over 50 tests of various types were given to different age groups. Using the statistical technique of factor analysis he isolated seven basic factors or 'primary mental abilities' which contributed independently to intellectual performance:—Spatial Ability (S), Perceptual Speed (P), Numerical Ability (N), Verbal Fluency (W),

Verbal Meaning (V), Memory (M) and Inductive Reasoning (R). Thurstone regarded these abilities as being independent of each other, and initially discounted the idea of a general intelligence factor.

In fact the argument about which of these two theories on the structure of intelligence provides the best explanation is, in the main, a statistical one. It has been shown that some degree of correlation exists between the 'primary mental abilities' isolated by Thurstone, thus supporting the idea of an over-riding general factor of intelligence.

GENETIC AND ENVIRONMENTAL FACTORS

Much of psychologists' work on intelligence in this century has been aimed at an evaluation of the respective contributions to intelligence made by hereditary and environmental factors. It is important to know whether intelligence is mainly determined by genetic factors, in much the same way as physical or bodily traits, or whether the environment is the predominant influence. This is a highly controversial topic in the study of intelligence, and the arguments are often characterized by emotion and dogma rather than objectivity, particularly with regard to postulated differences between races. However, it is an issue of great practical importance, since if environmental factors have a major role in determining a person's intelligence, it may be possible to arrange these so as to enable him to improve his intellectual performance.

A number of methods have been adopted in attempts to solve this problem, such as selective breeding in animals, comparison of intellectual performance by children and their parents, and studies of deprived groups such as orphanage children. It is the study of identical twins, however, which has provided the most valuable information in this area. Since they have identical heredity, they provide a convenient means for assessing the differential effects of genetic and environmental factors. Of particular interest are identical twins who have been reared apart, since with heredity held constant, any measured difference in intelligence can be attributed to the environment. Jensen (1970) collated the evidence from four major studies on the intelligence of identical twins reared apart following separation in early life. He reports that in over 70 per cent of the 122 cases studied, the difference in intelligence test scores was 8 IQ points or less, which is not significant (*see next section*). Extreme differences in test scores between twins were very rare. This compares with the average difference of 12 IQ points between full siblings reared together, and 11 IQ points between non-identical twins reared together. Thus, there is greater concordance among identical twins brought up in different environments than either non-identical twins or siblings reared together. Those who claim that the environment is the dominant influence would argue that there is no sure way of knowing that the environments of identical twins reared apart are any different from those of non-identical twins reared together, but most authorities now accept that heredity is the stronger influence in determining intelligence.

Attempts have been made to assess precisely the relative contributions of heredity and environment to intelligence. Burt, for example, concluded from complex genetic and statistical analysis that genetic factors contributed 80 per cent and the environment 20 per cent. In the individual case this kind of apportionment is not possible, and it is perhaps more meaningful to look upon heredity as providing innate intellectual potential, or capacity for development, and thus akin to 'g'. The process of interaction with the environment determines the extent to which that potential will be utilized. The environmental factors which exert an influence are multitudinous, but among the more obvious are nutrition, level of stimulation, social class, education and culture.

Severe mental handicap can be attributed to genetic factors in a number of conditions such as phenylketonuria, a metabolic disorder, and Down's syndrome, which is due to a chromosomal abnormality. The environmental factors which can result in mental handicap are many. Pre-natal causes include congenital syphilis in the mother. Hypoxia and injury at birth, and infection and head injury in the post-natal environment are common precipitants.

THE DEVELOPMENT OF INTELLIGENCE

Apart from general acceptance that intellectual ability increases up to adolescence and declines in old age, there is little precise information about the changes which occur in intelligence throughout the average human life-span. The major difficulty is a methodological one. Longitudinal studies, in which random samples of the population are followed up at intervals from birth throughout life, are obviously lengthy and expensive procedures, although they ultimately provide much valuable data. The alternative cross-sectional method whereby the results of samples from different age groups tested at the same time are compared, has practical advantages but is dependent upon the different age samples being alike on all the critical variables.

There is agreement among most authorities that intelligence cannot be reliably estimated before the age of two, although comparisons of developmental progress in terms of such aspects as language, motor ability and socialization are useful, especially for diagnosis. There is evidence, however, that from about the age of four years future ability can be assessed with some reliability. Intellectual ability accelerates rapidly until late adolescence when a levelling-off takes place for some years before it begins to decline. Longitudinal studies have tended to show very little change in intelligence during early adulthood and middle age, whereas cross-sectional studies frequently suggest a significant decline at a relatively early stage. These different findings may be explained to some extent on the one hand by a tendency for the less able to drop out of longitudinal studies as they proceed and on the other hand by the likelihood that older subjects in cross-sectional studies have had, on average, poorer education.

What has been clearly established is that different abilities decline at different rates. Verbal abilities such as vocabulary and general knowledge tend to show little change between early adulthood and old age, and in some cases may even increase. Non-verbal abilities generally show a deterioration from about age 30, which accelerates with advancing age (*see* Fig. 16).

It must be borne in mind, however, that these are *average* changes or trends which occur, and they will not apply in each individual case. There is evidence to suggest that the rate of decline varies in relation to initial intelligence level. With more intelligent individuals, the probability is that they will be better preserved intellectually later in life, and this has been attributed to a higher level of intellectual stimulation and general activity.

MEASUREMENT OF INTELLIGENCE

The first systematic attempts to measure individual differences in mental ability were carried out by Galton in the latter half of the last century. Galton concerned himself with basic mental processes such as reaction time and sensory perception, which he measured precisely in a large sample of subjects. While the abilities evaluated in these 'mental tests' would now be considered to be of limited relevance to intelligence, his application of a standard administration to each subject to obtain objective measures laid the basis of scientific method in the study of mental function. Furthermore, Galton's findings led him to conclude that mental characteristics are normally distributed throughout the population in the same way as physical traits, i.e. the majority of the population fall close to the average score, with roughly equal numbers on either side of the mean and fewer and fewer obtaining scores towards the extremes of the range. The result is that the curve showing the distribution of such traits as height, weight and intelligence in the population is roughly symmetrical and bell-shaped, and is known as the normal distribution curve.

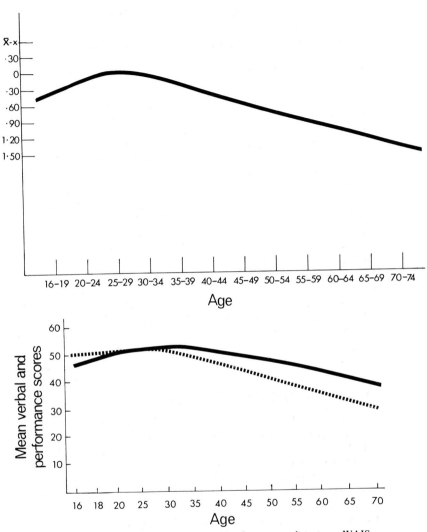

Fig. 16. Comparative decline of verbal and performance sub-tests on WAIS with age. Ages 16–75 and over (2052 cases). Solid line, verbal; broken line, performance. From Wechsler (1958) p. 202.

The next significant development in the measurement of intelligence emerged with the work of Binet, a French psychologist, at the turn of the century. Binet and his colleagues developed a scale for assessing children, in order to identify those unable to benefit from ordinary school instruction because of retardation so that they could be placed in special schools which would cater for their difficulties.

Binet continued the scientific approach adopted by Galton, but concentrated on the assessment of higher mental processes such as memory, concentration and comprehension. Batteries of tests involving problems of everyday life which required different aspects of mental function were given to large numbers of children of ages from 3 to 12, and only those which differentiated the brighter from the duller children, or the older from the younger were retained.

In 1905 Binet and Simon introduced the 'Scale of Intelligence', which comprised 30 items, graded in difficulty. The items ranged from following a moving object with one's eyes to defining abstract words. The average score for each age group was determined and it was then possible to compare any one child's performance with the average for his age group. A revised version appeared in 1908, in which the test items were grouped according to the age at which the majority of a large sample of children passed them. The child's mental age (MA) was derived from the highest group of tests he passed, irrespective of chronological age, so it was possible to determine whether the child was performing at an average level for his age, or above or below it. Thus an eight-year-old child who could pass items only up to the five-year-old level would be regarded as below average for his age group, and three years retarded in his intellectual development. This principle of comparing an individual's performance with the average for his age group remains the basis of intelligence testing today.

While comparison of mental age and chronological age (CA) was often useful as an index of a child's intellectual status, it could be misleading. A difference of two years between MA and CA in a five-year-old child would be of much greater significance than a similar discrepancy in a 14-year-old. A more meaningful method was introduced by Terman in 1916, whereby mental age was expressed as a ratio of chronological age to provide 'intelligence quotient' (IQ). The IQ formula is well known:

$$\frac{\text{Mental Age}}{\text{Chronological Age}} \times 100 = \text{IQ}.$$

Thus a child whose mental age is the same as his chronological age, i.e. he is average for his age group, would have an IQ of 100, which is the mean IQ score. The greater the discrepancy between MA and CA, whether higher or lower, the greater would be the deviation from 100.

The Binet–Simon scale was adapted for use in a number of different countries. It was revised and modified, and renamed as the Stanford–Binet or Terman–Merrill test, but many of the original features remained. It continues to have widespread use for ages between three and fifteen years, but the method of determining IQ scores changed with the 1960 revision.

The change was necessitated by the limitations of the concept of mental age. For example, it could not be applied to adults because the changes which occur in intelligence during adulthood are relatively minor over a period of time compared to those which occur in children over a similar period. Instead, the principle of 'deviation' IQ was utilized, based on statistical procedures. Tests were constructed so as to provide an average score of 100 when given to a large sample of a given age group, with 68 per cent of the sample obtaining IQ scores between 85 and 115. This is the average range of intelligence test scores. About 16 per cent of the population score below 85 (below average) and about 16 per cent above 115 (above average). Fig. 17 shows IQ scores are distributed throughout the population. Thus an individual's IQ score tells us where he stands in intelligence test performance relative to others of his age group. For example, a score of 130 places an individual within the top two per cent of the population in terms of intelligence.

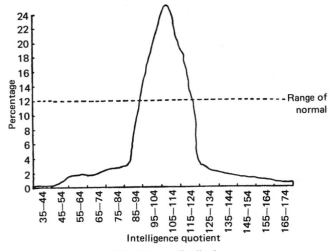

Fig. 17. Intelligence distribution curve.

It will be seen that, although the IQ distribution curve is roughly symmetrical, there are more individuals in the population with IQs below 50 than there are in the corresponding part of the curve above 150. This can be attributed to the effects of environmental factors. such as infection and brain injury, causing severe mental handicap in cases where the genetic endowment would otherwise have resulted in normal intelligence.

Before proceeding to a brief discussion of some of the commonly used intelligence tests, it is pertinent to consider factors which must be taken into account in their development and construction.

In intelligence testing, as with any other kind of psychological testing, the concepts of reliability and validity are crucial. Reliability in this context refers to consistency, and for a test to be considered reliable, it should provide the same results each time it is administered in identical conditions. Validity refers to whether a test actually measures what it is purported to measure, and since a definition of intelligence is elusive, there are difficulties in producing tests which can be said to give valid measurements of it. In practice, intelligence tests tend to be validated against an acceptable criterion, such as school achievement.

The construction of an intelligence test must involve definition of its purpose and scope. For example, the test may be intended to measure current intellectual level within a given age range and range of ability, or it may be used to predict future potential or attainment. The aim of the test may be to assess innate intellectual ability directly, or to obtain an indirect measure through acquired skills or abilities. Tests can be of verbal or non-verbal ability, and cultural factors should be taken into account. Generally, intelligence tests provide a sampling of different areas of ability rather than an assessment of global capacity, so selection of the abilities to be measured must be made.

The process of standardization is important. Basically, this means that appropriate test items are selected and administered in a standard procedure to a representative sample of the population for whom the test is intended, to yield a normal distribution of scores. This provides the norms against which individual performance can be compared. Tests should be standardized on as large a sample as possible, taking account of such variables as age, sex, socio-economic status, race and occupation. It is interesting to note that the Stanford–Binet test was standardized on a sample of over 3000 white children born in the United States, which raises doubts about its applicability to the coloured population in that country.

In addition to an adequate standardization sample, it is essential that the tests are administered and scored strictly in accordance with set procedures, even to the extent of exact wording of questions being used. Comparison of an individual's performance with the norm for his age group will not be valid if there is any variation in the administration or scoring.

Special problems arise in the intellectual assessment of the mentally handicapped, particularly those children categorized as severely or profoundly handicapped. Very often they will require to be assessed on tests or scales standardized on children from lower age groups. Most formal intelligence tests for children do not go below a mental age of 18 months, and require some speech development. Because many severely handicapped children are incapable of performing even the earliest items on these tests, assessment is often restricted to aspects of development, such as sensori-motor function.

Minor variations in an individual's IQ score often occur on repeat testing. A difference of up to five or six points greater or less than a previous score would not be considered unusual, and could be due to fatigue, nervousness or lack of confidence, rather than to a change in intellectual capacity. The tester should, therefore, allay anxiety and obtain the confidence of the subject as much as possible before proceeding with the test. Because of these variations, it is more meaningful to describe an individual's intelligence in terms of the range within which he falls, rather than the precise IQ score he obtains.

The intelligence classifications adopted by Wechsler (1958), with the percentage of the population included at each level, are as follows:

IQ	Classification	Per cent included
130+	Very Superior	2·2
120–129	Superior	6·7
110–119	Bright Normal	16·1
90–109	Average	50·0
80–89	Dull normal	16·1
70–79	Borderline Defective	6·7
69 and below	Mental Defective	2·2

The mentally retarded are commonly classified thus:

55–69	Mild retardation
40–54	Moderate retardation
25–39	Severe retardation
Below 25	Profound retardation

INTELLIGENCE TESTS

This section will be confined to a broad description of some of the tests in common use for assessment of intelligence. (*See also* Appendix 3.)

Merrill–Palmer Scale   Age range: 18–71 months
This scale consists of 93 items. The emphasis is on non-verbal abilities such as motor skill, and extra credit can be gained by performing tasks within specified time limits. Verbal items involve abilities such as comprehension, where the subject is required to carry out simple instructions or give word meanings. The non-verbal items include the Seguin form board and picture puzzles. Because many of the test items can be demonstrated by the tester rather than verbalized, it is useful for deaf children or those with poor language development.

Stanford–Binet Intelligence Scale   Age range: 2–18 years
The 1960 version of this scale is probably the most commonly used of the tests standardized on children. In addition to its extensive age range, it has broad application, covering the IQ range 30–170. The test consists of sets of six test items. For ages 2–5 there is a set for each half-year, and success on any one item contributes one month to the child's mental age. For ages 5–14 there is a set for each year, and two months is credited to mental age for each item passed. The mental age is then converted to a deviation IQ score.

Although the test does contain non-verbal items, these are applied at the younger age levels, and a common criticism of the Stanford–Binet is its heavy loading with verbal and educational material.

Wechsler Intelligence Scale for Children   (WISC) Age range: 5–15 years

Wechsler Adult Intelligence Scale   (WAIS) Age range: 16–75 years
These scales are very similar in content, the children's form being a scaled down version of the adult test. They consist of a series of verbal and 'performance' or non-verbal sub-tests, covering a range of abilities such as general knowledge, conceptualization and spatial orientation.

Items are arranged in order of difficulty, without reference to age levels, and a subject discontinues a sub-test after a prescribed number of consecutive failures. Scaled scores from each sub-test are combined to provide verbal and performance IQ scores, from which the full-scale IQ score is obtained. The scales are applicable within the IQ range 50–160. In addition to assessment of intelligence, the Wechsler scales can be of value as a diagnostic aid. Also, because of the greater emphasis on non-verbal abilities, they are usually regarded as being less vulnerable to the influences of cultural factors than the Stanford–Binet.

The sub-tests of the verbal scale involve general knowledge, comprehension, arithmetic, conceptualization, immediate recall of digits and vocabulary. The five performance sub-tests draw upon aspects of perceptual function, such as constructing jig-saw type puzzles, assembling visual designs and deducing the missing part from a picture. All performance sub-tests, and the arithmetic test, are timed and extra credit is gained from speedy responses, on the basis that more intelligent individuals can perform mental tests more quickly. Also the norms for the scales reflect the different rates of decline of verbal and non-verbal abilities with age.

In the majority of cases, verbal and performance IQs are similar. The influence of culture and education on the verbal sub-tests can lead to a disparity, however, in the case of deprived people whose verbal IQ may be an underestimate of their true potential. On the other hand, people with brain damage of different kinds are often found to perform at a significantly lower level on the performance scale than on the verbal scale.

Progressive Matrices Age range: 20–65 years
Coloured Progressive Matrices Age range: 5–11 years; 65–85 years
These are tests of logical reasoning, which require the subject to select the correct shape from a number of alternatives to complete a visual pattern. The adult form consists of five sets of twelve problems of increasing difficulty. For children and the elderly, there are three sets of problems which are in colour to provide extra clues. The Matrices test was specifically designed to measure Spearman's 'g' factor. It has been shown to be relatively unaffected by cultural factors, and is a useful tool for screening of intellectual level in the deaf and those with speech and communication disorders. It does not discriminate beyond the IQ range 70–130, however, and it does not cover the broad range of cognitive function of such tests as the WAIS.

Mill Hill Vocabulary Scale
Various forms of this vocabulary test are available, standardized for use with children, adults and the elderly. It is used to provide a measure of verbal ability for comparison with intellectual capacity as measured by the Progressive Matrices.

CONCLUSION

From a time when intelligence was regarded as fixed and unalterable, and the IQ test was looked upon as the ultimate criterion of mental development and potential, the pendulum has swung in the opposite direction. The usefulness of intelligence as a concept is doubled by many, and IQ tests are frequently viewed with hostility. In fact, intelligence tests are a useful guide to mental ability but their limitations must be acknowledged, particularly with regard to the content of tests and cultural influence. It is important that test scores be interpreted, not in isolation, but within the context of background information from various sources. For the future, there is a very clear need to isolate those environmental factors which contribute most towards intelligence, in order that individuals can benefit from optimum conditions.

CHAPTER 22

The Development of Thinking

ALTHOUGH INTELLIGENCE TESTS are constructed to take into account the changes which take place in thought processes at different stages in the development of children, neither the choice of test item nor the psychometric procedure gives much indication as to how these processes actually change. Probably the most comprehensive attempt to define the transitional phases in the development of logical thinking has been the work of Jean Piaget and his colleagues in Geneva. They have contributed greatly to our understanding of the mind of a child, and have many adherents in the fields of education and training. Their work is of considerable relevance to mental handicap. This chapter will provide a description of Piaget's views on the development of cognitive processes.

According to Piaget, normal cognitive development takes place in an ordered and unvaried chronological sequence from birth to adolescence, with each stage involving progressively more complex patterns of thinking and behaviour. Four periods of mental growth are isolated, during which new mental abilities became available at certain key points. The changes are subtle and often go unnoticed, but as a result of the acquisition of concepts such as time, space and number, the child is able to perceive his world more realistically. Critically involved in the transition is the child's development of language and capacity for symbolic representation.

The four main stages described by Piaget are the *sensori-motor* period, from birth to about 2 years; the *pre-operational* period, comprising the pre-conceptual stage (2–4 years), and the intuitive stage (4–7 years); the stage of *concrete operations*, from 7 to 11 years; and the stage of *abstract operations* (11 years onward). These stages are assumed to be mainly the result of maturation, but may be influenced by environmental or biological factors. The age levels are given only as a rough guideline, and are not intended to be precise indicators of transition.

THE SENSORI-MOTOR PERIOD

In this period the child's reactions change from that of a primarily reflexive organism to being relatively cohesive in response to the immediate environment. Throughout this period there is a move away from 'adualism', a term Piaget used to describe the inability of the infant to differentiate himself and his feelings from the objects and events of the outside world. Gradually he learns to adapt to his environment by taking in and adjusting to new experiences, and through these processes of *assimilation* and *accommodation* he builds up organized patterns of thought and action, known as *schemata*. An awareness of cause and effect develops, and some conception of external reality is acquired. Six sub-stages are distinguished:

(*i*) *0–1 month:* The infant shows little apart from reflexive behaviour.

(*ii*) *1–4 months:* Reflex activities are modified by experience, and the infant's repertoire is expanded by random body movements which will be repeated if he perceives that it leads to a certain result. He begins to co-ordinate his movements.

(*iii*) *4–8 months:* A transition occurs from body-centred activity to object-centred activity. The child begins to demonstrate goal-directed behaviour as a result of learning the association between his action and its perceived effect, such as shaking his rattle to make a noise. However, objects cease to exist for him if they are removed from view.

(*iv*) *8–12 months:* Behaviour patterns formed at sub-stage (*iii*) are co-ordinated. The child will change from one activity to another to achieve a goal, such as pushing aside an obstacle to get to a desired object. He uses previously learned behaviour in new situations. He will scrutinize and manipulate objects in different positions, thus learning about the three-dimensional nature of objects and the concept of space. He shows some awareness of the existence of unperceived objects, but cannot take account of changes of position which are shown to him. For example, he will retrieve a toy he sees hidden under A, but when he subsequently sees it hidden under B he will still look for it under A.

(*v*) *12–18 months:* The child now develops new patterns of behaviour as a result of deliberate experimentation. His manipulation of objects is more varied, so that he obtains new effects such as banging an object on different-sounding surfaces. He uses trial and error methods to solve such problems as obtaining objects out of reach. He can now take into account the change of position of hidden objects when searching. More is learned about the spatial relationship of objects by placing them one on top of the other, or putting small objects inside larger ones.

(*vi*) *18–24 months:* During this stage the child begins to invent solutions to problems, rather than using trial and error. By persistently searching for a well-hidden object he demonstrates a capacity for mental representation and memory. He will use one object to reach another which is out of reach, to show that his understanding of the spatial relationships is no longer based on direct perception.

At the end of the sensori-motor period the child has developed a concept of permanent objects, and distinguishes between himself and his environment. He is capable of symbolic representation of objects which are not present, by use of memory.

THE PRE-OPERATIONAL PERIOD

The Pre-conceptual Stage

The pre-conceptual stage (2–4 years) is given less attention by Piaget, but it is important as the child's acquisition of language and development of mental imagery provide him with new means of dealing with his environment. Symbolic processes begin to develop, evident in the make-believe playing which will later become creative imagination. However, the child's thinking is dominated by an egocentric quality. He interprets his world according to his own needs and viewpoint rather than the objective facts, and uses himself as the standard of judgement.

The face value of situations influences his thinking greatly, and he concentrates on one salient perceptual aspect of his environment to the exclusion of other equally important features. This has been demonstrated by an experiment carried out by Russian psychologists interested in language and behaviour. Three-year-old children were shown two pictures, one with a bright red circle on a pale yellow background, the other a bright green circle on a grey background. The children were asked to provide one response when shown the picture with the yellow background, and a different response when shown the picture with the grey background, which they duly did without trouble. The pictures were then changed, so that the red circle was on the grey background, and the green circle was on the yellow background, and the instructions given as before. The children changed their responses, thus indicating that they were not following the verbal instruction given to them, i.e. to respond to the *background* colour, but responded to the more impressive colour of the circles instead.

During this stage the child's ability to classify objects and to understand the relationship between objects belonging to the same class is limited, and will often lead him to false conclusions. Piaget uses the term 'transductive thinking' to describe the tendency to infer similarity between objects or events purely on perceptual grounds without any logical link. Because of these limitations of conceptualization, confusion often occurs for the child. For example, if he first learns the term 'dog' in reference to the family pet, he may be confused when it is also used for all other dogs, and left bemused as to whether all dogs are somehow the same animal. Conversely, seeing the same object under different conditions, such as the moon, may lead him to conclude that there are several moons.

The Intuitive Stage

The intuitive stage (from 4 to about 7 years) is still characterized by egocentric thinking and subjective judgements, but symbolic functioning continues to develop. Woodward (1967) writes, '... the child still centres his attention on one aspect of the situation and is still dominated by his own viewpoint, with consequent distortion and incorrect inferences. But the tendency to increased accommodation to reality means that the child is made increasingly aware of discrepancies between his judgements of the way objects will behave and what he observes of their actual behaviour. This continual correction of false beliefs by the facts of reality eventually leads to correct judgements and operational thinking'.

Piaget studied problem-solving behaviour in children of this age group. In fact, rather than demonstrating development which has occurred from the previous stage his work tends to highlight the limitations of conceptual thinking which are still evident. A number of experiments were devised to show the difficulty that children at this stage have in problems which require more than one factor to be taken into account to arrive at the correct solution. The most frequently quoted involves pouring a fixed volume of water from one beaker into another of different diameter and height. Pre-conceptual children will infer from the change in the visible water level that the amount of water has altered. They do not take into account the different width of the second beaker. Similarly, if a child is presented with a ball of Plasticine which is subsequently flattened out, he will reason that the amount has increased because it covers a larger area.

When the child learns from his failures to consider more than one factor at a time, he is said by Piaget to be acquiring *conservation*. This is the awareness that certain properties and characteristics of objects, such as quantity and weight, are unvaried even although simple changes might occur, for example in shape, appearance or location. By understanding conservation, the child's thinking is no longer dominated by the perceptual aspects of a situation.

According to Piaget, this critical point in the development of thinking and intelligence occurs round about seven years of age, and signals the transition to the next period.

THE PERIOD OF CONCRETE OPERATIONS

Having acquired conservation, the concrete-operational child (7–11 years) is now able to recognize relationships between objects and to use concrete concepts such as length, height and weight in a logical manner. He can classify objects according to common properties, and is able to arrange material in a sequence graded in value. His thinking now has a capacity for *reversibility*, defined by Piaget as 'the permanent possibility of returning to the starting point of the operation in question'. A child's awareness that 8 added to 4 is the same as 8 subtracted from 12 indicates reversible thinking.

Classification, seriation and reversibility are essential for the development of the concept of number. The child is also now capable of syllogistic reasoning, i.e. he can infer, for example, that when A = B, and B = C, then A = C, provided that concrete objects are available to assist the mental process involved. If two blocks of equal size and shape are shown to him to be of equal weight on a balance, and one of these is then demonstrated to be the same size, shape and weight as a third block, he can infer correctly that the two blocks not yet compared are also equal. However, if the child is asked to carry out this problem in a verbal or symbolic form he may well have great difficulty solving it, since according to Piaget the level of abstract thinking required demands a higher stage of development.

During the stage of concrete operational thinking there is a decrease in the egocentric quality manifest earlier. As a result of the process of *decentration* the child is less likely to concentrate only on one aspect of a situation, and a more objective view of the environment emerges from his growing awareness and appreciation of the needs and opinions of others. The concept of morality develops. Previously the child's attitude to incidents is dominated by material considerations, whereby he might consider the accidental breaking of four cups to be a worse offence than the deliberate smashing of one. As a clearer understanding of right and wrong is acquired, greater importance is attached to intent.

ABSTRACT OPERATIONAL THINKING

From about 11 years the child demonstrates a growing ability to deal with abstract concepts, and can handle several relevant variables simultaneously in problem-solving situations. He is increasingly able to carry out symbolic manipulations, and will formulate and evaluate hypotheses about the possible consequences of an action, in contrast to the concrete operational child who will carry out the action and draw conclusions from its effect. During this stage the adolescent takes the final step to full abstract thinking and conceptualization, as evidenced by the ability to carry out formal logical operations and tackle mathematical problems.

This stage is of very limited relevance in the context of mental handicap, however, since few within that category approach this level of thinking.

ASSESSMENT

Piaget's conclusions are based upon direct observation of children in a variety of situations. This method is particularly useful for assessing intellectual development in cases where the administration of formal tests is not desirable or not possible, although doubts about the reliability of assessments by different observers arise. The child's spontaneous responses in a play situation can be evaluated by observation from a distance if he is too disturbed or anxious to cope with a more structured setting. The level of sensori-motor behaviour can be readily assessed from the way in which he deals with toys and objects, and simple problems can be arranged. Training and education programmes can then be formulated to focus on the child's specific requirements, an important part of which should be provision of an adequate variety of stimuli to be experienced.

Piaget's work has given us a framework within which to formulate some understanding of the extent and limitations of thinking in children of different ages. While his original work was carried out on a small sample of normal children, its applicability to the problems of the mentally handicapped and to slow-learning children has been amply demonstrated in subsequent studies.

Legal Aspects of Mental Handicap

MENTAL HEALTH LEGISLATION is as subject to fashions and cycles as any other area of law. Most of the commitment laws stressing judicial or police involvement were enacted in the middle of the nineteenth century. Emphasis on formal structures and court review continued during the asylum era, in the course of which the mentally ill and the mentally handicapped were segregated and generally lost their legal capacity and civil rights. Not until the middle of this century did alterations in treatment methods and public attitudes have an effect on the law.

In 1954 a Royal Commission was set up to inquire into conditions within mental hospitals and hospitals for the mental defectives. As a result of this a new Act was placed before Parliament in 1959, which became law in 1960. Three important principles received emphasis in the Act:

1. That as much treatment as possible in and out of hospital be given as a voluntary measure, and that it will be as easy for the mentally disordered patient to obtain treatment in a suitable hospital as it is for the physically ill person.

2. That, where possible, treatment and training will be available in the community for all those patients who are not needing hospital care but who are able to live in their own homes or in a special home or hostel.

3. Only those who are ill enough to require care and treatment for their own sakes or for the sake of their families and the community and who are unwilling to go to hospital are now subject to any kind of compulsion. In such cases the recommendation of two doctors is all that is necessary.

However, to safeguard such patients from any risk of being kept in hospital unnecessarily each Health Authority has been empowered to provide a special tribunal to which patients or their relatives can appeal for a review of their case at certain phases of the detention period.

Prior to the inception of the Act there were many mental defectives who had spent many years in hospital because they had nowhere else to go and needed a certain amount of help and care. They did not require hospital treatment and would have been much happier and less likely to deteriorate mentally had they been allowed to live a more normal life and have a measure of independence in their own homes or in small hostels. A number of younger ones could have gone out to work and become self-supporting to some extent.

One of the redeeming features of the Act was that the relatively few laws that apply to mentally subnormal people apply only to the very small minority who are subject to detention orders. Local authorities were given greater powers to provide preventive and after-care services as well as community care for those patients who do not need to be treated or detained in hospital. This applied to adults and children.

Yet the English Mental Health Act has been much criticized and proposals for change have come from a number of bodies. As a result of these the DHSS (1976) produced a consultative document which was followed by a governmental white paper (1978). Subsequently in 1981 the Government placed before the House of Lords—

THE MENTAL HEALTH (AMENDMENT) BILL 1981

The major recommendations are as follows:

1. Subnormals and severe subnormals defined by reference to impairment of intelligence and social function (now to be renamed 'mentally handicapped') are to be allowed to be detained only if they are thought to be treatable. The government has expressed its intention once the bill becomes law to bring forward a consolidated Mental Health Act which will set out separately the provisions of the legislation which need to apply to mentally handicapped people.

2. A multiprofessional Mental Health Act Commission (clause 42) is to be established to provide a general protective function for all detained patients. The Commission will visit all psychiatric hospitals once or twice a year and each special hospital once a month. The Commission will also lay down guidelines about the giving of compulsory treatment to detained patients.

3. Access to Mental Health Review Tribunals is to be doubled. Local authorities are to approve social workers as mental health officers.

4. Emergency admission procedures are to be tightened up and Registered Mental or R.N.M.S. nurses are to have the power to detain an informal patient for 6 hours when it is considered that he is a danger to himself or to others in wishing to leave hospital.

5. Halving the period before the compulsory detention of any patient (except those on restriction orders) has to be either reviewed or ended.

6. Guardianship is retained, but with limited scope, simply giving the guardian (usually a local authority) the three essential powers of determining where a patient shall live, that he shall have treatment,

and that he may be visited at home. The period of such a Guardianship order, as with Section 26, is halved.

7. Restriction orders are to be applied to offender patients only 'for the protection of the public from serious harm'.

8. Remands to hospital will become possible for medical reports, treatment and assessment. Interim hospital orders for up to six months are to be introduced, and prisoners transferred to hospital are to become unrestricted at their earliest date of release instead of at the end of their nominal sentence as at present.

9. Treatments which are 'irreversible, hazardous or not fully established' should not be given without the informed consent of the patient and a concurring second medical opinion.

10. Clause 43, provides that Mental Welfare Officers shall within two years from the passage of the Bill be replaced by approved social workers, and these social workers must have 'appropriate competence in dealing with persons suffering from mental disorders'.

11. The principal changes concerning Mental Health Review Tribunals are set out in clauses 34 and 35 of the Bill. Tribunals must have regard to the same criteria as are specified for renewals of authority to detain. If a patient himself does not exercise his right to apply, the managers of the hospital must under certain conditions refer his case to a Tribunal. The patient may authorise a doctor to visit and examine him and inspect his records for the purpose of giving information to the Tribunal.

12. Withholding of patients' correspondence is limited to cases where the addressee has made a written request for letters not to be sent to him and this power will apply to detained patients only. Letters to patients in Special Hospitals may be withheld from them in a number of specified circumstances.

Lastly, it must be emphasised that this is an amending Bill, and so all changes are made by substitutions, additions or deletions to sections of the 1959 Act. It is intended that once the Bill becomes law a Consolidating Act will be prepared, as was done in 1980 following the Amendment Act of 1889. While this book is being written (1982) the Bill is still being discussed in the Lords, but it is expected to receive the Royal Assent in 1982 and the resultant Act become law in 1984.

Diseases cannot be cured by Act of Parliament. Such features which still discriminate against the mentally ill and the handicapped—e.g. inadequate facilities, poor food and poor staffing—are more likely to be corrected by a diversion of Health Service funds than by legislation.

THE MENTAL HEALTH ACT 1959

This was a completely new approach to the administrative problem of treatment, if necessary under compulsion, for mental patients and mental defectives, now known as mentally disordered persons.

Classification of Mental Disorder

In the Mental Health Act, mental disorder means:
1. Mental illness.
2. Arrested or incomplete development of the mind.
3. Psychopathic disorder.
4. Any other disorder or disability of the mind.

The classifications and definitions of mental subnormality are:

1. *Severe Subnormality*   A state of arrested or incomplete development of the mind which includes subnormality of the intelligence and is of such a nature or degree that the patient is incapable of living an independent life or of guarding himself against serious exploitation, or will be so incapable when of an age to do so.

2. *Subnormality*   A state of arrested or incomplete development of mind, not amounting to severe subnormality, which includes subnormality of intelligence, and is of a nature or degree which requires, or is susceptible to, medical treatment or other special care or training of the patient.

3. *Psychopathic Disorder*   A persistent disorder to disability of mind, whether or not including subnormality of intelligence, which results in abnormally aggressive or seriously irresponsible conduct on the part of the patient and requires, or is susceptible to, medical treatment.

Admission and Guardianship

Section 1   The Mental Health Act 1959 repealed the Lunacy and Mental Treatment Acts, 1890–1930 and the Mental Deficiency Acts, 1913–38, and made fresh provisions for the care and treatment of mentally disordered persons and the management of their property and affairs.

Section 2   The Board of Control was also dissolved.

Section 3   *Mental Health Review Tribunals*   To each Health Authority there is one Mental Health Review Tribunal. Each Tribunal must consist of:
1. A number of legal members approved by the Lord Chancellor.
2. A number of medical members appointed by the Lord Chancellor after consultation with the Minister.
3. A number of administrators who have experience of Social Services. The Chairman of the Tribunal must be a legal member.

Section 122—Powers and Proceeding of Mental Health Review Tribunals   All applications to the Mental Health Review Tribunals have to be made in writing to the appropriate Tribunal for the area in which the patient is residing either in hospital, or nursing home, or under guardianship.

Section 123   Where an application has been made to a Mental Health Review Tribunal in respect of a patient liable to be detained, the Tribunal may direct that the patient be discharged if they are satisfied that the patient is not suffering from mental illness, psychopathic disorder, subnormality, or severe subnormality, or that it is not necessary in the interests of his health or safety or for the protection of others for him to be detained, and that he is not likely to act in a manner dangerous to other persons or himself. The Tribunal may also direct that a patient under guardianship be discharged.

Section 28—The Application for Admission   An application for admission has to be based on the written recommendations on the prescribed form signed by two Medical Practitioners who have personally examined the patient.

One of the Medical Practitioners must be approved for the purpose as having special experience in the diagnosis or treatment of mental disorder by the Area Health Authority. If practicable, the other recommendation should be given by a Medical Practitioner who has acquaintance with the patient.

Section 30—Application for Admission in respect of a Patient already in Hospital   If in the case of a patient who is an in-patient in a hospital and not liable to be detained and it appears to the Responsible Medical Officer that an application for admission to hospital is necessary, he should furnish to the Managers a report in writing to that effect. In such a case, the patient may be detained in the hospital for a period of three days. The object of this provision is to allow time for an application for admission to be made.

Section 33—Guardianship   A guardianship application may be made in respect of a patient on the grounds that:

1. He is suffering from mental disorder, this being:

a. In the case of a patient of any age, mental illness or severe subnormality.

b. In the case of a patient under the age of 21 years, psychopathic disorder or subnormality, and that his disorder is of a nature or degree which warrants the reception of the patient into guardianship, and

2. It is necessary in the interests of the patient or for the

protection of other persons that the patient should be so received.

The application must be supported by two medical recommendations. The person named as guardian may be either an Area Health Authority, or any other person including the applicant.

Section 34   The application for guardianship has to be forwarded to the Area Health Authority within 14 days, beginning with the day the patient was last examined by a Medical Practitioner before giving medical recommendation.

If the application is accepted by the Area Health Authority, the application immediately confers on the named guardian the same powers over the patient as would be the case if he were the father of the patient and the patient were under the age of 14 years. The patient may apply to a Mental Health Review Tribunal within a period of 6 months beginning with the day on which the application is accepted, or with the day on which he attains the age of 16 years whichever is the later.

Section 5—*Informal Admission*   A mentally subnormal person may be admitted informally to any hospital or nursing home for treatment for mental disorder. A patient under the age of 16 years may be detained in hospital at his parents' or guardians' request, no matter what his wishes are. On reaching the age of 16 years and expressing his wish to leave the hospital, he may leave the hospital irrespective of the wishes of his parents or guardians.

COMPULSORY ADMISSION TO HOSPITAL

Section 25—*Admission for Observation*   A patient may be detained for observation with or without treatment for a period not exceeding 28 days, providing it can be shown that he is suffering from a mental disorder which warrants his detention in the interests of his own health and safety or for the protection of others.

Section 26—*Admission for Treatment*   Application for admission for treatment may be made in respect of a patient on the grounds that:

He is suffering from mental disorder, this being:

a. In the case of a patient of any age, mental illness or severe subnormality,

b. In the case of a patient under the age of 21 years, psychopathic disorder or subnormality,

of such a degree that it warrants his detention in hospital for medical treatment in the interests of the patient's health or safety, or for the protection of other persons.

The detention may be for a period not exceeding 1 year in the first instance.

Section 29—Admission for Observation in Case of Emergency   In the case of emergency, the social worker or any relative of the patient may make application for admission and detention in hospital for observation under Section 25. If going through the full procedure would involve unreasonable delay the application may be founded on one medical certificate but such application will cease to have effect after the expiration of 72 hours, unless a second medical recommendation is received by the Managers.

Section 60—Admission of Patients concerned in Criminal Proceedings and Transfer of Patients under Sentence   Where a person is convicted before a Court of Assize, or Quarter Sessions (in the case of a person convicted of an offence other than an offence for which the sentence is fixed by law), or a Magistrates' Court (in the case of a person convicted of an offence punishable on summary conviction with imprisonment), and the Court, being satisfied with the written or oral evidence of two Medical Practitioners that the person is suffering from mental illness, psychopathic disorder, subnormality, or severe subnormality, and the mental disorder is of a nature or degree which warrants his detention in hospital, or reception into guardianship, may order this form of care.

The Court must be satisfied that the hospital specified will be able to admit the patient within a period of 28 days or that the Area Health Authority or other person specified is willing to receive the patient into guardianship.

A Magistrates' Court may make an Order under this Section of the Act without convicting a person suffering from mental illness or severe subnormality, provided the Court is satisfied he committed the act.

Section 61   If a child or young person is brought before a Juvenile Court and the Court is satisfied that the child or young person is in need of care and protection, or that his parent or guardian is unable to control him, it may make a hospital or guardianship Order. Before making the Order the Court must be satisfied that the parent or guardian understands the results which will follow from the Order, and that they consent to its being made.

Leave of Absence from Hospital

Section 39   The Responsible Medical Officer may grant for any period leave of absence from hospital to a patient detained in hospital, subject to such conditions as the Officer considers necessary. A patient to whom leave of absence is granted shall not be recalled to hospital after he has ceased to be liable to be detained in hospital or after the expiration of six months, unless he has returned to the hospital.

Absence Without Leave

Section 40   If a patient, who is liable to be detained in hospital, absents himself from the hospital without permission or fails to return to the hospital on expiration of any leave, he may be taken into custody and returned to hospital by any social worker; by any Officer on the staff of the hospital; by any Constable or by any person authorized in writing by the Managers of the hospital. Patients subject to guardianship are dealt with in the same way.

Psychopathic and subnormal patients over the age of 21 years, on the first day of absence without leave, may be dealt with in this way at any time within a period of 6 months, beginning with that day. In other cases this period is limited to 28 days. After these periods have expired, the patient ceases to be liable to be detained or subject to guardianship.

Transfer of Patients

Section 41   A patient who is liable to be detained in hospital, or subject to guardianship, may be transferred to another hospital or into guardianship of another Area Health Authority. The transfer of the patient from hospital to guardianship, or vice versa, is permissible.

A patient, who, having attained the age of 16 years, is transferred from guardianship to a hospital, may apply to the Mental Health Review Tribunal within the period of 6 months.

Duration of Authority for Detention or Guardianship

Section 43   The period of detention in hospital or under guardianship is limited to a period not exceeding one year. Authority for detention or guardianship may be renewed for a further period of one year and from the expiration of this further period any further renewals are for periods of two years. A report recommending continued detention should be furnished to the Managers by the Responsible Medical Officer, or to the Area Health Authority by the nominated medical attendant of a patient under guardianship, stating that continued detention is necessary in the interests of the patient's health or safety, or for the protection of others, and the authority for continued detention is thereby renewed.

The Area Health Authority must notify patients over the age of 16 years of each renewal of authority, and the patient may apply to a Mental Health Review Tribunal within the period for which the authority is renewed.

Section 44   Upon attaining the age of 25 years, the authority for the detention or guardianship of a psychopathic or subnormal patient will cease to have effect unless in the case of a patient detained in hospital the Responsible Medical Officer, within the period of two months ending on the patient's 25th birthday, furnishes to the Area Health Authority a report that it appears to him that the patient would be likely to act in a manner dangerous to other persons or to himself if released from hospital. When such a report is furnished, the Area Health Authority are required to inform the patient and nearest relative who have the right within a period of 28 days, beginning with the patient's 25th birthday, to apply to the Mental Health Review Tribunal.

Discharge of Patients

Section 47   Orders for discharge may be made by:

   1. The Responsible Medical Officer, or the Area Health Authority in the case of a patient detained for observation.

   2. The Responsible Medical Officer, the Area Health Authority or the nearest relative in the case of a patient detained for treatment.

   3. The Responsible Medical Officer, the responsible Area Health Authority or the nearest relative in the case of a patient subject to guardianship.

ADDITIONAL AUTHORITIES FOR DISCHARGE

   1. The registration authority in the case of a patient liable to be detained in a Mental Nursing Home for observation or treatment.

   2. The Regional Health Authority if the patient is maintained under a contract with the Board.

RESTRICTION ON DISCHARGE BY THE NEAREST RELATIVE

Section 48   The nearest relative must give at least 72 hours' notice in writing to the Area Health Authority of his wish to discharge the patient. If the Responsible Medical Officer reports to the Area Health Authority within the period of notice that in his opinion the patient would be likely to be dangerous to others or himself if discharged, they may continue his detention against his nearest relative's wish. In this case the nearest relative may not order discharge during the next six months. The Area Health Authority must inform the relative of the report, and their right to apply to a Mental Health Review Tribunal within a period of 28 days.

   Where a report has been furnished by the Responsible Medical Officer that a psychopathic or subnormal patient having attained the age of 25 years would be likely to act in a manner dangerous to others or himself if released, then an Order for discharge may not be made by the nearest relative for a period of six months, beginning with the date of that report.

Section 52   In certain circumstances the functions of the nearest relative may be transferred to any specified person who, in the opinion of the County Court, is a proper person to act as the patient's nearest relative, and is willing to do so, and such an application may be made by:

1. Any relative of the patient.

2. Any other person with whom the patient is residing, or was last residing with before admission to hospital.

3. A social worker.

The nearest relative of this patient has the right to apply to a Mental Health Review Tribunal within the period of 12 months beginning with the date of the Order and in any subsequent period of 12 months.

The grounds upon which an Order may be made under this Section are:

1. That the patient has no nearest relative.

2. That the nearest relative of the patient is incapable of acting as such by reason of mental disorder or other illness.

3. That the nearest relative of the patient unreasonably objects to the making of an application for admission for treatment or a guardianship application in respect of the patient.

4. That the nearest relative of the patient has exercised, without due regard to the welfare of the patient or the interests of the public, his power to discharge the patient from hospital or guardianship.

ORDERS RESTRICTING DISCHARGE

Section 65   Where a hospital Order is made in respect of an offender by a Court of Assize or Quarter Sessions, and it appears to the Court having regard to the nature of the offence that there is risk of his committing further offences if set at large, the Court may order special restrictions either with or without a time limit or during such period as may be specified in the Order called 'Order Restricting Discharge'. Such an Order may not be made unless at least one of the Medical Practitioners gives oral evidence before the Court. Such patients cannot appeal to a Mental Health Review Tribunal, and they can only be discharged or transferred to another hospital with the consent of the Secretary of State.

Section 63   Relatives of a patient who is admitted to a hospital or placed under guardianship by virtue of an Order of Court may not exercise their power to order the patient's discharge. The Order also removes the age limits to the detention of psychopathic and subnormal patients in hospital or under guardianship. A patient admitted under a hospital or guardianship Order may apply to a Mental Health Review Tribunal within a period of six months, beginning with the date of the Order or with the day on which he attains the age of 16 years, whichever is the later. His relatives may make a similar application within the period of 12 months, beginning with the date of the Order and in any subsequent period of 12 months.

Section 66   The Secretary of State, on being satisfied that an Order restricting the discharge of a patient is no longer necessary for the protection of the public, may terminate the Restriction Order. He may also discharge the patient either absolutely or subject to conditions and, in the latter case, recall him to hospital at any time while the Order restricting discharge is still in force.

The Secretary of State is required to refer to a Mental Health Review Tribunal for their advice within 2 months of receiving a written request to do so from the patient whose Restriction Order has been in force for a year or more. The patient may apply to the Tribunal once during each period during which he could have applied to them had the order restricting his discharge not been in force. However, a patient recalled to hospital after being conditionally discharged may, in addition, make a request to the Secretary of State six months after the date of his recall to hospital.

Section 67   Any person over the age of 14 years convicted by a Magistrates' Court of an offence punishable by imprisonment, and it appearing to the Magistrates that a Restriction Order should be made, they may commit him in custody to Quarter Sessions to be dealt with. The Court of Quarter Sessions may make a hospital Order with or without an Order restricting discharge or deal with him in such a way that the Magistrates' Court might have done.

Section 68   The Magistrates' Court may order the patient's admission to hospital instead of committing him in custody until his case is dealt with by Quarter Sessions. The Order restricts the patient's discharge.

Section 69   Where an Order restricting discharge is made, the patient may appeal to the Court of Criminal Appeal against the Order.

Section 70   A patient subjected to a hospital or guardianship Order made by a Magistrates' Court may appeal against the Order to the Quarter Sessions. A child or young person brought before a Juvenile Court as in need of care and protection or as beyond control of his parent or guardian may also appeal to the Quarter Sessions against any Order the Court may make. His parent or guardian may also appeal.

Transfer to Hospital or Guardianship of Prisoners, etc.

Section 72   The Secretary of State, being satisfied by reports of at least two Medical Practitioners, one of whom is approved for the purpose by the Area Health Authority, that a person serving a sentence of imprisonment is suffering from mental illness, psychopathic disorder, subnormality or severe subnormality, and that the mental disorder warrants the patient's detention in hospital for medical treatment, may authorize his transfer to hospital.

A direction under this Section of the Act shall cease to have effect at the expiration of the period of 14 days beginning with the date on which it is given unless within that period the person with respect to whom it was given has been received into the specified hospital.

Section 75   The transfer of a patient back to prison may be authorized by the Secretary of State on notification by the Responsible Medical Officer that he no longer needs treatment for mental disorder, providing his prison sentence has not expired.

Section 79   The Secretary of State may order the reception into guardianship of a child or young person detained in an approved school, if he is satisfied that the child is suffering from mental illness, psychopathic disorder, subnormality, or severe subnormality, and that it is in the public interest.

LOCAL AUTHORITY SERVICES

Section 10   When a mentally disordered child or young person whose rights and powers of his parent are vested in the Area Authority is admitted to hospital or nursing home, the Department of Social Services of the Local Authority has to arrange for visits to be made to him on their behalf and to take any other steps as would be expected to be taken by his parent, whilst he is in hospital.

Section 11—Care and Training of Children in lieu of Education   A duty is imposed upon the Local Education Authority to ascertain what children in their area are suffering from a disability of mind of such a nature or extent as to make them unsuitable for education at school and to serve notice in writing to the parents of any child who has attained the age of 2 years to submit the child for examination by a Medical Officer of the Authority.

The parent may appeal to the Minister of Education against the decision of the Authority within a period of 21 days.

Section 12   The Area Health Authority is empowered to compel the regular attendance at a training centre, either daily or on a residential basis, of any child of compulsory school age ascertained by the Local Education Authority as being unsuitable for education at school.

The parents may appeal against this decision.

SPECIAL HOSPITALS

Section 97   The Minister provides such Institutions as appears to him necessary for patients requiring treatment under special security conditions, on account of their dangerous, violent, or criminal propensities.

Section 98   The special hospitals are under the control and management of the Minister.

Section 99   Any patient who for the time being is liable to be detained in a special hospital may, at the direction of the Minister, be removed into any other special hospital or any other type of hospital.

LEGAL POSITION OF THE MENTALLY SUBNORMAL

Section 126—*Ill-treatment*   Ill-treatment may include corporal punishment, causing physical or mental pain, and wilful neglect. No nurse or any other person employed in a hospital or mental nursing home or any of the Managers responsible for the care and treatment of mentally disordered patients shall ill-treat them. It is also an offence for any individual to ill-treat or wilfully neglect a mentally disordered person while he is subject to his guardianship under the Act, or in his custody or care. The penalty for this may be a term of imprisonment, not exceeding six months, on summary conviction, or a fine not exceeding £100, or both, or on conviction on indictment, a term of imprisonment not exceeding two years, or a fine, or both.

Section 127—*Carnal Knowledge*   It is illegal for a man to have sexual relationship with any female suffering from severe subnormality, providing he knows or has reason to suspect her to be severely subnormal.

Section 128   It is an offence for an Officer on the staff of a hospital or mental nursing home or any of the Managers to have sexual intercourse on hospital premises with a woman receiving treatment, either as an in-patient or as an out-patient.

It is also an offence for a man to have unlawful sexual intercourse with a patient subject to his guardianship. In each case it must be shown that the man knew or had reason to suspect that the woman was a mentally disordered person. The penalty for this offence on conviction or indictment is a term of imprisonment, not exceeding two years.

Assisting Patients to Absent Themselves Without Leave

Section 129   It is an offence to induce or knowingly assist a patient detained in hospital or subject to guardianship to absent himself without leave or to escape from legal custody or knowingly to harbour a patient absent without leave or prevent him being taken into custody.

The penalties for the offences are on summary conviction a term of imprisonment not exceeding six months, or a fine not exceeding £100, or both, or on conviction on indictment, a term of imprisonment not exceeding two years, or a fine, or both.

Warrant to Search For and Remove Patients

Section 135   A Justice of the Peace may issue a Warrant authorizing a Constable to enter, if need be by force, any premises within his jurisdiction, specified in the Warrant, and if thought fit, to remove him to a place of safety with a view to making an application for treatment or care any person if it appears to the Magistrate on information on Oath from a social worker that there is reasonable cause to suspect that the patient is suffering from mental disorder and to have been ill-treated, neglected, or not kept under proper control or in need of care. The Constable must be accompanied by a social worker and by a Medical Practitioner.

On sworn evidence of any Constable, a Justice of the Peace may issue a Warrant authorizing any Constable named in the Warrant to enter the premises, if need be by force, to retake and remove the patient to a place of safety. The Constable may be accompanied by a Medical Practitioner and/or the person authorized to take or re-take the patient.

A place of safety as defined in this Section of the Act is:

1. Accommodation provided by the Local Authority under Part III of the National Health Act 1940 or
2. Under Part III of the National Assistance Act 1948.
3. A hospital as defined by the Mental Health Act 1959.
4. A Police Station.
5. A Mental Nursing Home or residential home for mentally disordered persons.
6. Any other suitable place, the occupier of which is willing to receive the patient temporarily.

If a Constable finds in a public place a person who appears to him to be suffering from mental disorder and to be in immediate need of care or control, the Constable may, if he thinks it necessary for the interest of the patient or for the protection of others, remove him to a place of safety.

A person removed to a place of safety may be detained for a period not exceeding 72 hours, for the purpose of enabling him to be examined by a Medical Practitioner and to be interviewed by a social worker.

Marriage and Divorce

There is no law to prevent marriages between mentally subnormal people. Generally speaking these marriages are legal and binding unless the mentally subnormal person who has married can be proved to be incapable of comprehending the nature of the marriage contract and of fulfilling the physical conditions of marriage. This is a complex subject, however, and each case would need to be considered in the light of its individual circumstances.

Criminal Responsibility

To be a mentally subnormal person does not free the person from the responsibilities of complying with the laws of the land. If a mentally subnormal person commits a crime, he is still liable to conviction and punishment by law. His mental condition will be investigated by the Court, which may deal with him as a mentally subnormal person or as a responsible person.

Contracts

Unless it can be shown that the mentally subnormal person was incapable of comprehending the terms of the contract and that the other person knew that the mental state was such that the mentally subnormal person did not understand the terms of the contract, then the contract entered into is binding.

Testamentary Capacity

A Will is only valid if the Testator is able, at the time he makes his Will, to recall and keep clearly in his mind: (1) The nature and the extent of his property; (2) The persons who have claims on his bounty; (3) The relative strength of these claims.

Representation of the People Act 1949, Section 4, Paragraph 3

A certified mentally subnormal person undergoing hospital care as a detained patient has a legal right to vote, providing his name appears on the Register of Voters for the constituency which includes his place of residence immediately prior to his admission to hospital. Attempts are being made to extend voting rights to mentally handicapped people who are long term hospital residents.

Mental Health (Scotland) Act 1960

THE MENTAL HEALTH (SCOTLAND) ACT was passed to replace the old Lunacy and Mental Deficiency Acts with a more enlightened system. It set up a Mental Welfare Commission to oversee the interests of hospital patients, laid down criteria for compulsory admissions and gave local authorities wide powers to provide services for the integration of patients into the community.

The expressed concern at the inadequacies of the Act and the occasional abuses of it led to the Scottish Office promising a comprehensive review. An internal review was carried out, but the consultative document has been postponed indefinitely. 'It is clear that the 1960 Mental Health Act requires amendment in certain respects, but the Minister is not convinced that the matter is urgent enough to initiate the consultation process until more resources are available.' (Scottish Office 1980.)

PART I (SECTIONS 1–6): PRELIMINARY

Section 1—Repeal   Repeal of previous Lunacy and Mental Deficiency Acts (1857–1940).

Section 2—Mental Welfare Commission   Establishment of Mental Welfare Commission. Chairman, three Medical Commissioners, one Legal Commissioner and from two to four other Commissioners (there must be at least one woman Commissioner). No Commissioner shall be a civil servant.

By the National Health Service (Scotland) Act 1972 the maximum number of Commissioners is increased to eleven and the Commission is given powers to summon witnesses, take evidence on oath while the proceedings of any inquiry have the privilege of a court of law.

Section 4—Functions and Duties of Mental Welfare Commission   To enquire into any case where there may be ill-treatment, deficiency in care and treatment, or improper detention of any person who may be suffering from mental disorder, or where the property of such a person may be exposed to loss or damage.

To visit regularly patients in hospital or under guardianship and to afford opportunity of private interview to any patient.

To bring attention of any Area Health Authority or Local Authority facts of any case in which Area Health Authority or Local Authority should exercise any of their functions to secure the welfare of any patient.

To advise the Secretary of State on any matter arising out of this Act that he may refer to them and to bring to his attention any such matter of which, in the opinion of the Commission, he ought to be apprised.

Section 5—Duties of Secretary of State and Local Authorities   To afford the Commission all facilities necessary to enable them to carry out their functions in respect of any patient in a hospital or under guardianship.

Section 6—Definition of Mental Disorder   In the Act 'mental disorder' means mental illness or mental deficiency, however caused or manifested.

PART II (SECTIONS 7–14): LOCAL AUTHORITY SERVICES

Functions of Health Authorities

Section 27 of the National Health Service (Scotland) Act 1947 relates to the functions of Area Health Authorities with respect to the prevention of illness, care and after-care in relation to persons who are, or have been, suffering from mental disorder.

Section 7   Functions shall involve:

a. Provision, equipment and maintenance of residential accommodation and the care of persons for the time being resident in accommodation so provided (including such payment as Area Health Authority think fit for personal expenses).

b. Appointment of officers to act as social workers under the provisions of this Act.

c. Exercise by the Area Health Authority of their functions in respect of persons under guardianship.

d. Provision of any ancillary or supplementary services.

e. Ascertainment of mental deficiency in any person not of school age within the meaning of the Education (Scotland) Act 1946.

f. Supervision of persons suffering from mental deficiency who are neither liable to detention in a hospital nor subject to guardianship.

Section 12—The Training, etc. of Persons Unsuitable for Education and of Mental Defectives   Duty of the Area Health Authority to provide or secure the provision of suitable training and occupation for:

a. Persons under the age of 16 who have been reported by the Education Authority under Section 56 of the Education (Scotland) Act 1946 as having been found unsuitable for education or training in a Special School.

b. Persons suffering from mental deficiency who are over the age of 16.

This shall not apply:

    i. In any case where the report has been cancelled;

    ii. In the case of a person in hospital.

Duty of an Area Health Authority to make provision for transport of persons for training and occupation.

Where an Area Health Authority makes arrangements with any voluntary organization for the performance by that organization of any services in connexion with the duties of the Area Health Authority under this Section, the authority may make contributions to the funds of that voluntary organization.

Section 13—Powers to Compel Attendance at Training Centres Local Authority may direct that a child, if of school age, shall attend the centre for training and occupation if they are satisfied that:

a. The child is not receiving training comparable with that at the centre;

b. There is no reasonable cause for his failure to receive the training.

The parent, if aggrieved, may refer the question to the Secretary of State who may confirm, amend or withdraw the direction. Failure on the part of the parent to comply with the direction, unless exempted for a reasonable cause, shall be an offence. (First offence fine not exceeding £1, second offence fine not exceeding £5, third or subsequent offence fine not exceeding £10 or imprisonment not exceeding 1 month or both.)

PART III (SECTIONS 15–22)

Deals with Private Hospitals, Residential Homes, etc.

PART IV (SECTIONS 23–53): ADMISSION TO AND DETENTION IN HOSPITAL AND GUARDIANSHIP

Section 23—Patients liable to be detained in Hospital or Subject to Guardianship Person suffering from any mental disorder that requires, or is susceptible to, medical treatment may be admitted to a hospital or received into guardianship.

No person over the age of 21 years shall be admitted or received except where the mental disorder from which he suffers:

a. Is mental deficiency such that he is incapable of living an independent life or of guarding himself against serious exploitation, or

b. Is a mental illness other than a persistent disorder which is manifested only by abnormally aggressive or seriously irresponsible conduct.

A patient who has been admitted or received shall cease to be so liable or subject on the date on which he attains the age of 25 years unless:

    i. One of the exceptions (*a*) and (*b*) above applies to him, or

    ii. In the case of a patient liable to be detained in a hospital, he would be likely to act in a manner dangerous to himself or others.

Informal Patients Nothing in this Act shall be construed as preventing a patient who requires treatment for mental disorder from being admitted to any hospital or nursing home for that treatment without any application, recommendation or order rendering him liable to be detained under this Act, or from remaining in any hospital in pursuance of such arrangements if he has ceased to be so liable to be detained.

Section 24—Procedures for Admission and Detention of Patients
Applications for admission, in prescribed form, approved by the Sheriff.

Application for admission or guardianship application shall be founded on and accompanied by two medical recommendations, in prescribed form. Each such recommendation shall include the following statements, being statements of opinion, and the grounds on which each statement is based:

a. A statement of the form of mental disorder from which the patient is suffering, being mental illness or mental deficiency or both;

b. A statement that the said disorder requires or is susceptible to medical treatment and is of a nature or degree which warrants the patient's detention in a hospital for such treatment or his reception into guardianship;

c. A statement that the interests of the health or safety of the patient or the protection of other persons cannot be secured otherwise than by such detention or reception.

An application for admission or a guardianship application shall be of no effect unless the patient is described in each of the medical recommendations as suffering from the same form of mental disorder, whether or not he is described in either recommendation as suffering also from the other form.

Section 25—Guardianship. Procedure for Reception of Patients

Guardianship application, in prescribed form, approved by the Sheriff.

Application, after it is approved by the Sheriff, shall be forwarded to the Area Health Authority for the area in which the patient resides.

The person named as guardian in the application may be:

a. The Area Health Authority to whom the application is addressed;

b. A person chosen by that Authority;

c. Any other person who has been accepted as a suitable person by that Authority.

General Provisions as to Applications

Application for admission to Area Health Board, or guardianship application to Local Authority for area in which patient resides, may be made:

By the nearest relative, or

By a social worker.

Duty of social worker to inform nearest relative of proposed application, and of his right to object under Section 28 of this Act.

Person making an application must have personally seen patient within 14 days of date of submission to Sheriff.

Section 27—Medical Recommendations

a. Shall be signed on or before date of application by Medical Practitioners (neither being the applicant) who have personally examined patient separately at an interval of not more than 7 days, or where no objection by patient or nearest relative together.

b. One recommendation shall be given by a practitioner approved for the purpose by a Area Health Authority as having special experience in the diagnosis or treatment of mental disorder.

The other recommendation shall, if practicable, be given by the patient's General Practitioner or by another Practitioner who has had previous acquaintance with him.

c. Only one of the recommendations may be given by a Practitioner on the staff of the hospital named.

d. Not more than one of the recommendations may be given by a Medical Officer in the service of a Local Authority.

e. Recommendations shall state whether person signing recommendation is related to the patient and state any pecuniary interest the person may have in admission of patient to hospital or reception into guardianship.

Section 28—*Approval of Applications by the Sheriff*   Application shall be submitted to Sheriff within 7 days of date of last medical recommendation. In guardianship case there must be statement of willingness to act from the guardian named.

Sheriff may make such inquiries and hear such persons (including the patient) as he thinks fit. If nearest relative objects to application Sheriff shall afford that relative and any witness relative may call an opportunity of being heard. Sheriff shall not withhold approval to application without affording the applicant and any witness applicant may call an opportunity of being heard.

Sheriff may conduct proceedings in private.

Section 29—*Effect of Applications*   Application approved by Sheriff shall be sufficient authority for removal of patient to hospital named and admission within 7 days of Sheriff's approval and for detention in hospital within provisions of Act.

Where patient admitted to hospital or received into guardianship Area Health Authority or Local Authority concerned shall notify Mental Welfare Commission of admission or reception of patient, together with copy of application and medical recommendations within 7 days of admission or reception.

Duty of Responsible Medical Officer to examine patient or obtain report from another Medical Practitioner within the period of 7 days ending on the twenty-eighth day after admission or reception. If Responsible Medical Officer does not discharge patient he shall so inform Mental Welfare Commission, nearest relative and Area Health Authority.

Guardianship application approved by Sheriff and forwarded to the Area Health Authority within 7 days from date of approval confers on guardian named, to the exclusion of any other person, all such powers as if they or he were the father of the patient and the patient were a pupil child. Guardian has no power with respect to any property of the patient.

Guardian shall not administer corporal punishment to patient, or shall be guilty of offence, liable to fine not exceeding £50 (the court shall intimate conviction to the Mental Welfare Commission).

Section 30—*Rectification of Application and Recommendations*   If within 14 days after admission or reception of patient application or any medical recommendation found incorrect or defective it may within the next 7 days, with approval of Sheriff, be amended by person by whom it was signed.

Section 31—*Emergency Admission*   Emergency recommendation may be made by Medical Practitioner stating that by reason of mental disorder it is urgently necessary for patient to be admitted and detained in a hospital, but that compliance with Section 24 of the Act would involve undesirable delay.

Medical Practitioner must personally examine patient on day on which he signs emergency recommendation.

Recommendation shall be accompanied by statement that the consent of a relative or of a social worker has been obtained or by a statement of the reasons for failure to obtain that consent.

Emergency recommendation shall be sufficient authority for removal of patient to a hospital at any time within 3 days from date on which it was made and for his detention therein for a period not exceeding 7 days.

Duty of Area Health Authority where practicable to inform nearest relative or responsible person residing with patient without delay of patient's admission.

Section 32—Detention of Patients already in Hospital   Application for admission or emergency recommendation may be made notwithstanding that the patient is already in a hospital. In such a case the patient shall be treated for the purposes of this part of the Act as if he had been admitted on the date on which the application was forwarded to the Area Health Authority or, as the case may be, the recommendation was made.

Section 33—Regulations as to Guardianship   Secretary of State may make regulations as to exercise by guardians of their powers and may impose on guardians and on Area Health Authorities concerned such duties as he considers necessary or expedient in interests of the patients (including visitation by Local Authority).

Section 34—Correspondence of Patients   Responsible Medical Officer and guardian may use discretion. Communications from patient must be sent unopened to the nearest relative, the Secretary of State, the Lord Advocate, any Member of Parliament, the Mental Welfare Commission or any Commissioner, any Sheriff or Sheriff Clerk, the Area Health Authority.

Section 34 also applies to patients not subject to detention (Informal).

Section 35—Leave of Absence from Hospital   Responsible Medical Officer may grant leave of absence to a patient on specified occasions or for any specified period of not more than 6 months; leave may be extended for further periods of 6 months.

If leave is for more than 28 days Responsible Medical Officer shall inform Mental Welfare Commission giving patient's address and shall notify the Commission of the patient's return to hospital.

The Responsible Medical Officer may at any time in the interests of the health or safety of the patient or for the protection of others revoke the leave and recall the patient to hospital by notice in writing to the patient or to the person for the time being in charge of him.

Section 36—Return and Readmission of Patients Absent without Leave   Where a patient absents himself from hospital without leave or fails to return to hospital after a period of leave or absents himself from place in which he was required to reside during period of leave, he may be taken into custody and returned to the hospital or place by any social worker, by any Officer on the staff of the hospital, by any Constable, or by any person authorized in writing by the Area Health Authority.

In the case of a patient absent without leave from guardianship he may also be taken into custody and returned to his place of guardianship by the guardian.

A patient shall not be taken into custody after the expiration of the following period (beginning with the first day of his absence without leave):

a. In the case of a patient in hospital or guardianship because of mental deficiency, 3 months;

b. In the case of a patient detained under an emergency recommendation, 7 days;

c. In any other case, 28 days.

At the expiration of the period the patient shall cease to be liable to be detained or subject to guardianship.

Section 37—Transfer of Patients   Patients may be transferred from one hospital to another, from one guardian to another, from hospital to guardianship, and from guardianship to hospital.

The consent of the hospital or guardian receiving the transferred patient must be obtained and in the case of a guardianship case transferred to hospital, the consent of the Mental Welfare Commission.

All transfers shall be notified to the nearest relative and to the Mental Welfare Commission.

No patient shall be transferred from guardianship except with the consent of his guardian or, if that consent is refused, with the approval of the Sheriff to the transfer.

The original application for admission or guardianship application is the application used in every case of transfer.

Section 38—Transfer of Guardianship in Case of Death, Incapacity, etc., of Guardian   Guardianship shall rest in Area Health Authority concerned who may transfer patient to other guardian.

Section 39—*Duration of Authority* Authority for detention in hospital or guardianship must be renewed at end of first year, at end of second year and thereafter for periods of 2 years at a time.

Within 2 months of end of period of authority it shall be the duty of the Responsible Medical Officer to obtain from another Medical Practitioner a report on condition of patient in prescribed form and thereafter to assess the need for the detention to be continued.

If it appears that it is necessary in the interests of the health or safety of the patient or for the protection of others that detention should be continued, the Responsible Medical Officer shall furnish to the Area Health Authority or to the Local Authority concerned in a guardianship case and to the Mental Welfare Commission a report to that effect in the prescribed form, along with the report first mentioned.

The authority shall be thereby renewed for the period prescribed.

When the report is furnished the Area Health Authority shall, unless they discharge the patient, inform the patient, the nearest relative and (if a guardianship case) the guardian of the continued detention.

A patient who attains the age of 16 years may appeal to the Sheriff within the period for which detention or guardianship is authorized.

Section 40—*Detention or Guardianship of Certain Patients after the Age of 25* A similar action shall be taken by the Responsible Medical Officer, within 2 months before the patient attains his twenty-fifth birthday, to determine whether the patient ought to be detained in hospital or remain subject to guardianship after the date on which he attains the age of 25 in the case of:

a. A patient admitted to a hospital or received into guardianship by reason of his suffering from mental deficiency who has been continuously so detained or subject since he attained the age of 21; or,

b. A patient admitted to a hospital or received into guardianship by reason of his suffering from a mental disorder being a mental illness which is a persistent disorder manifested only by abnormally aggressive or seriously irresponsible conduct.

Where the authority is continued the patient and the nearest relative are informed and they may appeal to the Sheriff within 28 days after the patient attains the age of 25.

Section 41—*Special Provisions as to Patients Absent without Leave* If a patient is absent without leave and his case cannot be reviewed, he shall not cease to be liable to detention or subject to guardianship until the expiration of the period during which he can be taken into custody (*Section* 36).

If he is returned he shall not cease to be liable or subject until 1 week after he returns to allow time for furnishing of report.

Section 42—Special Provisions as to Patients Sentenced to Imprisonment, etc. Where a patient from hospital or guardianship is imprisoned for a period exceeding 6 months, he shall at the end of this period cease to be so liable or subject.

Where the period does not exceed 6 months he shall not cease to be liable or subject even if his case should have been reviewed during his period in prison. *Sections* 36 and 41 of this Act shall apply to the patient as if he had absented himself without leave on the day of his discharge from prison.

Section 43—Discharge of Patients An Order for discharge of patient from hospital or guardianship shall be made by the Responsible Medical Officer or the Mental Welfare Commission if he or they are satisfied:

a. That he is not suffering from mental disorder;

b. That, having regard to the care or supervision which would be available for the patient if he were discharged, it is not necessary in the interests of his health or safety or for the protection of other persons that he should continue to be liable or subject.

An Order for discharge may be made by the Responsible Medical Officer (but not in respect of a State hospital patient without the consent of the Area Health Authority, the Mental Welfare Commission or, after appeal, by the Sheriff).

An Order for discharge may also be made by the nearest relative of the patient, by the Area Health Authority and by the Area Health Authority concerned in a guardianship case. Order for discharge by Area Health Authority or by Local Authority concerned shall with the consent of the Responsible Medical Officer take effect on the expiration of 7 days from the Order.

If he does not consent he must furnish to Area Health Authority a report certifying that in his opinion the patient cannot be discharged without being a danger to himself or to others.

Section 44—Restriction on Discharge by Nearest Relatives Where a report under *Section* 40 (at age of 25) has been furnished, the nearest relative shall not make an Order for discharge during the period of 6 months thereafter. Nearest relative must give not less than 7 days' notice in writing to Area Health Authority or to Local Authority of an Order for discharge. If in that time Responsible Medical Officer furnishes a report against discharge the relative's Order for discharge shall be of no effect and no further Order for discharge shall be made by the relatives for 6 months thereafter.

But the relative may appeal to Sheriff within 28 days.

The nearest relative may not make an Order for discharge in respect of a State hospital patient.

(*Sections* 45–49) Refer to definition of relatives, children and young persons in care of Local Authority, nearest relative of child under guardianship, appointment by Sheriff of acting nearest relative.

Section 50—*Duty of Mental Health Officer to make Applications* Duty to make applications for admission to hospital or reception under guardianship within area of his Local Authority when he is of opinion that, having regard to any wishes expressed by relatives and to any other relevant circumstances, it is necessary or proper for the application to be made by him.

Section 51—*Appeals to Sheriff* Where a patient is to be continued in hospital or guardianship after review, it shall be the duty of the Area Health Authority or of the Local Authority to inform any person having a right to appeal (the patient or his nearest relative or both) of that right and of the period within which it may be exercised.

For purposes of the appeal any Medical Practitioner authorized by or on behalf of the patient or by the nearest relative may visit the patient and may examine him in private.

Section 53—*Responsible Medical Officer* In this Act Responsible Medical Officer means:

a. In relation to a patient in hospital, any Medical Practitioner employed on the staff of that hospital who may be authorized by the Area Health Authority to act (either generally or in any particular case or class of case or for any particular purpose) as the Responsible Medical Officer.

b. In relation to a patient under guardianship the Chief Area Medical Officer of the Area Health Authority concerned or any other Medical Practitioner authorized by that Authority to act (either generally or in any particular case or class of case or for any particular purpose) as the Responsible Medical Officer.

Area Health Authority Concerned Reference in this Act to an Area Health Authority concerned is a reference:

a. Where a guardianship application is effective, to the Local Authority to whom that application is addressed.

b. Where the patient has been transferred to guardianship by a Area Health Authority who received him into guardianship or approved his guardian.

PART V (SECTIONS 54–72): DETENTION OF PATIENTS CONCERNED IN CRIMINAL PROCEEDINGS, ETC., AND TRANSFER OF PATIENTS UNDER SENTENCE

Power of Court to Commit to Hospital

Where a Court remands or commits for trial a person charged with an offence who appears to be suffering from mental disorder, the Court may, instead of remanding in custody, commit him to a hospital (if available and suitable).

If Responsible Medical Officer is satisfied of nature and degree of mental disorder, the person shall be detained for the period for which he is remanded or for the period of committal unless before expiration of period he is liberated in course of law.

If the nature and degree of mental disorder are not such as to satisfy Responsible Medical Officer, the person will be dealt with by the Court.

No person shall be committed to a hospital except on the written or oral evidence of a Medical Practitioner.

Section 55—Powers of Courts to Order Hospital Admission or Guardianship   Where a person is convicted in High Court or Sheriff Court of an offence punishable by imprisonment, the Court may order his admission to hospital (specified) or place him under guardianship (specified):

a. If the Court is satisfied on the evidence of two Medical Practitioners that the offender is suffering from mental disorder of a nature and degree which, in the case of a person under 21 years of age, would warrant his admission to a hospital or his reception into guardianship.

b. If the Court is of opinion that the most suitable way of disposing of the case is by means of a hospital or guardianship Order.

Where a person is charged summarily in the Sheriff Court the Court may make an Order for admission to and detention in a hospital (specified).

The Court may, if it is satisfied that the person committed the offence, make a hospital Order without convicting him.

A Summary Court, other than a Sheriff Court, may remit a person to the Sheriff Court and the Sheriff Court may make an Order for hospital or guardianship.

It shall be the duty of the prosecutor in any Court, if it appears to him that the person may be suffering from mental disorder, to bring before the Court such evidence as may be available of the person's mental condition.

A State hospital shall not be specified in a hospital Order unless the Court is satisfied on the evidence of the Medical Practitioners that the offender, on account of his dangerous, violent or criminal propensities, requires treatment under conditions of special security, and cannot suitably be cared for in a hospital other than a State hospital.

Section 56—Additional Powers in respect of Children and Young Persons   A hospital or guardianship Order may be made in the case of a child or young person brought before a Juvenile Court or a Sheriff Court.

A Court shall not make a hospital or guardianship Order in respect of a person brought before the Court, as being beyond the control of his parent or guardian, unless the Court is satisfied that the parent or guardian understands the results which will follow from the Order and consents to it being made.

Where it appears to any person bringing a child or young person before any Court that the child or young person may be suffering from mental disorder, it shall be the duty of that person to bring before the Court such evidence as may be available of the mental condition.

Section 57—Requirements as to Medical Evidence   One at least of the Medical Practitioners whose evidence is taken into account by the Court shall be a Practitioner approved for the purposes of *Section* 27 of this Act by an Area Health Authority as having special experience in the diagnosis or treatment of mental disorder.

If the accused is represented, a copy of the medical report shall be given to his counsel or solicitor.

If the accused is not represented the substance of the report shall be disclosed to the accused or to his parent or guardian, if in court.

The accused may require that the practitioner by whom the report was signed be called to give oral evidence, and evidence to rebut this may be called by or on behalf of the accused.

Section 58—Effects of Hospital and Guardianship Orders   An Order shall be sufficient authority for any person directed to do so by the Court to convey the patient to the hospital specified in the Order within 28 days and for the Area Health Authority to admit him and to detain him in accordance with the provisions of this Act, or similar authority for guardianship.

Patient on a hospital or guardianship Order is not subject to review at 25 years and power to order discharge by nearest relative shall not apply.

Section 59—Supplementary Provisions as to Hospital Orders   The Court may direct conveyance of patient to a place of safety pending his admission to the hospital.

If within the period of 28 days it appears to the Secretary of State that it is not possible for the patient to be received into the hospital specified, he may give directions for the admission of the patient to such other hospital as appears to be appropriate.

Section 60—Power of Court to Restrict Discharge from Hospital
Where a hospital Order is made in respect of a person and it appears to the Court that it is necessary for the protection of the public, the Court may further order that the person shall be subject to special restrictions without limit of time or during such period as may be specified in the Order. An Order restricting discharge shall not be made unless the medical practitioner approved by the Area Health Authority has given evidence orally before the Court.

The special restrictions are as follows:

a. None of the provisions of Part IV of this Act relating to the duration, renewal and expiration of authority for the detention of patients shall apply, and the patient shall continue to be liable to be detained by virtue of the relevant hospital Order until he is absolutely discharged.

b. The following powers shall be exercisable only with the consent of the Secretary of State:

    i. Power to grant leave of absence (power to recall the patient shall be vested in the Secretary of State as well as in the Responsible Medical Officer).

    ii. Power to transfer the patient.

c. Power to take patient into custody and retain him may be exercised at any time (he is not discharged after 28 days' or 3 months' absence without leave).

A guardianship Order shall not be made where an Order restricting discharge is in force.

Other Powers
Section 61—Powers of Secretary of State in respect of Patients subject to Restriction Orders   The Secretary of State may direct that the patient shall cease to be subject to special restrictions. The provisions of this Act shall then apply as if the patient had been admitted by a hospital Order (without restriction) on the date on which the restriction Order ceased.

The Secretary of State may at any time, while an Order restricting discharge is in force, by warrant discharge the patient from hospital, either absolutely or subject to conditions.

If the patient is conditionally discharged the Secretary of State may at any time recall him by warrant.

If after the patient has been conditionally discharged an Order restricting discharge ceases to have effect, the patient shall be deemed to be absolutely discharged on the date when the Order ceases to have effect, unless previously recalled.

Section 62—Appeals   Where a hospital Order, guardianship Order or Order restricting discharge has been made by a Court, the person may, without prejudice to any other form of appeal, appeal against that Order as against a conviction.

Section 63—Procedure whereby Insanity stands in Bar of Trial or is the Ground of Acquittal of a Criminal Charge   Court shall direct finding of insanity at or during trial to be recorded.

Court shall direct jury to find whether person was insane at time of offence and to declare whether person was acquitted by them on account of his insanity.

Court shall order that the person to whom that finding or that acquittal relates shall be detained in a State hospital or such other hospital as for special reasons the Court may specify.

An Order for the detention of a person in a hospital under this Section shall have the like effect as a hospital Order with an Order restricting discharge, made without limitation of time.

The Court may order that the case be proceeded with in the absence of the accused if it is not practicable or appropriate for an accused person to be brought before it.

Section 64—Persons Ordered to be Kept in Custody during Her Majesty's Pleasure   The Secretary of State may by warrant direct that any such person be detained in a State hospital or such other hospital as he may specify and give directions for his removal there.

Section 65—Removal to Hospital of Persons in Prison Awaiting Trial, etc.   If it appears to the Secretary of State that a person in custody is suffering from mental disorder, he may apply to the Sheriff for an Order and the Sheriff, if satisfied by reports from two Medical Practitioners, may make an Order for removal and detention in hospital (specified).

This transfer Order must be acted on within 14 days.

Transfer Order has the like effect as a hospital Order together with an Order restricting discharge made without limit of time.

At least one of the Medical Practitioners shall be approved by a Area Health Authority for *Section* 27 of this Act. Transfer Order shall specify the form or forms of mental disorder.

Same form must be described by each of the practitioners.

Section 66—Removal to Hospital of Persons Serving Sentences of Imprisonment and Other Prisoners   If the Secretary of State is satisfied by the reports he may make a transfer direction.

This applies to persons suffering from mental disorder of a nature or degree which warrants their admission to hospital:

    a. Persons serving sentences of imprisonment (under a hospital Order);

    b. Civil prisoners (civil debt) (under Part IV of this Act);

    c. Aliens detained (under Part IV of this Act).

Within 3 months of his transfer to a hospital the person may appeal to the Sheriff to cancel the directions; if cancelled the person is returned to prison.

Section 67   There may be also a direction restricting discharge which shall have the like effect as an Order restricting discharge.

Section 69   Within a period of 28 days before a direction restricting the discharge of a person ceases to have effect, the Responsible Medical Officer shall assess the need for continued detention. If continued, patient shall be regarded as under a hospital Order (without restriction).

Section 71—*Reception into Guardianship of Persons Sent to Approved Schools*   If in the case of a child or young person in an approved school the Secretary of State is satisfied by reports (as in *Section* 65), he may by warrant direct that he be placed under guardianship of Area Health Authority or of other specified approved guardian.

Has the like effect as a guardianship Order.

PART VI (SECTIONS 73–88): REMOVAL AND RETURN OF PATIENTS WITHIN UNITED KINGDOM, ETC.

Reciprocity of arrangements for removal of patients within United Kingdom.

If absent without leave may be taken into custody within specified time anywhere in United Kingdom and returned.

PART VII (SECTIONS 89–90): STATE HOSPITALS

Section 89—*Provision of Hospitals for Patients Requiring Special Security*   Secretary of State shall provide such hospitals for those of dangerous, violent or criminal propensities.

Section 90—*Administrative Provisions*   The State hospitals shall be under the control and management of the Secretary of State.

The Secretary of State may constitute one or more committees to manage State hospitals on his behalf.

PART VIII (SECTIONS 91–93): DEALS WITH THE PROTECTION OF PROPERTY OF PATIENTS

Section 91—Duties of Local Authority   May petition the Court for appointment of Curator bonis to any person in their area who is incapable, on account of mental disorder, of managing his own affairs.

If the person is in hospital or under guardianship, Local Authority shall inform Area Health Authority or guardian of the granting of any such petition.

PART IX (SECTIONS 95–101): MISCELLANEOUS AND GENERAL

Section 95—Ill-treatment of Patients   Ill-treatment or wilful neglect of any patient in hospital or under guardianship shall be an offence.

(Six months' to 2 years' imprisonment and/or fine not exceeding £100–£500.)

Section 96—Protection of Female Defectives.   It is an offence:

  a. For a man to have unlawful sexual intercourse with a woman who is a defective;

  b. For any person to procure or encourage any woman who is a defective to have unlawful sexual intercourse;

  c. For any person to induce any woman who is a defective to resort to or to be upon premises for the purpose of unlawful sexual intercourse with any man.

A person shall not be guilty of an offence if he did not know and had no reason to suspect that the woman was a defective.

(Liable on conviction to imprisonment for term not exceeding 2 years.)

'Defective' in this section means girl or woman suffering from mental deficiency of such a nature or degree that she is incapable of living an independent life or of guarding herself against serious exploitation.

Section 97—Protection of Female Patients   Similar provisions in case of woman receiving treatment for mental disorder in hospital or under guardianship.

Section 98—Assisting Patients to Absent Themselves without Leave   It is an offence to induce or knowingly assist a person:

  a. Liable to be detained in hospital or being subject to guardianship, to absent himself without leave, or

  b. Being in legal custody, to escape from such custody.

It is an offence knowingly to harbour a patient who is absent without leave or to give him any assistance with intent to prevent, hinder or interfere with his being taken into custody or returned to the hospital or other place where he ought to be.

(Imprisonment not exceeding 6 months to 2 years and/or fine not exceeding £100–£500.)

Section 101—Provision of Pocket-money for In-patients in Hospital   Secretary of State may pay to in-patient (whether liable to be detained or not) in any hospital, other than a private hospital, wholly or mainly for the treatment of persons suffering from mental disorder, such amounts as he thinks fit in respect of their occasional personal expenses when it appears to him that they would otherwise be without such resources.

CRIMINAL PROCEDURE (SCOTLAND) ACT 1975

Prior to the passing of the Criminal Procedure (Scotland) Act of 1975, procedures dealing with crime and criminals were governed by forty separate Acts of Parliament, some dating from the sixteenth and seventeenth centuries.

The Criminal Procedure Act of 1975, which came into being on 16 May 1975, consolidates and collates all previous Acts under one Act. Therefore, any mentally disordered person involved in criminal proceedings will automatically be subject to the appropriate Section of the Criminal Procedure (Scotland) Act 1975. The only part of the Mental Health (Scotland) Act 1960 affected by this new Act is Part V, i.e. that part of the 1960 Act dealing with mentally disordered persons involved in criminal proceedings.

The Criminal Procedure (Scotland) Act 1975 is arranged in three Parts:

PART I.   *Solemn Procedure: Sections 1–282.*
  (a) Procedure prior to trial.
  (b) Procedure at trial of persons suffering from mental disorder.
  (c) Conviction and sentence.
       Adjournment and Remand.
  (d) Probation.   *Section 184.*
  (e) Further Provision as to Appeals.   *Section 280.*

PART II.   *Summary Procedure: Sections 283–457*
  (a) Procedure prior to trial.
  (b) Procedure at trial of persons suffering from mental disorder.

(c) Conviction and sentence.
   Adjournment and Remand.
(d) Probation.
(e) Review.
   Appeals.

The simple basic differences between Part I and Part II of the Criminal Procedure (Scotland) Act 1975 are:

PART I	PART II
'Major Crime'	'Minor Crime'
High Court	Sheriff Court
Indictment	Summary
Sheriff and Jury	Sheriff without Jury

Many cases starting off under Part I Procedure are subsequently reduced to Part II. This frequently happens with cases involving mentally disordered persons and causes some confusion due to multiplicity of Sections quoted.

PART III. *General: Sections* 458–464
   Section 462   Interpretation.
   Definition of child, convicted person, guardianship order, hospital, local authority, medical practitioner, place of safety, residential establishment, responsible medical officer, State hospital, etc.

   Schedule 9
   Amendments No. 17–29.
   The Mental Health (Scotland) Act 1960, amended in the following sections: *Sections* 58 (1), (2), (4); 59 (2); 60 (5); 64 (3); 66 (7)a; 67; 68; 72 (3); 111 (1); 111 (4).

   Schedule 10 Repealed Sections of Mental Health (Scotland) Act 1960.
   Sections 54; 55; 57(1)–(4); 59(1); 60(1), (2), (4); 62; 63; 96(5).

SUMMARY OF THE ACT WITH PARTICULAR REFERENCE TO MENTAL DISORDER

PART I. *Sections* 1–282

   Section 13 (1)(*b*)   A Sheriff or Justice may issue a warrant to arrest a convicted mental patient and bring him before any Sheriff.

Section 25   Prior to trial, instead of Custody the Court has power to commit a person suffering from mental disorder to hospital. The oral or written evidence of a medical practitioner is necessary and a hospital place must be available for admission.

Section 174 and *Section* 255(4)   Insane in Bar of Trial—Court shall order person to be detained in a State hospital or such other hospital as the Court may specify. This order automatically carries a restriction Order on discharge without limit of time. The case may be proceeded with in the absence of the person.

Section 175   Following conviction in the High Court or Sheriff Court a hospital Order may be granted by the Court. Two medical practitioners are necessary to give evidence which may be oral or written. The hospital Order must be acted upon within 28 days. State hospital shall not be specified unless the offender is dangerous, violent or has criminal propensities, supported by oral evidence. Guardianship Order is similar to above, but Court must be satisfied that Local Authority or guardian is willing to receive that person into guardianship.

Section 176   One practitioner must be approved under *Section* 27 of the Mental Health (Scotland) Act.

Section 176(4)   To rebut evidence, accused person may be examined by any medical practitioner. Examination may be made in private.

Section 177   Court may place person in a place of safety pending admission to hospital—28 days.

Section 178   Court may place Restrictive Order without limit of time or specified time on discharge. Restriction Order—may be recommended by approved doctor who must give oral evidence before the Court in addition to a written report.

Section 178(3)   When a restriction Order is made, a guardianship Order shall *not* be made.

Section 179   After accused person has been convicted, but before sentence is passed, three weeks' remand to determine most suitable method of dealing with the case.

Section 180 Charged before a Court with an offence. Court satisfied that the accused did the Act—mental and physical examination may be ordered. Three weeks' remand.

Section 180 If remanded on bail (S.180(2)) accused person must submit to a medical examination. (S.180(3)). Failure to comply—bail may be forfeited.

Section 184 Hospital Order as a condition of Probation— 1 year only.

Section 192 Probation report may *not* be given to accused person but to parent or guardian in Court.

Section 280 Hospital Order. Guardianship Order. Restriction Order—appeals against these Orders shall take the same form as for appeals against conviction. (This has nothing to do with appeals under the Mental Health (Scotland) Act 1960).

Section 143 Spouse may be called as a witness even against his/her wishes.

EQUIVALENT SECTIONS
Criminal Procedure (Scotland) Act 1975. Mental Health (Scotland) Act 1960.

PART I	PART II	
Section 13	322	36 & 106
25	330	54
174 (255(4))	375	63 (1) & (3)
175	376	55
176	377	57 (1) & (4)
177	378	59 (1)
178	379	60 (1) (2) (4)
179	380	54
180	381	54
184	385	55
280	443	62
143	348	96 (5)

Mental Health (Scotland) Act 1960. Part V. *Sections* 56, 64, 65, 66, 67, 69 and 71 have no equivalent in the Criminal Procedure (Scotland) Act 1975.

Psychological Tests used in the Field of Mental Handicap

THE USE OF STANDARD PSYCHOLOGICAL TESTS in mental handicap has changed over recent years. Intelligence tests have been supplanted by scales that measure social skills, independent living skills and coping behaviour.

ADAPTIVE BEHAVIOUR TESTS

The following are the most widely used measures of what is termed 'social competence' or 'adaptive behaviour'.

Progress Assessment Charts (PAC)

There are various levels of these scales covering the skills of young children up to adults. Four main areas are used: occupation, communication, socialization and self-help. A person is credited as to whether he or she can achieve a particular level of skill, and results are entered on a diagram so that deficits and progress can be seen at a glance. The latest version of the PAC II (for adults) includes a personality measure along the same lines.

Adaptive Behaviour Scale

This is an American scale measuring adaptive behaviour (including social skills, motor skills, language etc.) and maladaptive behaviour (including hyperactivity, stereotyped behaviour etc.). It is a very wide-ranging test, and provides a mass of information about a person. Like the PAC it is filled in from the information of somebody who is familiar with the person concerned.

Fairview Self-Help Scale

This rating scale of social skills measures five areas: motor dexterity, self-help skills, communication skills, social interaction and self-direction. From this is derived a behavioural age score in months. It is typical of many such scales that are used to measure similar skills. It is particularly useful with profoundly handicapped people.

343

Balthazar Scales of Adaptive Behaviour

These scales measure skills of independence in the severely and profoundly retarded including feeding, toileting and dressing. The second part of the scale looks at social behaviour including verbal communication, play activity and various self-directed behaviours. It is basically an observational scale.

The Vineland Social Maturity Scale

This test measures successive stages of social competence from infancy to adult life in eight areas of skill. Generally it is scored on the information given from parents, nurses and people who know the person well.

Developmental Check Lists

These cover a variety of tests, etc. that are available for assessing the mentally handicapped. Some of these are published whereas others are used in a specific situation and may have been devised by a psychologist or nurse to meet local needs. The newly introduced Paton's Assessment Schedules are fully described in Appendix 4.

INTELLIGENCE OR COGNITIVE TYPE TESTS

When intelligence or cognitive type tests are required, there are some which are particularly relevant to mentally handicapped people:

Coloured Progressive Matrices

This version of the Raven's Matrices Test is most used with the mentally handicapped and older people because it is simpler than the Standard Progressive Matrices tests. Norms exist to permit scoring of intelligence down to about IQ 40. It is usually used in conjunction with the Crichton Vocabulary Scale.

Leiter International Performance Scale

This is a purely non-verbal test in both tasks and instruction. It gives a mental age score and is particularly useful with mentally handicapped people as it is not biased by verbal ability. It is also useful with deaf people.

Columbia Mental Maturity Scale

This test requires no verbal response and a minimal motor response, and so is useful for groups who have impaired physical and/or verbal functioning.

Stanford–Binet: Terman–Merrill (Form LM)

This is the original intelligence measure, and is still occasionally used with mentally handicapped children and adults. It is divided into mental age categories, and consists of a number of sub-tests measuring various skills which indicate the mental age at which the person is functioning.

The Wechsler Tests

There are three main Wechsler tests—the Wechsler Adult Intelligence Scale, the Wechsler Intelligence Scale for Children and the Wechsler Pre-School and Primary Scale of Intelligence. They all have the same format, being divided into verbal and performance intelligence sections, with a number of sub-scales making up the overall total. The are the most commonly used scales in this country at present, although they do not really cover the mental handicap range adequately.

The British Ability Scales

These are new scales of abilities, which are designed to cover a wide range of skills and offer flexibility in use. Most of the new ideas in intellectual testing are incorporated and they cover the age range $2\frac{1}{2}$–17.

DEVELOPMENTAL TESTS

Assessment of severely handicapped children can be especially important and often with very young children developmental tests are used. The most common ones are:

The Bayley Scales of Infant Development

This test is suitable for babies and young children and is in three parts: the mental scale, the motor scale and infant behaviour record. It compares the childs' development with children of his own age.

The Griffiths Developmental Scale

This is a series of tests for the under two-year old much used in the

United Kingdom. It produces a development quotient which is a combination of motor development, hearing and speech development, hand co-ordination, social skills and performance skills.

Denver Development Screening Test

This is a short screening test of a child's development, divided into four sections: the Personal Social Scale, the Fine Motor Adaptive Scale, the Language Scale and the Gross Motor Scale. It provides a quick estimate of a child's developmental progress.

Behaviour Assessment Battery

This is a device based on learning procedures, and analyses the skills of profoundly handicapped children and adults at a very basic level. It is divided into a number of sections and is administered by actually teaching the tasks required. It is basically a device for developing programmes for profoundly severely handicapped children.

SPECIALIST ASSESSMENTS

Sometimes specialist assessments are required, in a particular aspect of a person's functioning. For this purpose the following tests might be used:

Reynell Developmental Language Scale

This is a test designed for children and assesses verbal expression and comprehension. It is used a lot by Speech Therapists and gives an idea of a child's level of development in language skills.

Illinois Test of Psycho Linguistic Abilities

This is a large complicated assessment device which looks at language along a number of dimensions. Its main use is as a specialist diagnostic tool for people with communication problems. It is linked to a teaching programme, known as the Peabody Language Development Kit.

Frostig Developmental Test of Visual Perception

This is a test that assesses a child's visual perceptual abilities again along a number of dimensions. It is a pencil and paper test involving mainly drawing tasks, and again is linked to a teaching kit aimed at developing a person's perceptual skills, eye–hand co-ordination and spatial awareness.

William's Intelligence Test for Children with Defective Vision

As the name implies this test is used mainly with people with visual difficulties. Its instructions and material are adapted for blind people, but are based on the Stanford–Binet and other tests. It is most useful for children with sensory problems as well as mental handicap.

OBSERVATIONAL ASSESSMENT

Many psychologists now use observational assessment as the primary source of data on an individual. The Balthazar Scales of Adaptive Behaviour are an example of a structured system for observing mentally handicapped people's behaviour. Many other systems exist, usually incorporating some sort of coding for behaviour occurring over a fixed period. Reference should be made to Chapter 20, *Training the Mentally Handicapped—a Behavioural Approach,* where the use of observation is described in more detail.

SCALES FOR EXAMINING ENVIRONMENT AND SERVICES

Lastly, there has been an increase recently in the number of scales that examine not the individually mentally handicapped person, but the environment he or she lives in and the services provided for them. Good examples are the PASS system (Programmed Analysis of Service Systems) developed by Wolfensberger in the USA, and the measures of the quality of care devised by amongst others Tizard, Raynes and Kushlick. These devices enable people planning new services and examining the functions of older ones to look at the quality and standard care provided for handicapped people and also analyse the way in which services are provided, according to the principle of normalization.

Paton's Assessment Schedules

THE AMERICAN ASSOCIATION on Mental Deficiency Adaptive Behaviour Scale (ABS) is a third-party behaviour-rating scale that was designed for use with mentally handicapped, emotionally disturbed and developmentally disabled individuals. It yields reasonably objective rating of an individual's effectiveness in dealing with the natural and social demands of the environment. Over the past few years the ABS has become one of the most popular of the approximately 300 behaviour rating-scales, in part because it has so many potential applications.

Although attempts have been made to modify the scale for British use the authors believe that the following Paton Schedules have a greater service utility in the United Kingdom for the following reasons:

1. They divide the profoundly mentally handicapped and/or very physically handicapped from the rest of the mental handicap population, thereby saving a great deal of administrative time and paper, as the two populations are very different, and therefore a high proportion of negative responses from the parents/caretakers are eliminated.

2. These Schedules go into a great deal more practical detail than other schedules. This instrument is designed to be used by professionals from several backgrounds, i.e. training centre managers, nurses, psychologists, teachers and social workers.

3. The ABS responses patterns are entirely 'closed' so there is no room for open-ended descriptions of the client. This may be satisfactory for a computer, but it is unsatisfactory for clinical and practical reasons. The Schedules have open-ended items for every sub-section so that a clear clinical picture is built up throughout.

4. Paton's Assessment Schedule 'C' provides a comprehensive educational attainments test for use by teachers, training centre instructors and further education tutors.

5. Printed copies of all the schedules can be obtained at a non-profit-making price from the Mental Handicap Team, Dingleton Hospital, Melrose, Roxburghshire, Scotland, U.K.*

* There is no copyright on this material.

CLIENT'S NAME: ....   IN CONFIDENCE

.... MENTAL HANDICAP SERVICE

PATON'S ASSESSMENT SCHEDULE 'A'

For use with ALL MENTALLY HANDICAPPED CLIENTS *except* those who are Profoundly MH and/or Physically Handicapped. (Paton's Assessment Schedule 'B' should be completed for this category.)

DESCRIPTION OF SCHEDULE 'A' AND INSTRUCTIONS FOR COMPLETION

The purpose of this Schedule is to give as full a picture of the client's abilities, disabilities and potential for further training as is possible. SHOULD THE CLIENT BE ADMITTED FOR CARE AT ANY TIME, A COPY OF THIS SCHEDULE SHOULD BE GIVEN TO THE NEW 'CARETAKERS' so that the client suffers minimal discomfort on transfer.

The questions should be answered by the person(s) who presently care daily/nightly for the client.

The person responsible for completing the Schedule should note the following:

1. Give the Respondent a blank copy of the Schedule so that he/she can follow the text. Explain the purpose of the interview. In order to minimize anxiety make it clear that the procedure is a routine one.

2. Circle *every* relevant item as your colleagues will only obtain a clear clinical picture as to how to care properly for the client if you do this intelligently and conscientiously. Check your circling before you leave the Respondent.

3. The item 'Has not learned this skill' might cause Interviewers some confusion. It is a diplomatic way of saying 'Could learn but has not been taught', so the Interviewer must probe the Respondent appropriately.

4. No Schedule can be fully comprehensive. Do not hesitate to write in any extra information you think important. Use the 'Comments on Interview' section to state if you think the Respondent is unreliable in any way.

5. The basic data questions on the Client and his/her main caretaker have been placed last in this Schedule. Interviewers have found that Respondents cope best with these questions at the end of the interview rather than at the beginning. You are advised to follow this order of working. THIS 'SENSITIVE' SECTION SHOULD ONLY BE COMPLETED BY RESPONDENT'S SOCIAL WORKER OR DOCTOR OR A PSYCHOLOGIST.

6. When you have completed the Schedule, read through what you have recorded, imagining that this client about whom you know nothing will have to be cared for on the basis of the information you have just recorded. HAVE YOU MADE A COMPREHENSIVE RECORD?

7. DO NOT FORGET TO COMPLETE THE SUMMARY OF CLIENT'S PERFORMANCE which you will find below. This Summary should indicate the areas in which the Client would benefit from further training.

Client's Name: *THIS IS A CONFIDENTIAL DOCUMENT*
Date:

Summary of Client's Performance

A fairly common method of summarizing assessment results is to provide some form of 'profile' or percentile scores on the Client's abilities/deficits. Although the provision of such data may be interesting and useful for research purposes, the author is of the opinion that their incorporation into a summary provides a disincentive to the instructor to look sufficiently closely at the actual results obtained by the Client on each test item. This is what really matters in order to prepare an individualized remedial teaching plan. Bearing in mind that Schedule 'A' is intended to suggest the parameters of a training curriculum for the adult M.H. Client, the person who fills in the form may find the following headings useful in the preparation of his summary.

1. Areas of relatively useful practical ability where very little further teaching is indicated.

2. Problem learning areas which should be given high priority when planning a remedial teaching programme. The instructor is advised to consider the Client's **immediate** practical and social learning needs when including items under this heading.

3. Problem learning areas which should be given a lower priority than in 2 (above) but whose remediation will ultimately be appropriate and necessary if the Client is to cope with the practical demands of his day-to-day living situation.

CLIENT'S NAME/INITIALS: ....

I. **LEISURE ACTIVITIES** (Whether organized or not—tick ANY
appropriate item)
TV/Gramophone/Radio/Pub/Disco/Dominoes/Knitting/Swim-
ming/Sports/Any other—please specify............................

....

II. TRAVEL (Circle ANY appropriate items)
Journeys:
   1. Makes unfamiliar journeys by self (e.g. on a bus)
   2. Makes familiar journeys by self (e.g. on a bus)
   3. Finds way around own neighbourhood by self
   4. Visits one or two very familiar places/shops etc. very near own home by self
   5. Should not go out without a supervisor
   6. No opportunity to make journeys by self but might learn this skill

Road Crossing:
   1. Crosses busy main road reliably by self
   2. Crosses fairly traffic-free road reliably by self
   3. Uses 'Zebra' pedestrian crossing reliably by self
   4. Uses 'Green Man' crossing reliably by self
   5. Should ALWAYS be accompanied when crossing ANY type of road
   6. No opportunity for crossing roads but might learn this skill

    Extra comments on Journeys/Road Crossing:

III. SHOPPING (Circle ANY appropriate items)
Purchasing:
   1. Shops independently for *any* items he/she requires
   2. Can shop for own food
   3. Shops for clothing accessories (tights/socks etc.)
   4. Shops only for simple items like sweets/cigarettes etc.
   5. Should be supervised when shopping
   6. Has not learned shopping skills

Errands (e.g. to a shop or neighbour)
   1. Goes on several non-routine errands reliably without a note or 'line'
   2. Goes on one non-routine errand reliably without a note
   3. Goes on *routine* errands without a note
   4. Always needs a note when sent on an errand
   5. Has not learned this skill

    Extra comments on Purchasing/Errands:

IV. TELEPHONE (Circle appropriate item)
   1. Uses private/public telephone (DELETE APPROPRIATELY)
   2. Can only *answer* telephone
   3. Has not learned this skill

    .Extra comments on Telephone:

CLIENT'S NAME/INITIALS: ....

V. DOMESTIC ACTIVITY (Circle appropriate item)

Cooking:
1. Cooks adequate meals without help (give details below)
2. Cooks adequate meals with supervision
3. Makes elementary meals without help (give details below)
4. Has not learned this skill

   Describe what items etc. Client can cook/make (e.g. toast/eggs etc.):

Cleaning:
1. Cleans a room adequately without help
2. Cleans a room under supervision
3. Has not learned this skill

   Extra comments on Cleaning:

Laying Table:
1. Lays a table completely without any help
2. Lays a 'place' only without help (e.g. knife/fork/spoon/side plate etc.)
3. Lays a table with supervision
4. Has not learned this skill

Clearing Table:
1. Clears a table without any help
2. Clears a table with supervision
3. Has not learned this skill

   Extra comments on Laying/Clearing Table:

Washing Dishes:
1. Washes dishes efficiently by self
2. Washes dishes with supervision
3. Has not learned this skill

Drying Dishes:
1. Dries dishes efficiently by self
2. Dries dishes with supervision
3. Has not learned this skill

   Extra comments on Washing/Drying Dishes:

Bed-Making:
1. Makes bed efficiently by self
2. Makes bed with supervision
3. Has not learned this skill

   Extra comments on Bed-Making:

Laundry:
1. Uses washing machine by self
2. Uses washing machine under supervision
3. Hand-washes by self
4. Hand-washes under supervision
5. Has not learned this skill

   Extra comments on Washing:

Ironing:
1. Uses iron efficiently by self
2. Uses iron with supervision (see below)

CLIENT'S NAME/INITIALS: ....

V. DOMESTIC ACTIVITY CONTD.

Ironing contd. (Circle as appropriate)

3. Has not learned this skill

   Extra comments on Ironing and describe any special safety precautions necessary:

VI. CLOTHING (Circle appropriate items)

Dressing:

1. Dresses self completely
2. Dresses self completely if given verbal guidance only
3. Dresses self completely if given physical guidance
4. Dresses self completely except for zips/buttons/laces (Circle items of DIFFICULTY)
5. Has not learned this skill
6. Will always need overall help with dressing

Undressing:

1. Undresses self completely
2. Undresses self completely with verbal direction only
3. Undresses self completely except for zips/buttons/laces (circle items of DIFFICULTY)
4. Has not learned this skill
5. Will always need overall help with undressing

   Extra comments on Dressing/Undressing

Clothing—Miscellaneous: (Circle ANY appropriate item)

1. Changes dirty clothes—with/without reminder (DELETE as appropriate)
2. Keeps clothes tidy in room and house—with/without reminder (DELETE as appropriate)
3. Needs supervision with regard to care of clothing
4. Needs advice about the right clothes to wear

   Extra comments on Clothing:

VII. EATING/DRINKING ETC. (Circle appropriate item)

Eating:

1. Uses knife/fork etc. in a normal way
2. Uses knife but can't cut with it
3. Only uses knife for spreading
4. Only uses spoon and fork
5. Only uses spoon by self
6. Has to be fed
7. Has not learned this skill

Drinking:

1. Drinks in a normal way
2. Has to be helped to drink
3. Has not learned this skill

   Extra comments on Eating/Drinking and describe special needs (e.g. diet/eating problems):

Table Manners:

Describe any objectionable table manners here: ....

....

CLIENT'S NAME/INITIALS: ....

VIII. PERSONAL HYGIENE (Circle appropriate item)

Toilet—Continence:
1. Never has toilet accidents by day
2. Occasionally has toilet accidents by day (not more than once per week)
3. Frequently has toilet accidents during the day
4. Only has toilet accidents by day when he/she has a fit

1. Never has toilet accidents when in bed
2. Occasionally has toilet accidents when in bed (not more than once per week)
3. Frequently has toilet accidents when in bed
4. Only has toilet accident when in bed when he/she has a fit

Toilet—Self Care: (Circle appropriate items)
1. Goes to toilet unaided
2. 'Wipes' self efficiently
3. Remembers to flush toilet
4. Remembers to wash hands

Specify any help needed with toileting:

Washing:
1. Washes and dries hands and face efficiently by self
2. Washes and dries hands and face with supervision—verbal/physical prompt (DELETE appropriately)
3. Has not learned this skill

Bathing/Showering:
1. Baths and dries self unaided
2. Baths and dries self unaided but needs bath run
3. Needs supervision while bathing and drying self
4. Has not learned this skill

Toothbrushing:
1. Cleans own teeth/dentures efficiently
2. Needs supervision when cleaning teeth/dentures
3. Has not learned this skill

Extra comments on Washing/Bathing/Toothbrushing:

Shaving:
1. Shaves self unaided
2. Shaves self with supervision
3. Has not learned this skill

Circle type of shaver used here—(a) Electric/battery (b) Safety
Extra comments on Shaving:

Menstruation:
1. Copes by self with all menstrual hygiene
2. Copes except for purchase of towels
3. Copes if supervised
4. Has not learned this skill

Extra comments on Menstruation: (e.g. indicate type of help required)

Nails:
1. Cuts own nails/toenails efficiently (and without reminder Yes/No)
2. Has not learned this skill

CLIENT'S NAME/INITIALS: ....

Hair—Brushing/Combing:
1. Brushes/combs hair efficiently (and without reminder Yes/No)
2. Brushes/combs hair with supervision
3. Has not learned this skill

Hair—Shampooing:
1. Shampoos/dries own hair efficiently (and without reminder Yes/No)
2. Shampoos/dries hair with supervision
3. Has not learned this skill

   Extra comments on Nails/Hairbrushing and Shampooing:

General Body Hygiene:
1. Needs no reminder regarding regular attendance to personal body hygiene
2. Needs occasional reminders on this item
3. Needs close supervision on this item

IX. PHYSICAL CONDITION (Circle appropriate items)

Limb Function:
1. Has no limb function disability
2. Suffers from some form of walking disability which impedes function but needs no help (*see* below)
3. Needs a helping hand to move from A to B (*see* below)
4. Has to use a wheelchair/Zimmer/stick etc. (DELETE appropriately)
5. Suffers from some form of hand disability which impedes function but needs no help (*see* below)
6. Needs help because of impaired hand function (*see* below)

   Describe any help needed due to disabilities noted above and also give brief description of dysfunction:

Sleep Pattern:
1. Usually easy to settle to bed
2. Usually difficult to settle to bed
3. Usually sleeps undisturbed
4. Intermittent/poor sleeper

   Extra comments about settling/sleeping:

   Does the patient presently sleep alone/in the same room/bed as any member of the family/staff etc?—(DELETE appropriately)—please describe here:

Epilepsy:
1. Has never had epileptic fits
2. Had epileptic fits as a child
3. Still has epileptic fits
4. Has nocturnal fits

   Please state frequency and type of fits here:

Medication:
1. Receives no medication
2. Receives *regular* medication prescribed by doctor
3. Receives any other medication (e.g. from chemist without prescription)

   Extra comments on medication including indication of what the medication is treating (e.g. epilepsy, sleeplessness etc):

CLIENT'S NAME/INITIALS: ....

Speech/Communication—Expression:
1. Speaks normally
2. Difficult but possible to understand what he/she says
3. Only possible to understand the odd word
4. Uses Bliss/Makaton/any other system (give details below)
5. No speech but can communicate basic needs by gesture
6. Does not even use gesture

Speech/Communication—Comprehension:
1. No trouble in understanding anything that is said to him/her
2. Can comply with non-routine instructions
3. Can only comply with simple *routine* instructions
4. Needs constant repetition to ensure understanding
5. No apparent understanding

   Extra comments on Speech:

Hearing:
1. Has no impairment of hearing function
2. Hearing aid in right/left ear (DELETE appropriately)

   Describe any hearing difficulties in detail:

Vision:
1. Has no impairment of visual function
2. Glasses for reading etc. only
3. Glasses all the time

   Describe any visual difficulties in detail:

X. WORK PERFORMANCE (To be completed by ATC staff or work place)
Level of Supervision Required:
1. No supervision of work required
2. Intermittent supervision required
3. Regular supervision required
4. Continuous supervision required

   Describe the Client's attitude to being supervised:

Task Perseverance (if left to own devices):
1. Will persevere for more than 30 minutes
2. Will presevere from 10/30 minutes
3. Will persevere for up to 10 minutes
4. No perseverance

Task Perception (i.e. ability to perceive what needs to be done to complete the task efficiently):
1. Recognizes own mistakes and corrects same unaided
2. Recognizes own mistakes and asks for help to correct same
3. Will occasionally recognize mistakes and request help
4. Does not recognize mistakes

Task Organization (ability to organize materials, tools, time etc. to complete the task effectively):
1. Requires no help in organizing work given
2. Requires guidance *initially* to organize work given

CLIENT'S NAME/INITIALS: ....

X. WORK PERFORMANCE CONTD.
Task Organization contd.

3. Requires constant guidance in relation to task organization
4. Cannot be given work which needs organization

   Describe the Client's attitude to supervision/work etc.

   Describe the type of training/work experience the Client already has (woodwork/metalwork/craftwork/assembly work etc.):

XI. SOCIAL ACCEPTABILITY

Social Acceptability with relatives/staff etc. (i.e. how easy is the Client to live and/or work with):
1. Socially acceptable all the time
2. Socially acceptable most of the time
3. Difficult and temperamental now and then
4. Difficult and temperamental most of the time

Social Acceptability with other mentally handicapped people (i.e. how well does the Client 'get on' with these people):
1. Very well
2. Averagely well
3. Not very well
4. Not at all well

   Extra comments on this section (*Please explain* if you have circled 3 or 4 on *either* of the above sub-sections):

XII. BEHAVIOURAL DESCRIPTION

Interviewer: the following list covers items of behaviour which could be dangerous either to other mentally handicapped people or to staff or to the client himself. Explain (if the parent is the respondent) that you are aware that this is an unpleasant list which may not apply to their child but that it is most important that they should try to be as truthful as possible to protect everyone, including their child, against possible future dangers.

	State Frequency:		
Circle the Numbers	**Weekly**	**Monthly**	**Other**
1. Can be physically aggressive towards other MH people			
2. Can be physically aggressive towards staff/family etc.			
3. Can be physically aggressive with objects in a dangerous way (throwing etc.)			
4. Can be physically aggressive against self in a dangerous way (biting, headbanging etc.)			
5. Has tantrums—not dangerous to self or others			
6. Uses verbal threats			
7. Uses obscene language.			
8. Steals regularly.			
9. Tells lies regularly.			
10. Runs away (to own danger)			

CLIENT'S NAME/INITIALS: ....

XII. BEHAVIOURAL DESCRIPTION CONTD.
Circle the Numbers—contd.

State Frequency:
Weekly Monthly   Other

11. Has threatened to commit suicide . . .
12. Has tried to commit suicide . . . . .
13. Expresses fantastic ideas not rooted in reality . . . .
14. Is sexually promiscuous. . . . . . .
15. Is sexually at risk—could be exploited .
16. Exposes self. . . . .
17. Masturbates in public . . . .
18. Is inclined to drink too much. . . . .
19. Any other alarming or anti-social behaviour—please specify briefly here: .

Extra comments on the above section:

Then give:—
General Behavioural Description:
Interviewer: It is very important that an accurate behavioural description of the Client should be given here including—(a) any undesirable behaviour not already mentioned in the Schedule and (b) a thorough description of the Client's 'good points'.

The purpose of this section is to fill in any gaps left by omissions in the Schedule and to give a rounded, thumb-nail sketch of the Client's personality as seen by the respondent.

Comments on Interview:

Subsequent Notes (e.g. a record of any items required to keep the Schedule up-to-date)

Please date and sign each entry
Go over the page if necessary:—

(Mrs) X W R Paton
Principal Clinical Psychologist
Borders Area Health Board
Melrose
Scotland

Acknowledgements to all who helped revise the Schedule—especially the Borders Mental Handicap Team, St Aidan's Team, Mrs Mary Rhodes, Craigmillar ATC., Edinburgh, and Dr W I Fraser, Consultant Psychiatrist, Gogarburn Hospital, Edinburgh.

Private and Confidential

PATON'S ASSESSMENT SCHEDULE

.... Mental Handicap Service

BASIC INFORMATION ON CLIENT: (This is Sensitive Information—Interviewer for this Section should be Respondent's Social Worker or Doctor or a Psychologist)

Surname...................................... Christian Name ....

Home Address..

Present place of residence of Client (if not living in own home) ....

....

Date of Birth..Religion ....

Name of Respondent and Relationship to Client
    (e.g. Mrs Brown/Mother or Miss Jones/Charge Nurse, Hospital, etc.)...

....

Diagnosis (if any)..

Present State of Client's Health ....

....

Medication—please specify exactly including dosage and times of administration (obtain from GP or Doctor) ....

....

Name of/Place of Practice of Client's Medical Practitioner........................

....

Describe Client's place of work/frequency of attendance ....

....

Describe place and frequency of Holiday Relief Service (if any).................

....

Who is main caretaker for Client now? CIRCLE AS APPROPRIATE
1. Mother 2. Father 3. Any other (describe clearly)...................................

If caretaker is an individual (as opposed to an institution) please complete the following:

Name of main Caretaker ....

PATON'S ASSESSMENT SCHEDULE CONTD.

.... Mental Handicap Service

Date of birth of main Caretaker (Year will do) ....

Address of main Caretaker ....

Brief note on present state of health of main Caretaker:

(a) From Caretaker ....

....

(b) From GP ....

....

Who would be Client's official next of kin in the event of the death of the present main Caretaker? Give full name and address of this person who would then have to deal with legal/medical enquiries etc.

Name...

Address (with telephone number if any) ....

....

Relationship to Client..

How does the present main Caretaker *wish* the Client to be managed in the event of his/her death or incapacity to cope with the Client?

1. By a surviving parent
2. By a relative (see Note below)
3. In a hospital for the mentally handicapped
4. In a closely supervised small group home (i.e. day/night care-staff and domestic help)
5. In a warden-controlled hostel where the Warden lives in
6. In sheltered housing with night and day telephone connection to Warden
7. In a flat with other mentally handicapped and with Social Work supervision

Note: If by a relative please obtain the following particulars:

Full Name (Mr/Mrs etc.) ....

Home Address (with telephone number if any)...

Date of Birth (Year will do)...

Name of/Place of Practice of this person's GP ....

Has the agreement of this person been obtained? YES/NO (tick)
This Schedule completed by:

....
Name   Designation   Date of Completion

CLIENT'S NAME:................................ IN CONFIDENCE

.... MENTAL HANDICAP SERVICE

PATON'S ASSESSMENT SCHEDULE 'B'

FOR USE WITH ALL PROFOUNDLY MENTALLY HANDICAPPED AND/OR VERY PHYSICALLY HANDICAPPED CLIENTS

NOTE:
- (i) Paton's Assessment Schedule 'A' should be used for all other mentally handicapped clients (except see note *ii* below)
- (ii) If the client is *not* Profoundly Mentally Handicapped but is very Physically Handicapped it may be necessary to use appropriate sections from *BOTH* Schedules 'A' and 'B'.

Description of Schedule and Instructions for Completion:

The purpose of this Schedule is to give as full a picture of the client's abilities, disabilities and potential for further training as is possible. The Schedule also describes any special physical or other aids the client uses in his present situation and gives detailed information as to how he should be cared for. SHOULD THE CLIENT HAVE TO BE ADMITTED FOR CARE AT ANY TIME, A COPY OF THIS SCHEDULE SHOULD BE GIVEN TO THE NEW 'CARETAKERS' so that he suffers minimal discomfort on transfer.

The questions should be answered by the person(s) who presently care daily/nightly for the client.

The person responsible for completing the Schedule should note the following:

1. Give the Respondent a blank copy of the Schedule so that he/she can follow the text. Explain the purpose of the interview. In order to minimize anxiety make it clear that the procedure is a routine one.

2. Circle *every* relevant item as your colleagues will only obtain a clear clinical picture as to how to care properly for the client if you do this intelligently and conscientiously. Check your circling before you leave the Respondent.

3. No schedule can be fully comprehensive. Do not hesitate to write in any extra information you think important. Use the 'Comments on Interview' section to state if you think the Respondent is unreliable in any way.

4. The basic data questions on the Client and his/her main caretaker have been placed last in this Schedule. Interviewers have found that Respondents cope best with these questions at the end of the interview rather than at the beginning. You are advised to follow this order of working. THIS 'SENSITIVE' SECTION SHOULD ONLY BE COMPLETED BY RESPONDENT'S SOCIAL WORKER OR DOCTOR OR A PSYCHOLOGIST.

5. When you have completed the Schedule, read through what you have recorded, imagining that this Client about whom you know nothing will have to be cared for on the basis of the information you have just recorded. HAVE YOU MADE A COMPREHENSIVE RECORD?

CLIENT'S NAME/INITIALS:..
Brief diagnostic description of client including prognosis (if known):

I. **LIMB EFFICIENCY/AMBULATION** (Circle below as appropriate)
1. Uses hands normally
   Specify any hand/arm dysfunction/help needed here:
2. Uses legs normally
   Specify any leg dysfunction/help needed here:
3. Sits without support
   Specify any sitting dysfunction/help needed here (including head control):
4. Uses Zimmer/stick etc. (DELETE appropriately)
5. Chairfast—with/without restraining straps (DELETE appropriately)
6. Can 'hand-wheel' own chair
7. Always has to be pushed in chair
8. Can transfer self from wheelchair to bed/toilet/ordinary chair (DELETE appropriately)
9. Bedfast
   If bedfast, describe any special nursing management routines here (e.g. 'turning' etc.):

   Any additional comments on this *section* here:

II. **MECHANICAL AND OTHER SPECIAL AIDS**
—in each case specify any special type/adaptations used etc. (if known)
1. Wheelchair:
2. Bed (e.g. cot sides/net/straps//waterproof sheet):
3. Protective headware:
4. Walking aids:
5. Lifting aids:
6. Positioning aids (e.g. sandbags):
7. Hearing aids:
8. Glasses:
9. Adapted Clothing:
10. Boots/Shoes:
11. Calipers:
12. Splints:

   Specify any other mechanical/physical aids used:

   Give particulars of any specialist who regularly maintains aids for client here:

III. **HEARING/VISION**
1. Appears to have normal hearing
2. Defective hearing—specify difficulties here:
3. Unable to assess due to handicap

1. Appears to have normal vision
2. Defective vision—specify difficulties here:
3. Unable to assess due to handicap

   Any extra information on hearing/vision here:

CLIENT'S NAME/INITIALS:...

IV. ABILITY TO COMMUNICATE
1. Normal communication ability
2. Does not communicate well/normally (describe below)
3. Does not communicate at all

Describe briefly client's method of communication (especially distress/hunger/pain etc.):

V. EPILEPSY
1. Has never had fits
2. Had fits in childhood but not now
3. Has occasional fits GM/PM (DELETE appropriately)—state frequency here:
4. Has frequent fits GM/PM (DELETE appropriately)—state frequency here:

Any extra information regarding fits and their nursing management here:

VI. NEUROLOGICAL DISORDERS
Describe briefly any neurological disorders from which the client suffers (e.g. Cerebral Palsy, Spina Bifida, Muscular Dystrophy, Multiple or Disseminated Sclerosis, Polio, Paralysis of any kind, etc.):

VII. PHYSICAL DEFORMITIES
Describe briefly any physical deformities from which the client suffers (e.g. hydrocephalus, hare-lip, cleft palate, congenital hip deformity, positional deformities, etc.)

VIII. MEDICATION
(Details of dosage and times of administration included on basic information sheet)
1. Receives no medication
2. Receives *regular* medication prescribed by doctor
3. Receives any other medication (e.g. from chemist without prescription)

Extra comments on medication including indication of what the medication is treating (e.g. epilepsy, sleeplessness, etc.):

IX. SLEEP PATTERN
1. Usually easy to settle to bed
2. Usually difficult to settle to bed
3. Usually sleeps undisturbed
4. Intermittent/poor sleeper
5. Client sleeps alone/in the same room/bed as other members of the family (DELETE appropriately)

Describe any difficulties in settling/sleeping/waking—including time client normally goes to bed/gets up:

CLIENT'S NAME/INITIALS:...

X. URINATION/DEFAECATION
1. Is continent of urine
2. Is incontinent of urine—state approximate frequency:
   (a) By day
   (b) By night
3. Is continent of faeces
4. Is incontinent of faeces—state approximate frequency:
   (a) By day
   (b) By night
5. Is not toilet trained at all
6. Might learn to toilet self if given special attention

Specify any urination/defaecation needs (e.g. incontinence pads/nappies/kanga pants/enemas/suppositories/special care systems including frequency of toileting and receptacles used):

Describe any nursing routines for urination/defaecation management here:

XI. MENSTRUATION
1. Does not menstruate
2. Menstruates—state frequency:

Describe in detail what menstruation care is required:

XII. FEEDING/DRINKING
Feeding:
1. Is right-handed/left-handed (DELETE appropriately)
2. Uses knife/fork etc. normally
3. Feeds self with spoon and fork—cleanly
4. Feeds self with spoon and fork—spillage
5. Feeds self with spoon only—cleanly
6. Feeds self with spoon only—spillage
7. Feeds self with fingers only
8. Must be fed
9. Might learn to feed self if given special attention

Specify briefly any relevant *physical or mental* disabilities which interfere with feeding (e.g. swallowing/chewing etc.):

Specify any special feeding aids (e.g. deep plate/special cutlery/bib etc.):

How long does client take to feed/be fed?

Describe any special food likes/dislikes:

Specify any special dietary needs:

Drinking:
1. Drinks normally
2. Uses both hands/right hand/left hand for holding cup/glass (DELETE appropriately)
3. Drinks by self—spillage using cup/glass (DELETE appropriately)

CLIENT'S NAME/INITIALS:...

XII. FEEDING/DRINKING CONTD.
Drinking contd:
4. Sucks from bottle/cup/spoon (DELETE appropriately)
5. Must be helped to drink
6. Might learn to drink by self if given special attention

   Specify briefly any relevant *physical or mental* disabilities which interfere with drinking:

   Specify any special drinking aids (e.g. special cup/straw/bib etc.). Any special hints on drinking:

   Describe any special drink likes/dislikes:

XIII. TOILETING
Washing and Bathing:
1. Can wash hands/face without supervision—water must be run YES/NO (DELETE appropriately)
2. Can bath without supervision—water must be run YES/NO (DELETE appropriately)
3. Will co-operate actively when washed/bathed by caretaker
4. Must be washed/bathed
5. Might learn to wash/bath self if given special attention

   Specify briefly any relevant *physical or mental* disabilities which might interfere with washing/bathing:

   Specify any special washing/bathing care required (e.g. eye care/opening out tight hands, positioning etc.):

   Specify any special washing/bathing aids required (e.g. bath seat etc.):

Teeth:
1. Own teeth/dentures/no teeth (DELETE appropriately)
2. Brushes own teeth without supervision
3. Brushes own teeth under supervision
4. Might have teeth brushed
5. Might learn to brush teeth if given special attention

   Specify any oral care required (e.g. care of gums etc.):

Hair:
1. Brushes/combs own hair unaided
2. Brushes/combs hair under supervision
3. Must have hair brushed/combed
4. Might learn to brush/comb hair if given special attention

   Specify any hair care required—include comments on shampooing hair here:

Skin Care:
1. Normal skin care requirements

   Specify any special skin care here:

CLIENT'S NAME/INITIALS:...

Shaving:
1. Can shave self
2. Needs to be shaved

Specify any special shaving needs here:

XIV. DRESSING/UNDRESSING
1. Dresses self with assistance appropriate to handicap
2. Co-operates when being dressed e.g. puts out arms/legs (DELETE appropriately)
3. Must be dressed
4. Might learn to dress self if given special attention

Specify any help required with dressing here:

1. Undresses self unaided
2. Undresses self with assistance appropriate to handicap
3. Co-operates when being undressed e.g. puts out arms/legs (DELETE appropriately)
4. Must be undressed
5. Might learn to undress self if given special attention

Specify any help required with undressing here:

XV. SOCIAL ACCEPTABILITY
Social Acceptability with relatives/staff etc. (i.e. how easy is the client to live and/or work with):
1. Socially acceptable all the time
2. Socially acceptable most of the time
3. Difficult and temperamental now and then
4. Difficult and temperamental most of the time

Social Acceptability with other mentally handicapped people (i.e. how well does the client 'get on' with these people):
1. Very well
2. Averagely well
3. Not very well
4. Not at all well
5. Too handicapped to notice other mentally handicapped people

Extra comments on this section (*please explain* if you have circled 3 or 4 on *either* of the above sub-sections):

XVI. BEHAVIOUR—DANGEROUS TO SELF OR OTHERS
Please describe in detail any behaviour which might be dangerous—
(a) To the clients;   (b) To other mentally handicapped people;   (c) To staff—

XVII. BEHAVIOUR—GENERAL
Please describe in detail below any other unusual behaviour which a person caring for the client ought to know about (e.g. hyperkinetic, stereotypical, autistic, psychotic or any idiosyncratic unusual behaviours):

CLIENT'S NAME/INITIALS: ....

XVIII. MANAGEMENT

Please describe below any particular way you think the client should be managed for his own comfort and well-being which has not already been covered by the Schedule—include any likes/dislikes which the client may have about the way he is managed.

(Mrs) X. W. R. Paton
Principal Clinical Psychologist
Borders Area Health Board
Melrose
Scotland

Acknowledgements to all who helped revise the Schedule—especially to the Borders Mental Handicap Team, A Benicki, Nursing Officer, Gogarburn Hospital, Edinburgh and Dr W. I. Fraser, Consultant Psychiatrist, Gogarburn Hospital, Edinburgh

Subsequent Notes
  (e.g. record of any items required to bring this Schedule up-to-date)
Please date and sign each entry:—

PATON'S ASSESSMENT SCHEDULE

For exact wording of this schedule *see* p. 349

THIS IS A CONFIDENTIAL DOCUMENT

INTRODUCTION TO PATON'S SCHEDULE 'C'

An Educational Attainments Assessment Schedule for Adult Mentally Handicapped People

GENERAL

Schedule 'C' is designed to supplement information already obtained from Paton's Schedule 'A' which assesses the mentally handicapped adult on self-care skill levels, physical/medical condition, work performance, social acceptability and behaviour. Schedule 'A' also includes a section which elicits basic information on the Client, e.g. address/place of work/diagnosis/how the parent ultimately wishes the mentally handicapped person to be cared for, etc., etc.

If the Client is either profoundly mentally handicapped or very physically handicapped, Paton's Schedule 'B' should be completed as it covers this population separately. It seeks information on the Client's physical status and on the kind of nursing care he will require. A severely physically handicapped person who is otherwise able (e.g. a paraplegic) may require to have both Schedule 'A' and 'B' completed for him.

These Schedules will give the professional caretaker/administrator a very detailed picture of the Client's abilities/disabilities and potential for further training. The completed Schedules should always accompany the Client if he is moved from one care system to another. They also provide a useful basis for any large-scale forward-planning exercises which may be necessary for the adult mentally handicapped population.

SCHEDULE 'C'

One of the main problems in assessing educational attainments in the mentally handicapped is how to discover at what level to start testing. Schedule 'C' eases this problem by being organized at three levels of Client function as follows:—

Level 1—for assessment of the lowest-functioning MH Clients
Level 2—for the middle-range of function
Level 3—for the most competent MH person.

Unless the Client is obviously low-functioning, it is recommended that the assessment should commence at Level 2 and move on to Level 3 as appropriate. It may of course be necessary to move from Level 2 to Level 1 if the Client's responses indicate this. The best person to administer this test is the student's teacher or Training Centre instructor or further education tutor.

The questions throughout Schedule 'C' are of a practical nature in that they are testing the Client's 'social-survival' skills. The Schedule attempts to cover the basic literacy, numeracy and practical social coping skills the Client would ideally require to learn, so in that sense it is also intended to suggest the parameters of a teaching curriculum. Most MH Clients will not, of course, achieve full competence, so the teacher must adjust his teaching targets according to his post-test estimates of his Client's actual and potential ability.

Finally, it is important to acknowledge that Schedule 'C' in no way claims to replace the many excellent standardized tests already available to psychologists and teachers. It merely claims to be a useful screening device for ATC instructors and other teachers of the mentally handicapped who may not have easy access to psychologists. **Any Client who demonstrates specific learning disabilities should be referred to an educational or clinical psychologist for professional assessment and advice.**

Advice on Testing Techniques

Here are some 'tips' for testers.

1. Make sure your student is seated opposite you in a comfortable working position. You may have to get him to push his chair up to the table.

2. Make sure that all the items you need for the test are properly organized and readily available to you. Make the testing material exactly as described in the Schedule as far as this is possible.

3. Spend about 5 minutes talking in an informal way to your student. Try to assess his reactions to you as a person and attempt to get him as relaxed and comfortable as possible with you.

4. Remember there is a relatively high incidence of deafness in mentally handicapped people so ensure that the lighting is good so that non-verbal clues can be picked up.

5. Speak slowly and clearly, using short sentences and don't worry if there are pauses while you prepare for the next test. Mentally handicapped people are usually far more tolerant of pauses than you are! Get your student to help you gather up test material at the end of each test.

6. In the writer's experience, most mentally handicapped students will tolerate about one hour's uninterrupted testing at a time. If you need longer, you can test for, say, 45 minutes then both break for a cup of tea, then resume for a further 45 minutes, but not longer. Most mentally handicapped people clearly enjoy being assessed and getting the undivided attention this entails.

7. Be natural, friendly and encouraging during the test, but keep the student answering the questions and do not allow him to divert you from the task in hand.

8. Do not change your facial expression if he fails to answer correctly. Stop testing once it is clear he is out of his depth.

9. Do not *help* the student to give you the correct answer—this is a common failing in people who are learning to test the mentally handicapped. Do not fix your gaze on the correct answer if you are displaying a series of alternatives. In the writer's experience, mentally handicapped people are suprisingly good at picking up such non-verbal cues.

10. It is important to avoid the distraction of a third person being present during testing. In particular, anxious parents and others emotionally involved in the student should be politely and tactfully excluded.

THIS IS A CONFIDENTIAL DOCUMENT

Particulars of Student

Name of Organization administering Test...

....

Name and Designation of Tester:..

....

Date of Test: ....

Name of Student:..

Date of Birth: ....

Name of Student's Parent/Guardian: ....

Home Address/Telephone Number: ....

....

Place of Work: ....

Any other Relevant Information on Student

e.g. If epileptic, type (GM/PM), durations and frequency of fits should be known by the teacher.

Any gross speech impairment should be noted here.

Any physical disabilities which obviously interfere with the teaching/learning situation — hearing/vision/manipulation/mobility etc.

Any gross behavioural problems which might interfere with teaching.

Student's Name: *THIS IS A CONFIDENTIAL DOCUMENT*
Date:

Summary of Student's Performance

A fairly common method of summarizing test results is to provide some form of 'profile' or percentile scores on the Client's abilities/deficits. Although the provision of such data may be interesting and useful for research purposes, the author is of the opinion that their incorporation into a summary provides a disincentive to the teacher to look sufficiently closely at the actual results obtained by the student on each test item. This is what really matters in order to prepare an individualized remedial teaching plan. Bearing in mind that Schedule 'C' is intended to suggest the parameters of a teaching curriculum for the adult MH student, the tester may find the following headings useful in the preparation of his summary.

1. Areas of relatively useful practical ability where very little further teaching is indicated.

2. Problem learning areas which should be given high priority when planning a remedial teaching programme. The teacher/instructor is advised to consider the student's *immediate* practical and social learning needs when including items under this heading.

3. Problem learning areas which should be given a lower priority than in 2 (above) but whose remediation will ultimately be appropriate and necessary if the student is to cope with the practical demands of his day-to-day living situation.

Student's Name: THIS IS A CONFIDENTIAL DOCUMENT
Date:

PATON'S SCHEDULE 'C'

Level One

Designed for testing educational attainment levels of the low-functioning Adult Mentally Handicapped Student.

Q/1(a). COMMON OBJECTS—REAL OBJECTS—IDENTIFICATION
Instructions to Tester:

Materials: A spoon, an apple, a watch (own will do), a cup.

Administration: Place these objects on the table in front of the student. *Say 'Show me X'* (in the order given below). Tick successes below.

Total Score

spoon   apple   watch   cup   =

Comments on performance here:

Q/1(b). COMMON OBJECTS—PICTURES—IDENTIFICATION
Instructions to Tester:

Materials: 2 copies Ladybird First Picture Book (cat on cover), price 50p each. Published Ladybird Books Ltd., Loughborough, Leicestershire, England. White card and adhesive. Protective 'see-through' covering material.

Method: Cut out 2 sets×12 pictures listed below. Stick the 24 pictures on separate pieces same-sized card. Cover with protective 'see-through' material.

Administration: Lay out one set of pictures of cup, watch, apple, spoon only (in that order). *Say 'Show me X'.* Tick successes below.

Total Score

cup   watch   apple   spoon   =

Comments on performance here:

Q/2(a). COMMON OBJECTS—MATCHING
Instructions to Tester:

Materials: As for Q/1(b).

Administration: Lay out one set of the cards randomly right way up in front of the student. Offer each duplicate card in the order given below. *Say 'Find me another one just like this—where's the other one?'*
Once the student has matched the picture, note results, remove your offered card and offer the next one, etc., etc. Tick successes below.

Total Score

shoe	orange	ball	car	banana	spoon	=
cup	tap	watch	apple	stairs	chair	

Comments on performance here:

Student's Initials: **THIS IS A CONFIDENTIAL DOCUMENT**
Date:

Q/2(b). COMMON OBJECTS—NAMING
Instructions to Tester:

Materials: One set of cards used in Q/1.

Administration: Place pictures one by one in front of student in the order given below. Remove each card before presenting the next. *Say 'What is this called, tell me what it is'.* Tick successes on the list below.

Total Score

shoe	orange	ball	car	banana	spoon	=
cup	tap	watch	apple	stairs	chair	

Comments on performance here:

Q/3. COMMON SHAPES—MATCHING
Instructions to Tester:

Materials: Thick white cardboard, ruler, pair of compasses, covering material.

Method: Using ruler/compass etc., cut out a duplicated set of the 5 shapes below. Shapes should be approximately 2″ in diameter. Cover with protective 'see-through' material. The cardboard should be hard and thick.

Administration: Lay out one set of shapes randomly in front of student. Offer each duplicate shape in the order given below. *Say 'Find me another one just like this—where's the other one?'* Once the student has 'matched' the shape, note results, remove your offered card and offer the next one, etc., etc. Tick successes below.

Total Score

circle	square	triangle	oblong	diamond	=

Comments on performance here:

Q/4. BASIC COLOURS—MATCHING
Instructions to Tester:

Materials: White card. Set of coloured felt-tipped pens as follows: red/blue/green/yellow/black. Covering material.

Method: Draw 2 sets of 2″×2″ squares on the card—colour squares except leave one white square. Cut out the 12 squares and stick them on to same-sized white card. Cover with 'see-through' material.

Administration: Lay out one set of cards randomly in front of student. Offer each duplicate card in the order given below. *Say 'Find me another one just like this—where's the other one'.* Once the student has 'matched' the card, note results, remove your offered card and proceed to test for the next colour-match, etc. Tick successes below.

Total Score

red	blue	green	yellow	black	white	=

Comments on performance here (describe any confusions in detail):

Student's Initials: **THIS IS A CONFIDENTIAL DOCUMENT**
Date:

Q/5. BASIC COLOURS—NAMING
Instructions to Tester:

Materials: One set of cards used in Q/4.

Administration: Place the cards one by one in front of student in the order given below. Remove each card before presenting the next. *Say 'What colour is this— tell me the colour?'* Tick successes below.

Total Score

red   blue   green   yellow   black   white   =

Comments on performance here:

Q/6. SINGLE LETTER SHAPES—MATCHING
(*Note*: success in Q/6, Q/7 and Q/8 does not necessarily indicate student can **read!**)

Instructions to Tester:

Materials: White card. Black felt-tipped pen. Covering material.

Method: Using same-sized cards (not less than 2″ square), write the following 4 alphabet letters below in clear *lower case* lettering. Cover with protective 'see-through' material. Duplicate the set.

Administration: Lay out one set of cards randomly in front of student right way up. Offer each duplicate card in the order given below. *Say 'Find me another letter just like this—where's the other one?'* Remove each card before presenting the next. Tick successes on the list below.

Total Score

j   b   m   s   =

Comments on performance here (note any confusions):

Q/7. WHOLE WORD SHAPES—MATCHING
Instructions to Tester:

(*a*) Matching—Upper-Case Lettering

Materials: White card. Black felt-tipped pen. Covering material.

Method: Using same-sized cards, write the words below in clear *upper-case* lettering. Cover with protective 'see-through' material. Duplicate the set.

Administration: Lay out one set of cards randomly in front of student right way up. Offer each duplicate card in the order given below. *Say 'Find me another word just like this—where's the other word?'* Remove each card before presenting the next. Tick successes on the list below.

Total Score

UP   COME ON   LANTERN   AXES   =

Comments on performance here:

Student's Name: *THIS IS A CONFIDENTIAL DOCUMENT*
Date:

Q/7. WHOLE WORD SHAPES—MATCHING CONTD.

(b) Matching—Lower-Case Lettering

Materials, Method and Administration: As above but write the words in clear *lower-case* lettering and present them to student. Tick successes on list below.

Total Score

    jam   happiness   collect   ship   =

    Comments on performance here:

Q/8. OWN FORENAME—DISCRIMINATION FROM OTHER FORENAMES

Instructions to Tester:

(a) Forename Discrimination

Materials: White card. Black felt-tipped pen. You cannot use covering material this time.

Method: Using one piece of card only, make a list of the following forenames—Bob/Caroline/Student's forename/Edward/Dick. Make sure the student's forename is in the middle position.

    Use suitable common forenames of varying length if you come from outside the UK.

Administration: Offer the card right way up to the student. *Say 'Find your name on this card—which is your name?'*

Results: (tick appropriately)   CORRECT/INCORRECT

    Comments on performance here:

(b) Whole-Name Discrimination—from other whole-names

Materials, Method and Administration: As above. Write the 4 forenames again but add the following surnames—Jones/Pilkington/Rodd/Griffiths. Put the student's whole name in the 4th position this time.

    Use suitable common surnames of varying length if you come from outside the UK.

Results: (tick appropriately)   CORRECT/INCORRECT

    Comments on performance here:

Student's Initials: *THIS IS A CONFIDENTIAL DOCUMENT*
Date:

Q/9(a). BASIC NAME-WRITING ABILITY

Materials: Mediumly sharpened pencil. Broad-lined paper. A piece of unlined paper.

Administration: Say *'Write your name for me—can you write your name?'* (Use the broad-lined paper for this.)

Results: (tick appropriately)—Forename only
　　　　　　　　　　　　　　　Full name
　　　　　　　　　　　　　　　Unable to write

　　　Comments on performance here:

Q/9(b).

If student is unable to write own name, make the following controlled marks on the piece of unlined paper. Place the pencil directly in front of student and say *'Pick up your pencil'*. Pointing to each mark in the order given below, say *'Make me a circle/line/mark just like this—do it here'* (pointing). Tick successes below.

　　　Circle　　　Vertical Line　　　Series of joined letters m or w or curves

　　　Now indicate which hand is dominant—　　　　　　RIGHT/LEFT (tick)

　　　Is pencil held properly?　　　　　　　　　　　　YES/NO (tick)

　　　Comments on performance here:

Q/10. COMPREHENSION OF THE SIMPLE SPOKEN WORD
Instructions to Tester:

Read the following sentences to the student. Follow each reading with the question given. Note results. *Say each time 'Listen to me—I am going to tell you something—are you listening?'*

(*a*)　*Read:*　　　The girl had an egg for her tea.
　　　Question:　What did the girl have for her tea?
　　　Results:　　Correct/Incorrect (tick).

(*b*)　*Read:*　　　The boy went to the shop to buy some matches.
　　　Question:　Where did the boy go?
　　　Results:　　Correct/Incorrect (tick).

(*c*)　*Read:*　　　The man fell off the ladder and had to go to hospital
　　　　　　　　　with a broken leg.
　　　Question:　What did the man fall off?
　　　Results:　　Correct/Incorrect (tick).

　　　Comments on performance here:

Student's Name: *THIS IS A CONFIDENTIAL DOCUMENT*
Date:

Q/11. ABILITY TO COUNT OBJECTS TO 20
Instructions to Tester:

Materials: 20 counters.

Administration: Put all the counters in front of the student. *Say 'I want you to count these for me out loud'.* Demonstrate by moving the first one over and saying *'One',* then *say 'Go on, count the rest for me—out loud'.*

Note number counted in correct sequence here:.....................................

Comments on performance here (especially whether or not student understands one-to-one correspondence):

Q/12. ABILITY TO RECOGNIZE NUMBERS 1–20
Materials: White card. Black felt-tipped pen. Covering material.

Method: Write the numbers 1–20 on separate 2" squares of card. Number one must be written as a straight line in all cases (to avoid confusion with seven).

Administration: Offer the 20 cards *randomly* to the student. *Say 'What number is this?—tell me the number'.* Remove card and proceed with the next number, etc. Tick successes on list below.

Total Score

    1   2   3   4   5   6   7   8   9 10   =
   11 12 13 14 15 16 17 18 19 20

Comments on performance here:

(Mrs) X W R Paton
Principal Clinical Psychologist
Borders Area Health Board
Dingleton Hospital
Melrose, Scotland

DON'T FORGET TO COMPLETE SUMMARY

Student's Initials: **THIS IS A CONFIDENTIAL DOCUMENT**
Date:

Level Two
Designed for testing educational attainment levels of the averagely functioning Adult Mentally Handicapped Student.

LITERACY SECTION

Q/1. SOCIAL SIGHT VOCABULARY (SSV)—RECOGNITION SKILLS

Instructions to Tester:
Using 10 white cards 6″ × 2″, write the following 10 SSV words in black:—
    (*a*) 5 words in upper-case lettering
    (*b*) 5 words in lower-case lettering.
Use covering material.

Administration: Lay the first 5 cards out right way up in front of student. *Say 'Can you read these?'* Then remove cards and repeat performance with the second group of 5 cards. Tick successes below.

Total Score

1st Group: POST-OFFICE   TOILETS   CROSS NOW   =
               DANGER   PRIVATE

2nd Group: cafe   poison   no smoking   push   enquiries

Comments on performance here:

Q/2(a). READING ABILITY—MECHANICAL

Instructions to Tester:
Write the following sentences in clear bold script on a single piece of white card. Number the sentences. Cover.

Administration: *Say 'I want you to read this for me—read as many sentences as you can'.* Stop student when he is clearly faltering. Tick successes below.

    1. Can the big dog jump?
    2. He is a very good man.
    3. Will you play with me?
    4. Please hide this book from my sister.
    5. Cut the string and open the parcel.
    6. We travelled at high speed so we got there quickly.
    7. I could telephone all the people we know to suggest they come to our party.
    8. I was engaged to James but the marriage didn't take place.
    9. My knowledge and experience warned me to be careful and not to obstruct him.
    10. My secretary should acknowledge the receipt of the substantial subscription you forwarded to our Society.

Comments on performance here:

Note: If the student can read sentence 8 onwards, he may well be able to read a simply written newspaper, etc., from the mechanical reading point of view.

Student's Initials: *THIS IS A CONFIDENTIAL DOCUMENT*
Date:

Q/2(b). READING ABILITY—PHONIC BLENDS

Note: This test to be given only to students who *cannot* cope with sentence 6 onwards in Q/2(a) above.

Using six pieces of white card write the following 6 nonsense words in black lower-case lettering. Cover.

Administration: Lay the cards right way up in front of the student. *Say 'These words make a sound. Tell me what sounds they make'.* Point to each in turn. Tick successes below.

    1—fax; 2—bom; 3—oosh; 4—theek; 5—ching; 6—trud.

Comments on performance here:

Q/3. READING ABILITY—COMPREHENSION
(Often well below mechanical reading ability)

Instructions to Tester: Copy the 3 paragraphs below on to 3 same-sized pieces of white card. Cover.

Administration: (THIS TEST IS FOR STUDENTS WHO CAN AT LEAST READ SENTENCES 4/5 FROM Q/2(a) ABOVE). Offer one card at a time. *Say 'Read this to me, please, you can read it out loud—then answer the question about it'.* Allow student to read silently if he naturally does this.

You may have to prompt student again to answer the question. *Note especially* whether student has to search text again for answers or if he gives answers without having to do this.

Card 1: I live at home. I have two brothers and three sisters. We live near the shops. My mother lets me go shopping for her.

    Question: How many sisters does he have?
    Results: (tick) Correct/Incorrect.

Card 2: My father told me how to get to my granny's new house. We live in a big town. I must catch the 23 bus to Green Street then cross the road and go down Black Street and first left into Red Street. Then I must look for house number 42 at the end of the street. That is my granny's new house.

    Question: Which bus must he catch to Green Street?
    Results: (tick) Correct/Incorrect.

Card 3: I have been on holiday at a farm and took the train to get there. I was telling my mother what the farm looked like. The farm had a white gate in front of it and two houses for the cows at the side of it. Behind it were some old apple trees and further up the hill there was a big barn full of hay and a shed which had a blue tractor in it. There were horses in the field beside the tractor shed.

    Question: What colour was the farm gate?
    Results: (tick) Correct/Incorrect.

Comments on performance here (especially re-searching test—see above):

Student's Initials: *THIS IS A CONFIDENTIAL DOCUMENT*
Date:

Q/4(a). BASIC NAME-WRITING ABILITY

Materials: Mediumly sharpened pencil. Broad-lined paper. A piece of unlined paper.

Administration: Say *'Write your name for me—can you write your name?'* (Use the broad-lined paper for this.)

Results: (tick appropriately)—Forename only
                                    Full name
                                    Unable to write.

Comments on performance here:

If student is unable to write own name, make the following controlled marks on the piece of unlined paper. Place the pencil directly in front of student and say *'Pick up your pencil'*. Pointing to each mark in the order given below say *'Make me a circle/line/mark just like this—do it here'* (pointing). Tick successes below.

Circle   Vertical Line   Series of joined letter m or w or curves

Now indicate which hand is dominant—   RIGHT/LEFT (tick)
Is pencil held properly?   YES/NO (tick)

Comments on performance here:

Q/4(b). SIMPLE WRITING ABILITY

(ONLY FOR STUDENTS WHO CAN AT LEAST READ SENTENCES 4/5 FROM Q/2(a) ABOVE. Many mentally handicapped people cannot write at all. This test is a crude screen to check whether student has learned to write at a simple level.)

Instructions to Tester: Have a mediumly sharpened pencil and a sheet of broad-lined writing paper for the student.

Administration: Say *'We'll pretend you're on holiday and you're writing a postcard to your home—write what I say—are you ready?'* Then dictate at a speed to suit student.

We are having a good time.   We have been on a bus trip.   See you soon.

Comments on results here (noting errors):

Q/5. RETENTION ABILITY WITH THE SPOKEN WORD

Instructions to Tester: Most of us are inclined to use sentences which are too long when teaching our MH students. Many mentally handicapped people have great difficulty in retaining what you *tell* them. It is obviously important for the teacher to be aware of the level of his student's difficulty on this parameter so that he can choose the best method for teaching him. Just 'telling' him may not be the best method if he is a poor 'retainer' of the spoken word. Find out how many of the following sentences your student can repeat without error. You may be in for a salutary shock! You must now limit the span of your spoken teaching instructions to suit your student's ability. This will be especially important if your student is also a poor 'processor' of the spoken word (see Q/6 below).

Student's Initials: *THIS IS A CONFIDENTIAL DOCUMENT*
Date:

Q/5. RETENTION ABILITY WITH THE SPOKEN WORD—CONTD.

Administration: Give these sentences *once only*.
1. *Say, 'Listen and say exactly what I say—are you listening?'*
    (*a*) 'John likes to give his friend a nice present'
    (*b*) 'We are going home to see our mum and dad'
    (i.e. 9/10 simple words).

Describe results:

2. *Say 'Listen and say exactly what I say—are you listening?'*
    (*a*) 'Peter will play his new pop record to his friends this evening'
    (*b*) 'Mary is making a red dress to wear at the disco tomorrow'
(i.e. 12 words).

Describe results:

3. *Say 'Listen and say exactly what I say—are you listening?'*
    (*a*) 'Those people are going to the shops to get their food for
    the week-end' (14 words).
    (*b*) 'Tomorrow we will go for a bus trip in the country and
    come back home for tea' (17 words).

Describe results:

NB If your student can only manage to repeat the sentences in question 1, he is probably a poor 'retainer' of the spoken word. You should always *show* him rather than tell him what to do, or show and tell. If he can manage to repeat the long sentences in question 3 without error—he is probably relatively competent at retaining the spoken word so teaching by simple 'telling' will not be a waste of time, although 'showing how' should always be used at least initially.

Q/6. PROCESSING ABILITY WITH THE SPOKEN WORD

Instructions to Tester: Our students also often have difficulty in *processing* what you tell them. Read your student the following little story and then see how many of the comprehension questions he can answer. If he can answer most of them, he is demonstrating a reasonable ability at processing what you tell him as long as this is simple.

Administration: *Say 'Here is a story about a dog. Listen carefully while I read it because I'm going to ask you some questions about it. What am I going to do?'* When the student answers this question satisfactorily *say 'Here's the story—are you ready?'*
Once there was a boy whose name was John. He lived with his sister Jessie. Their father gave them a dog for a present. They called the dog Rover. They took the dog out for a walk one day. Rover the dog chased a cat up a tree. The man next door had to come with a ladder to get the cat down from the tree. John and Jessie were very angry with Rover and gave him a good smacking for being so naughty.

Now ask the student the following questions:

(*a*) What was the boy's name? (John)	Correct/Incorrect (tick)
(*b*) Who gave John and Jessie the dog? (Father)	Correct/Incorrect (tick)

Q/6. PROCESSING ABILITY WITH THE SPOKEN WORD—CONTD.

(*c*) What was the dog's name? (Rover)	Correct/Incorrect (tick)
(*d*) What did the dog do? (Chased a cat up a tree)	Correct/Incorrect (tick)
(*e*) Who got the cat down from the tree? (Man next door)	Correct/Incorrect (tick)
(*f*) What did John and Jessie do to Rover then? (Smacked him)	Correct/Incorrect (tick)

Comments on performance here:

NUMERACY SECTION

Q/7. COUNTING TO 100—USING COUNTERS

Instructions to Tester: Provide 100 counters. *Say 'Count these for me out loud'.* Demonstrate by moving the first one over and saying 'One'. Encourage student to go as far as possible.

Note here to what number student can count in correct sequence ....

Comments on performance here:

Q/8. RECOGNITION OF NUMBERS 1–100

Instructions to Tester: Write the numbers 1–100 in 10 lines of 10 (e.g. 1–10, 11–20, etc.) on a large piece of white card. Always write number one as a straight line (to avoid confusion with number seven). Cover. Give the card to the student. *Say 'Can you find the number X for me—where is X?'* Use the list of numbers given below. Tick successes.

Total Score

67	29	84	15	48	=
95	6	71	32	53	

Comments on performance (note any reversals, e.g. 59 for 95 or 9 for 6):

Q/9. UNDERSTANDING RELATIVE VALUES—NUMBERS 1–100

Instructions to Tester: Make up a set of number flashcards 2″ square as follows: first 8 and 24, then 17/46/73, then 68/39/55/14/92.

Administration: Lay out numbers 8/24 in front of student. *Say 'If I gave you this number of chocolates (pointing to 8), or this number of chocolates (pointing to 24)—which would give you more chocolates?'*

Results: Correct/Incorrect. (tick)

If the student is successful, remove 8 and 24 then lay out 17/46/73 *randomly*. *Say 'Which is the biggest/highest number—put it here—which is the next biggest—put it below the other one'* and so on until student has the numbers arranged in a column in *his* order of relative value.

Student's Initials: *THIS IS A CONFIDENTIAL DOCUMENT*
Date:

Q/9. UNDERSTANDING RELATIVE VALUES—NUMBERS 1–100—CONTD.

Results: If correct—tick Correct.
                 If incorrect—note errors here:

If the student is still successful, remove 17/46/73, then repeat the instructions immediately above using numbers 68/39/55/14/92.

Results: If correct—tick Correct.
                 If incorrect—note errors here:

Comments on performance here:

Q/10. ABILITY TO WRITE NUMBERS 1–20

Instructions to Tester: Provide a mediumly sharp pencil and broad-lined paper.

Administration: *Say 'Please write these numbers for me'.* Give numbers 1–20 *randomly.* Tick successes below.

                                                        Total Score

   1   2   3   4   5   6   7   8   9 10 =
11 12 13 14 15 16 17 18 19 20

Comments on performance here:

Q/11. RECOGNITION OF DECIMAL COINS

Instructions to Tester: Lay out a set of REAL coins *values face-upwards* in a row. Pointing to each coin in turn with the butt of a pencil *say 'What is that—what's it worth?'* Tick successes below.

   50p   10p   5p   2p   1p $\frac{1}{2}$p

Comments on performance here:

Q/12. ADDING DECIMAL COINS

Instructions to Tester: Using REAL coins, check that student can add the following combinations: If student is obviously competent—ask for all coins. The most common failures occur when student has to add 2p/1p to 65p! Tick successes.

2p, 5p, 10p, 50p—ask student to add 1p to each of these.

2p, 5p, 10p, 50p—ask student to add 2p to each of these.

50p+10p.

50p+10p+5p.

All coins, i.e. 50p+10p+5p+2p+1p+$\frac{1}{2}$p = 68$\frac{1}{2}$p.

10p+10p+10p+10p+10p = 50p.

50p+50p = £1.

Comments on performance here:

Student's Initials: THIS IS A CONFIDENTIAL DOCUMENT
Date:

Q/13. MONEY CHANGE—COUNTING IN 10'S AND CONCEPT OF 'NEAREST 10 ABOVE'

(*a*) **Counting in 10's with 10p pieces.**

Instructions to Tester: You need 10×10p REAL coins (or equivalent in your appropriate currency if outside UK).

Administration: Place 10×10p on the table *randomly* in front of student. *Say 'Count these for me, please'.* If correctly counted, *say 'How much does that make?'* (i.e. £1).

> **Results:**   10's correctly counted YES   NO   (tick)
>   Makes £1 correctly   YES   NO   (tick)
> Comments on performance here:

(*b*) **Concept of 'Nearest 10 above'** (only administer to students who have passed 13(a) above).

Instructions to Tester: Very few mentally handicapped can ever subtract 'in their heads' but they *can* learn to offer exact amounts for purchases or to offer 'the nearest 10 above' the correct amount. It is crucial to teach this skill to those who can count in 10's.

Administration: Have 10×10p. Lay out 4×10p in front of student. *Say 'How much is that?'* Then *say, 'I'm the shopkeeper; you come to my shop and buy something costing 20p—how many of these (pointing) would you give me?'* Then test for a purchase worth 15p, then 22p. Then add 6×10p to the 40p and test for the other amounts given below: Tick successes.

> 20p   15p   22p   54p   78p   81p
> Comments on performance here:

Q/14. UNDERSTANDING RELATIVE VALUES—SHOP PRICE TAGS

Make up 6 price-tags on 2″ square cards as follows (or equivalent if working in another currency); £1·20   £11·30   £4·90   75p   £3·05   £0·45.

Administration: *First* using £4·90/£1·20 and 75p, *say 'Tell me the prices of these cards',* then *say 'Which is the highest/dearest price—put it here—Which is next highest/dearest—put it below the other one'*—and so on.

> **Results:**   Price-reading   Correct/Incorrect (tick)
>   Value-order   Correct/Incorrect (tick)

If the student is successful—repeat test using all 6 cards *randomly* placed in front of him.

> **Results:**   Price-reading   Correct/Incorrect (tick)
>   Value-order   Correct/Incorrect (tick)
> Note type of error here:

THIS IS A CONFIDENTIAL DOCUMENT

Date:

Q/15. UNDERSTANDING OF SIMPLE SHARING

Instructions to Tester: Very few Adult Mentally Handicapped can cope with division 'in their heads'. Use any sets of 24 common objects, e.g. sweets/dominoes, etc.

Administration: Say *'I want you to share these out between 4 people—so each person gets the same number'.*

> **Results:**   If correct—tick Correct.
> If incorrect—describe errors:
>
> Comments on performance here:

Q/16. UNDERSTANDING OF BASIC LIQUID MEASUREMENT

Instructions to Tester: (Choose pints or litres as appropriate). A 'see-through' litre or pint/quart measuring jug. Access to a tap.

Administration: Say *'Go to the tap and measure $\frac{1}{2}$ litre/$\frac{1}{2}$ pint, 1 litre/1 pint, 1 quart/2 litres for me'.*

Results: (tick as appropriate)
  half-litre   1 litre   2 litres
  half-pint   1 pint   1 quart

If incorrect—describe errors:

Comments on performance here:

Q/17. KNOWLEDGE OF OWN CLOTHES/SHOE SIZES

Instructions to Tester: Say *'Do you know what size of shirt/trousers/dress you wear—is it small, medium or large?'*

> **Results:** YES/NO (tick)—Small   Medium   Large   (tick)

'Do you know what size of shoe you wear?'

> **Results:** YES/NO (tick)
>
> Comments on performance here:

TIME SECTION

Q/18. ORIENTATION IN TIME/PLACE, ETC.

Does student know:
  (*a*) His: Age; Birthday; Year of Birth (tick)
  (*b*) Home Address; Address of Workplace (tick)
  (*c*) What day it is; Date (within 7 days) (tick)
  (*d*) Names of Weekdays; Names of Months (tick)
  Say *'I want you to tell me the names of the weekdays . . . Monday—names of the months . . . January'.*

Comments on performance here:

THIS IS A CONFIDENTIAL DOCUMENT

Date:

Q/19. TELLING TIME

Instructions to Tester: Use a geared clock if possible—otherwise a clock with all the numbers on it. Set the clock at the following times. *Say 'What time does it say—tell me the time?'* Tick successes.

4 o'clock	8 o'clock	10.30 (or half past ten)
5.15 (quarter past 5)	3.10 (10 past 3)	9.45 (quarter to 10)
1.25 (25 past 1)	7.40 (or 20 to 8)	5.35 (or 25 to 6)

If student cannot tell time properly, test as follows: TICK

1. Does student recognize the numbers 1–12 and know their order?   YES/NO

2. Does he know the positions of these numbers on the clock-face? (some clocks have dots or Roman numerals)   YES/NO

3. Can he discriminate the big/long hand from the little/short hand?   YES/NO

4. Does he understand the function of each hand—big hand minutes, little hand hours?   YES/NO

5. Can he count to 30 in fives (fluently), starting with 0? Can he apply this skill to the clockface?   YES/NO

6. In relation to the long hand's function—does he realize there are 5 minutes between each figure?   YES/NO

7. Does he realize the hands move in one direction only and does he know which direction this is?   YES/NO

8. Does he understand the principle of 'past' and 'to' sides on the clock?   YES/NO

Comments on performance here:

(Mrs) X W R Paton
Principal Clinical Psychologist
Borders Area Health Board
Dingleton Hospital
Melrose, Scotland

DON'T FORGET TO COMPLETE SUMMARY

THIS IS A CONFIDENTIAL DOCUMENT

Date:

Level Three

Designed for testing educational levels of the more advanced Mentally Handicapped student—AN EXTENSION OF LEVEL 2 WHICH MUST BE GIVEN FIRST.

INTRODUCTION

Level 3 is differently constructed from Levels 1 and 2 in that it is more in the nature of a teaching check-list for the Instructor. It assumes that the student will be a candidate for semi-independent living and reminds the Instructor of the social skills which the student will need in order to survive without loss of dignity. The Instructor may find that the list is not comprehensive for his particular student whose life-style may require other social skills not mentioned here. The Instructor should add to the questions below if this is the case. It would clearly be very difficult to formalize tests in this Section so it is left to the individual Instructor to make use of the checklist below in the way which suits him and his student best.

1. **ADDRESS**

Own—
Social Worker's (or contact person)—
Place of Work—

(*a*) Does he know them verbally?
(*b*) Can he write them?

2. **BUSES**

Own bus numbers—names of own bus stops—price of fares—how to pay in: (*a*) one-man, (*b*) two-man buses. Where (in bus) to get on and off. How to cope in bus station—ask for correct 'stand' etc.

3. **CAFE**

How to order and pay—how to behave in a self-service cafe.

4. **COOKERY SCALES**—use of Dial Setting Skills

i.e. cooker/washing machine/radio/T.V./cassette player/iron. Simplified coding systems may be necessary.

5. **COUNCIL HOUSE**

How to pay rent, rates, make complaints.

6. **DICTIONARY**—how to use.

7. **ELECTRICITY**—how to use/pay for.

8. **ENTERTAINMENTS**

i.e. cinema/disco/bingo/fairground—how to cope—including the hazards.

9. **GAS**—how to use/pay for.

10. **HEALTH CENTRE**—how to make an appointment.
how to behave.

11. **HIRE PURCHASE/MAIL ORDER**—advise Client **not** to get involved!

12. **JOB CENTRE**—how to cope with help of contact person.

13. **LAUNDERETTE**—how to cope.

14. **MONEY**—care of
(*a*) looking after purse/money in pocket.
(*b*) depositing and withdrawing money in Post Office/Bank, etc.

15. **POLICE**—how they can help.

THIS IS A CONFIDENTIAL DOCUMENT

Date:

16. **QUEUEING**—how to do it—how to wait your turn.

17. **RECIPES**—devise some basic ones Client can 'decode'.

18. **REFRIGERATOR**—(*a*) maintenance/defrosting, etc.
      (*b*) care of food/dating/covering, etc.

19. **SOCIAL SECURITY BENEFITS**
    (*a*) claiming them,
    (*b*) drawing them.

20. **SHOPPING/SUPERMARKET**
How to collect trolley/basket—find and collect goods—pay for goods.

21. **TELEPHONE DIRECTORY**—how to use.

22. **TELEPHONE**—how to use: (*a*) private 'phone; (*b*) pay 'phone. Knowing contact person and doctor's telephone numbers. How to dial in an emergency and when NOT to dial! Knowledge of **own** telephone number.

23. **TIME OF DAY**
Understanding concepts like morning/afternoon/evening/a.m. versus p.m.

24. **TIME OF YEAR**
Understanding concepts like Spring/Summer/Autumn/Winter.

25. **TIME**—especially concepts like 'half an hour ago—in an hour's time'.

26. **TRAFFIC**—street-crossing drill.

27. **TV AND RADIO PROGRAMMES**—how to read.
    TV—how to adjust. How to pay for licence.
    RADIO—how to adjust.

(Mrs) X W R Paton
Principal Clinical Psychologist
Borders Area Health Board
Dingleton Hospital
Melrose, Scotland

DON'T FORGET TO COMPLETE SUMMARY

Bibliography

Allport G. W. (1937) *Personality and Psychological Interpretation*. New York, Hope.

Baltaxe C. (1981) Prosodic abnormalities in autism. In: Mittler P. (ed.) *Frontiers of Research*. Proceedings of Vth IASSMD Conference. Baltimore, University Park Press.

Baltaxe C. and Simmonds J. Q. (1975) Language and childhood psychosis. *J. Speech Hear. Disord.* **40**, 439.

Baltaxe C. and Simmonds J. Q. (1977) Language patterns of adolescent autistics. In: Mittler P. (ed.), *Research to Practice*. Proceedings of IVth IASSMD Conference. Baltimore, University Park Press.

Barton R. (1976) *Institutional Neurosis,* 3rd ed. Bristol, Wright.

Bentovin A. (1972) Handicapped pre-school children and their families: effects on child's emotional development. *Br. Med. J.* **3**, 634–7.

Bijou S. W. (1966) A functional analysis of retarded development. In: Ellis N. (ed.), *International Review of Research in Mental Retardation,* Vol. 1. New York, Academic Press.

Bliss C. (1966) *Semantography*. Sydney, Australia, Blissymbolics.

Bliss C. (1975) *Teaching Guidelines*. Sydney, Australia, Blissymbolics.

Bliss C. (1976) *Provisional Dictionary* (revised ed.). Sydney, Australia, Blissymbolics.

Boswell D. M. and Wingrove J. M. (1974) *The Handicapped Person and the Community*. A Reader and Source Book. London, Open University.

Bowlby J. (1969) *Attachment and Loss*: I, Attachment: London, Hogarth Press.

Bowness S. and Zadik T. D. (1981) Implementing the nursing process at a unit for mentally handicapped children. *Nursing Times*, 16 April, pp. 695–6.

Brown K. (1971) Paper at (Camphill) Conference, Aberdeen. Unpublished Proceedings, Rudolf Steiner.

Burt C. (1949) The structure of the mind: a review of the results of factor analysis. *Br. J. Educ. Psychol.* **19**, 100–14, 176–99.

Carrier J. K. (1977) Application of a non-speech language system with the severely language handicapped. In: Lloyd L. L. (ed.), *Communication, Assessment and Intervention Strategies*. London, University Park Press.

Clark D. F. (1958) A reassessment of the role of the clinical psychologist in the mental deficiency hospital. *J. Ment. Subnormal*, **14**, 3–17.

Clark D. F. (1970) The psychologist and interpersonal relationships in a mental subnormality hospital. *J. Ment. Subnormal*, **16**, 33–44.

Clark D. F. (1974) In: Clarke A. M. and Clarke A. D. B.

Clarke A. M. and Clarke A. D. B. (ed.) (1974) *Mental Deficiency*. London, Methuen.

Committee of Enquiry into the Education of Handicapped Children and Young People (1978) *Special Educational Needs*. (The Warnock Report.) London, HMSO.

Court Report (1976) *Fit for the Future*. Report of the Committee on Child Health Services. London, HMSO.

Craft M. (ed.) (1979) *Tredgold's Mental Retardation*, 12th ed. London, Baillière Tindall.

Craft M. and Craft A. (ed.) (1978) *Sex and the Mentally Handicapped*. London, Routledge & Kegan Paul.

Critchley M. (1974) Cited in Brain, Lord: *Speech Disorders, Aphasia, Apraxia and Agnosia*, 4th ed. London, Butterworths.

Cunningham C. C. (1979) The Down's baby. Paper delivered at National Conference of APMH, Edinburgh.

Cunningham C. C. and Sloper P. (1979) *Helping Your Handicapped Baby*. London, Souvenir.

Darcy P. T. (1980) The nursing process: a base for all nursing developments. *Nursing Times*, 20 March, pp. 497–501.

Deich R. F. and Hodges P. M. (1977) *Language without Speech*. London, Souvenir.

Department of Education and Science (1980) *Special Educational Needs*. London, HMSO.

Department of Health and Social Security (1971) Better Services for the Mentally Handicapped. London, HMSO, Cmnd 4683.

Department of Health and Social Security (1976) A Review of the Mental Health Act 1959. London, HMSO.

Department of Health and Social Security (1978) Review of the Mental Health Act. London, HMSO, Cmnd 7320.

Dodd B. (1972) Comparison of babbling patterns in normal and Down's syndrome infants. *J. Ment. Defic. Res.* **21**, 103.

Duff R. S. and Campbell A. G. M. (1973) Moral and ethical dilemmas in the special care nursery. *N. Engl. J. Med.* **289**, 890.

Duncan A. S., Dunstan G. R. and Wellbourne R. B. (1981) *Dictionary of Medical Ethics*, 2nd ed. London, Longman & Todd.

Edgerton T. (1967) *The Cloak of Competence: Stigma in the Lives of the Mentally Retarded*. U.C.L.A.

Editorial (1973) *Development. Med. Child Neurol.* 15.

Editorial (1980) *Br. Med. J.* 281, 18 October.

Educational Institute of Scotland (1981) *Scottish Ed. J.* 13 February.

Egan D. F., Illingworth R. S. and Mackeith R. G. (1969) Developmental screening 0–5 years. *Clinics in Developmental Medicine*, No. 30. London, SIMP with Heinemann.

Family Fund Analysis (1979) National Children's Bureau. London.

Fernald W. E. (1912) The burden of feeble-mindedness. *Med. Commun. MASS Med. Soc.* **23**, 30.

Finnie N. R. (1974) *Handling the Young Cerebral Palsied Child at Home*. London, Heinemann.

Fraser W. I. and Grieve R. (ed.) (1981) *Communicating with Normal and Retarded Children*. Bristol, Wright.

Frostig M. and Horne D. (1964) *The Frostig Programme for Development of Visual Perception*. Chicago, Follet.

Gardiner R. A. and Gardiner B. T. (1969) Teaching sign language to a chimpanzee. *NY Science*, **165**, 664.

Gardner W. I. (1971) *Behaviour Modification in Mental Retardation*. London, University of London.

Gibson D. (1978) *Down's Syndrome.* Cambridge, Cambridge University Press.

Gillham B. (1979) *The First Words Language Programme.* Beaconsfield, Allen & Unwin.

Goddard H. (1919) *Feeblemindedness: Its Cause and Consequences.* New York, Macmillan.

Griffith M. (ed.) (1980) *Prevention of Mental Handicap.* BIMH Conference Proceedings.

Grossman (1973) *A Manual on Terminology and Classification in Mental Retardation.* Series 2. Washington D. C., American Association on Mental Deficiency.

Grove N. (1980a) *Research Information Service,* Vol. 1, No. 1. Farnborough, MVDP.

Grove N. (1980b) *Research Information Service,* Vol. 1, No. 5. Farnborough, MVDP.

Grunewald K. (1974) *The Mentally Retarded in Sweden.* Stockholm, Swedish Institute.

Grunewald K. (1978) *The Mentally Handicapped: Towards Normal Living.* London, Hutchinson.

Gunzburg H. C. (1973) *Social Competence and Mental Handicap.* London, Baillière Tindall.

Gunzburg H. C. (1973) *Advances in the Care of the Mentally Handicapped.* London, Baillière Tindall.

Gunzburg H. C. and Gunzburg L. (1973) *Mental Handicap and Physical Environment.* London, Baillière Tindall.

Habgood J. S. (1980) *A Working Faith.* London, Darton, Longman & Todd.

Henderson V. (1960) *Basic Principles of Nursing Care.* London, International Council of Nurses.

Hewett F. M. (1965) Teaching speech to an autistic child through operant conditioning. *Am. J. Ortho. Psychiat.* 35(5), 927–36.

Hewett S. and Newson J. E. (1970) *The Family and the Handicapped Child.* London, Allen & Unwin.

Hollis K. (1977) *Progress to Standing.* London, British Institute for Mental Handicap.

Hollis K. (1977) *Progress to Good Movement.* London, British Institute for Mental Handicap.

Hoogenrad R. (1981) In: Fraser W. and Grieve R. (ed.), *Communicating with Normal and Retarded Children.* Bristol, Wright.

Jay Committee (1979) *Report of Committee on Mental Handicap Nursing and Care.* Edinburgh, HMSO.

Jeffree D. M. and McConkey R. (1976) *Let me Speak.* London, Souvenir.

Jeffree D. M. and McConkey R. (1977) *Let me Play.* London, Souvenir.

Jensen A. R. (1970) IQs of identical twins reared apart. *Behav. Genet.* 1, 133–46.

Kiernan C. (1977) Alternative to speech. A review of research on manual and other forms of communication with the mentally handicapped and other non-communicating populations. *Br. J. Ment. Subnormal,* 23, 6–28.

Kiernan C. and Jones M. (1977) *Behaviour Assessment Battery.* London, NFER.

Kiernan C., Jordan R. and Saunders C. (1978) *Starting Off.* London, Souvenir.

Kilma E. S. and Bellugi U. (1979) *The Signs of Language.* Cambridge, Mass., Harvard University Press.

Kirman B. and Bicknell J. (1975) *Mental Handicap.* London, Churchill Livingstone.

Kratz C. R. (ed.) (1979) *The Nursing Process.* London, Baillière Tindall.

Kron T. (1976) *The Management of Patient Care.* Philadelphia, Saunders.

LaPage C. P. (1910) *Feeblemindedness in Children of School Age.* Manchester, Manchester University.

Lindsley O. R. (1964) The direct measurement and prothesis of retarded behaviour. *J. Ed.* **147**, 60–8.

Loring J. (1966) *Teaching the Cerebral Palsied Child.* London, National Spastics Society. In association with Heinemann.

McConkey R. and Jeffree D. M. (1981) *Let's Make Toys.* London, Souvenir.

MacGillivray R. C. (1956) The larval psychosis of idiocy. *Am. J. Ment. Defic.* **60**, 570.

MacKay G. F. and Dunn W. R. (1981) *Early Communicative Skills.* Glasgow, University of Glasgow.

Malin N. (1975) *Staff Attitudes to Mental Handicap.* Scottish Society for the Mentally Handicapped. Glasgow, Bell & Bain.

Marks-Maran D. (1978) Patient allocation *v.* task allocation in relation to the nursing process. *Nursing Times,* 9 March, pp. 413–16.

Menolascino F. J. (1968). Parents of the mentally retarded. *J. Am. Acad. Child Psychol.* October, pp. 589–601.

Mittler P. (1972) *The Psychological Assessment of the Physically and Mentally Handicapped Child.* London, Methuen.

Mittler P. (1978) *Helping Mentally Handicapped People in Hospital.* London, DHSS.

Morris P. (1969) *Put Away: A Sociological Study of Institutions for the Mentally Retarded.* London, Routledge & Kegan Paul.

Murdoch J. C. (1980) Hypothalamo-pituitary target organ function in adults with Down's syndrome. In: Mittler P. (ed.), *Frontiers of Knowledge in Mental Retardation.* Baltimore, University Park Press.

Nay R. W. (1975) A systematic comparison of instructional techniques for parents. *Behaviour Therapy,* **6**, 14–21.

Nihira K. (1969) Factorial dimensions of receptive behaviour in adult retardant. *Am. J. Ment. Defic.* **73**(6), 868.

Nirge B. (1970) The normalization philosophy. *J. Ment. Subnormal,* **16**, 62.

O'Connor N. (ed.) (1975). *Language, Cognitive Deficits and Retardation.* London, Butterworths.

O'Connor N. and Hermelin D. (1963) *Speech and Thought in Severe Subnormality.* Oxford, Pergamon Press.

O'Donohoe N. (1979) *Epilepsies of Childhood.* London, Butterworths.

Office of Health Economics (1973) *Mental Handicap.* London, Office of Health Economics.

O'Hara J. (1968) The role of the nurse in subnormality: a re-appraisal. *J. Ment. Subnormal,* **14**(1), 19–24.

Olshansky S. (1965) Chronic sorrow: a response to having a mentally defective child. *Social Casework,* **43**, 190–3.

Orlick T. (1978) *The Cooperative Sports and Games Book.* New York, Pantheon.

Paget R., Gorman P. and Paget G. (1968) *A Systematic Sign Language.* London, RNID.

Piaget J. (1926) *Language and Thought of the Child.* New York, Basic Books.

Piaget J. (1953) *The Origins of Intelligence in the Child.* Cook M. (trans.). London, Routledge.

Piaget J. (1973) *Problem Orientated Medical Records.* Scottish Hospital Centre Symposium.

Premack D. and Premack A. J. (1974) Teaching visual language to apes and language deficient persons. In: Schiefelbusch R. L. and Lloyd L. L. (ed.), *Language Perspectives. Acquisition, Retardation and Intervention.* London, University Park Press.

Reid A., Aungle P. and Maloney A. F. (1978) Dementia in ageing mental defectives: a clinical and physiological survey. *J. Ment. Defic. Res.* **22**, 170.

Reid A. H. (1980) Diagnosis of psychiatric disorder in the severely and profoundly retarded patient. *J. R. Soc. Med.* **73**, 607.

Richards B. W. (ed.) (1970) *Mental Subnormality.* Modern Trends in Research. London, Pitman.

The Report of the Committee on Local Authority and Allied Personal Social Services (1968) The Seebohm Report. Cmnd 37030. London, HMSO.

Roberts J. A. F. and Pembrey M. E. (1976) *An Introduction to Medical Genetics,* 7th ed. London, Oxford University Press.

Roper N., Logan W. W. and Tierney A. (1980) *The Elements of Nursing.* Edinburgh, Churchill Livingstone.

Scottish Education Department (1973) *The Training of Staff for Centres for the Mentally Handicapped:* (The Melville Report.) Edinburgh, HMSO.

Scottish Education Department (1977) The Structure of the Curriculum in the Third and Fourth Years of the Scottish Secondary School. (The Munn Report.) Edinburgh, HMSO.

Scottish Education Department (1980) *Special Educational Needs in Scotland.* Edinburgh, HMSO.

Seguin E. (1866) *Idiocy and its Treatment by Physiological Method.* Reprinted in 1907 by Teachers College, Columbia University, New York.

Shennan V. (1978) *Help Your Child to Learn at Home.* London, NSMHC.

Sherridan M. D. (1975) *Children's Developmental Progress from Birth to Five Years: The Stycar Sequences.* London, NFER.

Simon G. (ed.) (1981) *Local Services for the Mentally Handicapped: The Community Team.* British Institute for Mental Handicap.

Sirvio P. and Michelson K. (1976) Sound spectrographics and analysis of normal and abnormal newborn infants. *Folia Phoniatr.* **72**, 161.

Skelly M. (1979) *Amer-Ind Gestural Code based on Universal American Indian Hand Talk.* Oxford, Elsevier.

Skinner B. F. (1972) Compassion and ethics in the case of the retarded. In: *Cumulative Record,* 3rd ed. New York, Appleton-Century-Crofts.

Skinner B. F. (1976) *Walden Two,* 2nd ed. New York, Macmillan.

Smith G. F. and Berg J. M. (1976) *Down's Anomaly.* London, Churchill Livingstone.

Sparrow S. and Zigler E. (1978) Evaluation of a patterning treatment for retarded children. *Paediatrics,* **62,** 137–49.

Spearman C. E. (1927) *The Abilities of Man.* London, Macmillan.

Stephens Beth (1974) *Am. J. Ment. Defic.* **79,** 113.

Stevens H. A.—quotation from his address at 4th International Congress of the International Association for the Scientific Study of Mental Deficiency, Washington, August 1976.

Stevens M. (1976) *The Educational and Social Needs of Children with Severe Handicap.* London, Edward Arnold.

Stokoe W. C. (1978) Sign language research: what it knows and whither it leads. *British Deaf News,* August.

The Specialised Health Visitor for the Handicapped Baby, Young Child and School Child (1979). London, Disabled Living Foundation.

Thomas A. (1979) Applying the nursing process to the care of the mentally handicapped. *Nursing Mirror* 8 March, pp. 26–8.

Thurstone L. L. (1938) *Primary Mental Abilities.* Psychometric Monograph No. 1. University of Chicago Press.

Touwen B. C. and Prechtl H. F. (1970) The neurological examination of the child with minor nervous dysfunction. *Spastic International.* London, Heinemann.

Tyson M. (1971) The design of remedial programmes. In: Mittler P. (ed.), *The Psychological Assessment of Mental and Physical Handicaps.* London, Methuen.

Van Witsen B. (1967) *Perceptual Training Activities Handbook.* New York, Teachers College.

Walker M. (1973) An Experimental Evaluation of the Success of a System of Communications for Deaf Mentally Handicapped Adults. Unpublished MSc Thesis, University of London.

Walker M. (1976) Language Programme for use with the Revised Makaton Vocabulary. MVDP, 31 Firwood Drive, Camberley, Surrey.

Walker M. and Armfield A. (1981) What is the Makaton vocabulary? *Special Education—Forward Trends* Vol. 8, No. 3.

Wasz-Hockert D., Lind T., Vuorenkoski V. et al. (1968) The infant cry. In: *Clinics in Developmental Medicine.* London, Heinemann Medical.

Watson I. S. (1973) *Child Behaviour Modification: A Manual for Teachers, Nurses and Parents.* New York, Pergamon.

Wechsler D. (1958) *The Measurement and Appraisal of Adult Intelligence,* 4th ed. London, Baillière, Tindall & Cox.

Wehman P. (1979) *Curriculum Design for the Severely and Profoundly Handicapped.* New York, Human Sciences.

Whelan E. and Speake B. (1979) *Learning to Cope.* London, Souvenir.

Wolfensberger W. (1970) In: Menolascino F. J. (ed.), *Psychiatric Approaches to Mental Retardation.* New York, Basic Books.

Woodward M. (1967) Piaget's Theory. In: Howells J. G. (ed.), *Modern Perspectives in Child Psychiatry.* Edinburgh, Oliver & Boyd.

Younghusband E. (1970) *Living with Handicap.* London, National Children's Bureau.

Index

X, fragile chromosome, 71
X-rays, pre-natal, 218
XYY syndrome, 70–71, 270

Young persons work preparation
    courses, 20
Youth opportunities programme, 20

zarontin, 225, 230